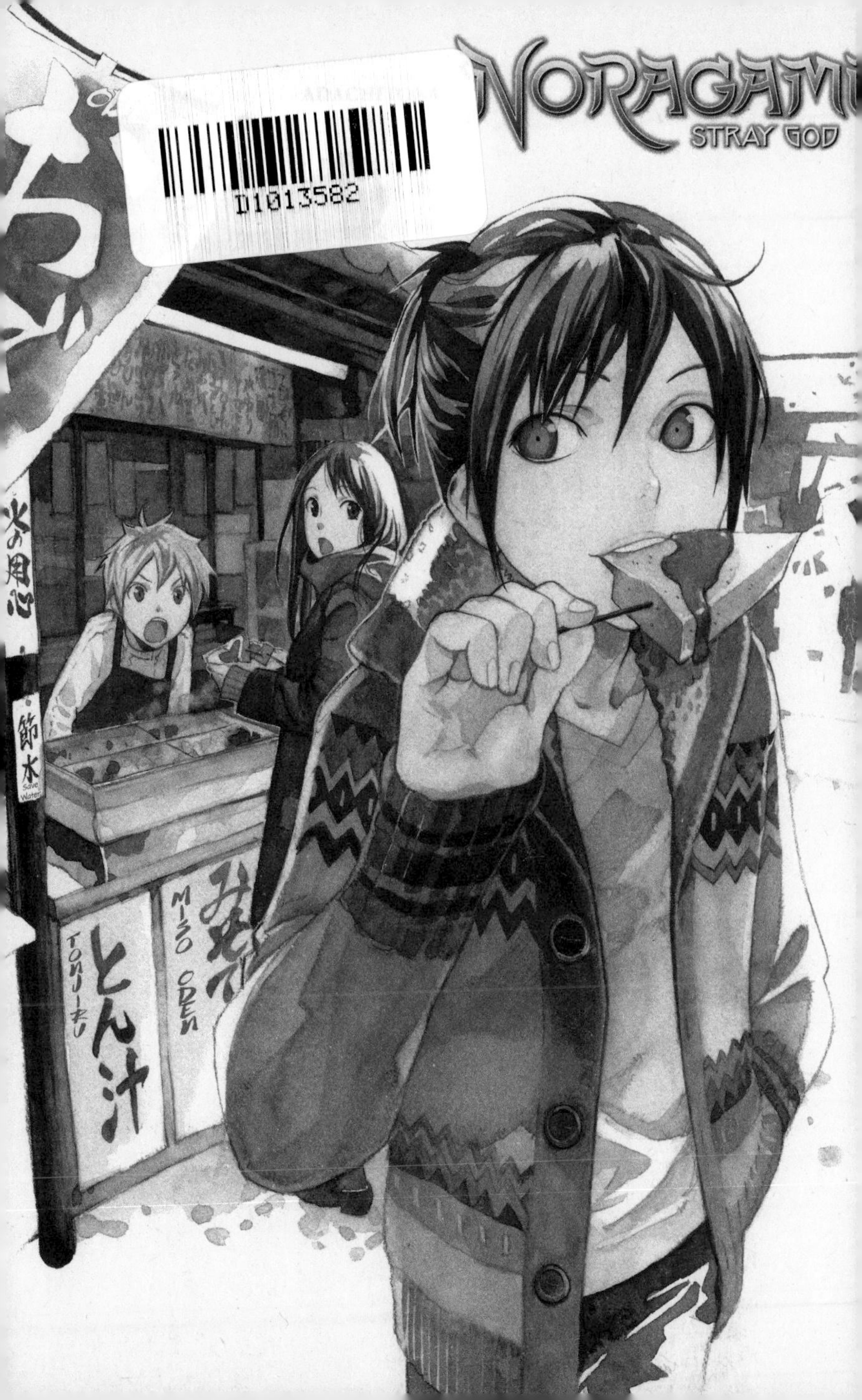
NORAGAMI
STRAY GOD
火の用心
節水
Save Water
みそでん
MISO ODEN
とん汁
TONJIRU

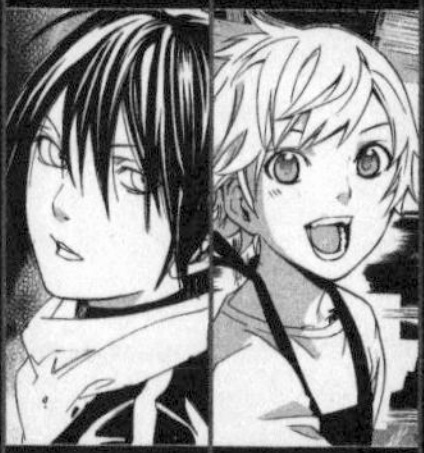

YATO
A minor deity who always wears a sweatsuit.

YUKINÉ
Yato's shinki who turns into swords.

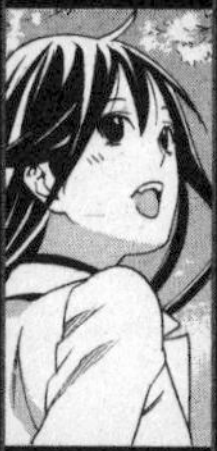

HIYORI IKI
A high school student who has become half ayakashi.

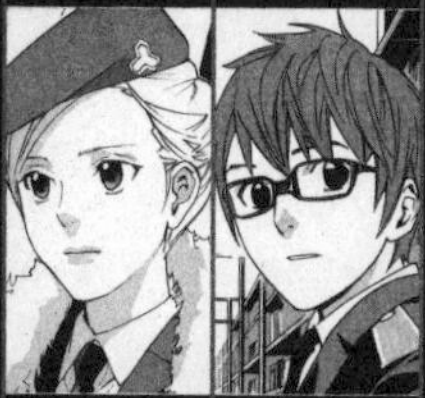

BISHA-MONTEN
A powerful warrior god, one of the Seven Gods of Fortune.

KAZUMA
A navi-gational shinki who serves as guide to Bishamon.

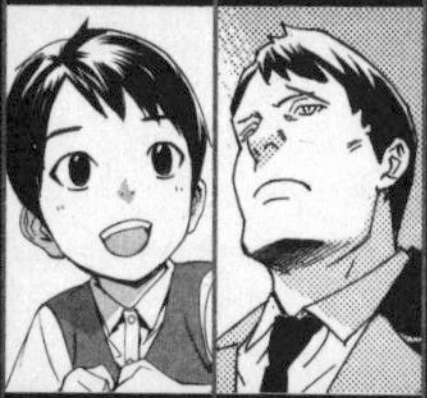

EBISU
A business-god in the making, one of the Seven Gods of Fortune.

KUNIMI
A shinki who enhances Ebisu's motor skills.

characters

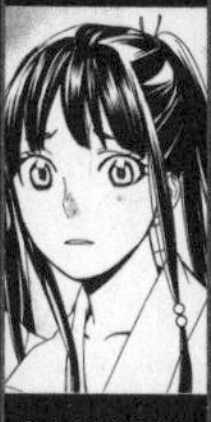

SAKURA
A shinki who remains in Yato's heart to this day.

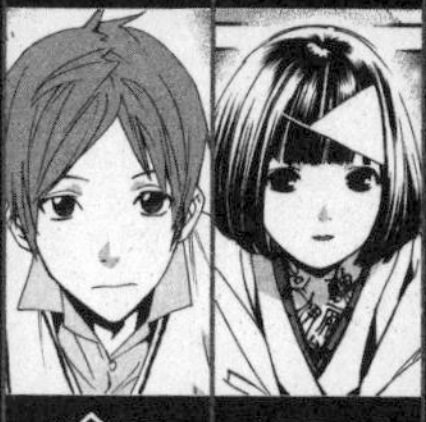

KÔTO FUJISAKI
Yato's "father."

STRAY
A shinki who serves an unspecified number of deities.

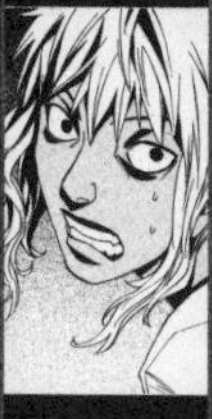

KUGAHA
A shinki who once deceived Bishamon.

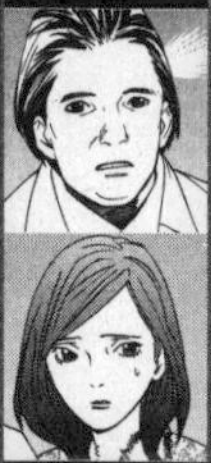

HIYORI'S PARENTS
They run a hospital.

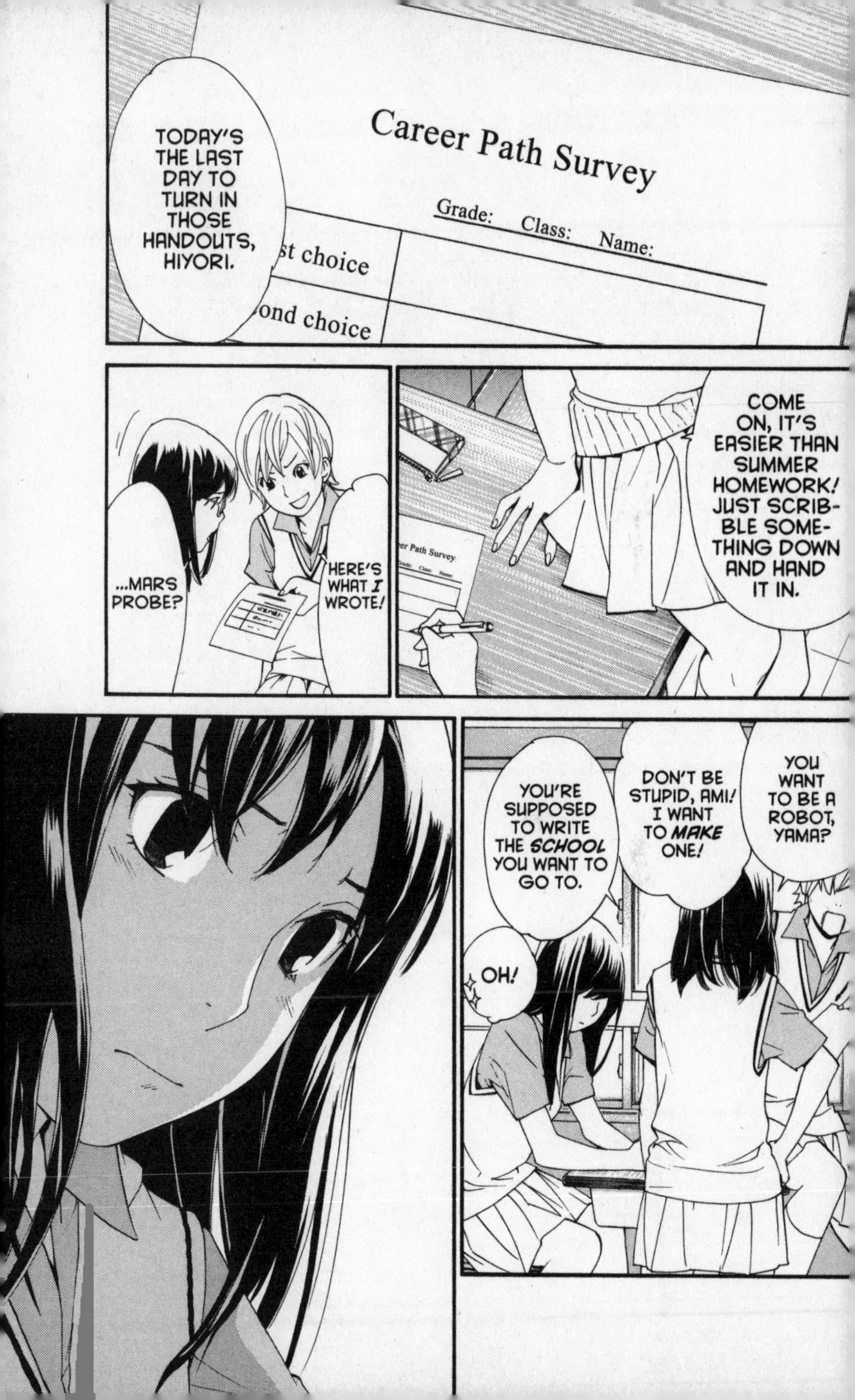
Career Path Survey
Grade: Class: Name:
TODAY'S THE LAST DAY TO TURN IN THOSE HANDOUTS, HIYORI.
COME ON, IT'S EASIER THAN SUMMER HOMEWORK! JUST SCRIBBLE SOMETHING DOWN AND HAND IT IN.
HERE'S WHAT *I* WROTE!
...MARS PROBE?
YOU WANT TO BE A ROBOT, YAMA?
DON'T BE STUPID, AMI! I WANT TO *MAKE* ONE!
YOU'RE SUPPOSED TO WRITE THE *SCHOOL* YOU WANT TO GO TO.
OH!

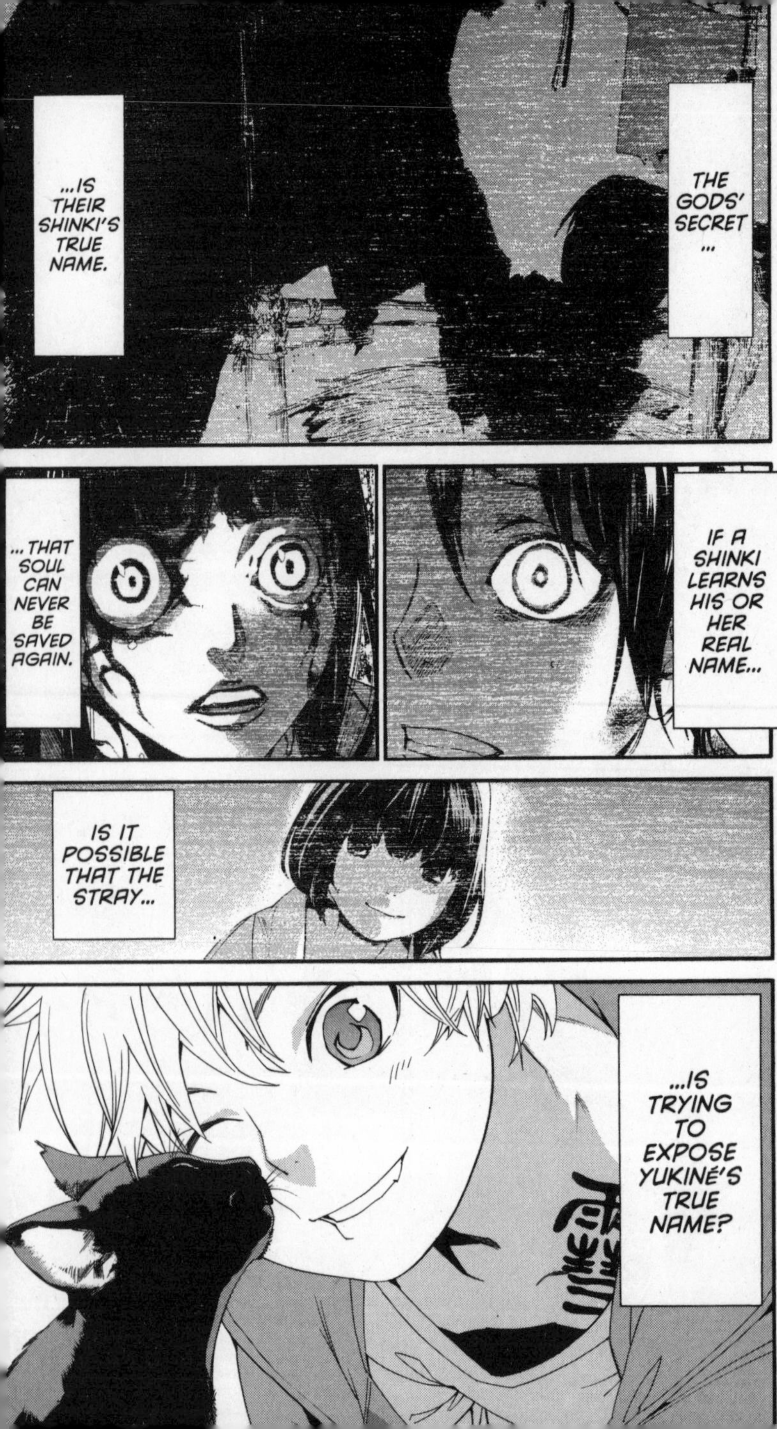
THE GODS' SECRET...
...IS THEIR SHINKI'S TRUE NAME.
IF A SHINKI LEARNS HIS OR HER REAL NAME...
...THAT SOUL CAN NEVER BE SAVED AGAIN.
IS IT POSSIBLE THAT THE STRAY...
...IS TRYING TO EXPOSE YUKINÉ'S TRUE NAME?

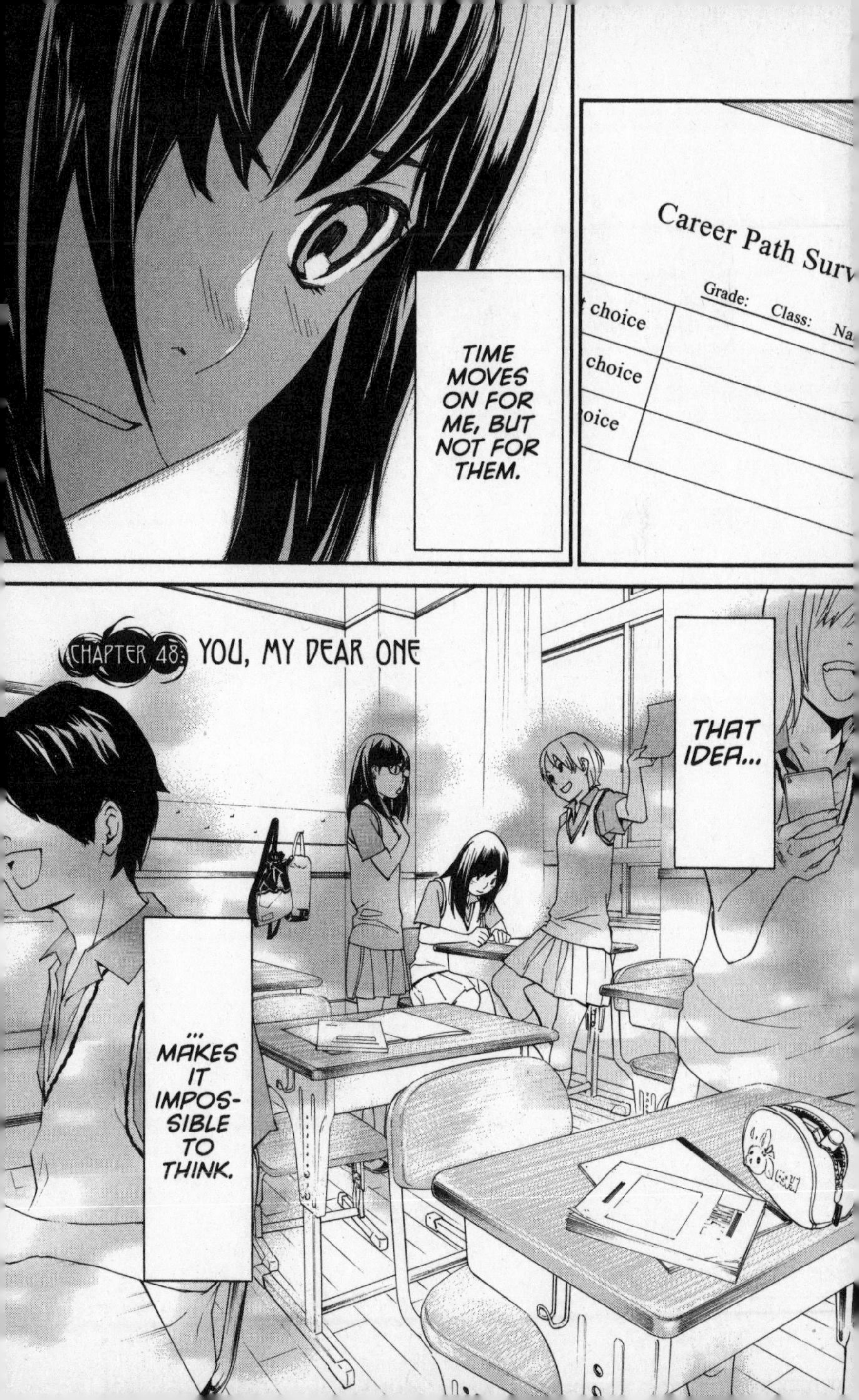
Career Path Surv
Grade: Class: Na
t choice
choice
oice
TIME MOVES ON FOR ME, BUT NOT FOR THEM.
CHAPTER 48: YOU, MY DEAR ONE
THAT IDEA...
...MAKES IT IMPOSSIBLE TO THINK.

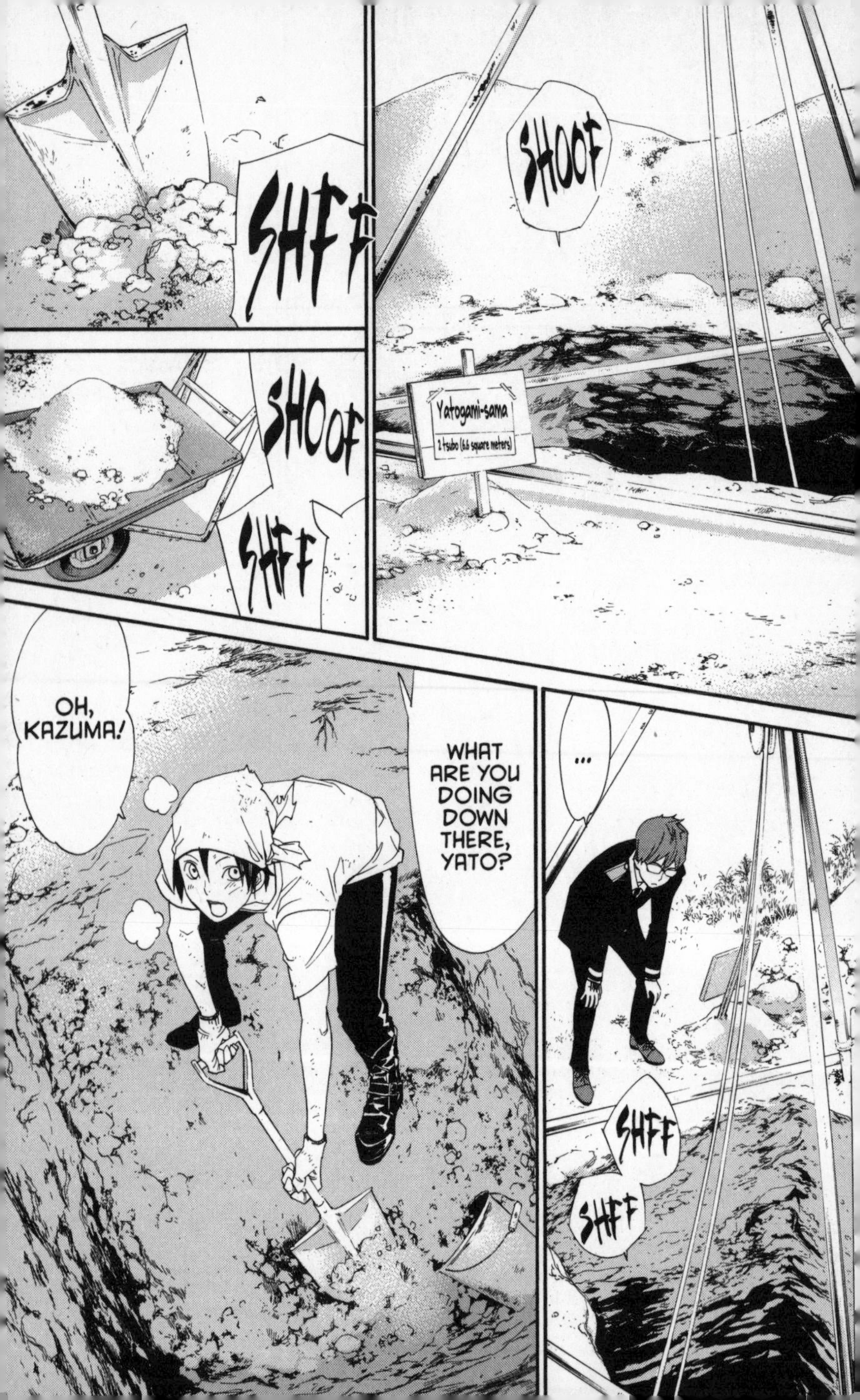
SHOOF
Yatogami-sama
2 tsubo (6.6 square meters)
SHFF
SHOOF
SHFF
...
SHFF
SHFF
WHAT ARE YOU DOING DOWN THERE, YATO?
OH, KAZUMA!

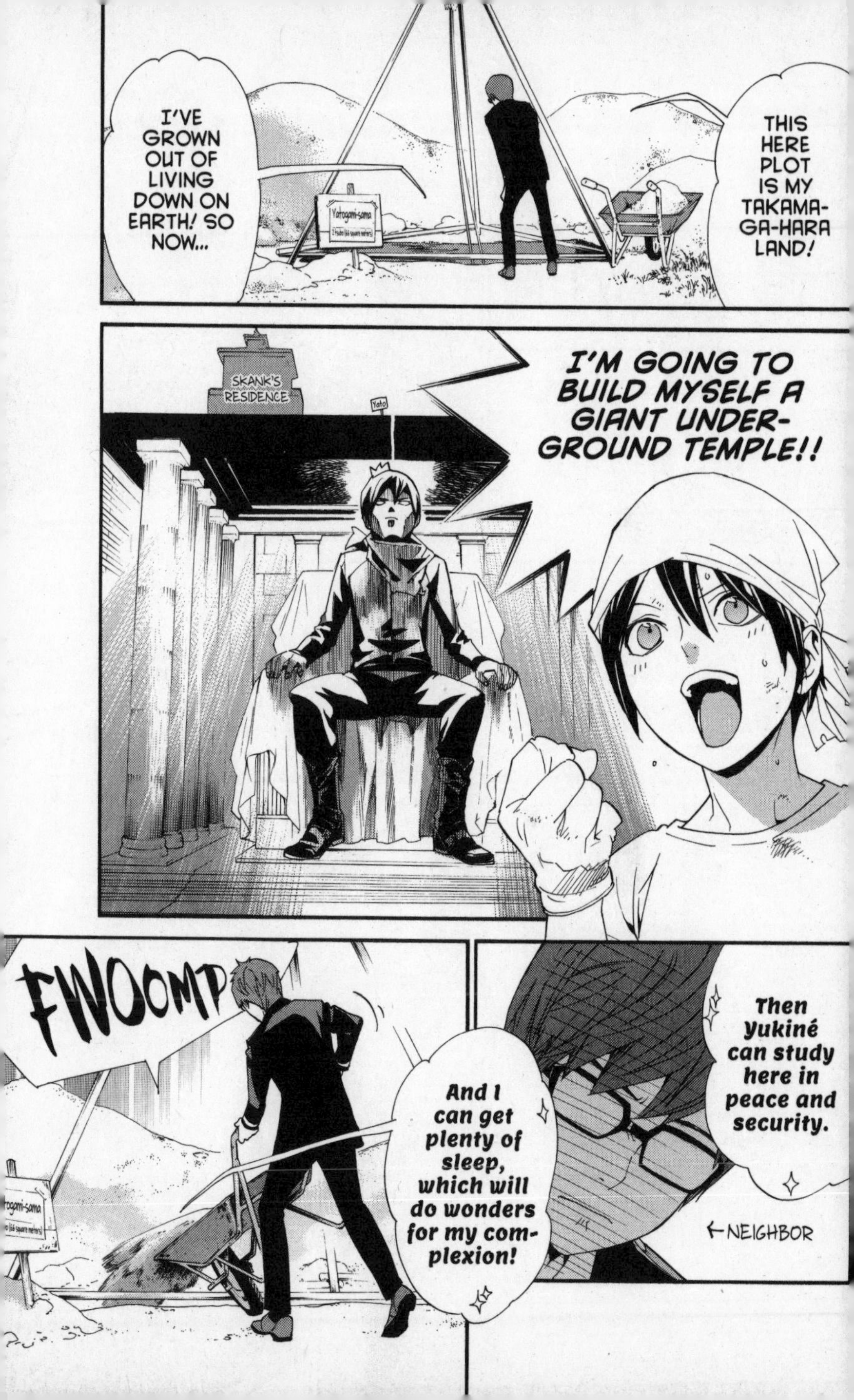
THIS HERE PLOT IS MY TAKAMA-GA-HARA LAND!
I'VE GROWN OUT OF LIVING DOWN ON EARTH! SO NOW...
Yatogami-sama
SKANK'S RESIDENCE
Yato
I'M GOING TO BUILD MYSELF A GIANT UNDER-GROUND TEMPLE!!
Then Yukiné can study here in peace and security.
←NEIGHBOR
FWOOMP
And I can get plenty of sleep, which will do wonders for my complexion!

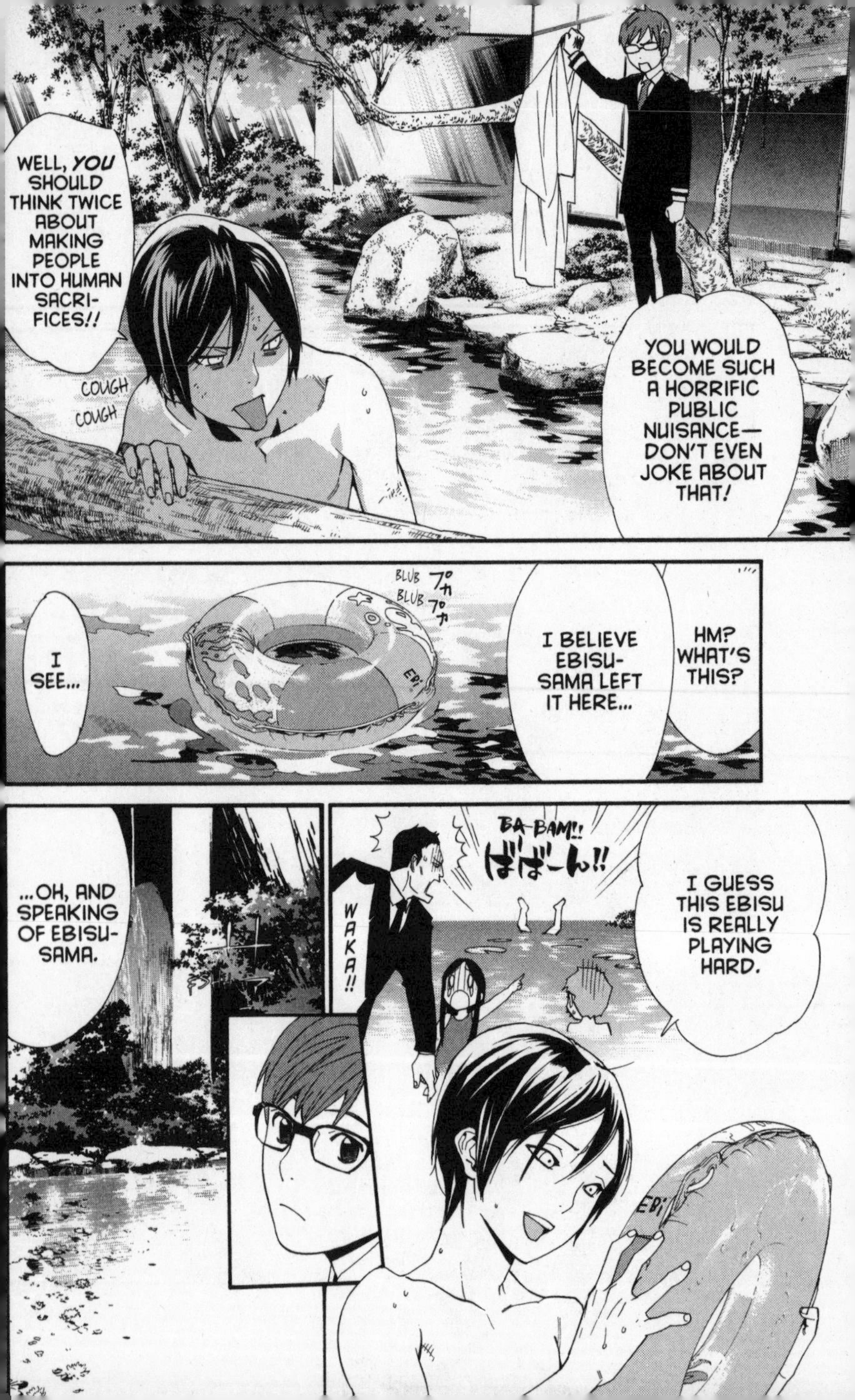
YOU WOULD BECOME SUCH A HORRIFIC PUBLIC NUISANCE—DON'T EVEN JOKE ABOUT THAT!
WELL, *YOU* SHOULD THINK TWICE ABOUT MAKING PEOPLE INTO HUMAN SACRI-FICES!!
COUGH
COUGH
HM? WHAT'S THIS?
I BELIEVE EBISU-SAMA LEFT IT HERE...
BLUB プカ
BLUB プカ
EBI
I SEE...
I GUESS THIS EBISU IS REALLY PLAYING HARD.
BA-BAM!!
ばばーん!!
WAKA!!
EBI
...OH, AND SPEAKING OF EBISU-SAMA.

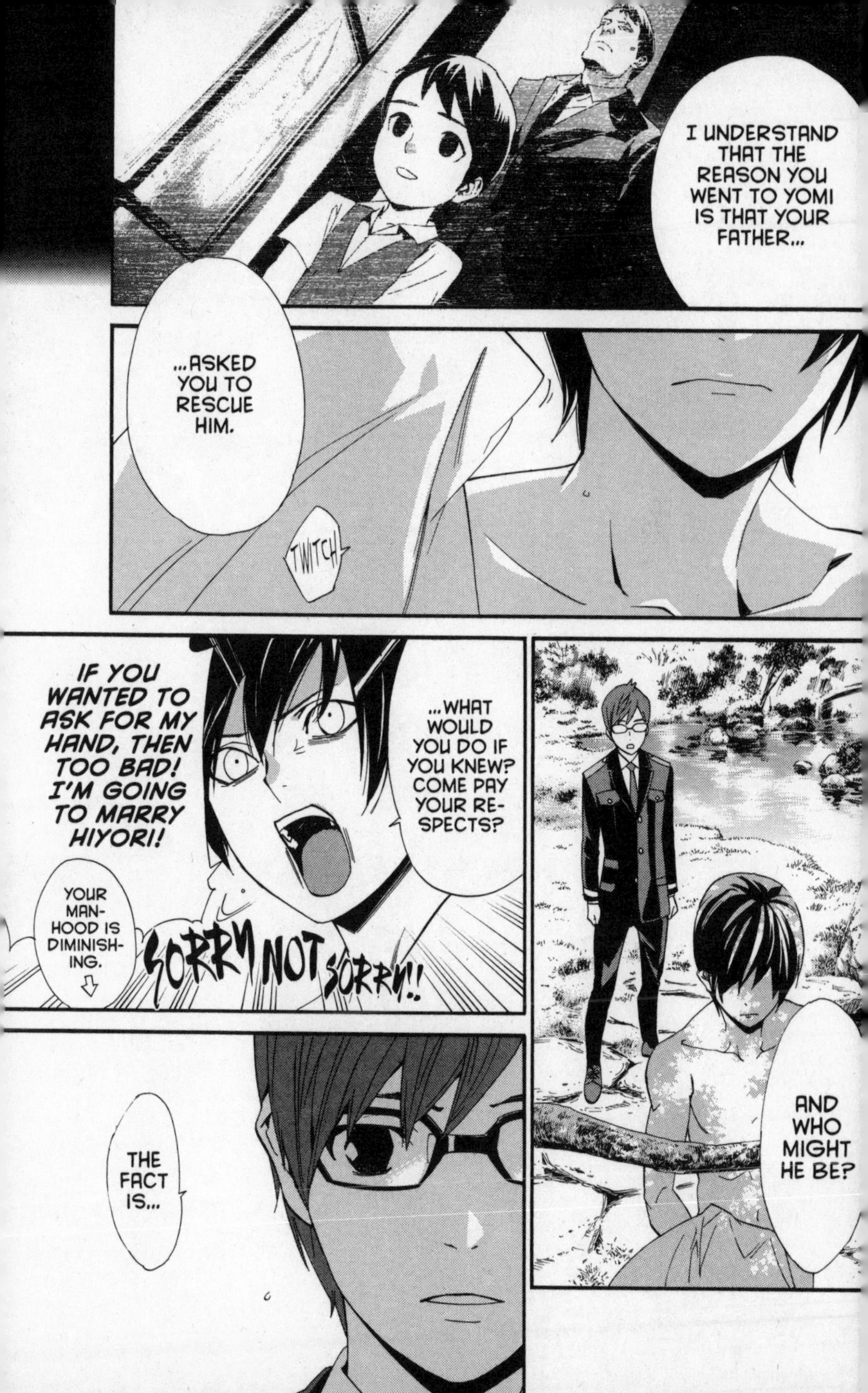
I UNDERSTAND THAT THE REASON YOU WENT TO YOMI IS THAT YOUR FATHER...
...ASKED YOU TO RESCUE HIM.
TWITCH
AND WHO MIGHT HE BE?
...WHAT WOULD YOU DO IF YOU KNEW? COME PAY YOUR RE-SPECTS?
IF YOU WANTED TO ASK FOR MY HAND, THEN TOO BAD! I'M GOING TO MARRY HIYORI!
YOUR MAN-HOOD IS DIMINISH-ING.
SORRY NOT SORRY!!
THE FACT IS...

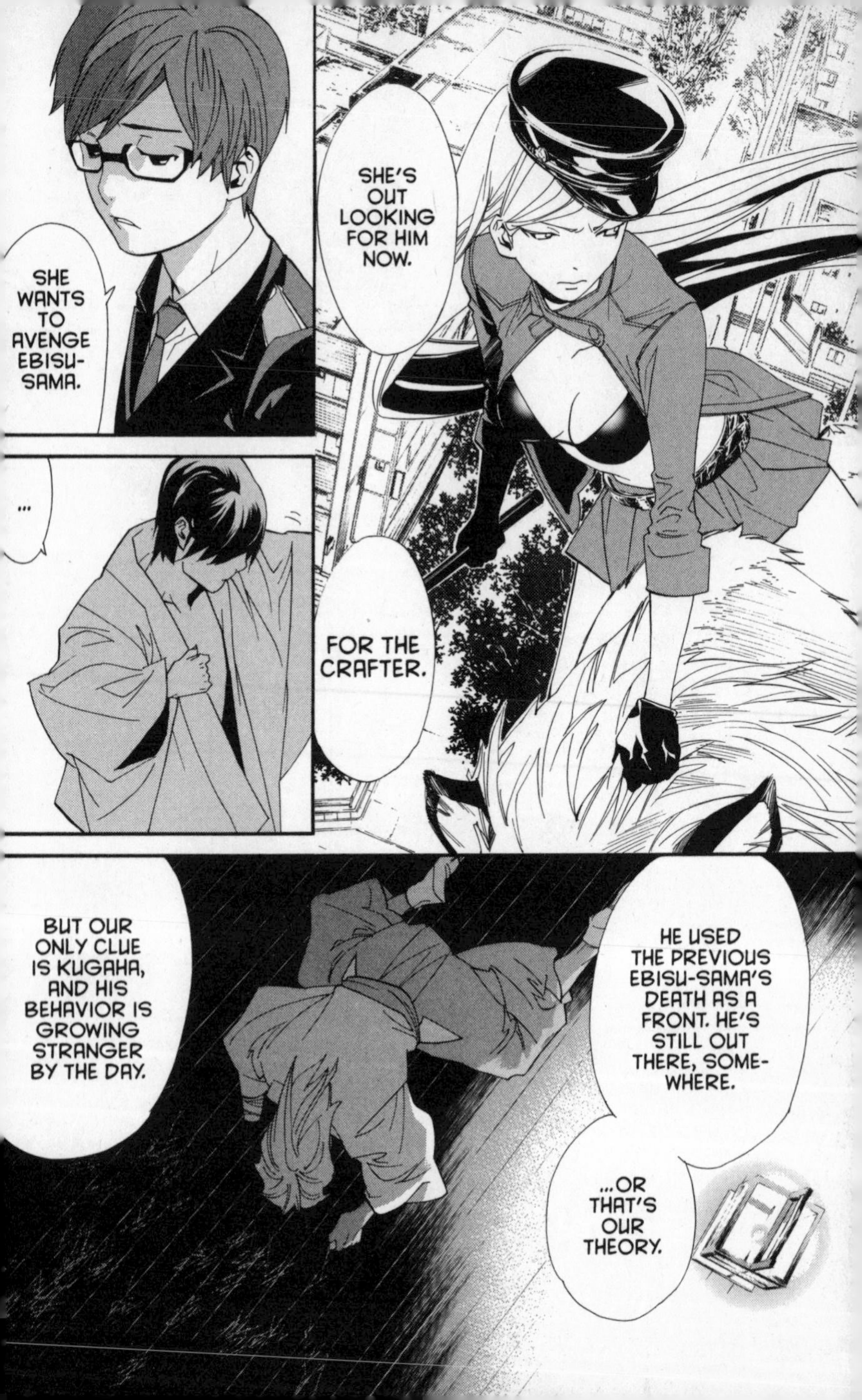
SHE'S OUT LOOKING FOR HIM NOW.
FOR THE CRAFTER.
SHE WANTS TO AVENGE EBISU-SAMA.
...
HE USED THE PREVIOUS EBISU-SAMA'S DEATH AS A FRONT. HE'S STILL OUT THERE, SOME-WHERE.
...OR THAT'S OUR THEORY.
BUT OUR ONLY CLUE IS KUGAHA, AND HIS BEHAVIOR IS GROWING STRANGER BY THE DAY.

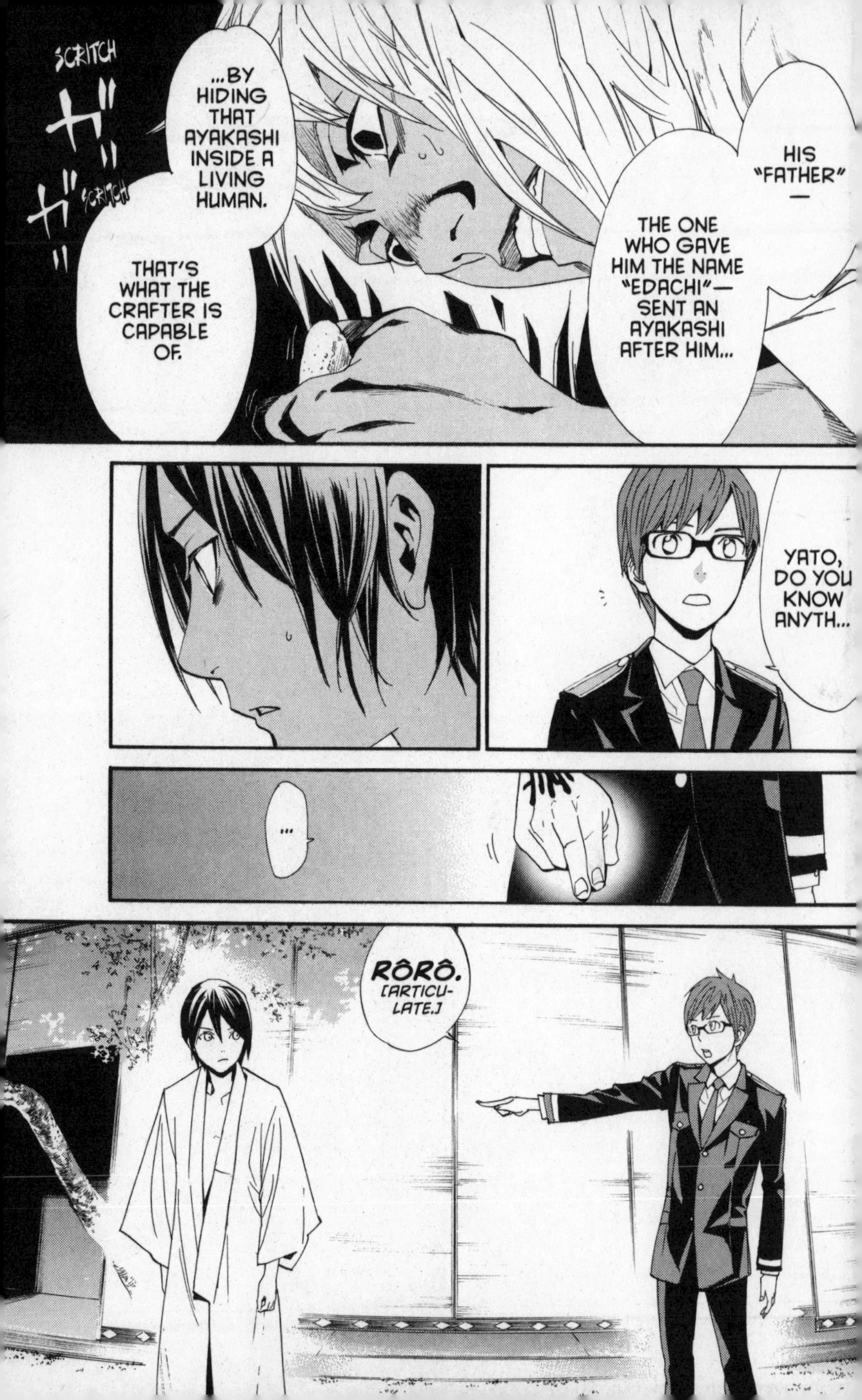
HIS "FATHER"—
THE ONE WHO GAVE HIM THE NAME "EDACHI"— SENT AN AYAKASHI AFTER HIM...
...BY HIDING THAT AYAKASHI INSIDE A LIVING HUMAN.
SCRITCH
SCRITCH
THAT'S WHAT THE CRAFTER IS CAPABLE OF.
YATO, DO YOU KNOW ANYTH...
...
RÔRÔ.
[ARTICU-LATE.]

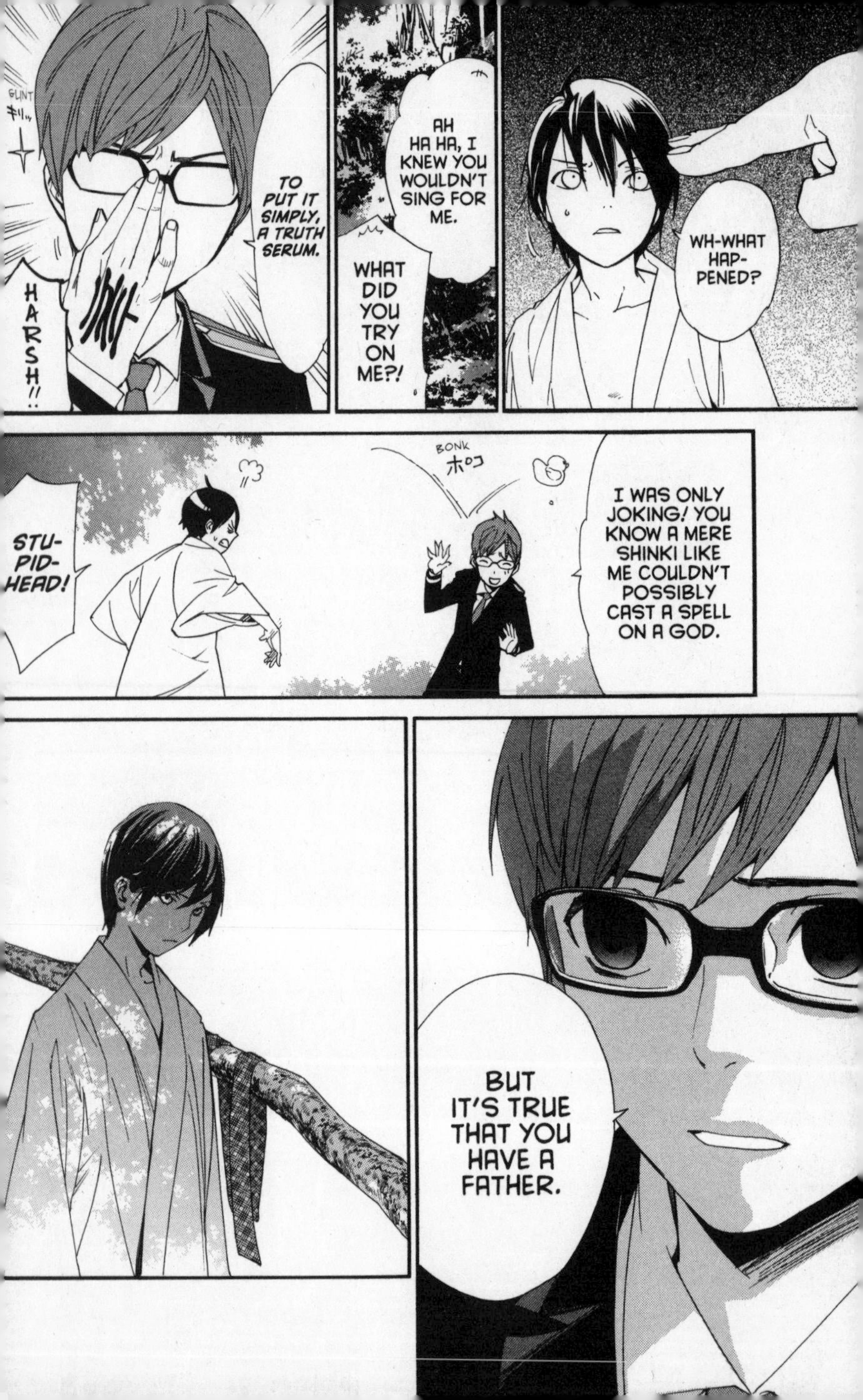
WH-WHAT HAP-PENED?
AH HA HA, I KNEW YOU WOULDN'T SING FOR ME.
WHAT DID YOU TRY ON ME?!
TO PUT IT SIMPLY, A TRUTH SERUM.
GLINT キリッ
HARSH!!
I WAS ONLY JOKING! YOU KNOW A MERE SHINKI LIKE ME COULDN'T POSSIBLY CAST A SPELL ON A GOD.
BONK ポコ
STU-PID-HEAD!
BUT IT'S TRUE THAT YOU HAVE A FATHER.

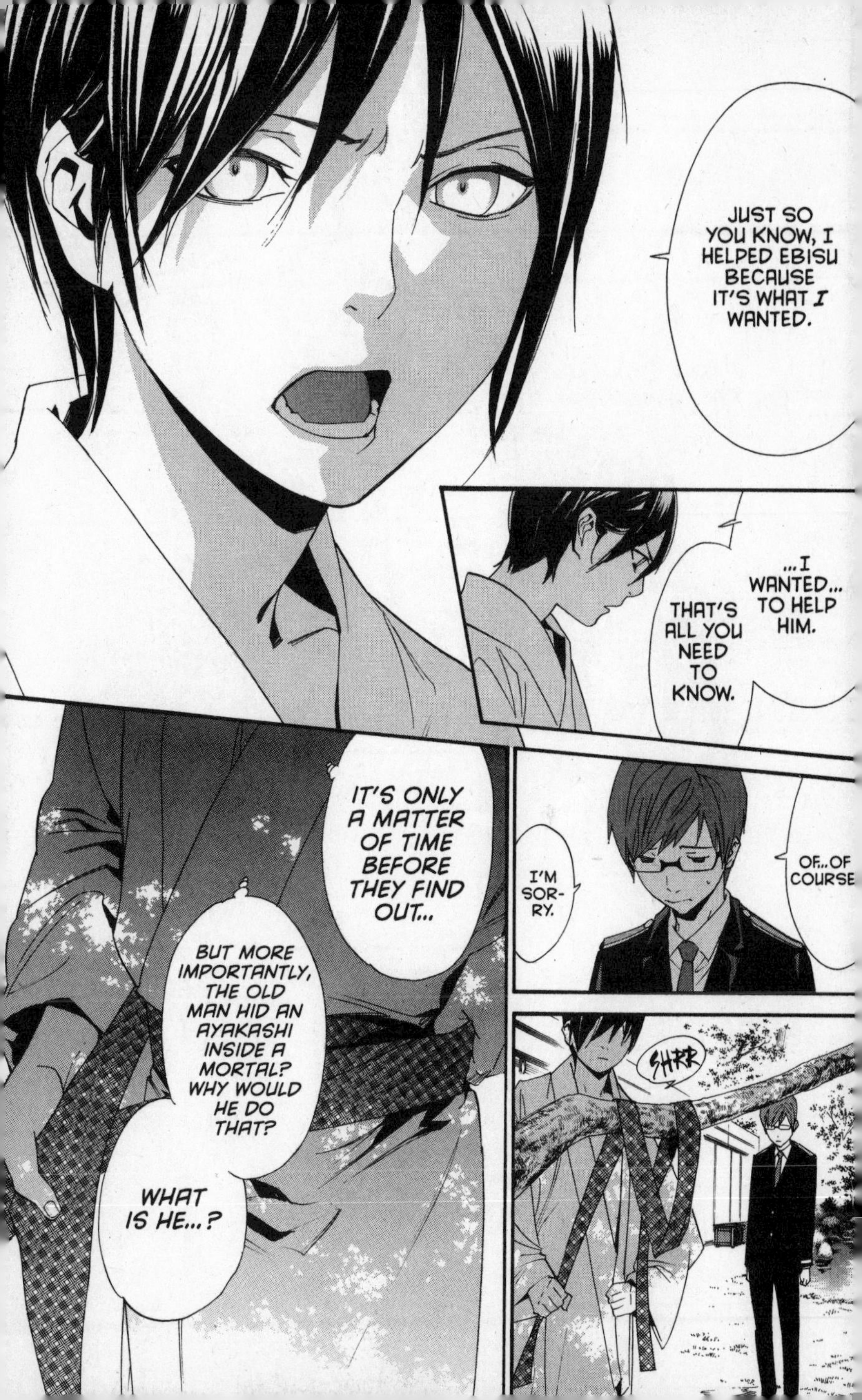
JUST SO YOU KNOW, I HELPED EBISU BECAUSE IT'S WHAT I WANTED.
...I WANTED... TO HELP HIM.
THAT'S ALL YOU NEED TO KNOW.
OF...OF COURSE
I'M SOR-RY.
SHRR
IT'S ONLY A MATTER OF TIME BEFORE THEY FIND OUT...
BUT MORE IMPORTANTLY, THE OLD MAN HID AN AYAKASHI INSIDE A MORTAL? WHY WOULD HE DO THAT?
WHAT IS HE...?

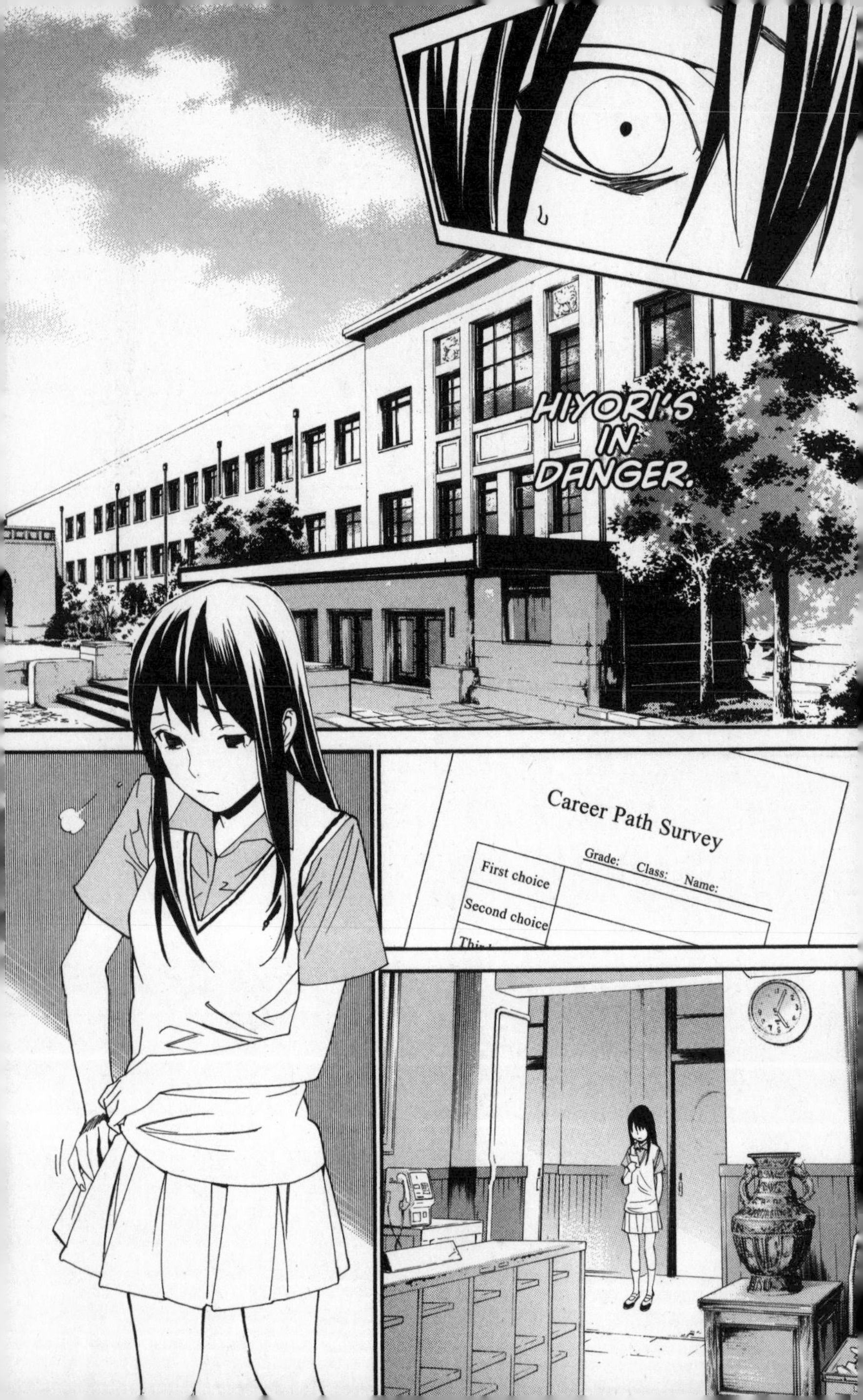
HIYORI'S IN DANGER.
Career Path Survey
Grade: Class: Name:
First choice
Second choice

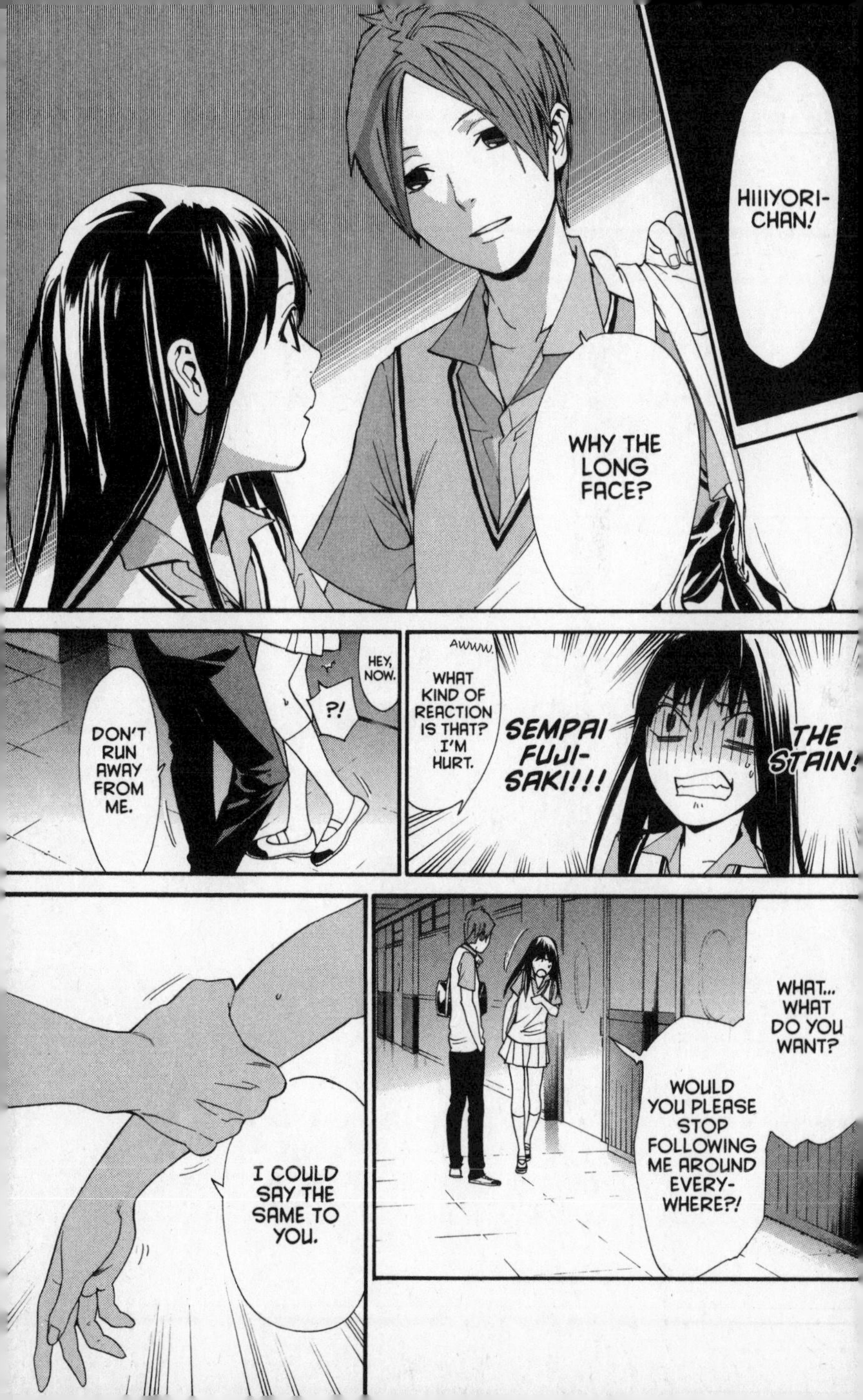
HIIIYORI-CHAN!
WHY THE LONG FACE?
THE STAIN!
SEMPAI FUJI-SAKI!!!
AWWW.
WHAT KIND OF REACTION IS THAT? I'M HURT.
HEY, NOW.
?!
DON'T RUN AWAY FROM ME.
WHAT... WHAT DO YOU WANT?
WOULD YOU PLEASE STOP FOLLOWING ME AROUND EVERY-WHERE?!
I COULD SAY THE SAME TO YOU.

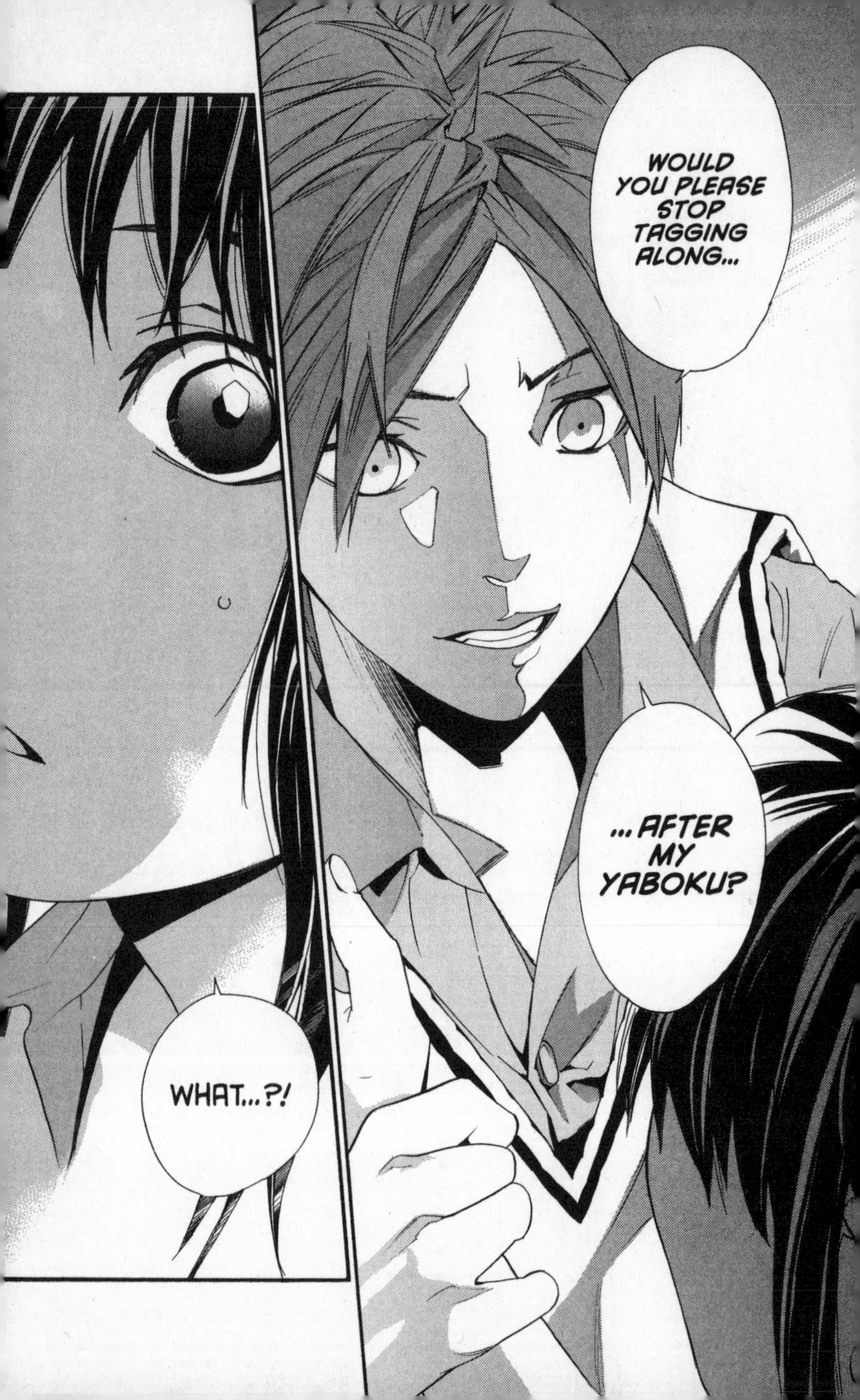
WOULD YOU PLEASE STOP TAGGING ALONG...
...AFTER MY YABOKU?
WHAT...?!

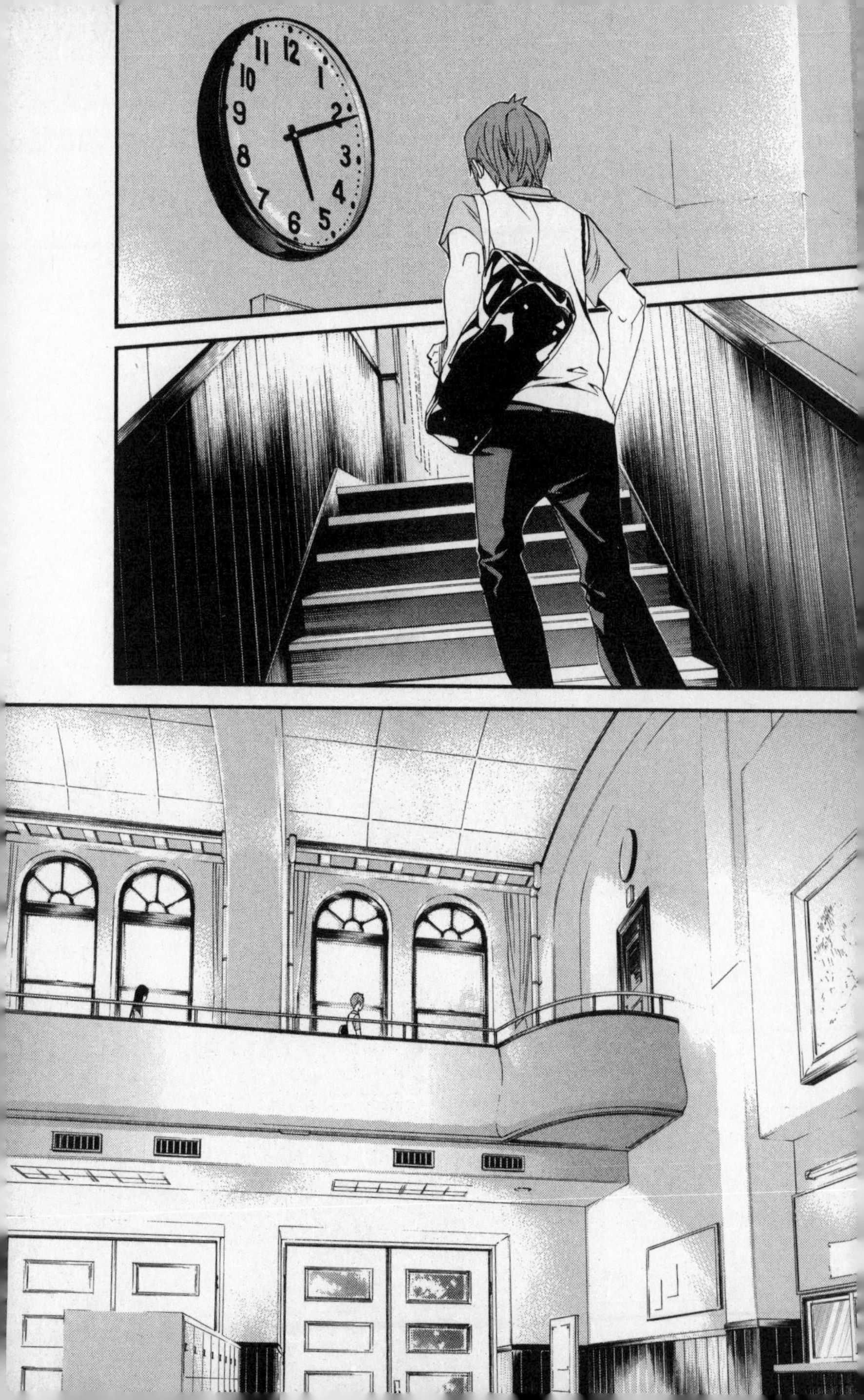

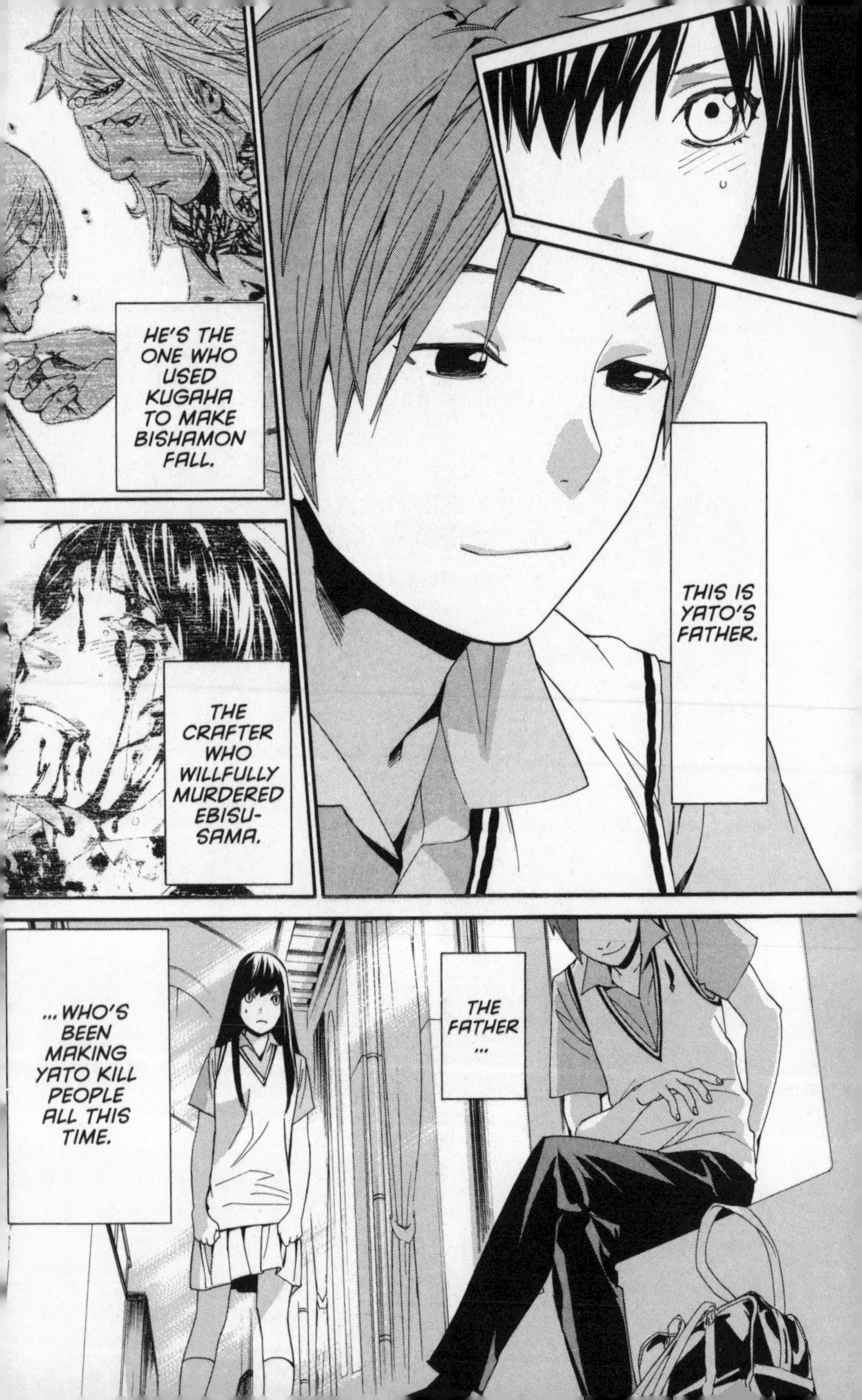
THIS IS YATO'S FATHER.
HE'S THE ONE WHO USED KUGAHA TO MAKE BISHAMON FALL.
THE CRAFTER WHO WILLFULLY MURDERED EBISU-SAMA.
THE FATHER...
...WHO'S BEEN MAKING YATO KILL PEOPLE ALL THIS TIME.

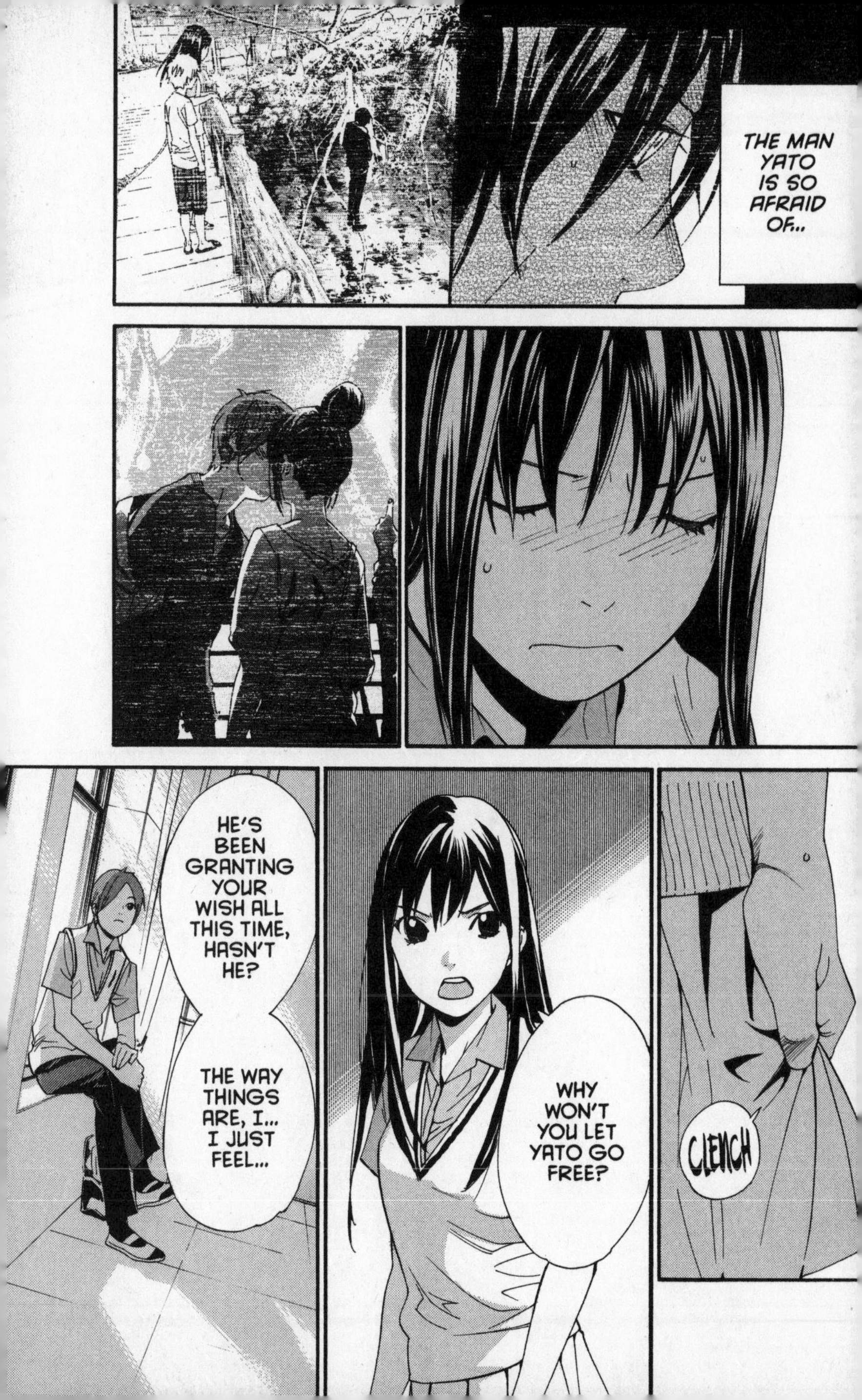
THE MAN YATO IS SO AFRAID OF...
WHY WON'T YOU LET YATO GO FREE?
CLENCH
HE'S BEEN GRANTING YOUR WISH ALL THIS TIME, HASN'T HE?
THE WAY THINGS ARE, I... I JUST FEEL...

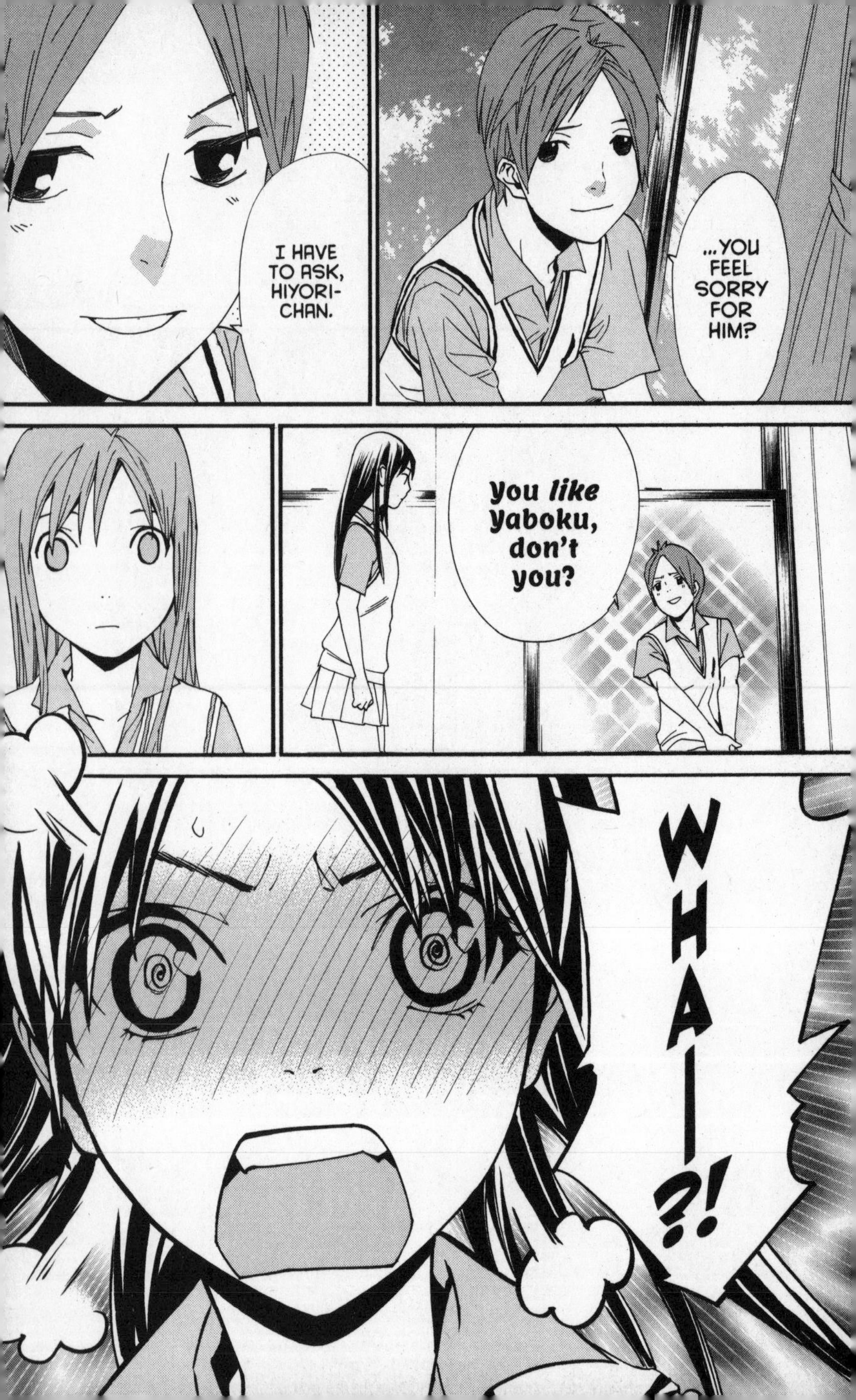
...YOU FEEL SORRY FOR HIM?
I HAVE TO ASK, HIYORI-CHAN.
You *like* Yaboku, don't you?
WHA—?!

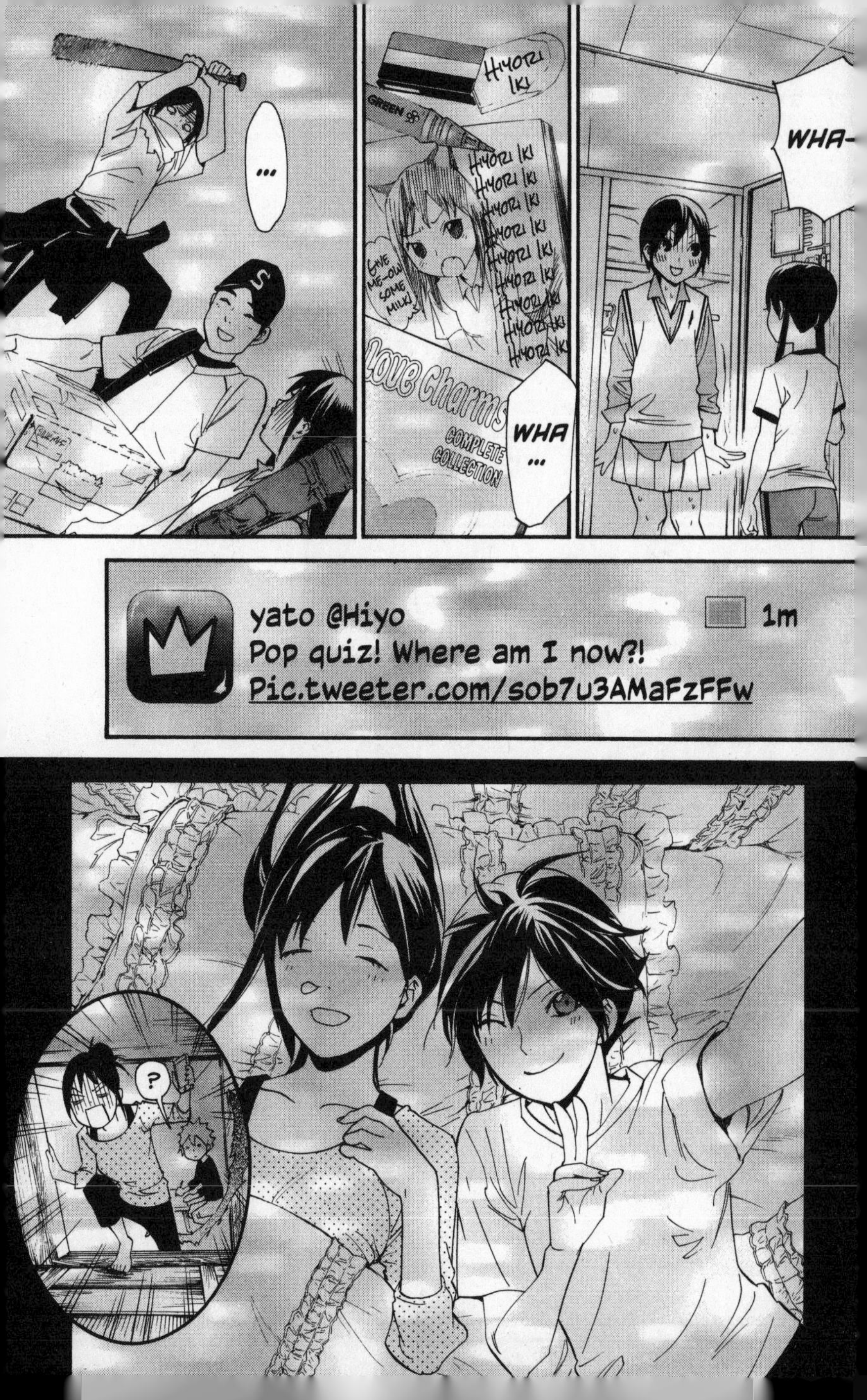
WHA-
HIYORI IKI
HIYORI IKI HIYORI IKI HIYORI IKI HIYORI IKI HIYORI IKI HIYORI IKI HIYORI IKI HIYORI IKI HIYORI IKI HIYORI IKI
GIVE ME-OW SOME MILK!
Love Charms COMPLETE COLLECTION
WHA ...
...
yato @Hiyo 1m
Pop quiz! Where am I now?!
Pic.tweeter.com/sob7u3AMaFzFFw
?

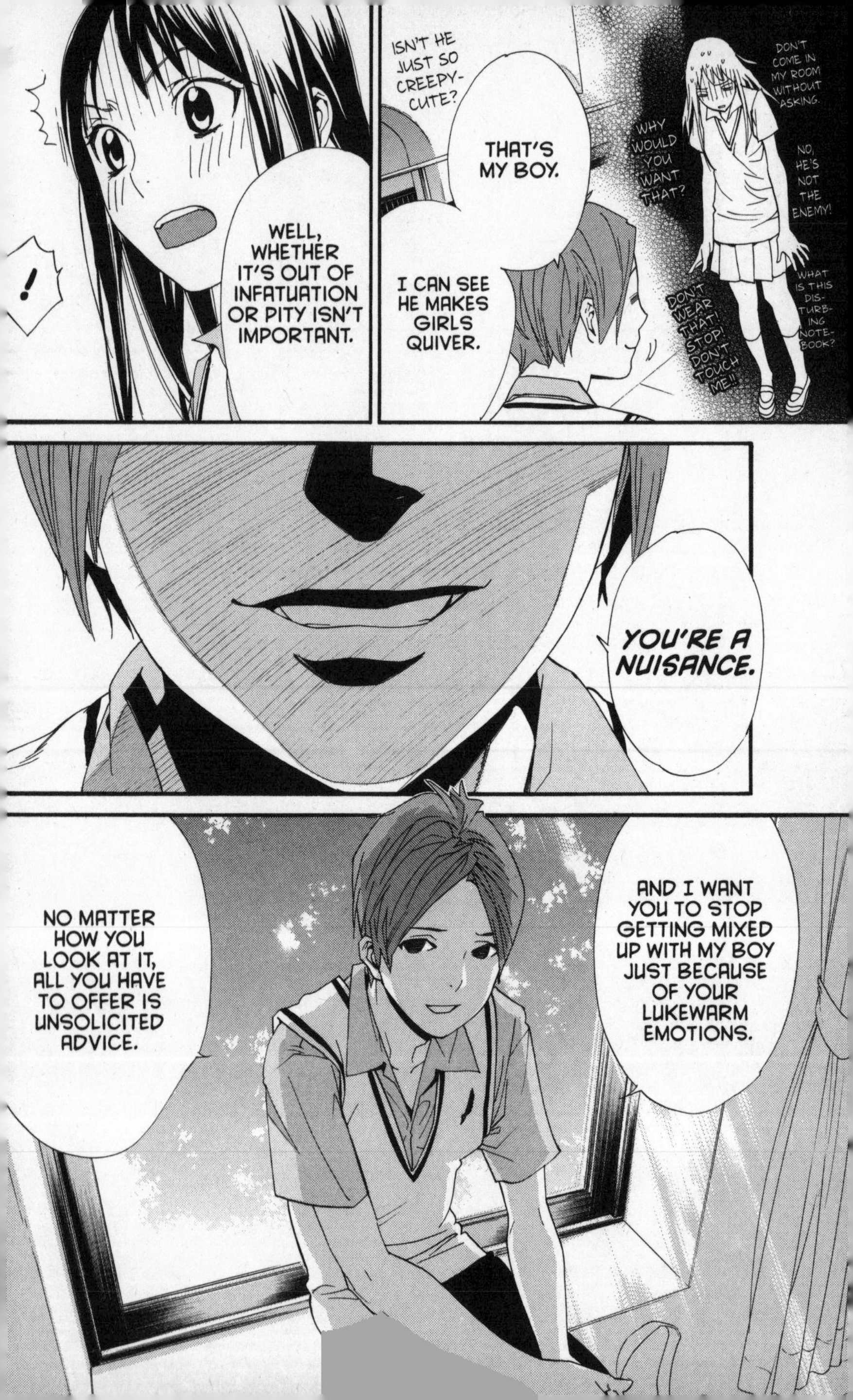
DON'T COME IN MY ROOM WITHOUT ASKING.
NO, HE'S NOT THE ENEMY!
WHAT IS THIS DIS-TURB-ING NOTE-BOOK?
WHY WOULD YOU WANT THAT?
DON'T WEAR THAT! STOP! DON'T TOUCH ME!!
ISN'T HE JUST SO CREEPY-CUTE?
THAT'S MY BOY.
I CAN SEE HE MAKES GIRLS QUIVER.
!
WELL, WHETHER IT'S OUT OF INFATUATION OR PITY ISN'T IMPORTANT.
YOU'RE A NUISANCE.
AND I WANT YOU TO STOP GETTING MIXED UP WITH MY BOY JUST BECAUSE OF YOUR LUKEWARM EMOTIONS.
NO MATTER HOW YOU LOOK AT IT, ALL YOU HAVE TO OFFER IS UNSOLICITED ADVICE.

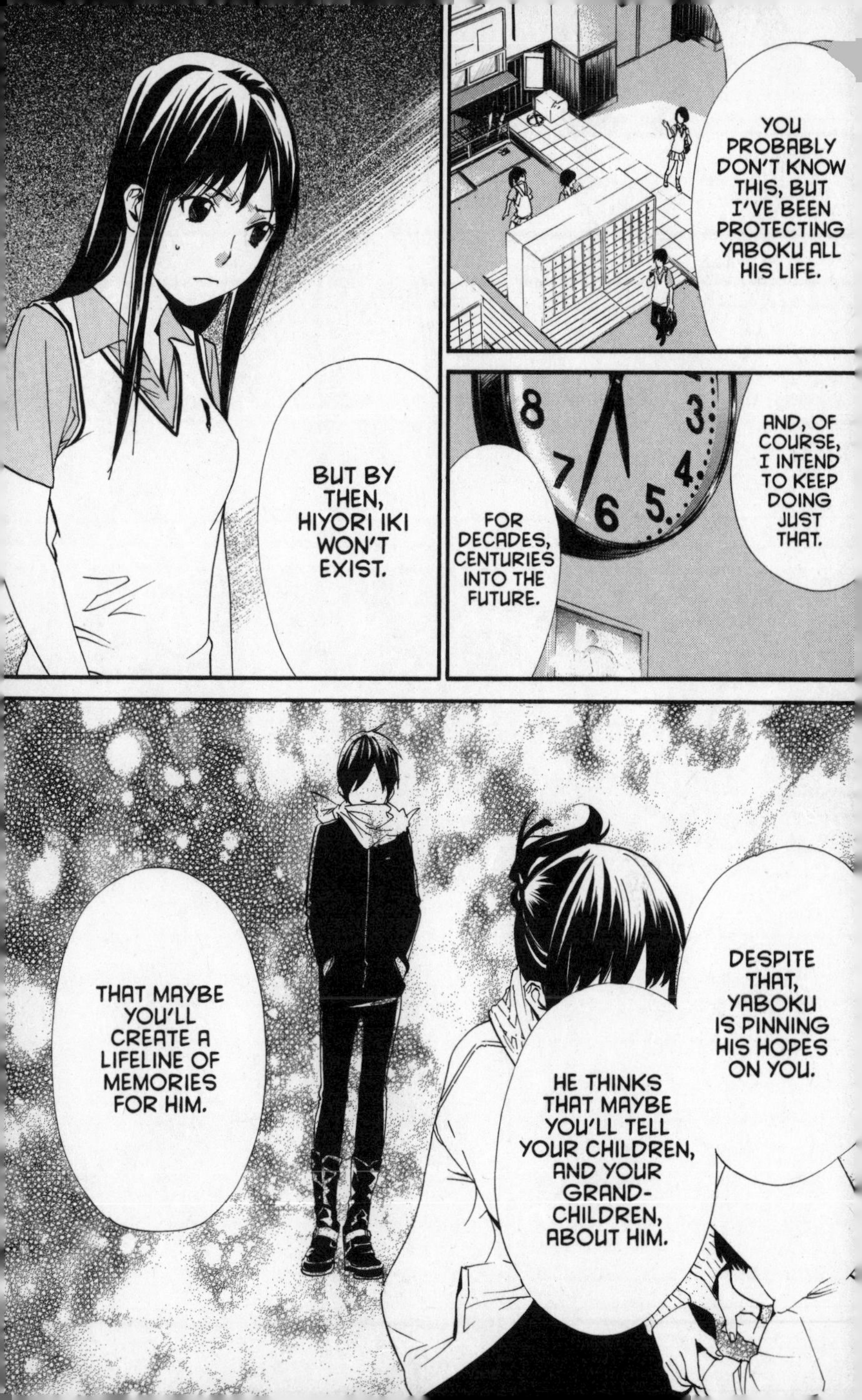
YOU PROBABLY DON'T KNOW THIS, BUT I'VE BEEN PROTECTING YABOKU ALL HIS LIFE.
AND, OF COURSE, I INTEND TO KEEP DOING JUST THAT.
FOR DECADES, CENTURIES INTO THE FUTURE.
BUT BY THEN, HIYORI IKI WON'T EXIST.
DESPITE THAT, YABOKU IS PINNING HIS HOPES ON YOU.
HE THINKS THAT MAYBE YOU'LL TELL YOUR CHILDREN, AND YOUR GRAND-CHILDREN, ABOUT HIM.
THAT MAYBE YOU'LL CREATE A LIFELINE OF MEMORIES FOR HIM.

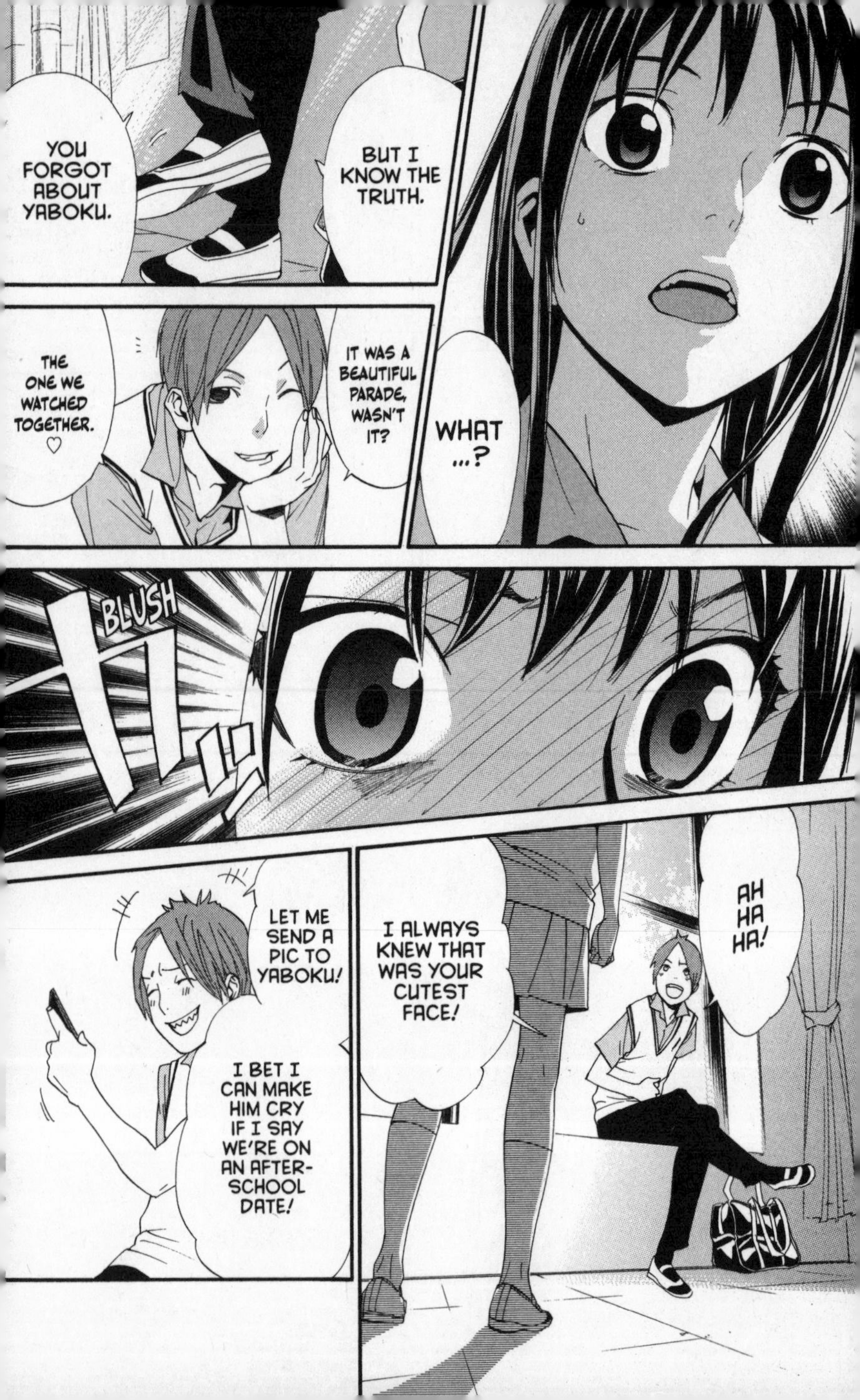
WHAT ...?
BUT I KNOW THE TRUTH.
YOU FORGOT ABOUT YABOKU.
IT WAS A BEAUTIFUL PARADE, WASN'T IT?
THE ONE WE WATCHED TOGETHER. ♡
BLUSH
AH HA HA!
I ALWAYS KNEW THAT WAS YOUR CUTEST FACE!
LET ME SEND A PIC TO YABOKU!
I BET I CAN MAKE HIM CRY IF I SAY WE'RE ON AN AFTER-SCHOOL DATE!

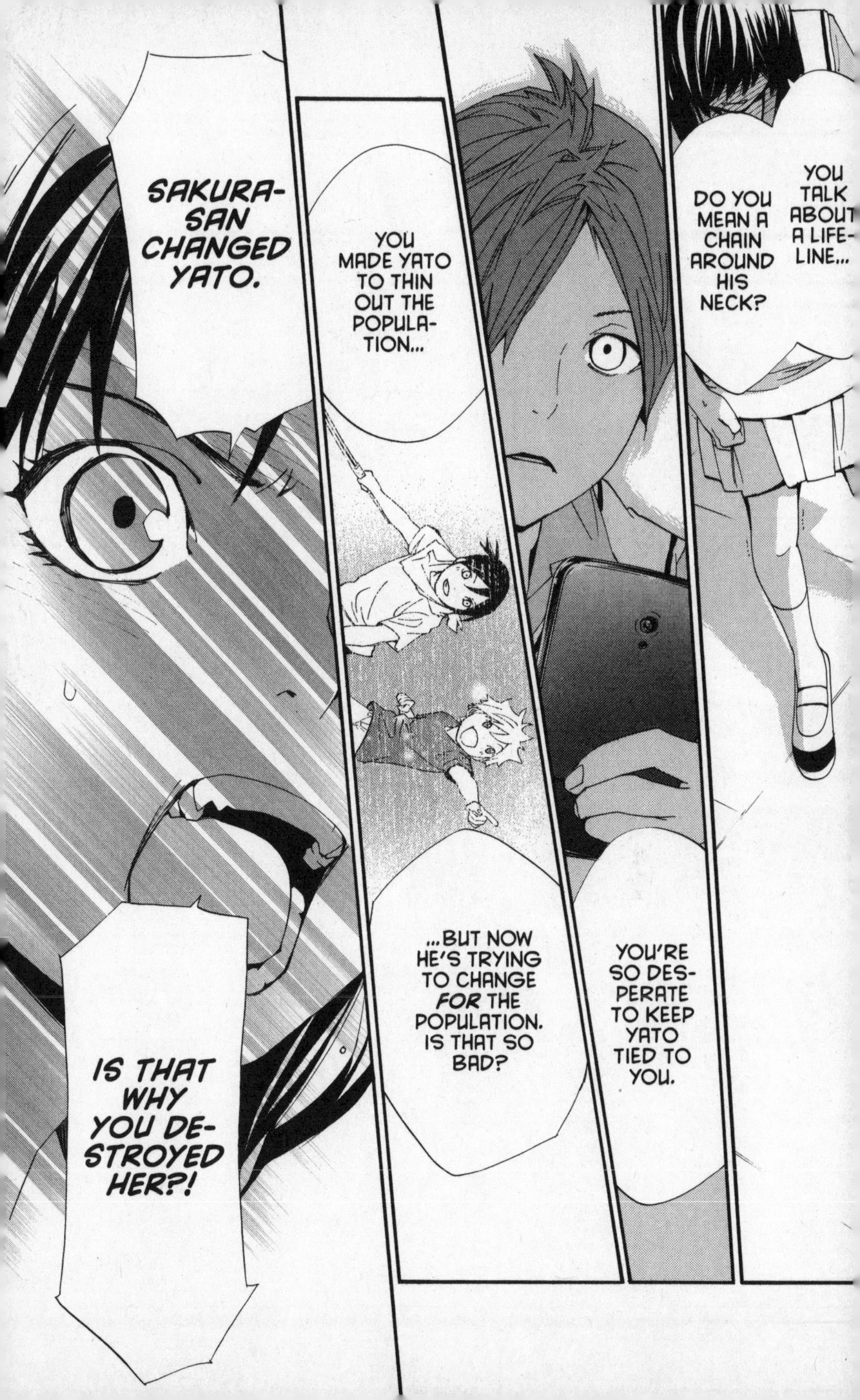
YOU TALK ABOUT A LIFE-LINE...
DO YOU MEAN A CHAIN AROUND HIS NECK?
YOU'RE SO DES-PERATE TO KEEP YATO TIED TO YOU.
YOU MADE YATO TO THIN OUT THE POPULA-TION...
...BUT NOW HE'S TRYING TO CHANGE *FOR* THE POPULATION. IS THAT SO BAD?
SAKURA-SAN CHANGED YATO.
IS THAT WHY YOU DE-STROYED HER?!

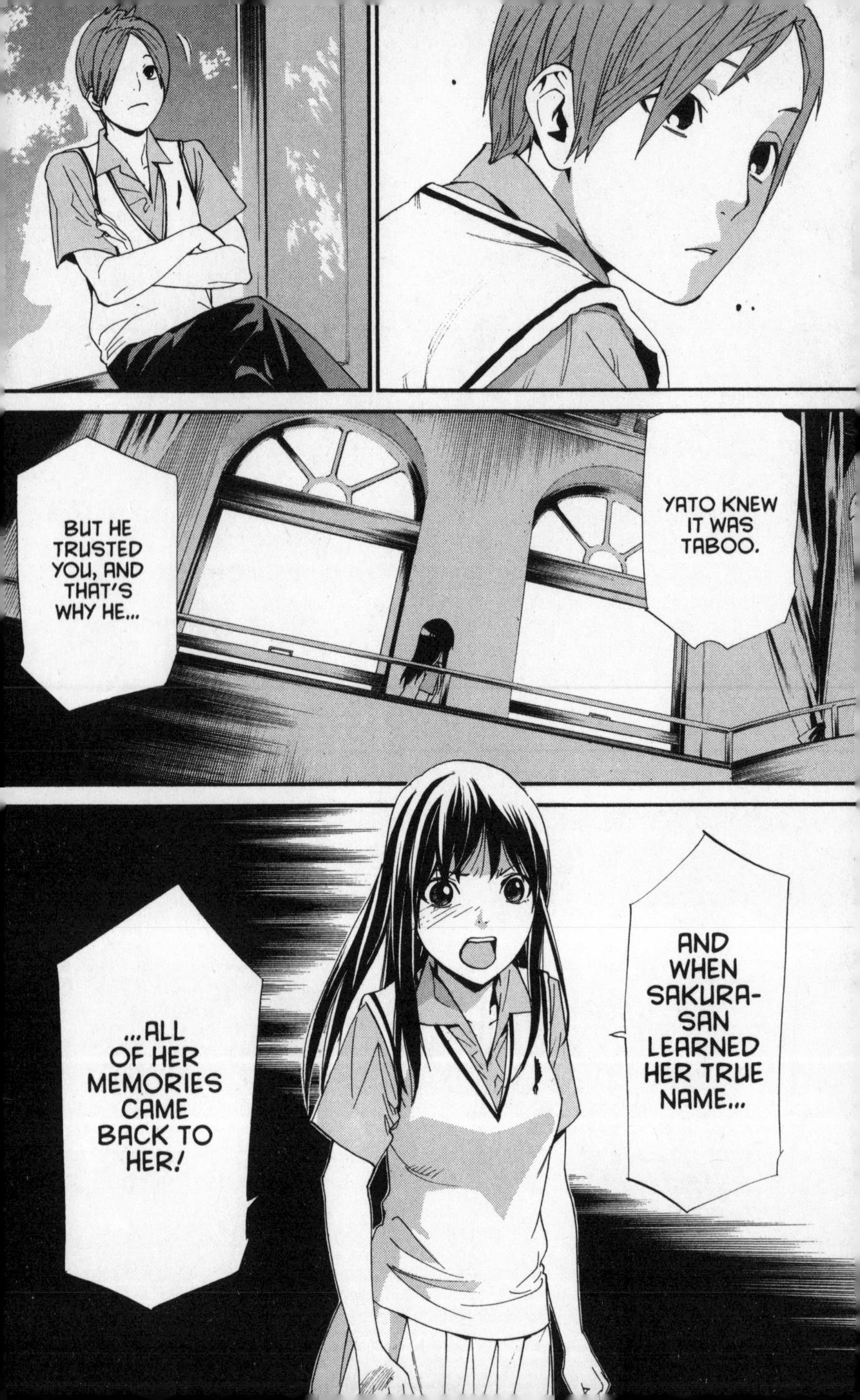
YATO KNEW IT WAS TABOO.
BUT HE TRUSTED YOU, AND THAT'S WHY HE...
AND WHEN SAKURA-SAN LEARNED HER TRUE NAME...
...ALL OF HER MEMORIES CAME BACK TO HER!

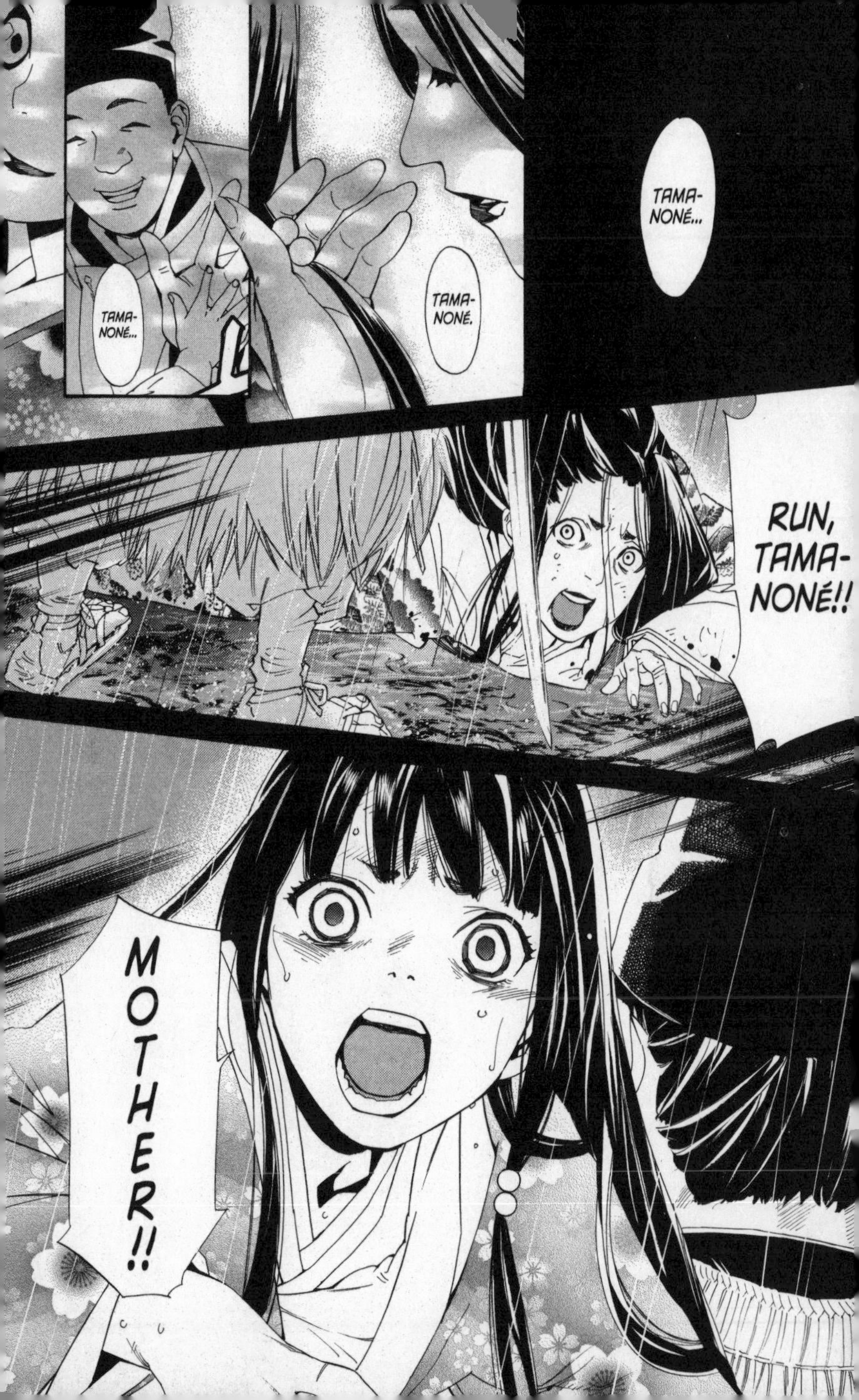
TAMA-NONÉ...
TAMA-NONÉ.
TAMA-NONÉ...
RUN, TAMA-NONÉ!!
MOTHER!!

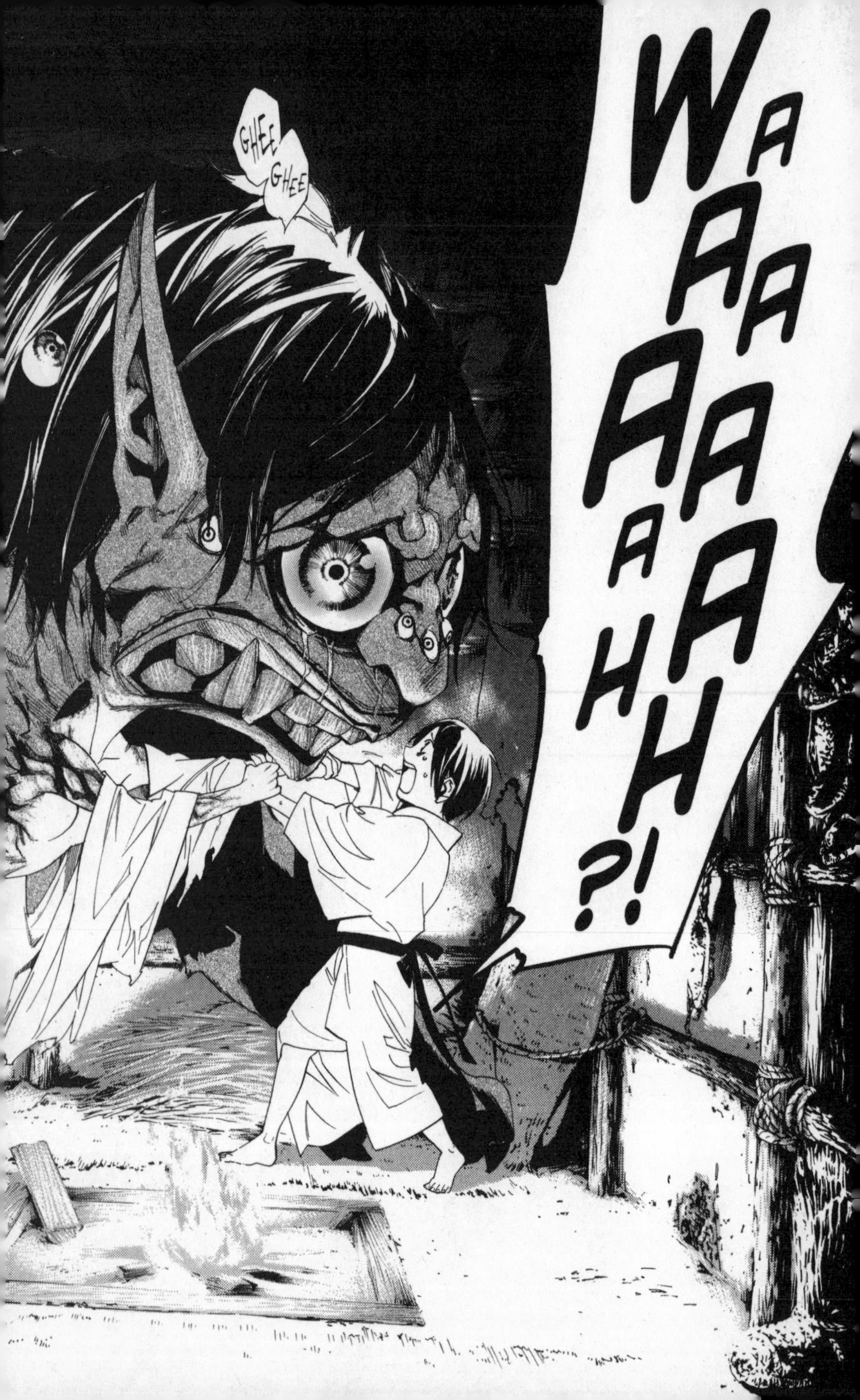
WAAAAAAAAAHHH?!
GHEE GHEE

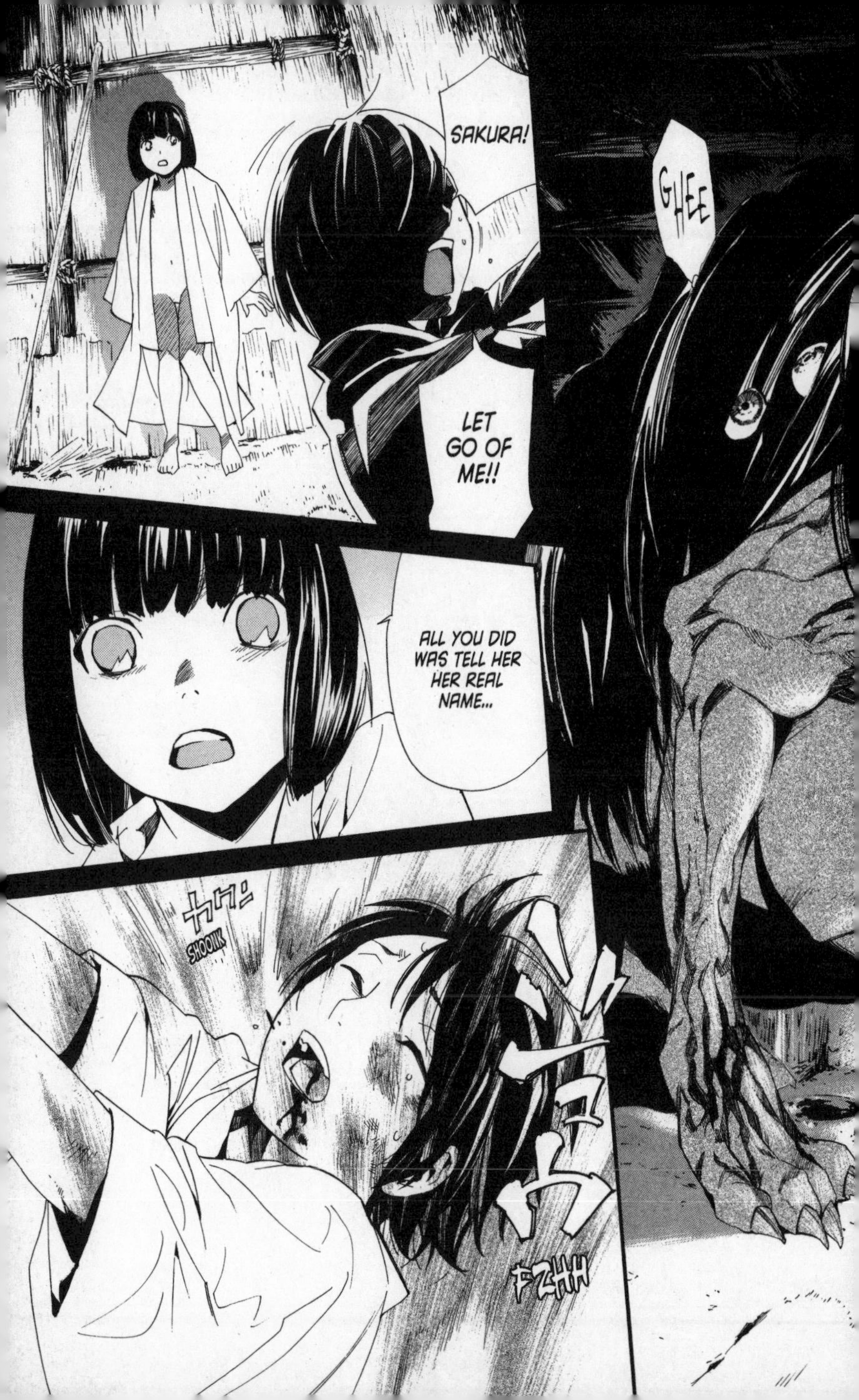
GHEE
SAKURA!
LET GO OF ME!!
ALL YOU DID WAS TELL HER HER REAL NAME...
SHOONK
FZHH

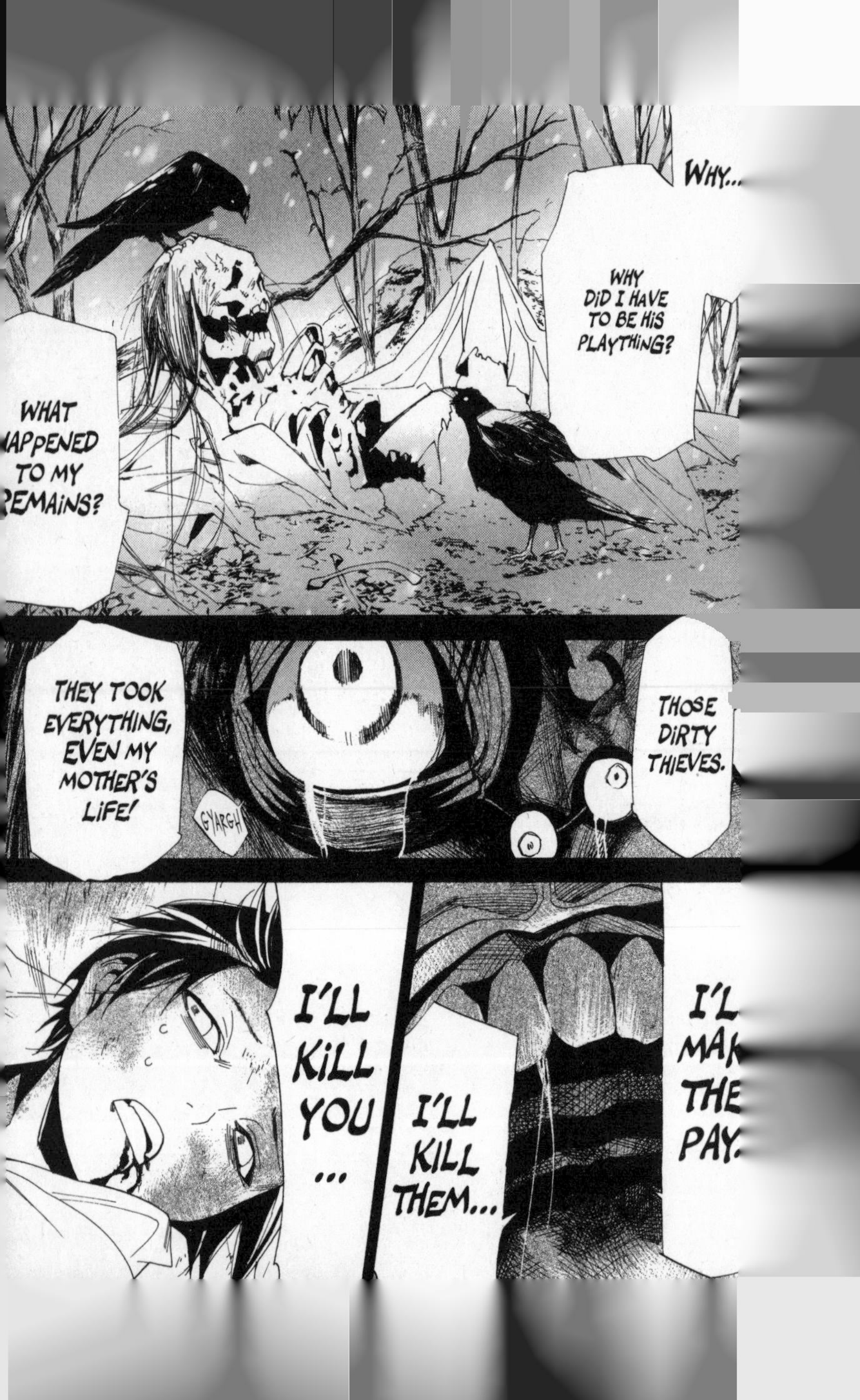
WHY...
WHY DID I HAVE TO BE HIS PLAYTHING?
WHAT APPENED TO MY EMAINS?
THOSE DIRTY THIEVES.
GYARGH
THEY TOOK EVERYTHING, EVEN MY MOTHER'S LIFE!
I'L MAK THE PAY.
I'LL KILL THEM...
I'LL KILL YOU ...

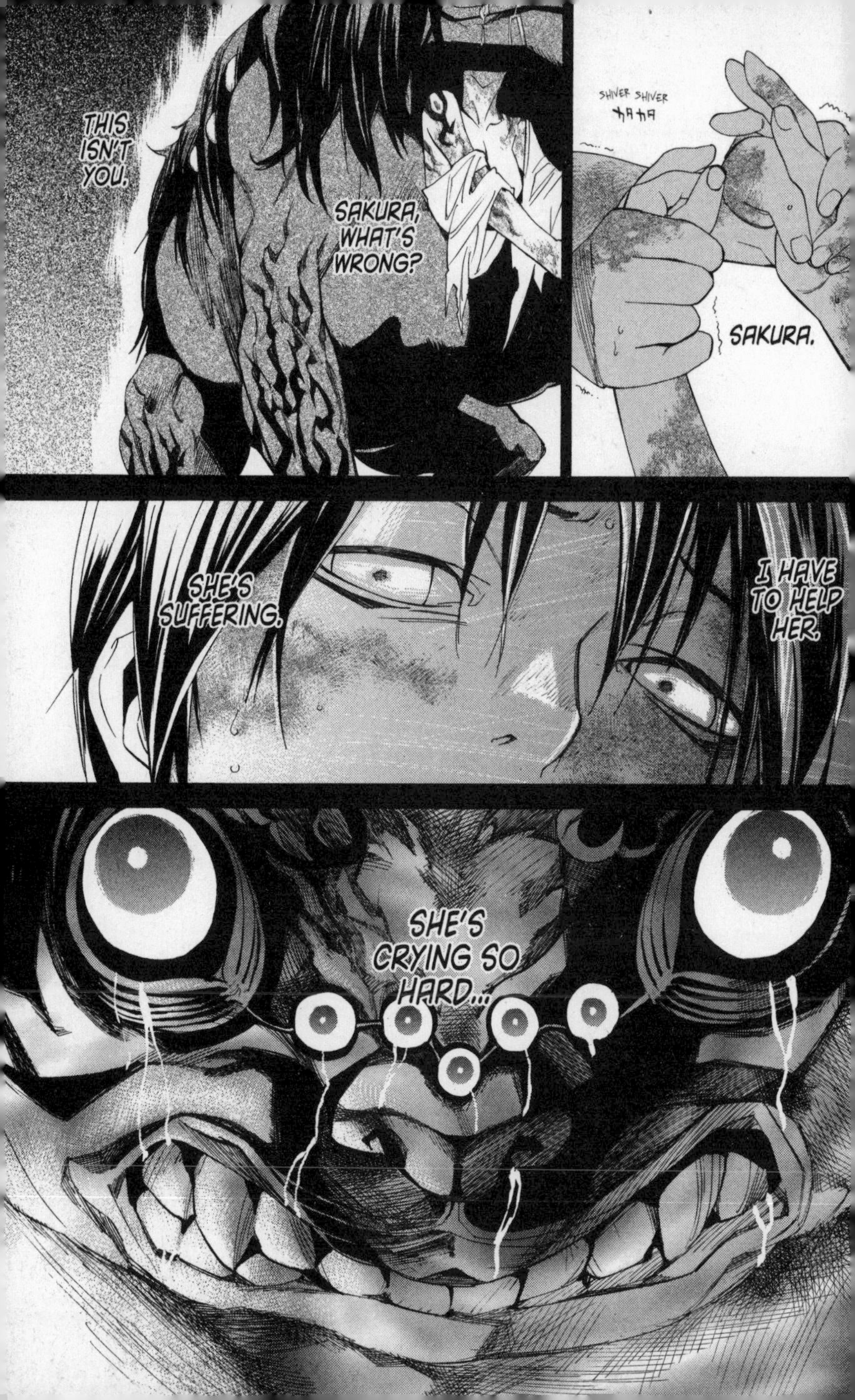
SHIVER SHIVER
カタカタ
SAKURA.
SAKURA, WHAT'S WRONG?
THIS ISN'T YOU.
I HAVE TO HELP HER.
SHE'S SUFFERING.
SHE'S CRYING SO HARD...

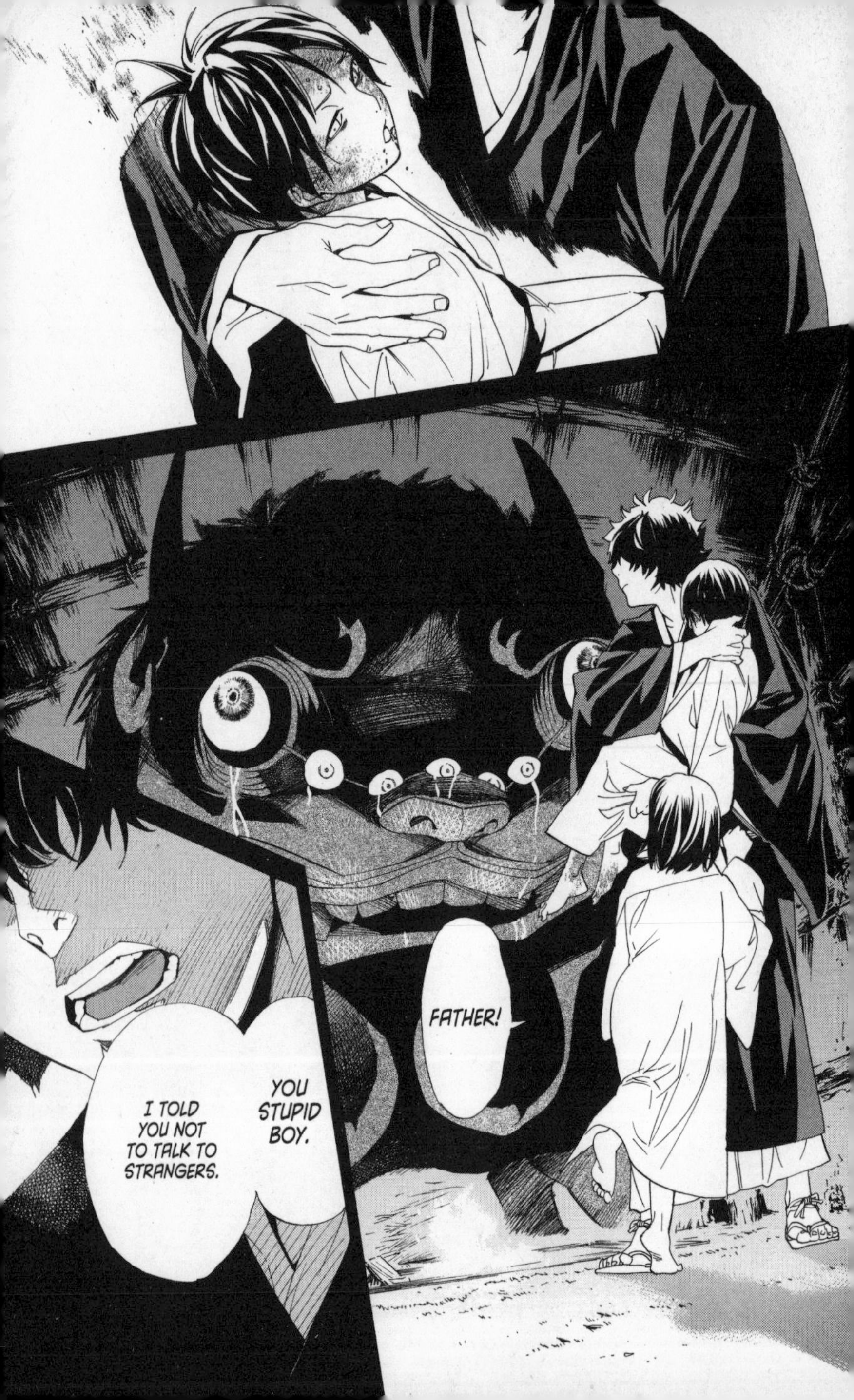
FATHER!
YOU STUPID BOY.
I TOLD YOU NOT TO TALK TO STRANGERS.

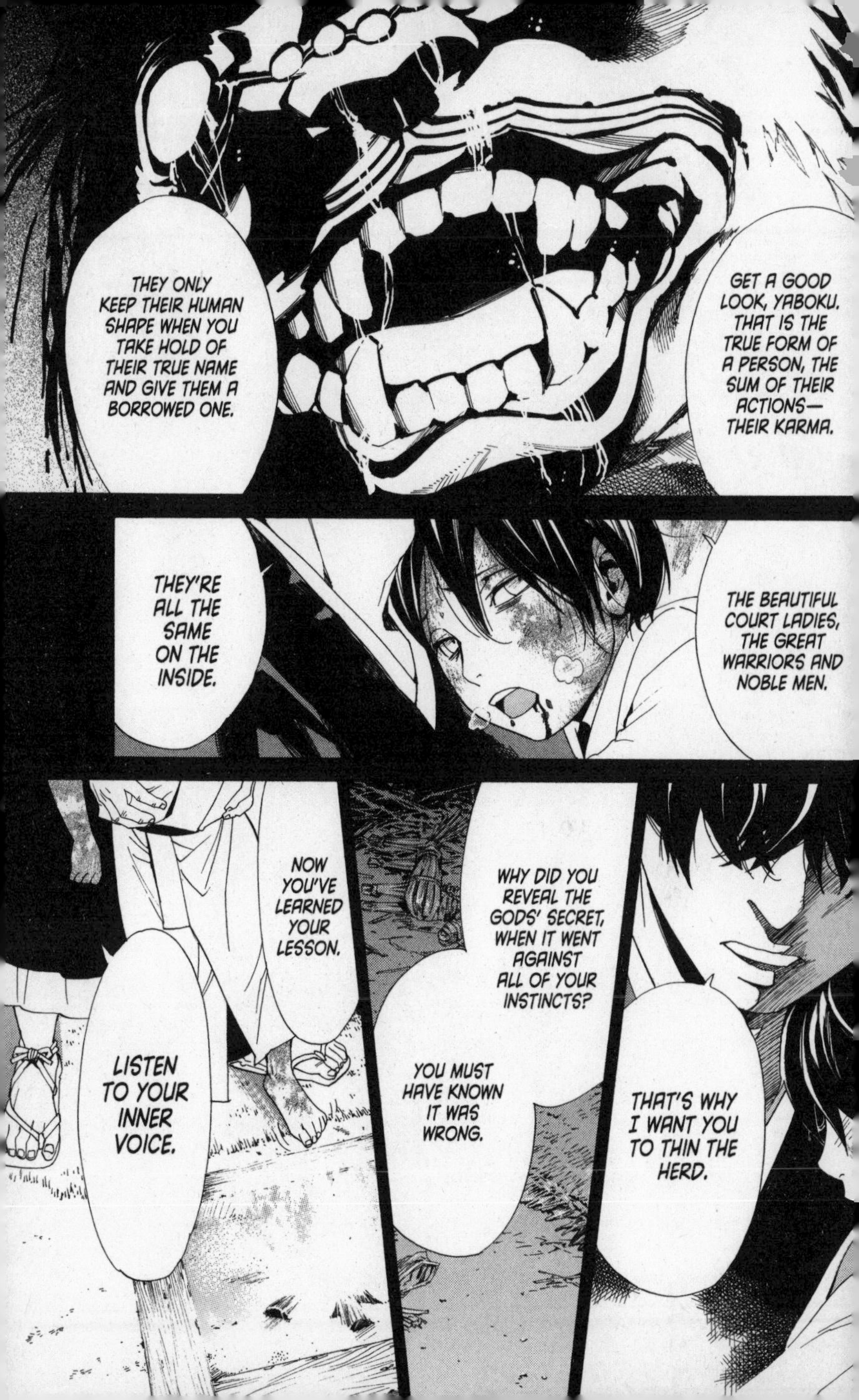
GET A GOOD LOOK, YABOKU. THAT IS THE TRUE FORM OF A PERSON, THE SUM OF THEIR ACTIONS— THEIR KARMA.
THEY ONLY KEEP THEIR HUMAN SHAPE WHEN YOU TAKE HOLD OF THEIR TRUE NAME AND GIVE THEM A BORROWED ONE.
THE BEAUTIFUL COURT LADIES, THE GREAT WARRIORS AND NOBLE MEN.
THEY'RE ALL THE SAME ON THE INSIDE.
THAT'S WHY I WANT YOU TO THIN THE HERD.
WHY DID YOU REVEAL THE GODS' SECRET, WHEN IT WENT AGAINST ALL OF YOUR INSTINCTS?
YOU MUST HAVE KNOWN IT WAS WRONG.
NOW YOU'VE LEARNED YOUR LESSON.
LISTEN TO YOUR INNER VOICE.

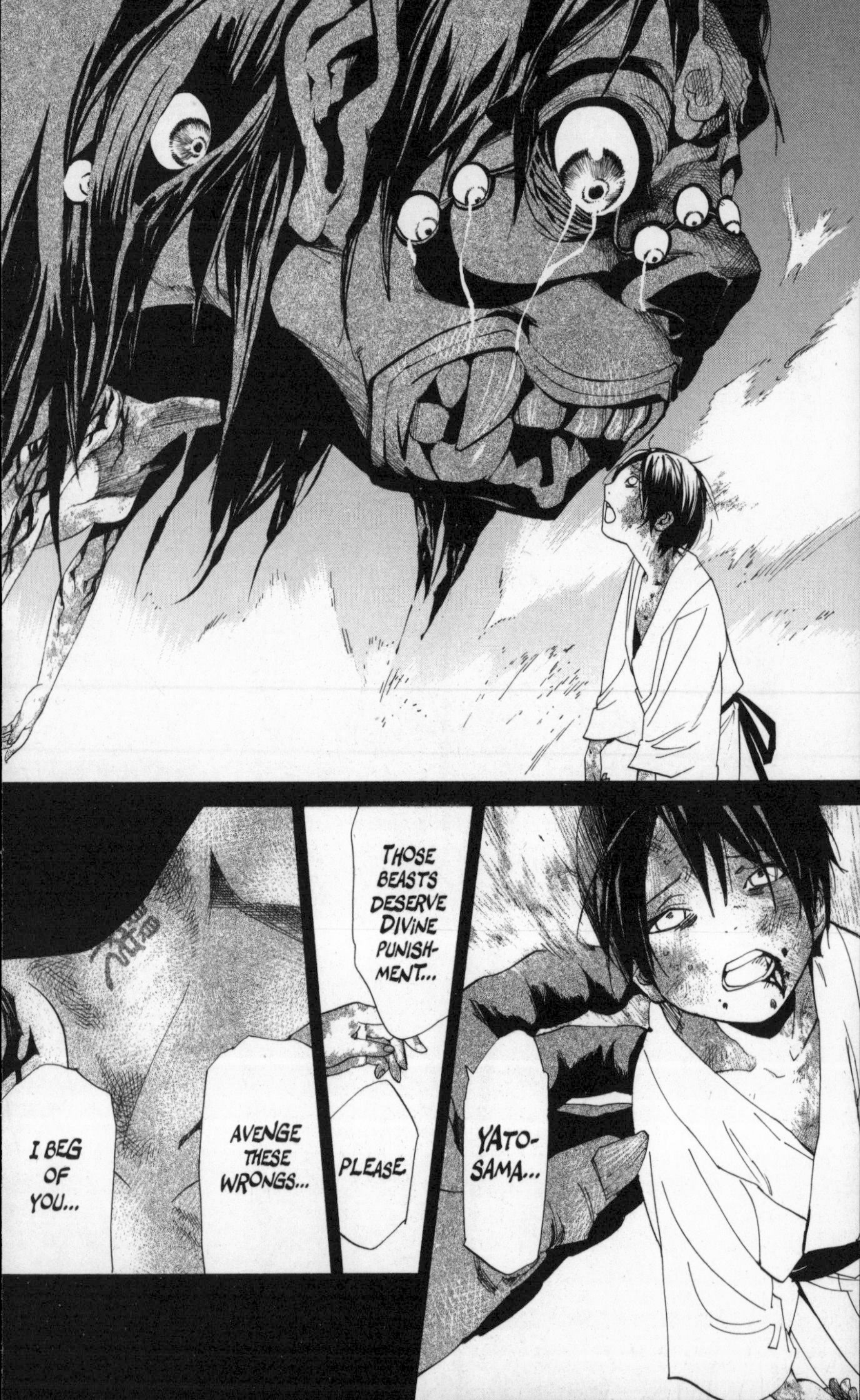
YATO-SAMA...
THOSE BEASTS DESERVE DIVINE PUNISHMENT...
PLEASE
AVENGE THESE WRONGS...
I BEG OF YOU...

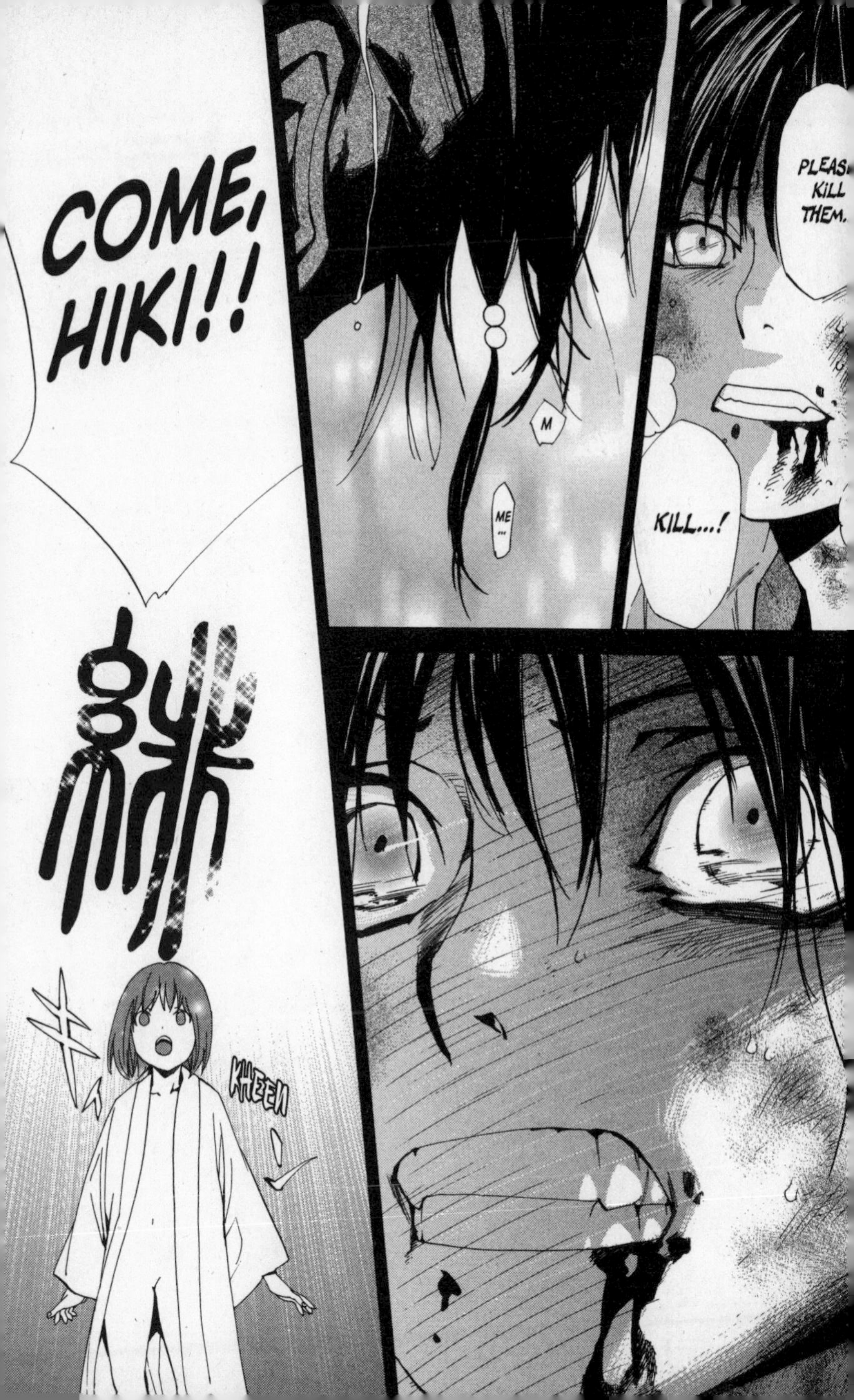
PLEAS KILL THEM.
KILL...!
M
ME...
COME, HIKI!!
KHEEN

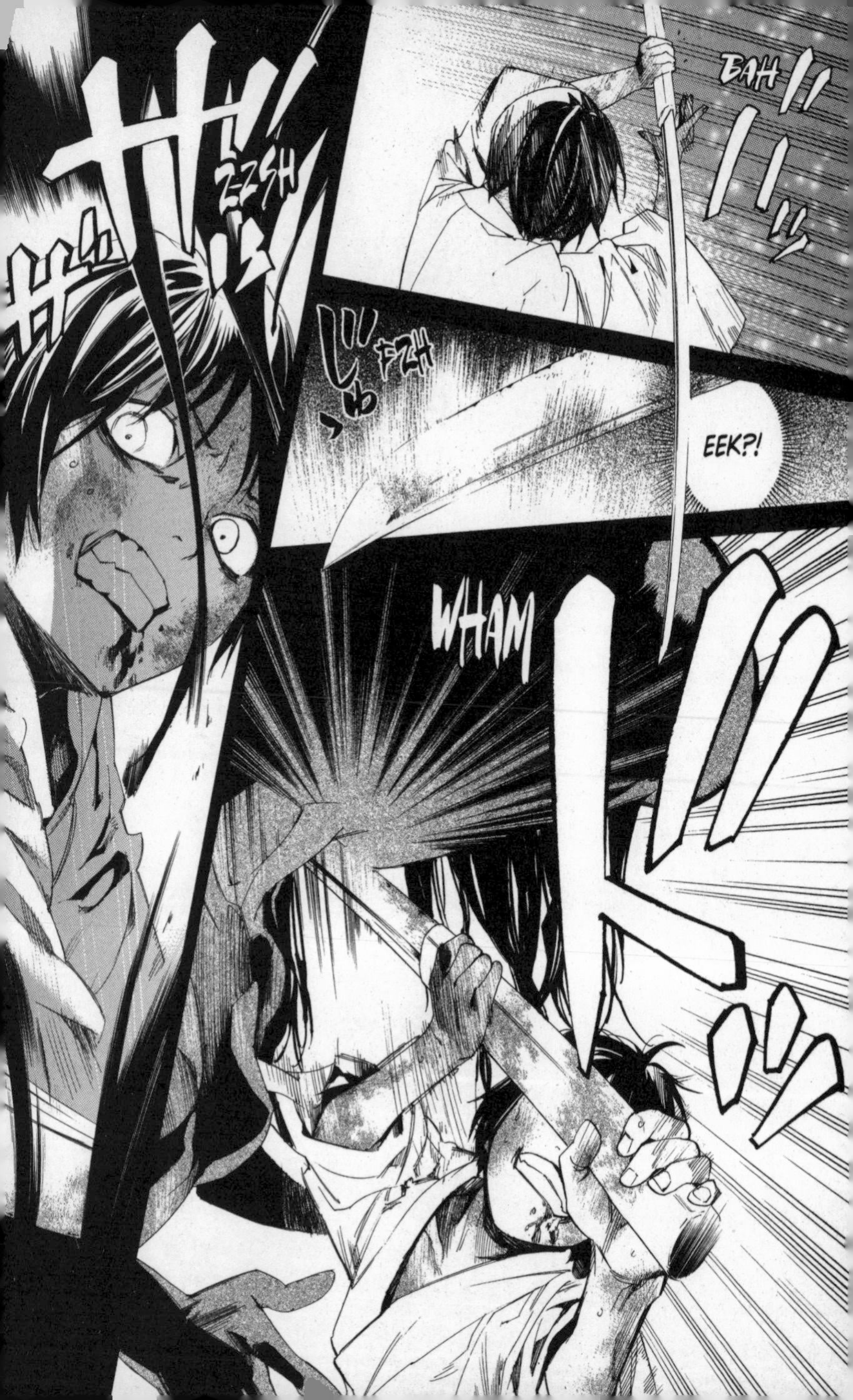
BAH
EEK?!
FZH
WHAM
Z-ZSH

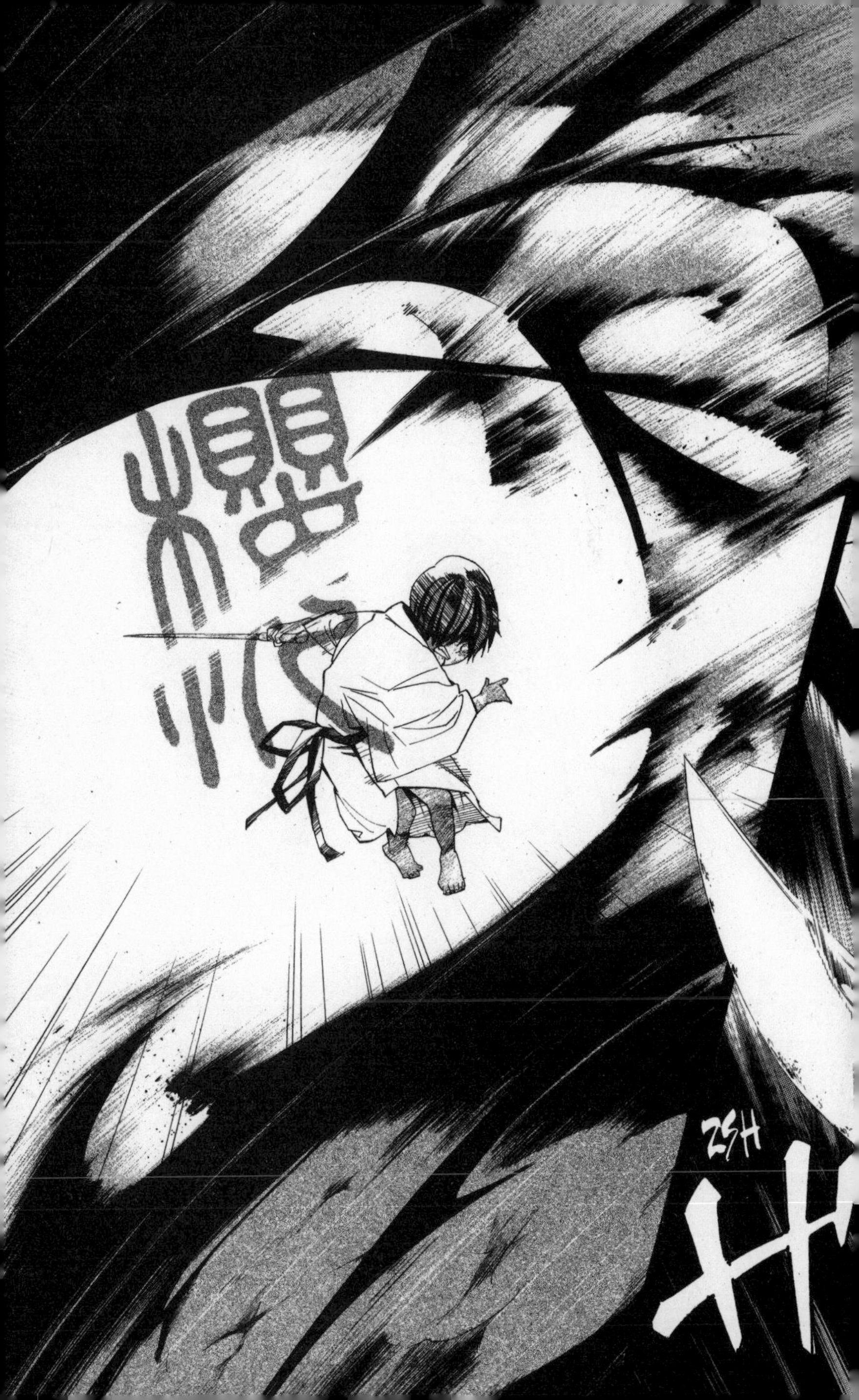
ZSH

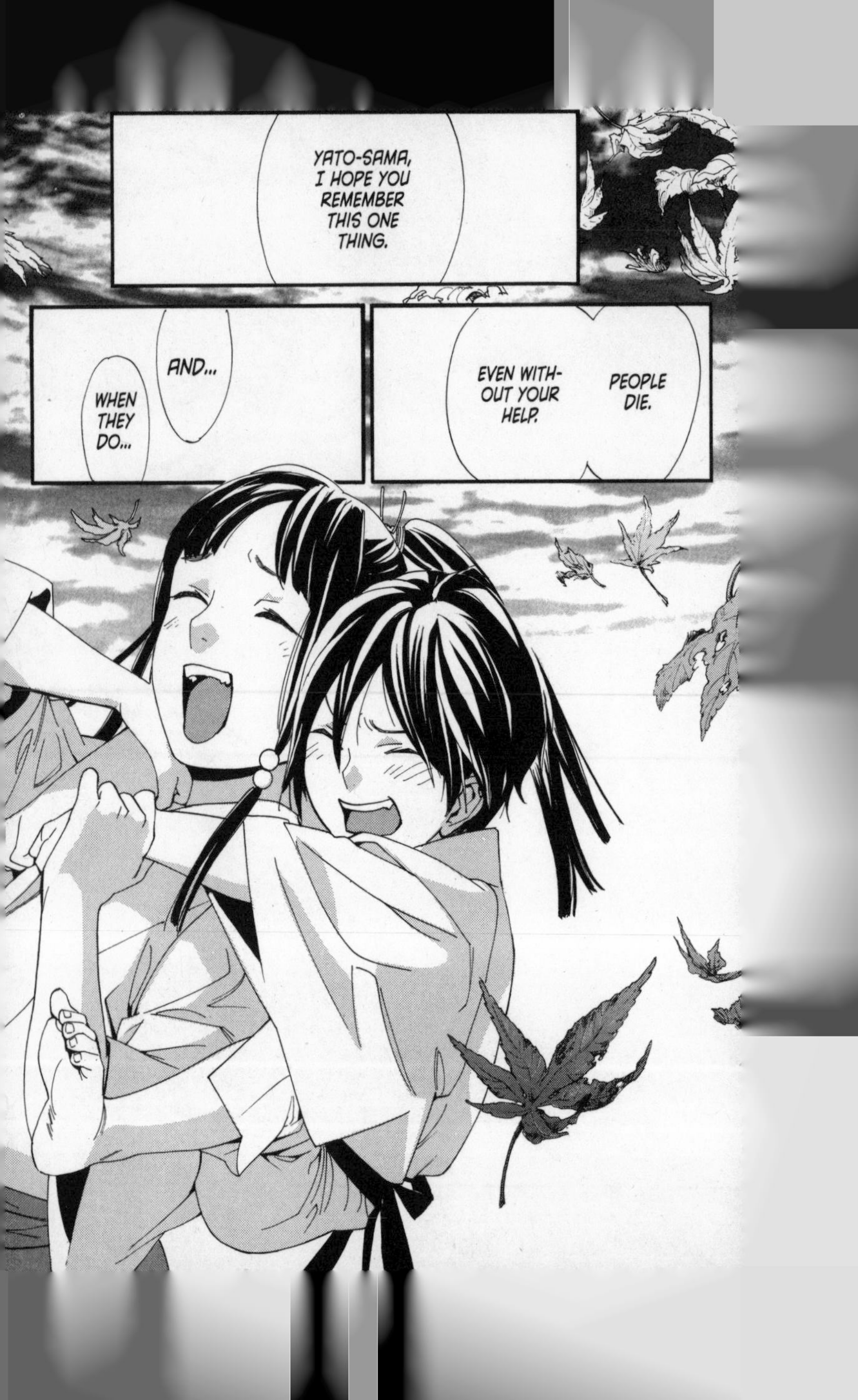
YATO-SAMA, I HOPE YOU REMEMBER THIS ONE THING.
PEOPLE DIE.
EVEN WITH-OUT YOUR HELP.
AND...
WHEN THEY DO...

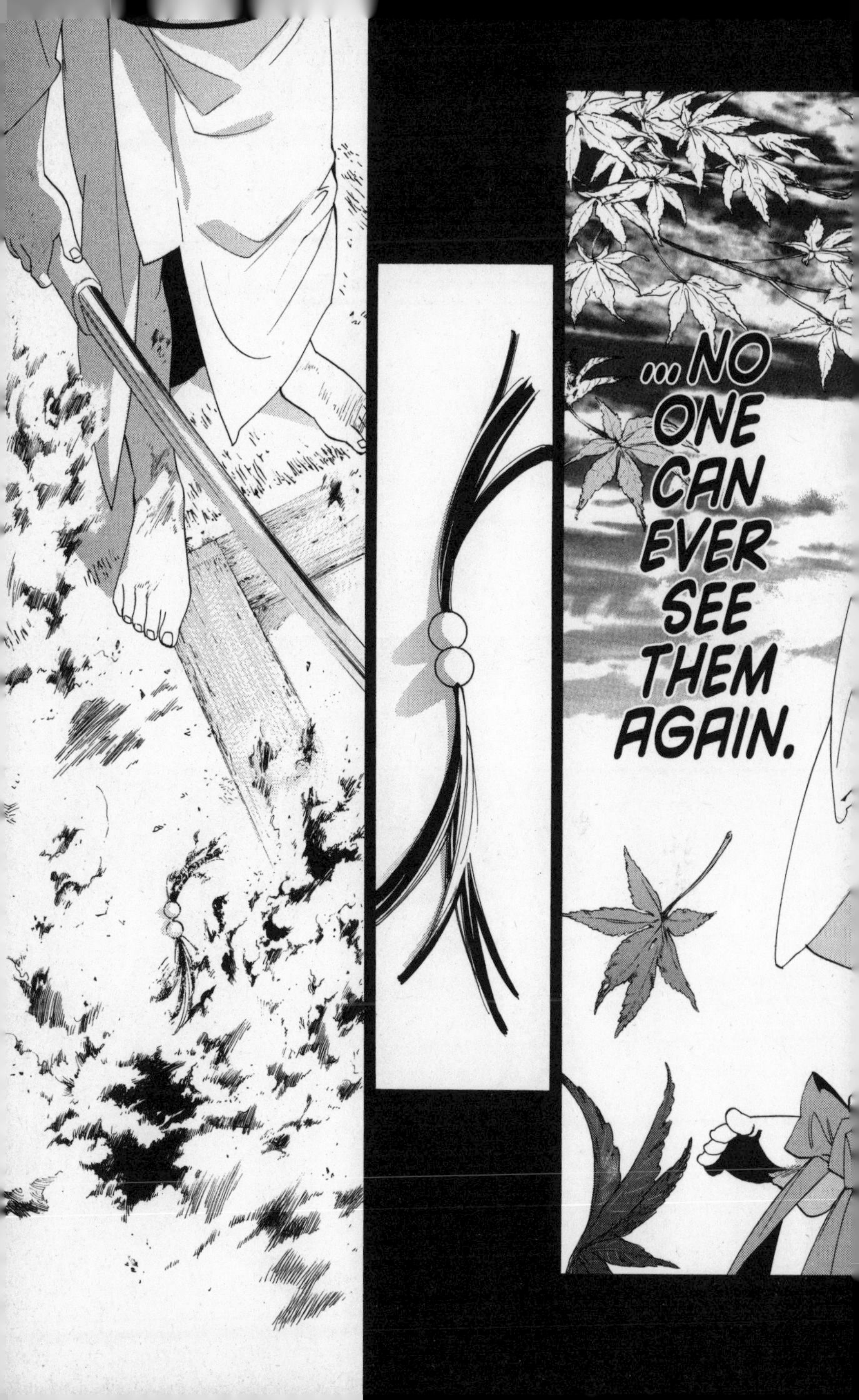
...NO ONE CAN EVER SEE THEM AGAIN.

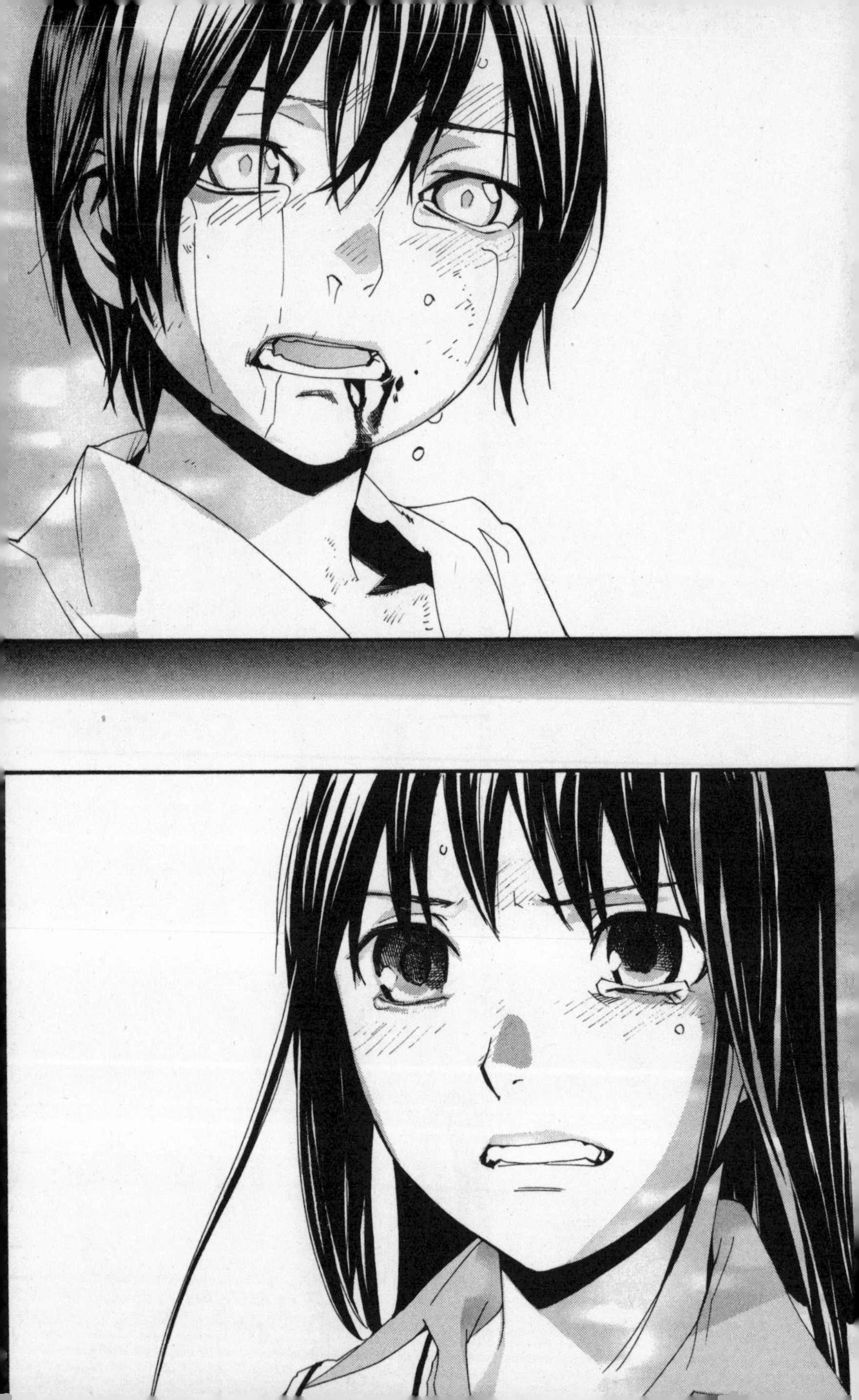

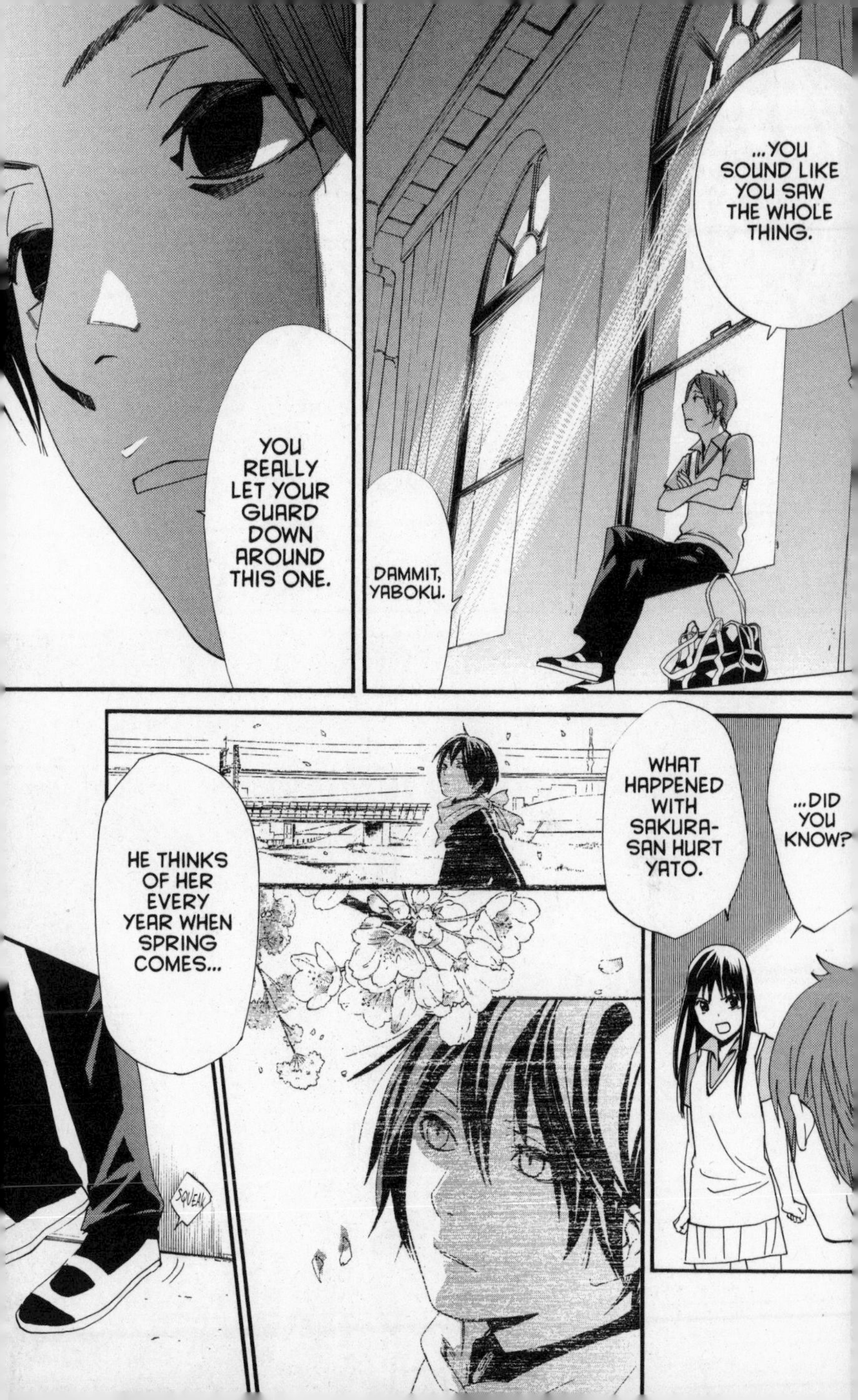
...YOU SOUND LIKE YOU SAW THE WHOLE THING.
DAMMIT, YABOKU.
YOU REALLY LET YOUR GUARD DOWN AROUND THIS ONE.
...DID YOU KNOW?
WHAT HAPPENED WITH SAKURA-SAN HURT YATO.
HE THINKS OF HER EVERY YEAR WHEN SPRING COMES...
SQUEAK

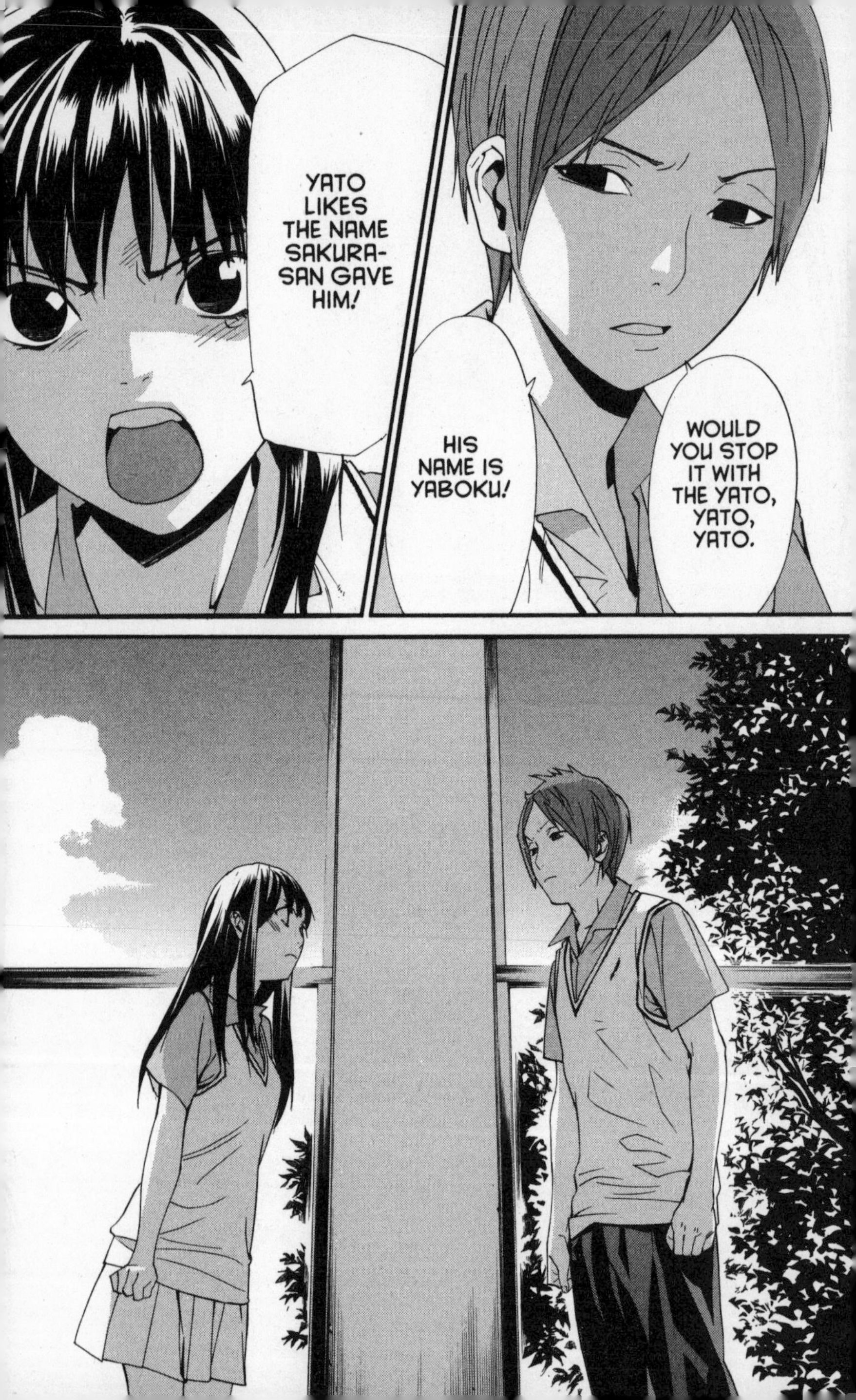
WOULD YOU STOP IT WITH THE YATO, YATO, YATO.
HIS NAME IS YABOKU!
YATO LIKES THE NAME SAKURA-SAN GAVE HIM!

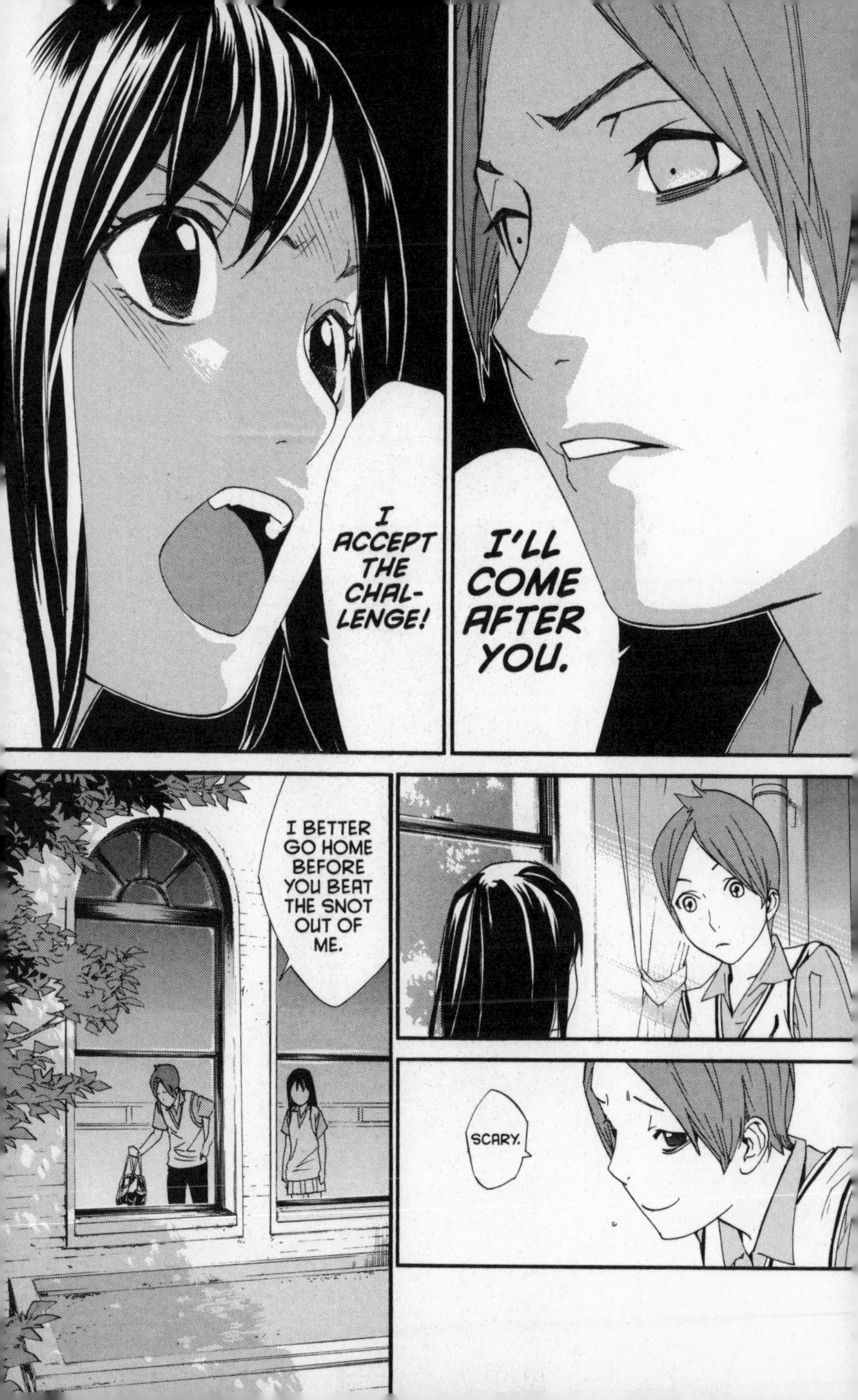
I'LL COME AFTER YOU.
I ACCEPT THE CHAL-LENGE!
SCARY.
I BETTER GO HOME BEFORE YOU BEAT THE SNOT OUT OF ME.

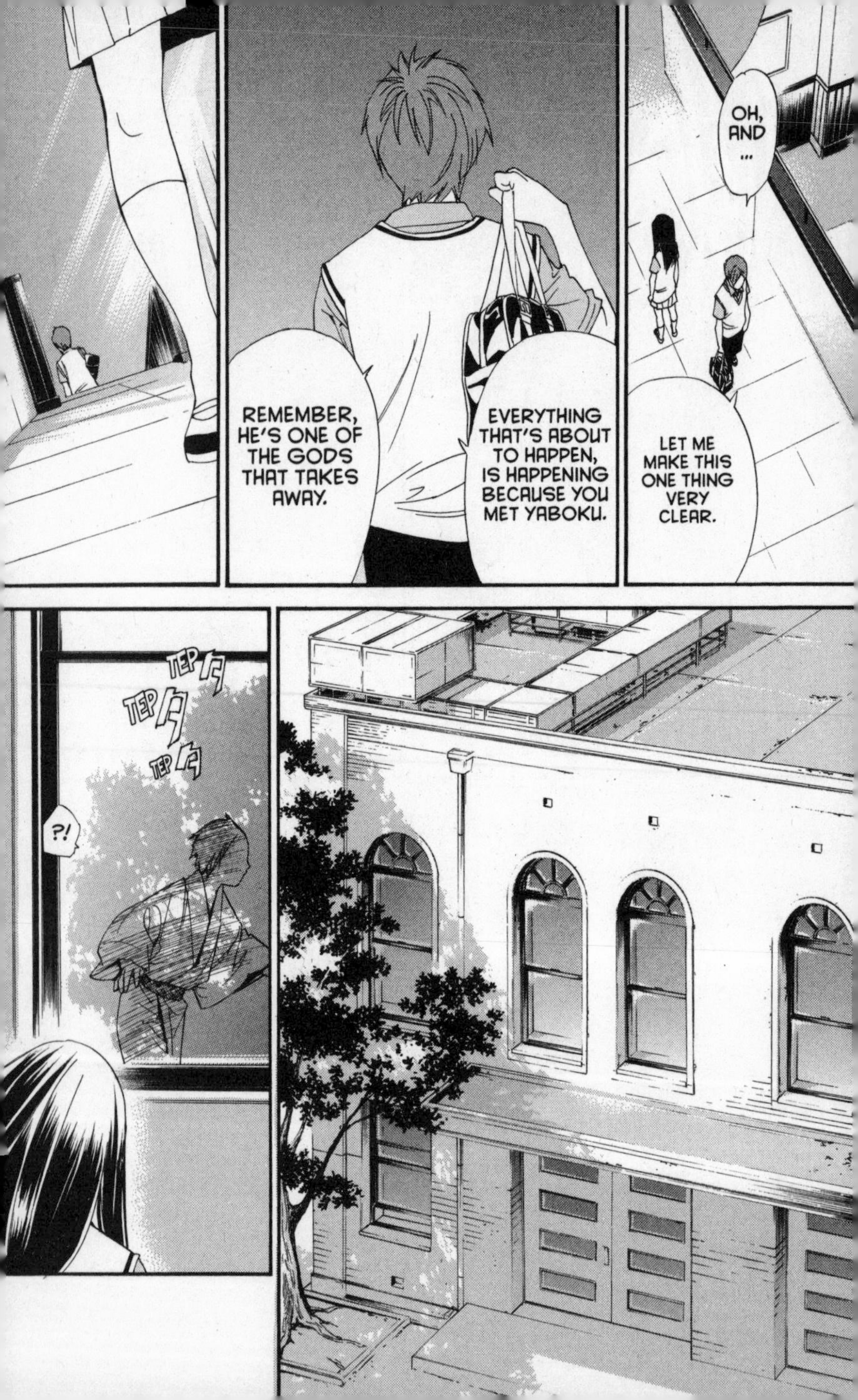
OH, AND ...
LET ME MAKE THIS ONE THING VERY CLEAR.
EVERYTHING THAT'S ABOUT TO HAPPEN, IS HAPPENING BECAUSE YOU MET YABOKU.
REMEMBER, HE'S ONE OF THE GODS THAT TAKES AWAY.
TEP
TEP
TEP
?!

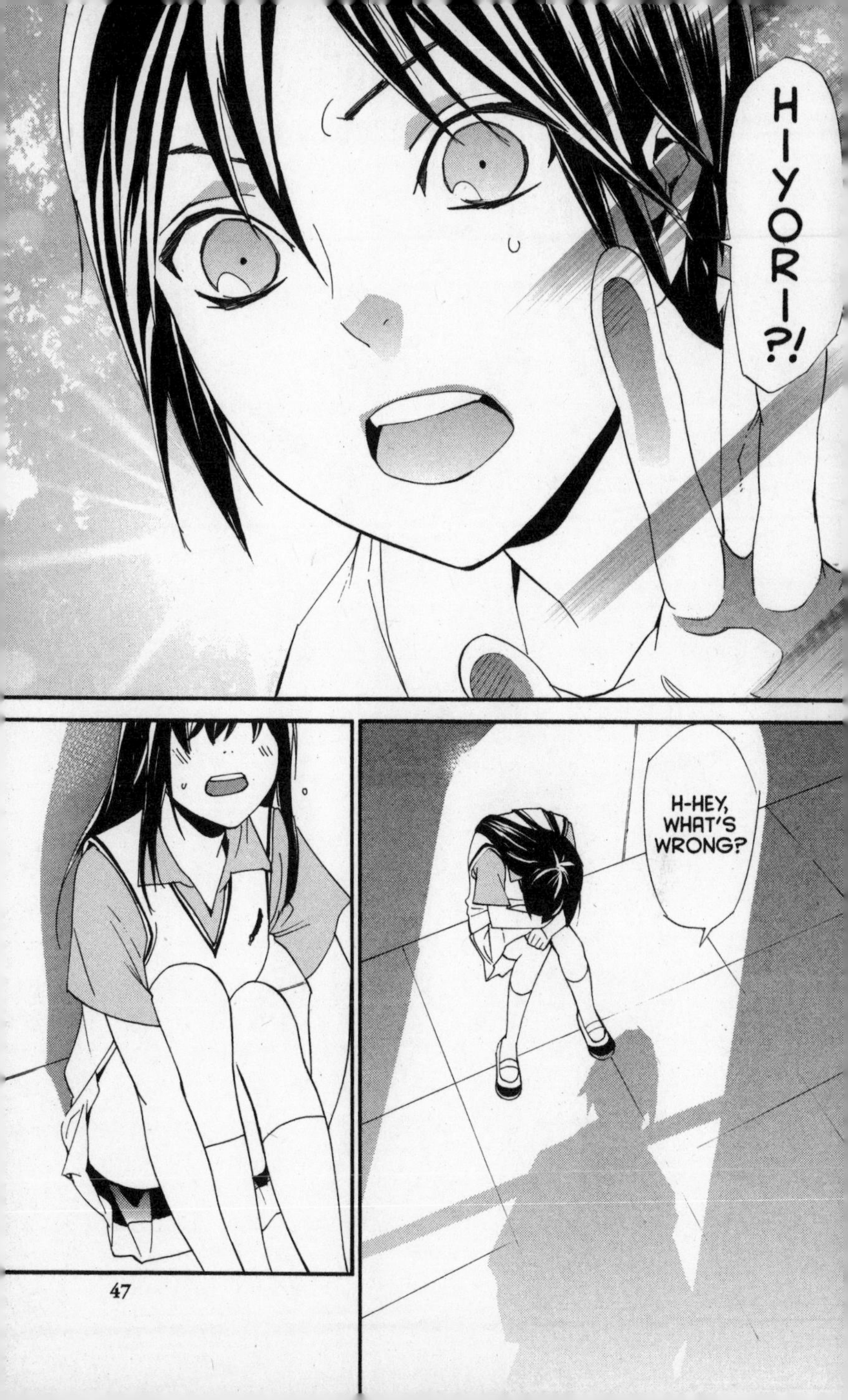
HIYORI?!
H-HEY, WHAT'S WRONG?

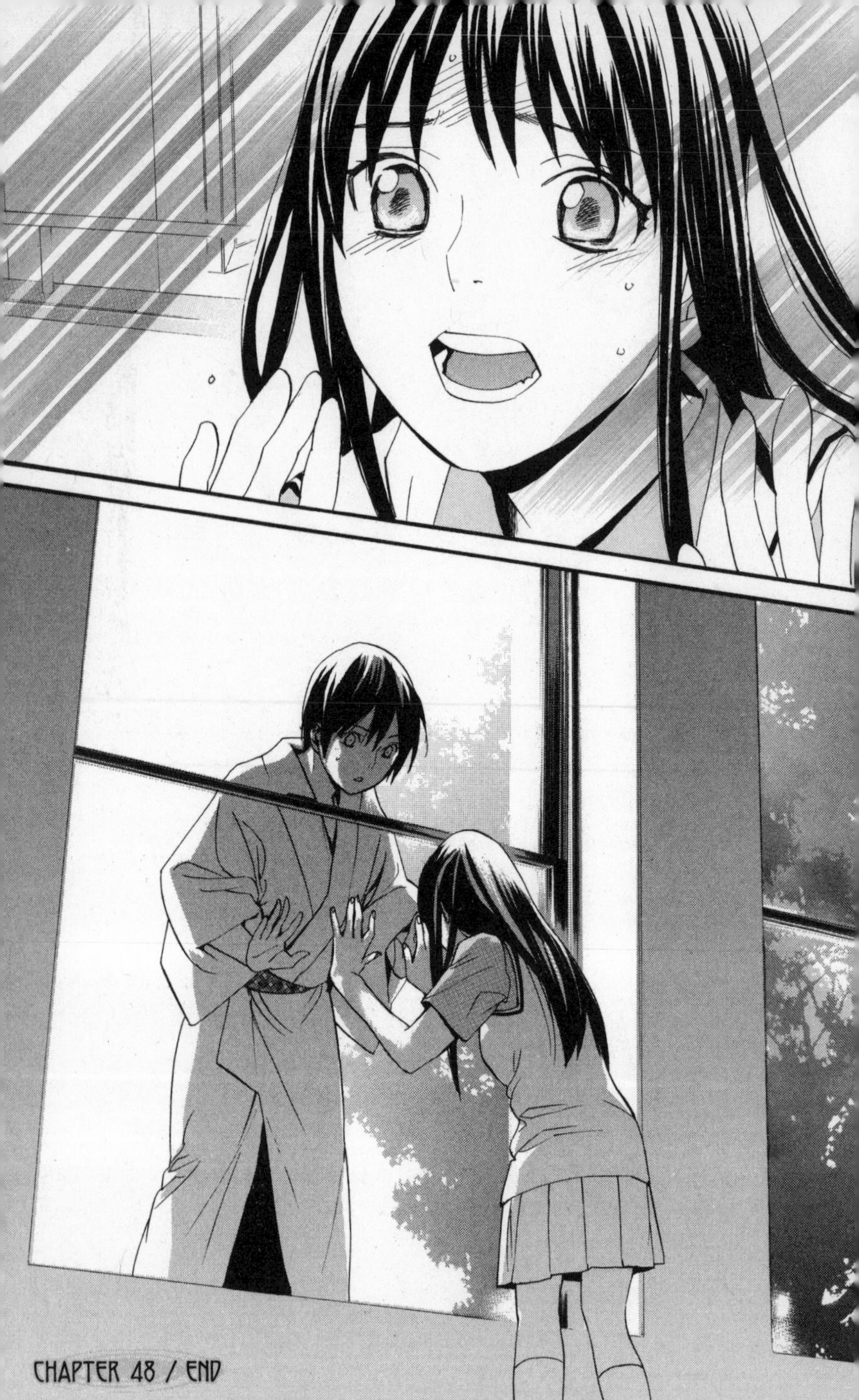
CHAPTER 48 / END

野

兑

神

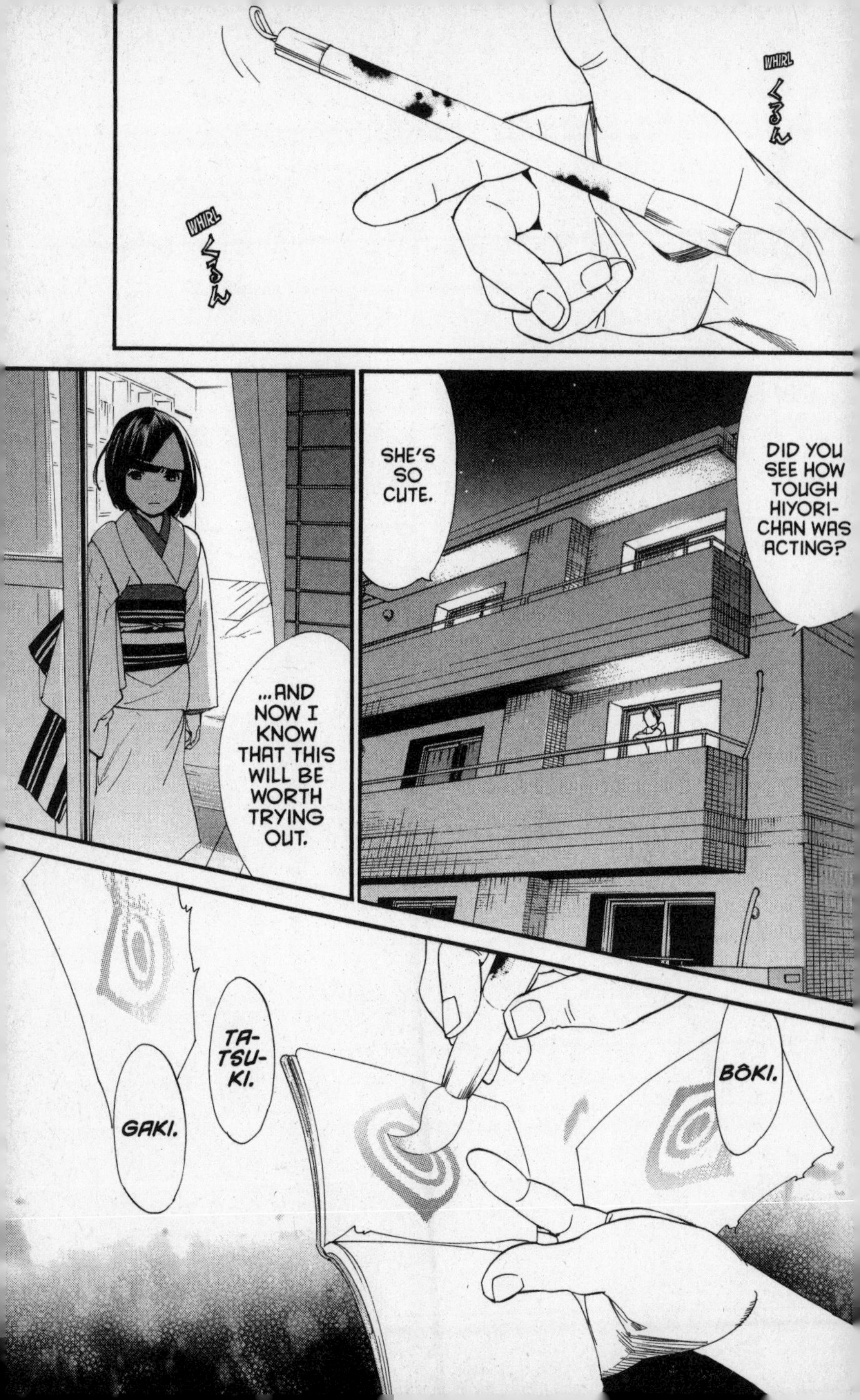
WHIRL
くるん
WHIRL
くるん
DID YOU SEE HOW TOUGH HIYORI-CHAN WAS ACTING?
SHE'S SO CUTE.
...AND NOW I KNOW THAT THIS WILL BE WORTH TRYING OUT.
BÔKI.
TA-TSU-KI.
GAKI.

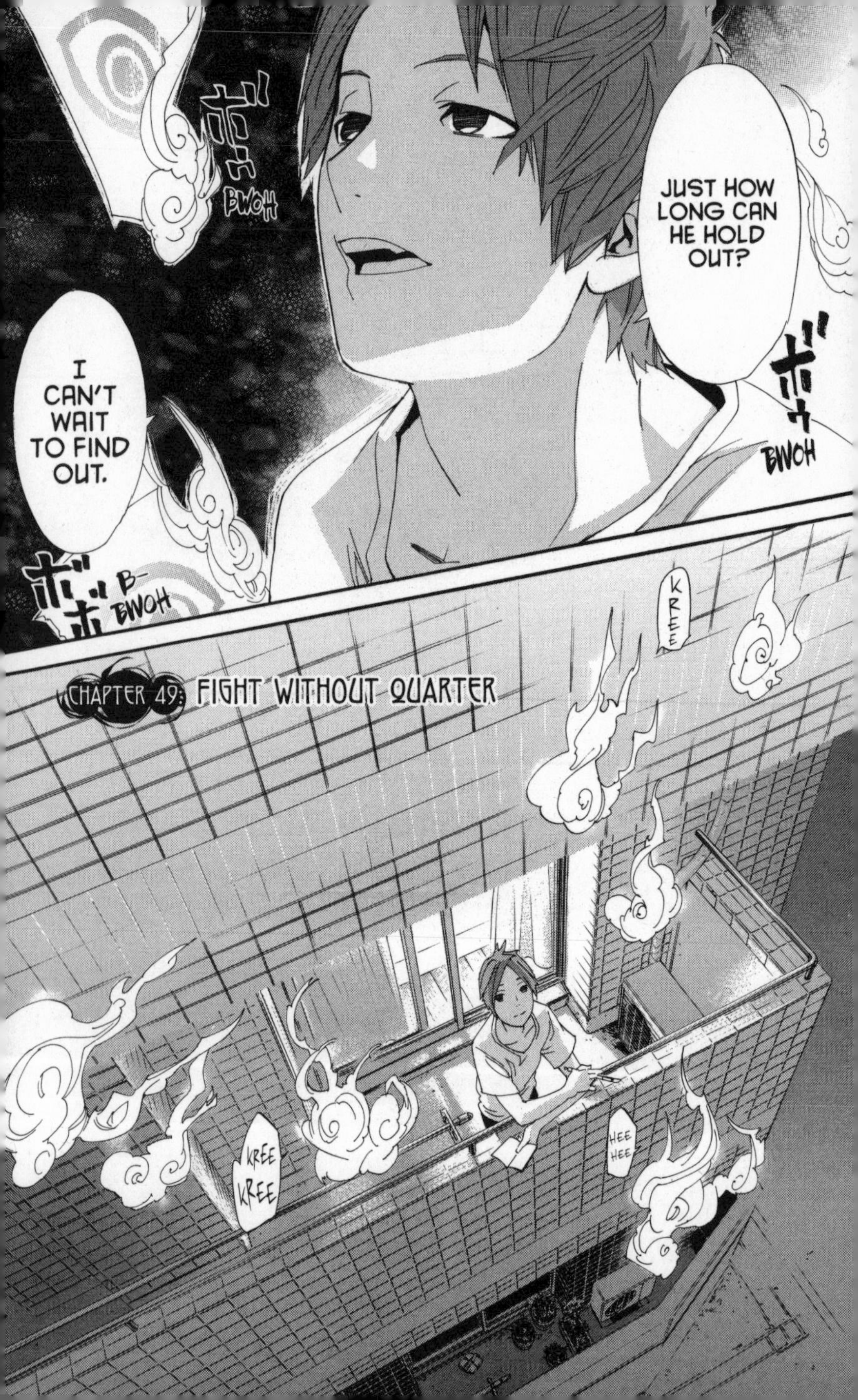
JUST HOW LONG CAN HE HOLD OUT?
BWOH
BWOH
I CAN'T WAIT TO FIND OUT.
B-BWOH
CHAPTER 49: FIGHT WITHOUT QUARTER
KREE
HEE HEE
KREE KREE

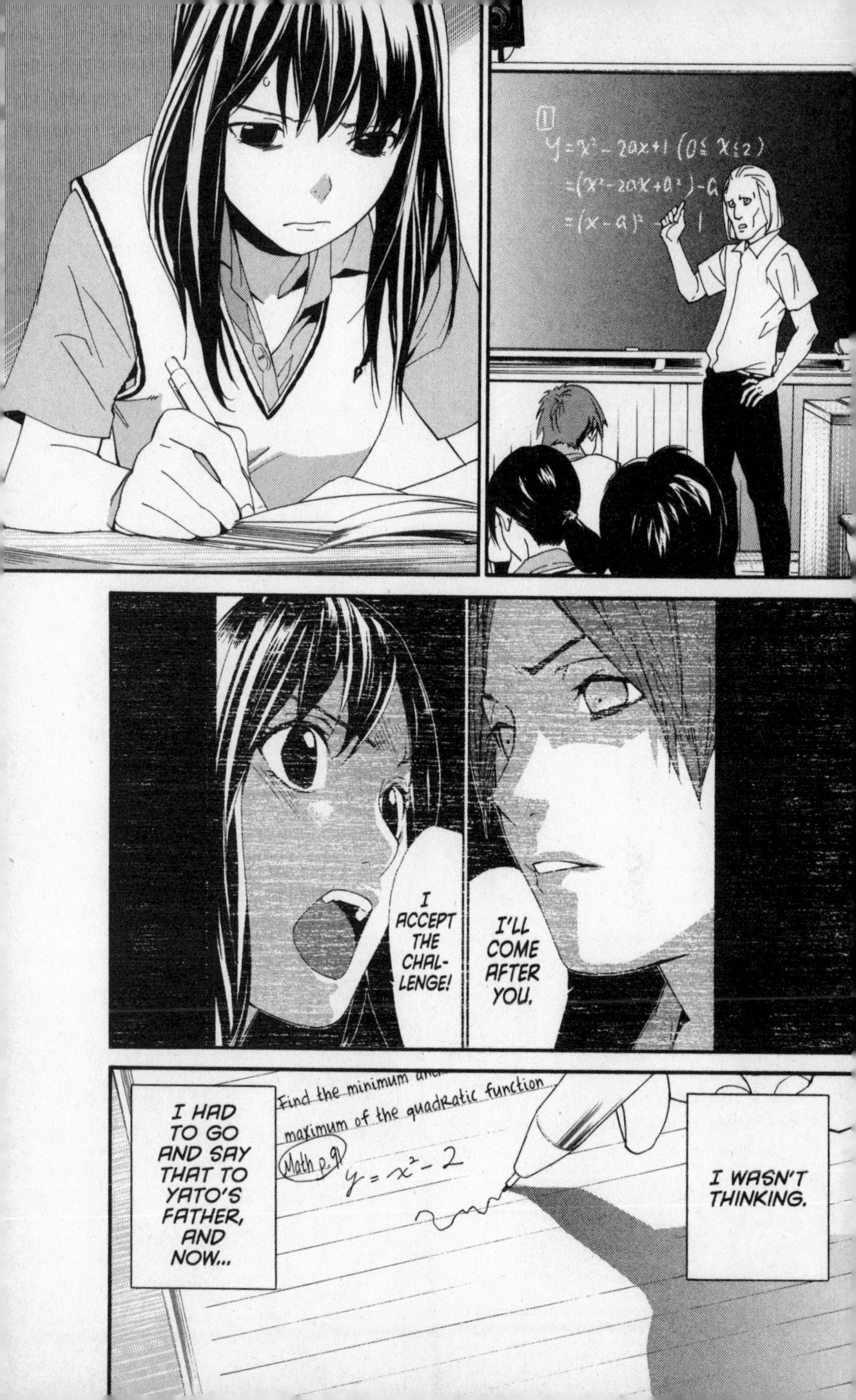
I'LL COME AFTER YOU.
I ACCEPT THE CHAL-LENGE!
I HAD TO GO AND SAY THAT TO YATO'S FATHER, AND NOW...
Find the minimum
maximum of the quadratic function
Math p.91
y = x² − 2
I WASN'T THINKING.

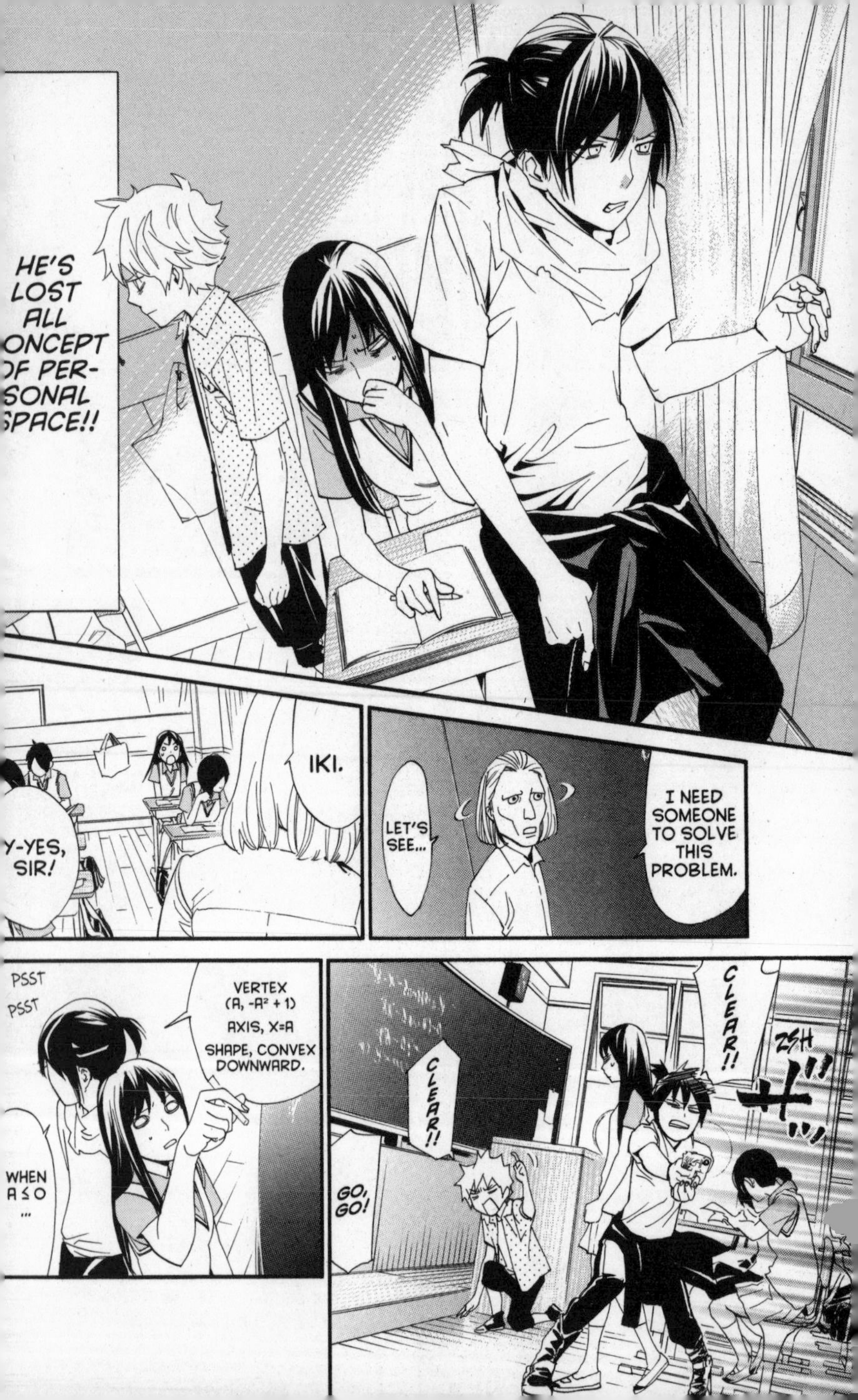

HE'S LOST ALL CONCEPT OF PER-SONAL SPACE!!
I NEED SOMEONE TO SOLVE THIS PROBLEM.
LET'S SEE...
IKI.
Y-YES, SIR!
CLEAR!!
ZSH
CLEAR!!
GO, GO!
PSST PSST
VERTEX (A, -A² + 1) AXIS, X=A SHAPE, CONVEX DOWNWARD.
WHEN A ≤ 0 ...

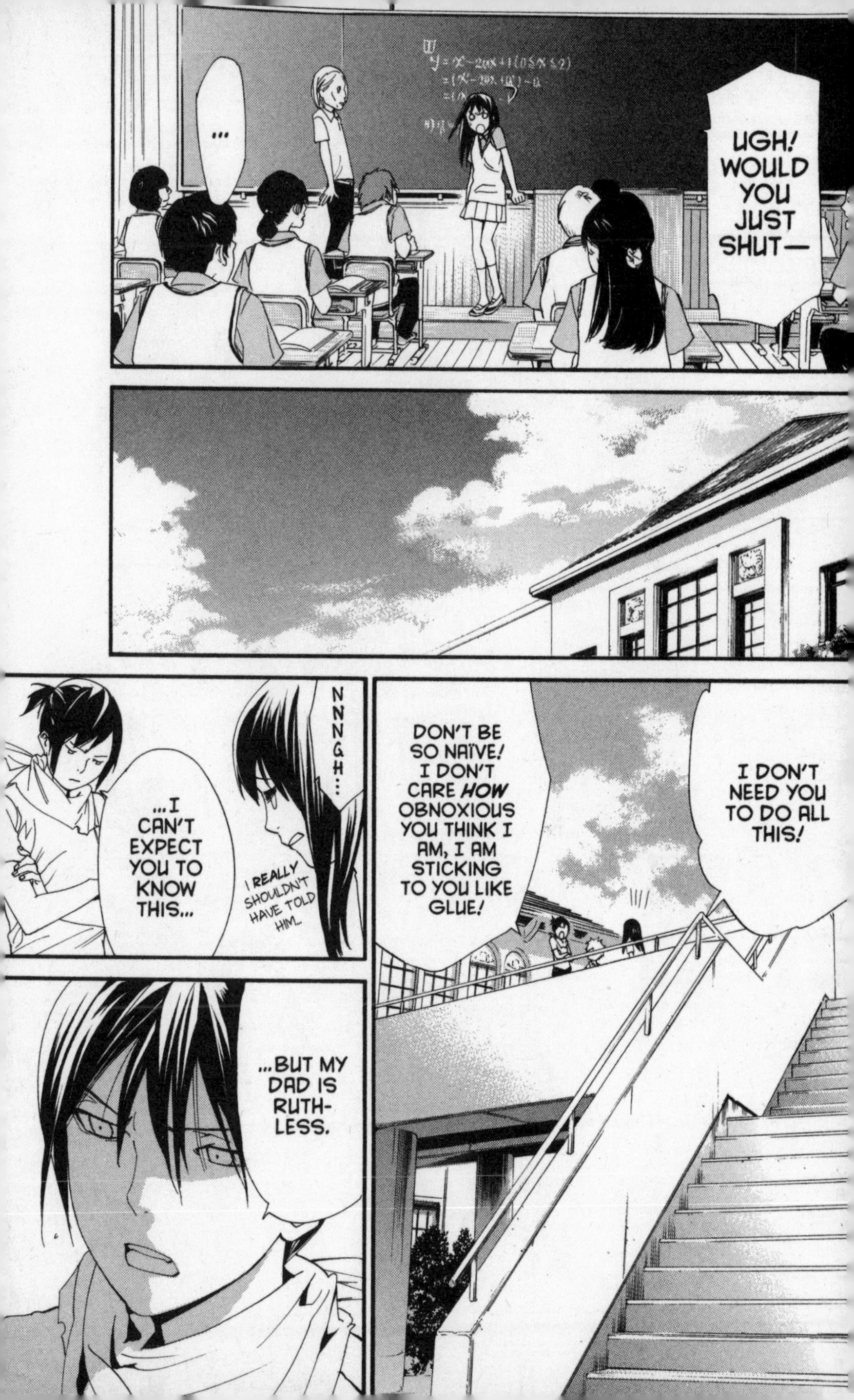
UGH! WOULD YOU JUST SHUT—
...
I DON'T NEED YOU TO DO ALL THIS!
DON'T BE SO NAÏVE! I DON'T CARE *HOW* OBNOXIOUS YOU THINK I AM, I AM STICKING TO YOU LIKE GLUE!
NNNGH...
I **REALLY** SHOULDN'T HAVE TOLD HIM...
...I CAN'T EXPECT YOU TO KNOW THIS...
...BUT MY DAD IS RUTH-LESS.

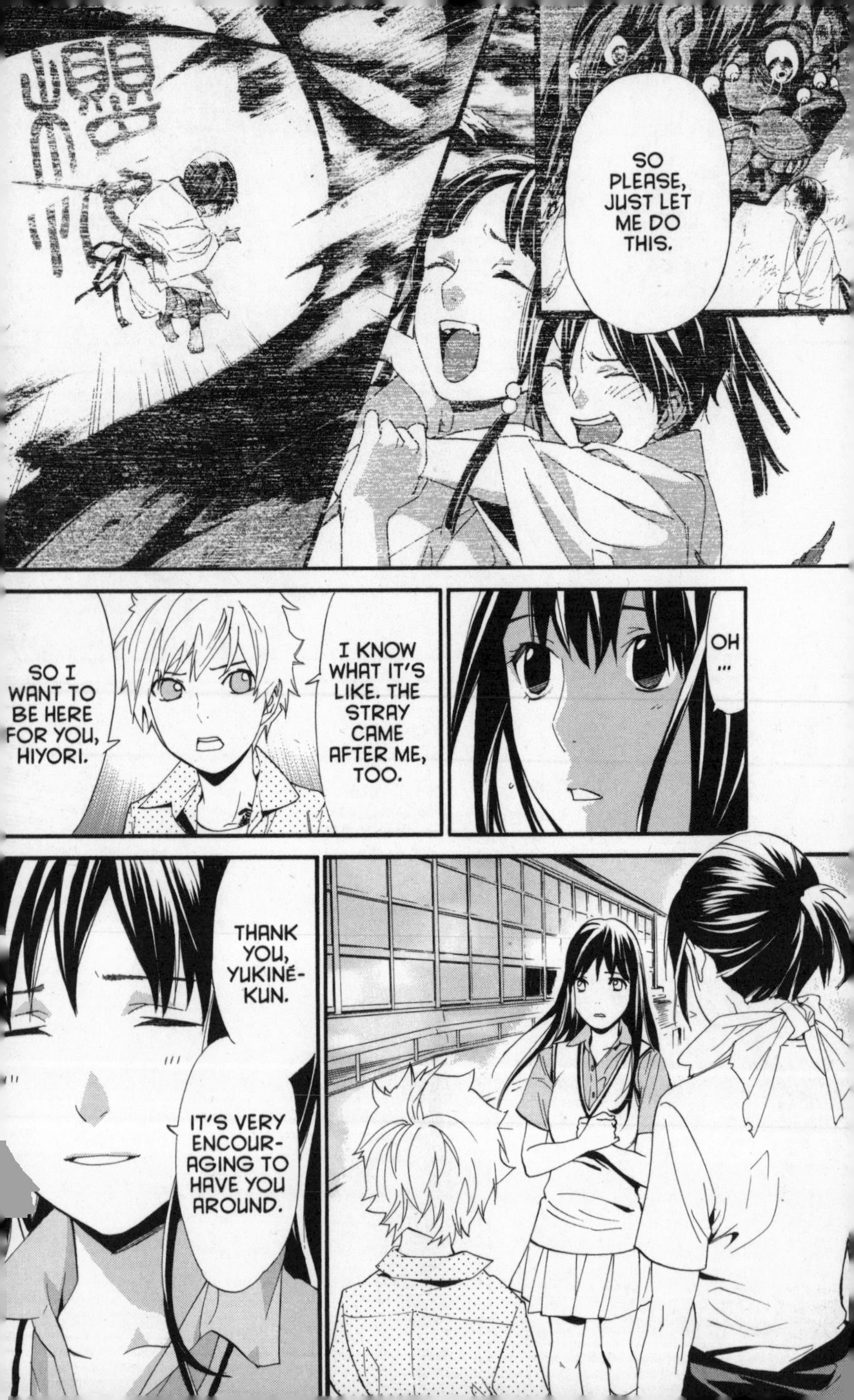
SO PLEASE, JUST LET ME DO THIS.
OH ...
I KNOW WHAT IT'S LIKE. THE STRAY CAME AFTER ME, TOO.
SO I WANT TO BE HERE FOR YOU, HIYORI.
THANK YOU, YUKINÉ-KUN.
IT'S VERY ENCOURAGING TO HAVE YOU AROUND.

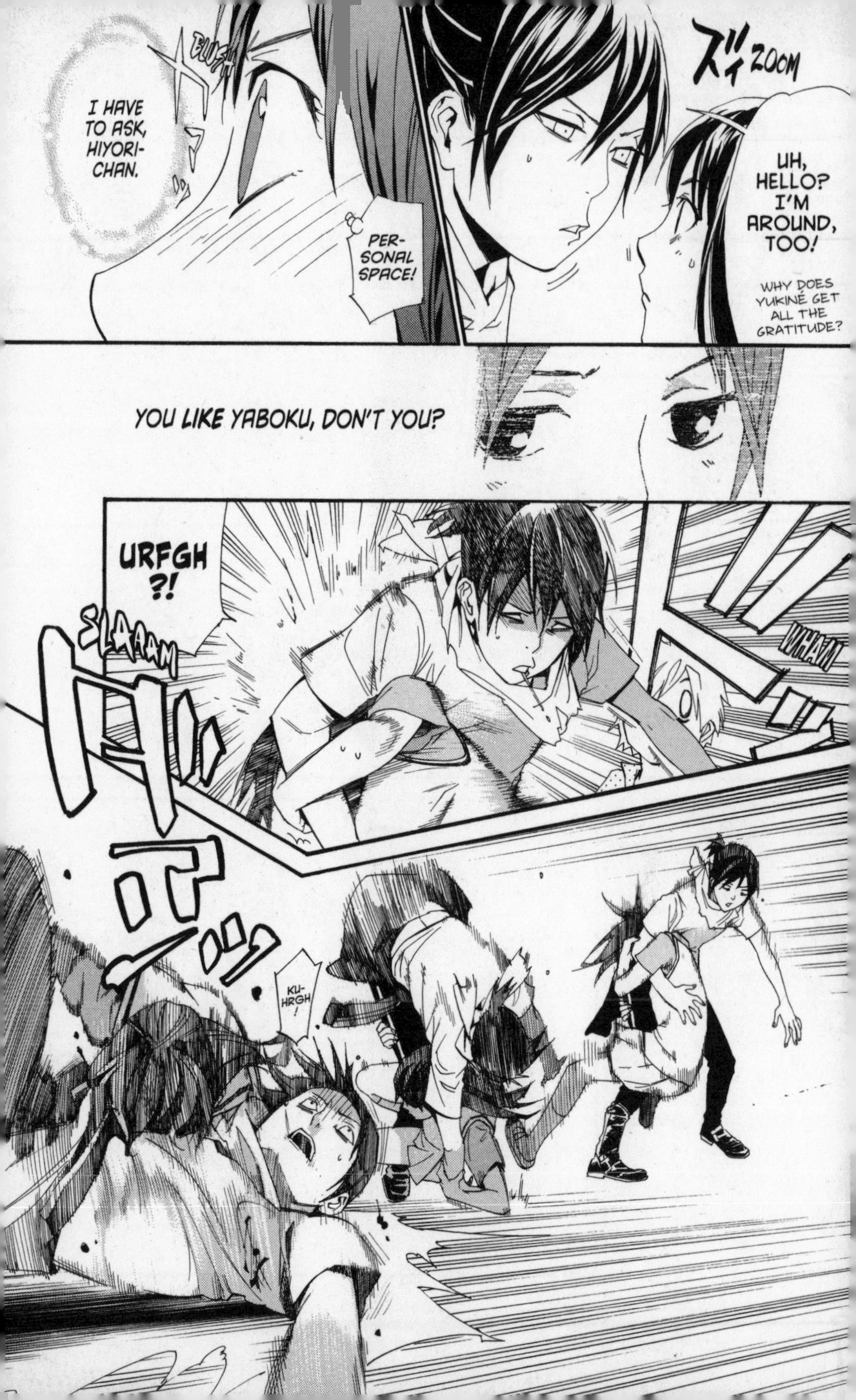
ズィ ZOOM
UH, HELLO? I'M AROUND, TOO!
WHY DOES YUKINÉ GET ALL THE GRATITUDE?
PER-SONAL SPACE!
BLUSH
I HAVE TO ASK, HIYORI-CHAN.
YOU LIKE YABOKU, DON'T YOU?
WHAM
URFGH ?!
SLAAAM
KU-HRGH!

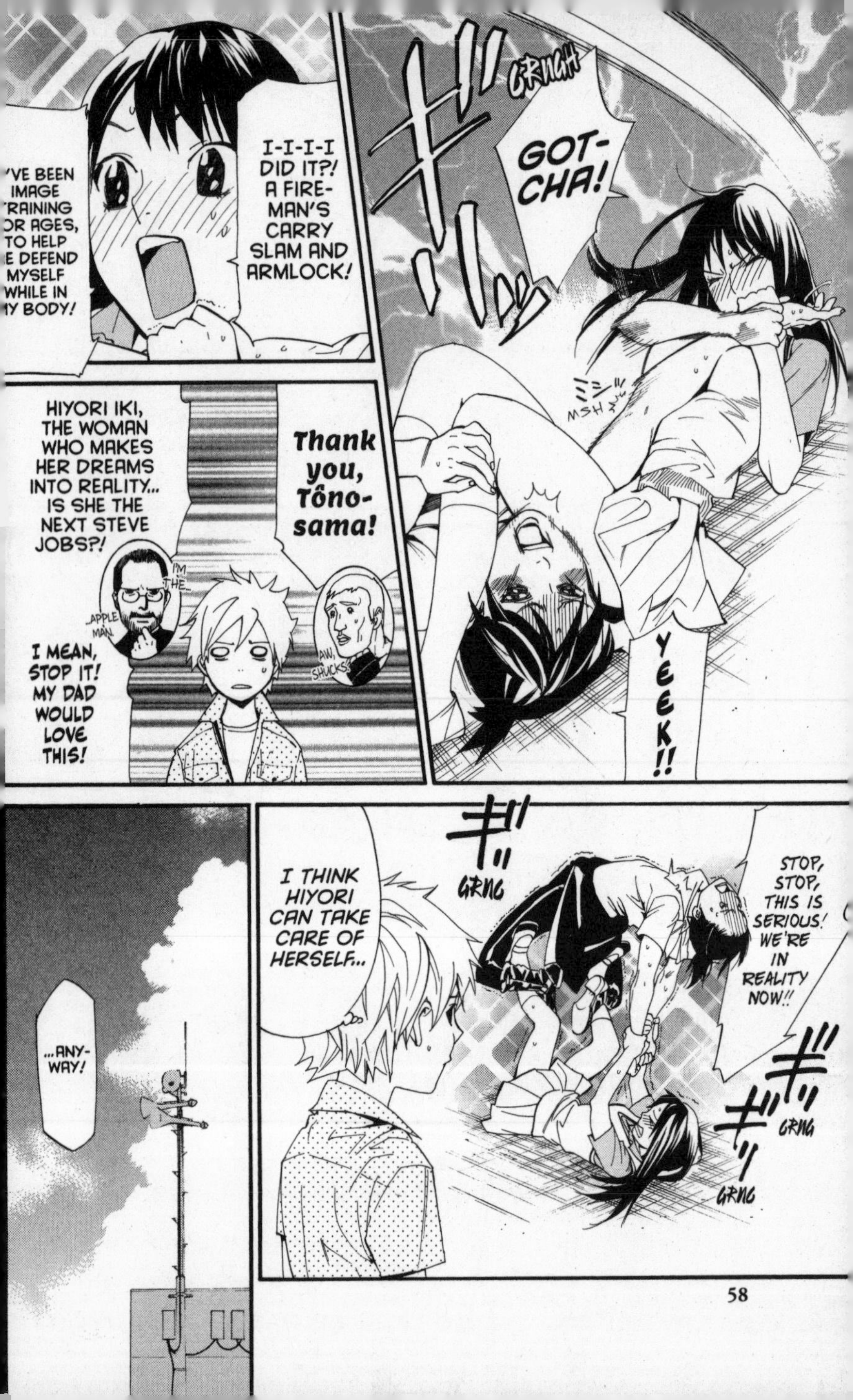
CRUNCH
GOT-CHA!
MSH
YEEEK!!
I-I-I-I DID IT?! A FIRE-MAN'S CARRY SLAM AND ARMLOCK!
'VE BEEN IMAGE TRAINING OR AGES, TO HELP E DEFEND MYSELF WHILE IN Y BODY!
Thank you, Tôno-sama!
HIYORI IKI, THE WOMAN WHO MAKES HER DREAMS INTO REALITY... IS SHE THE NEXT STEVE JOBS?!
I'M THE... ...APPLE MAN.
AW, SHUCKS
I MEAN, STOP IT! MY DAD WOULD LOVE THIS!
STOP, STOP, THIS IS SERIOUS! WE'RE IN REALITY NOW!!
GRNG
GRNG
GRNG
I THINK HIYORI CAN TAKE CARE OF HERSELF...
...ANY-WAY!

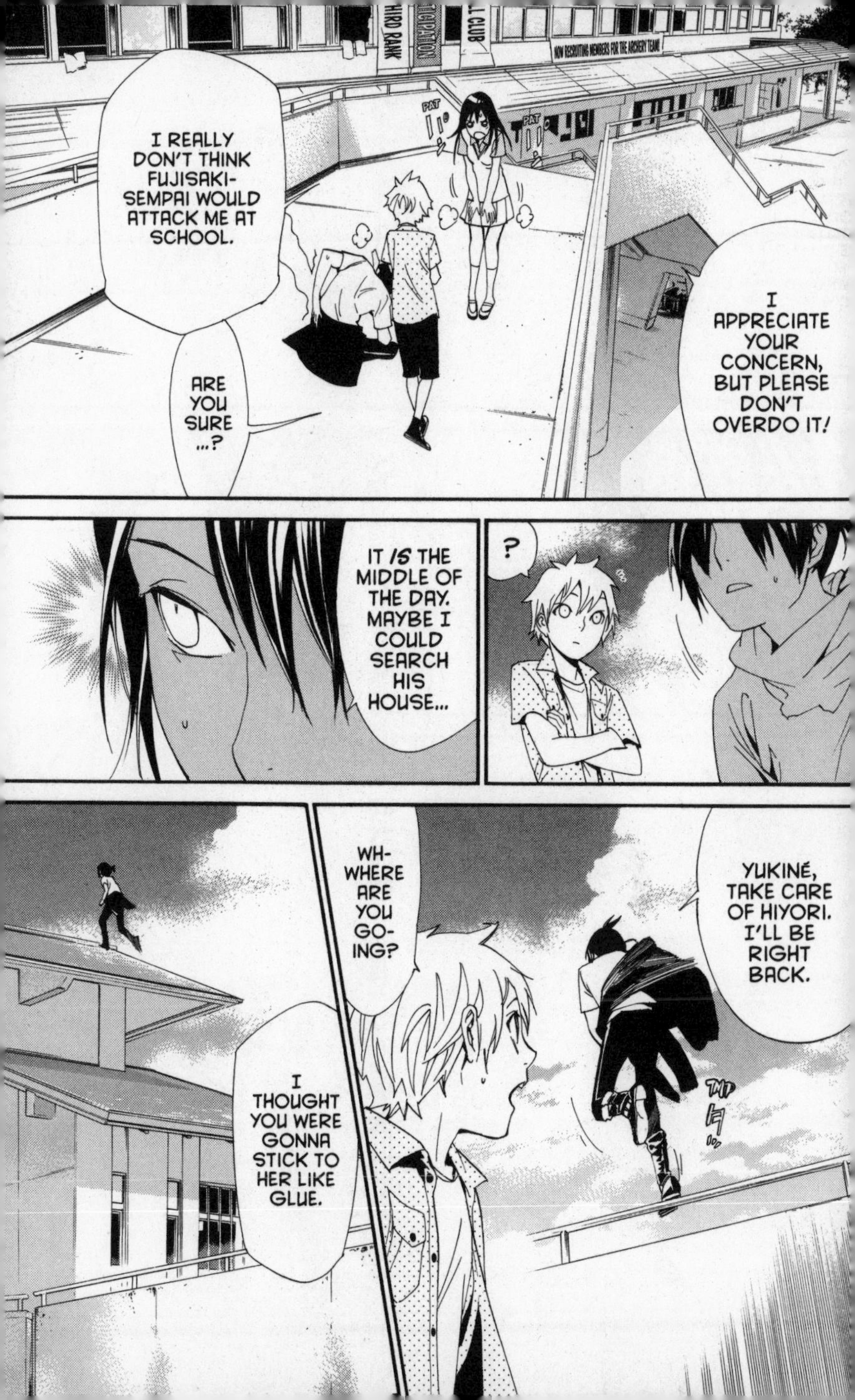
NOW RECRUITING MEMBERS FOR THE ARCHERY TEAM!
HIRD RANK
PAT
PAT
I REALLY DON'T THINK FUJISAKI-SEMPAI WOULD ATTACK ME AT SCHOOL.
ARE YOU SURE ...?
I APPRECIATE YOUR CONCERN, BUT PLEASE DON'T OVERDO IT!
?
IT *IS* THE MIDDLE OF THE DAY. MAYBE I COULD SEARCH HIS HOUSE...
YUKINÉ, TAKE CARE OF HIYORI. I'LL BE RIGHT BACK.
TMP
WH-WHERE ARE YOU GO-ING?
I THOUGHT YOU WERE GONNA STICK TO HER LIKE GLUE.

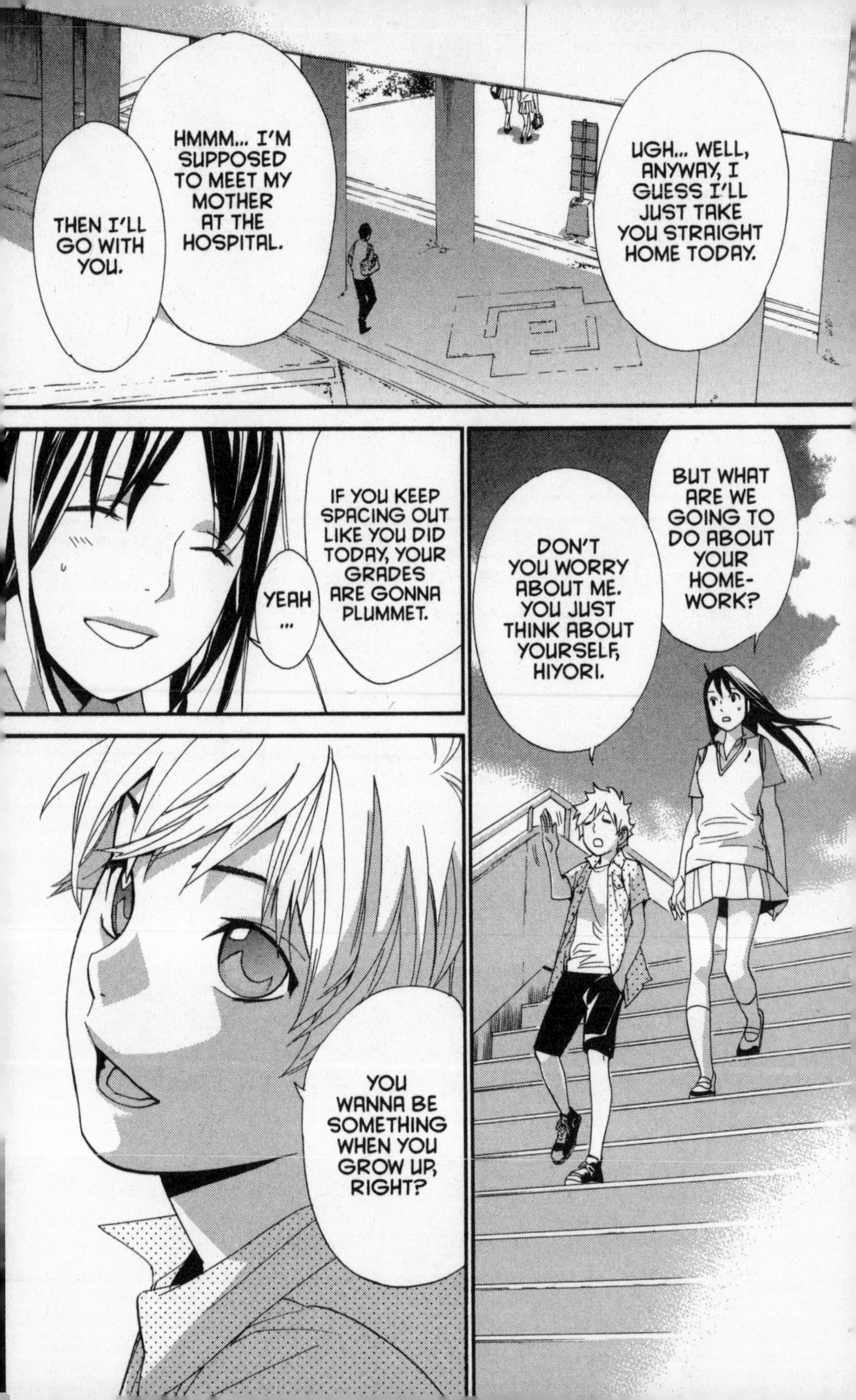
UGH... WELL, ANYWAY, I GUESS I'LL JUST TAKE YOU STRAIGHT HOME TODAY.
HMMM... I'M SUPPOSED TO MEET MY MOTHER AT THE HOSPITAL.
THEN I'LL GO WITH YOU.
BUT WHAT ARE WE GOING TO DO ABOUT YOUR HOME-WORK?
DON'T YOU WORRY ABOUT ME. YOU JUST THINK ABOUT YOURSELF, HIYORI.
IF YOU KEEP SPACING OUT LIKE YOU DID TODAY, YOUR GRADES ARE GONNA PLUMMET.
YEAH ...
YOU WANNA BE SOMETHING WHEN YOU GROW UP, RIGHT?

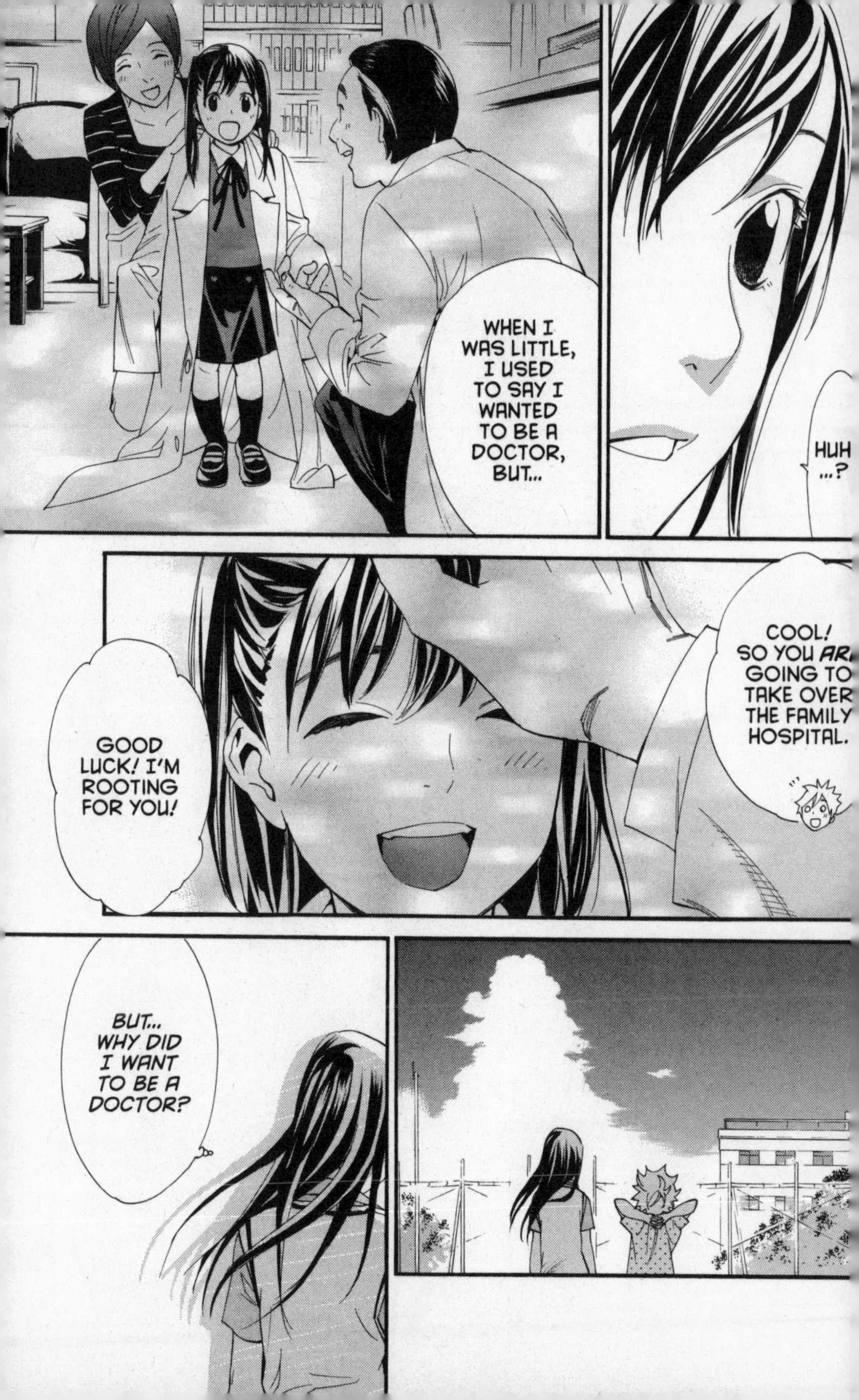
HUH ...?
WHEN I WAS LITTLE, I USED TO SAY I WANTED TO BE A DOCTOR, BUT...
COOL! SO YOU AR GOING TO TAKE OVER THE FAMILY HOSPITAL.
GOOD LUCK! I'M ROOTING FOR YOU!
BUT... WHY DID I WANT TO BE A DOCTOR?

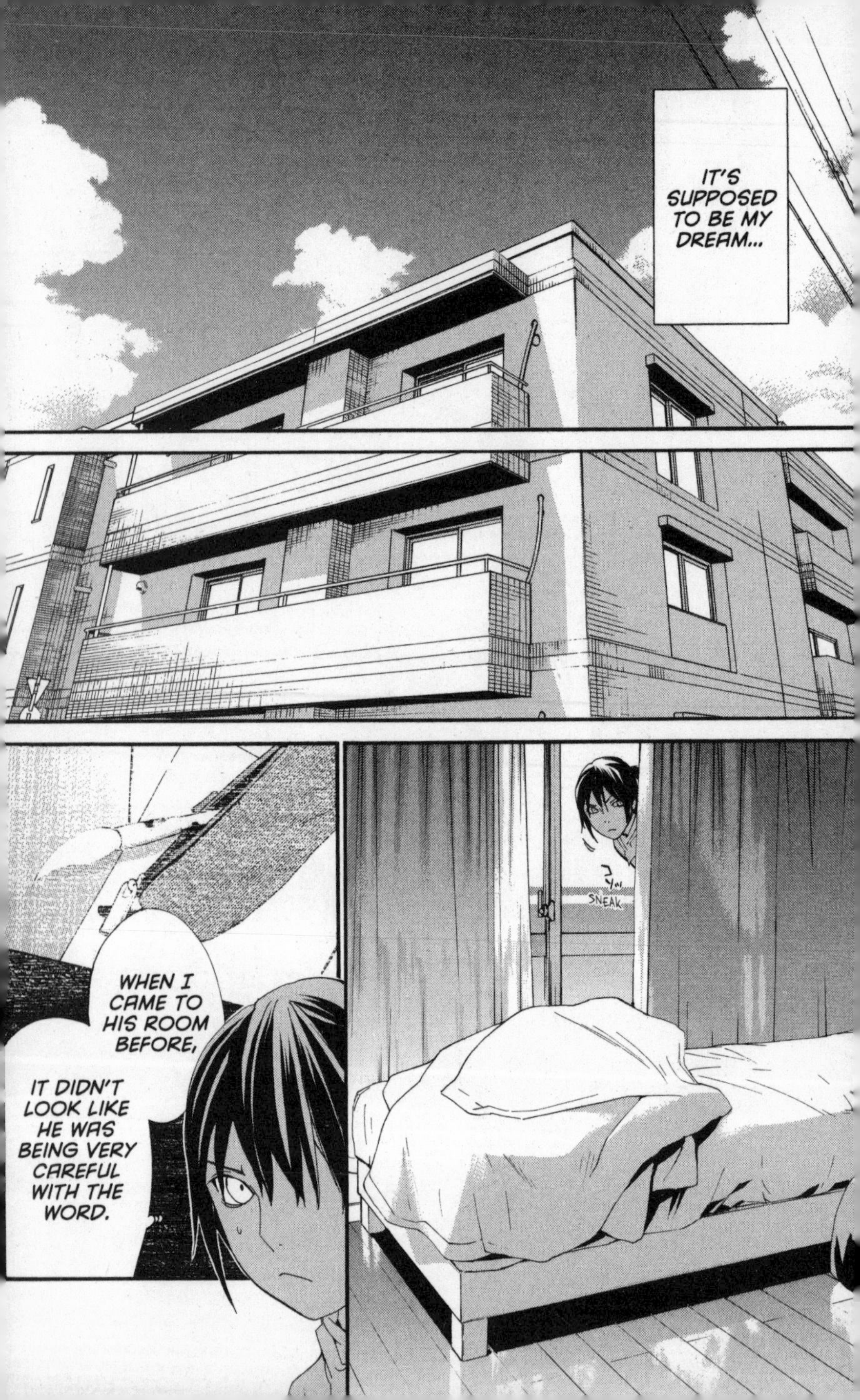
IT'S SUPPOSED TO BE MY DREAM...
SNEAK
WHEN I CAME TO HIS ROOM BEFORE,
IT DIDN'T LOOK LIKE HE WAS BEING VERY CAREFUL WITH THE WORD.

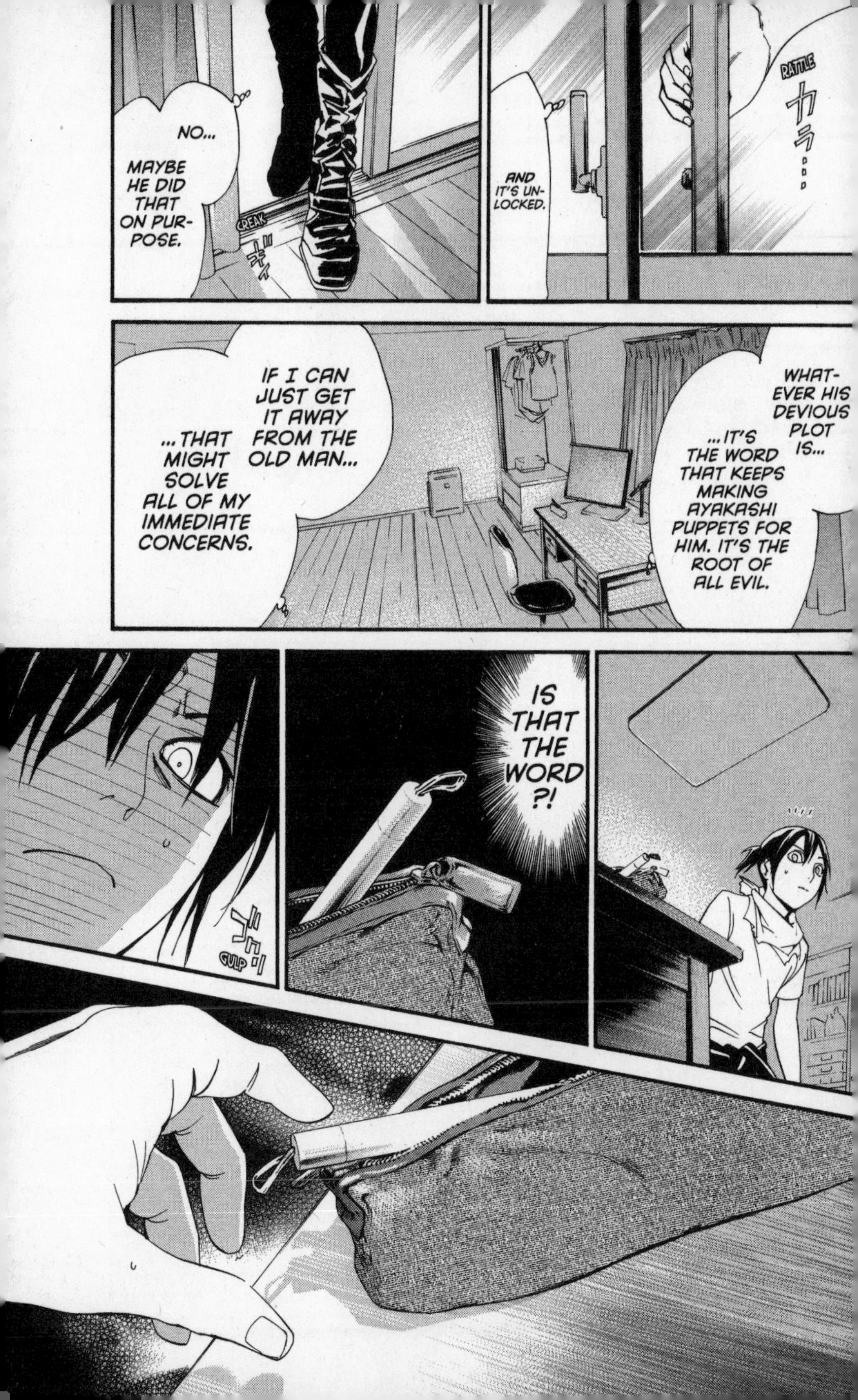
RATTLE
カラ
AND IT'S UN-LOCKED.
NO...
MAYBE HE DID THAT ON PUR-POSE.
CREAK
ギィ
WHAT-EVER HIS DEVIOUS PLOT IS...
...IT'S THE WORD THAT KEEPS MAKING AYAKASHI PUPPETS FOR HIM. IT'S THE ROOT OF ALL EVIL.
IF I CAN JUST GET IT AWAY FROM THE OLD MAN...
...THAT MIGHT SOLVE ALL OF MY IMMEDIATE CONCERNS.
IS THAT THE WORD?!
GULP

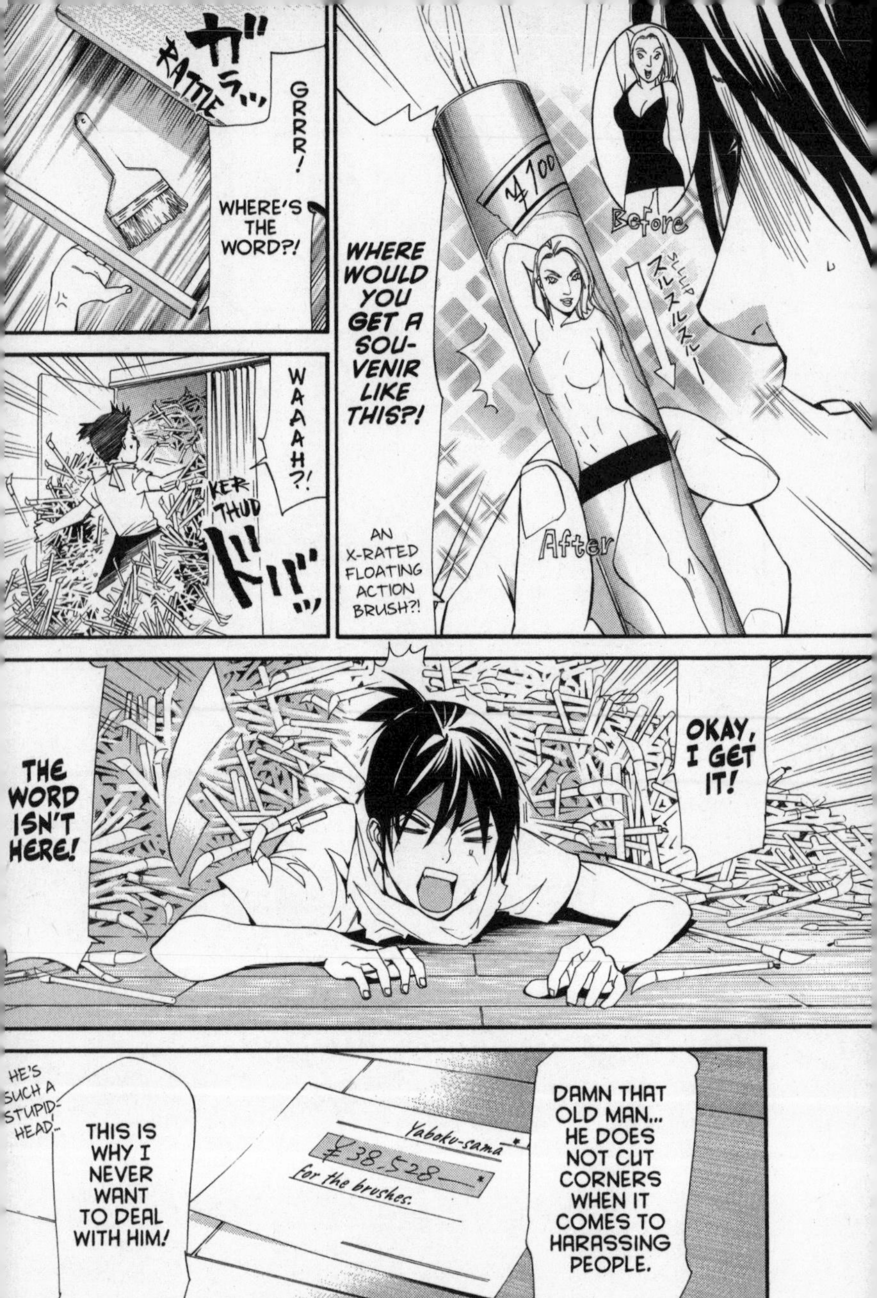
¥100
Before
SLLLIP
スルスルスルー
After
WHERE WOULD YOU GET A SOUVENIR LIKE THIS?!
AN X-RATED FLOATING ACTION BRUSH?!
RATTLE
ガラッ
GRRR!
WHERE'S THE WORD?!
WAAAH?!
KER THUD
ドドッ
OKAY, I GET IT!
THE WORD ISN'T HERE!
DAMN THAT OLD MAN... HE DOES NOT CUT CORNERS WHEN IT COMES TO HARASSING PEOPLE.
Yaboku-sama
¥38,528—*
for the brushes.
THIS IS WHY I NEVER WANT TO DEAL WITH HIM!
HE'S SUCH A STUPID-HEAD...

*ABOUT $385.

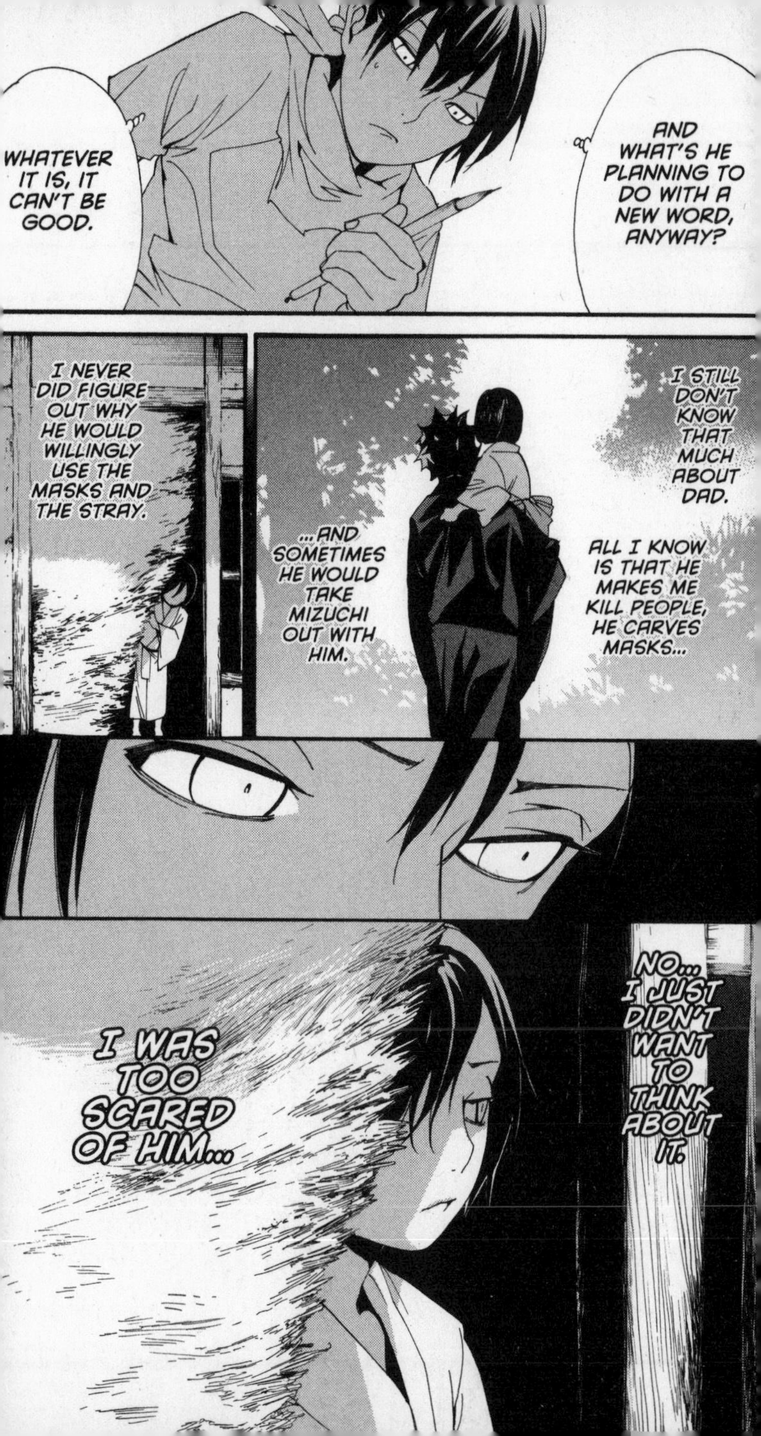
AND WHAT'S HE PLANNING TO DO WITH A NEW WORD, ANYWAY?
WHATEVER IT IS, IT CAN'T BE GOOD.
I STILL DON'T KNOW THAT MUCH ABOUT DAD.
ALL I KNOW IS THAT HE MAKES ME KILL PEOPLE, HE CARVES MASKS...
...AND SOMETIMES HE WOULD TAKE MIZUCHI OUT WITH HIM.
I NEVER DID FIGURE OUT WHY HE WOULD WILLINGLY USE THE MASKS AND THE STRAY.
NO... I JUST DIDN'T WANT TO THINK ABOUT IT.
I WAS TOO SCARED OF HIM...

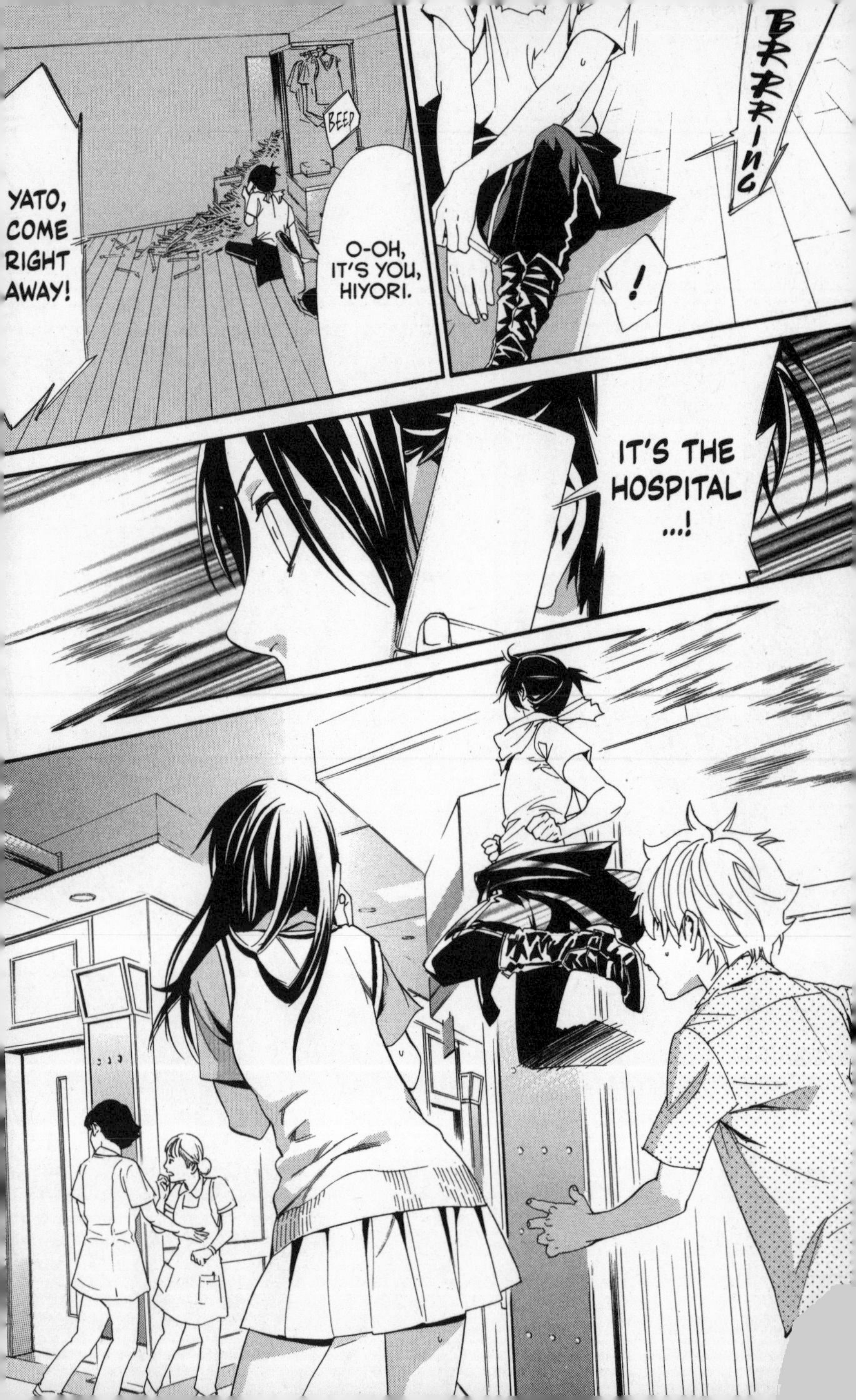
BRRRING
!
BEEP
O-OH, IT'S YOU, HIYORI.
YATO, COME RIGHT AWAY!
IT'S THE HOSPITAL ...!

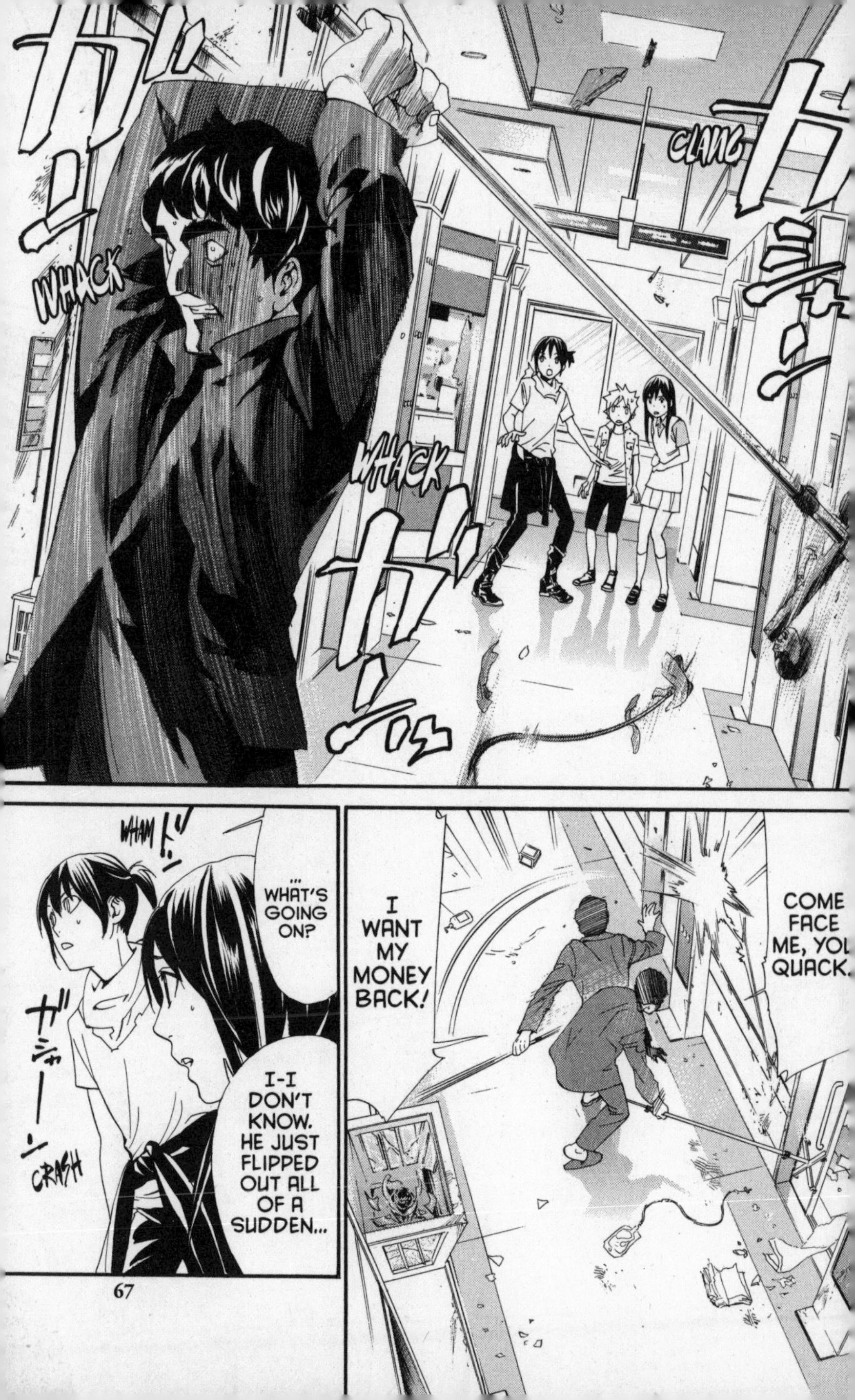
CLANG
WHACK
WHACK
COME FACE ME, YOU QUACK.
I WANT MY MONEY BACK!
WHAM
...WHAT'S GOING ON?
I-I DON'T KNOW. HE JUST FLIPPED OUT ALL OF A SUDDEN...
CRASH

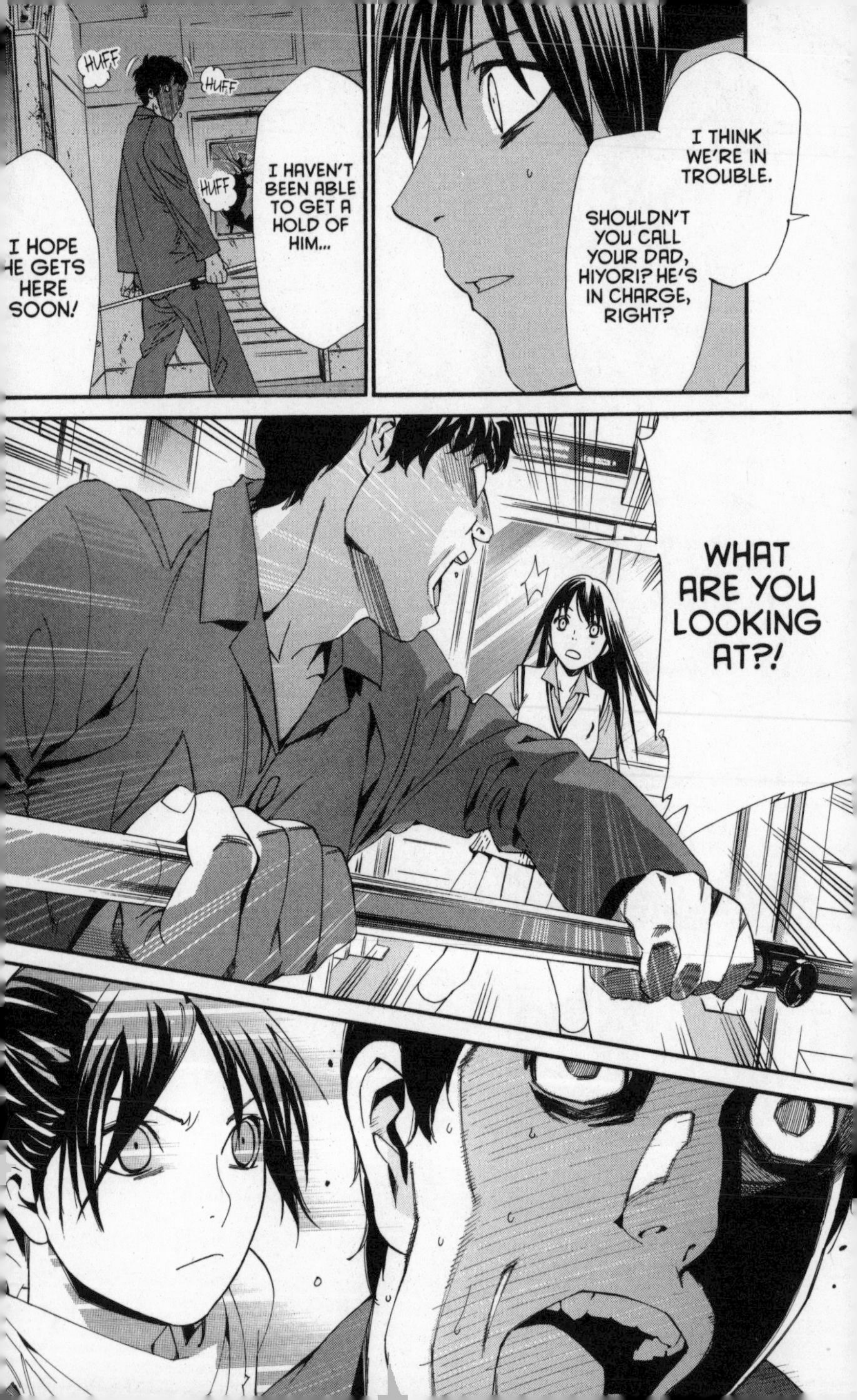
I THINK WE'RE IN TROUBLE.
SHOULDN'T YOU CALL YOUR DAD, HIYORI? HE'S IN CHARGE, RIGHT?
I HAVEN'T BEEN ABLE TO GET A HOLD OF HIM...
HUFF
HUFF
HUFF
I HOPE HE GETS HERE SOON!
WHAT ARE YOU LOOKING AT?!

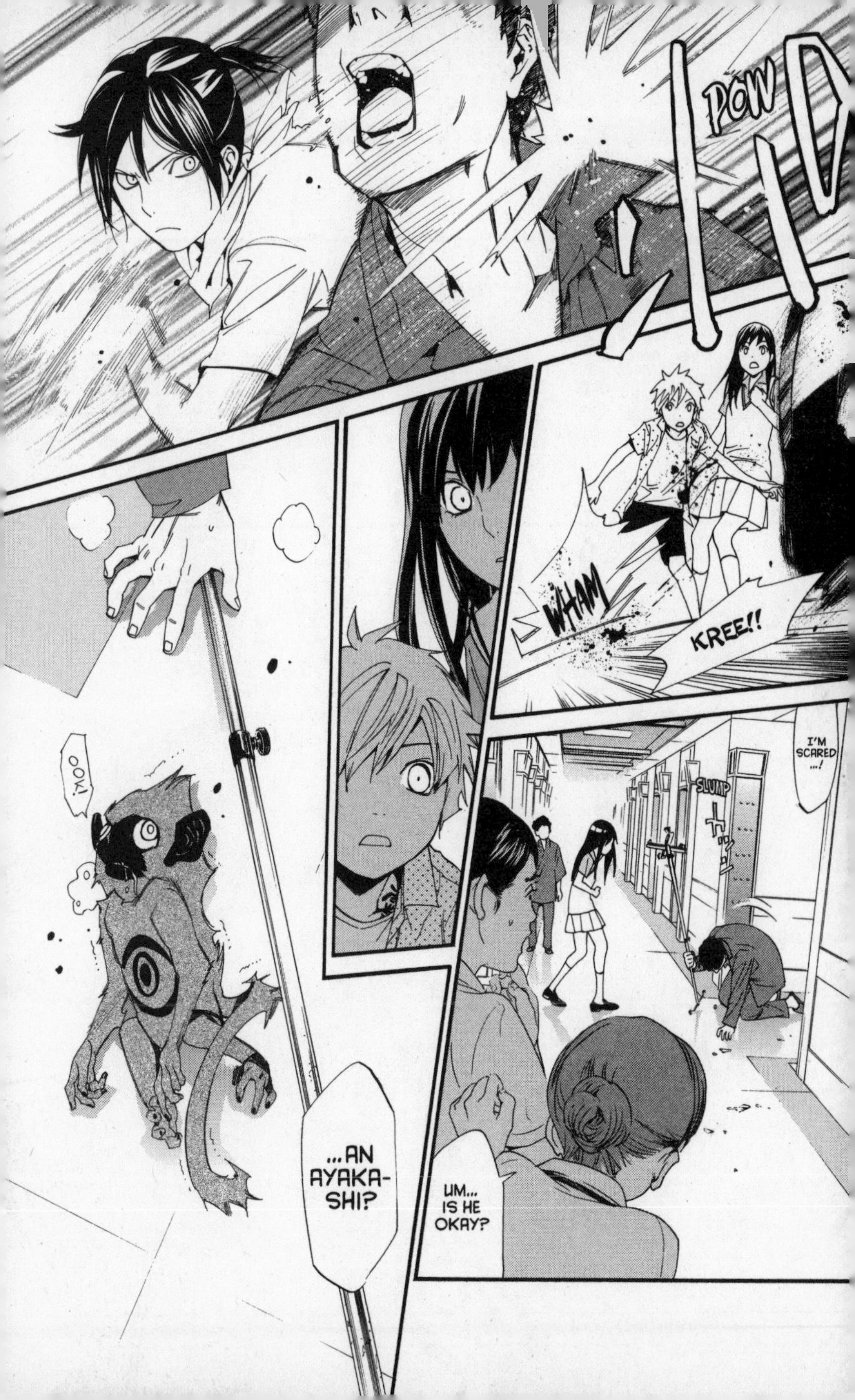
POW
WHAM
KREE!!
I'M SCARED...!
SLUMP
UM... IS HE OKAY?
OOK!
...AN AYAKASHI?

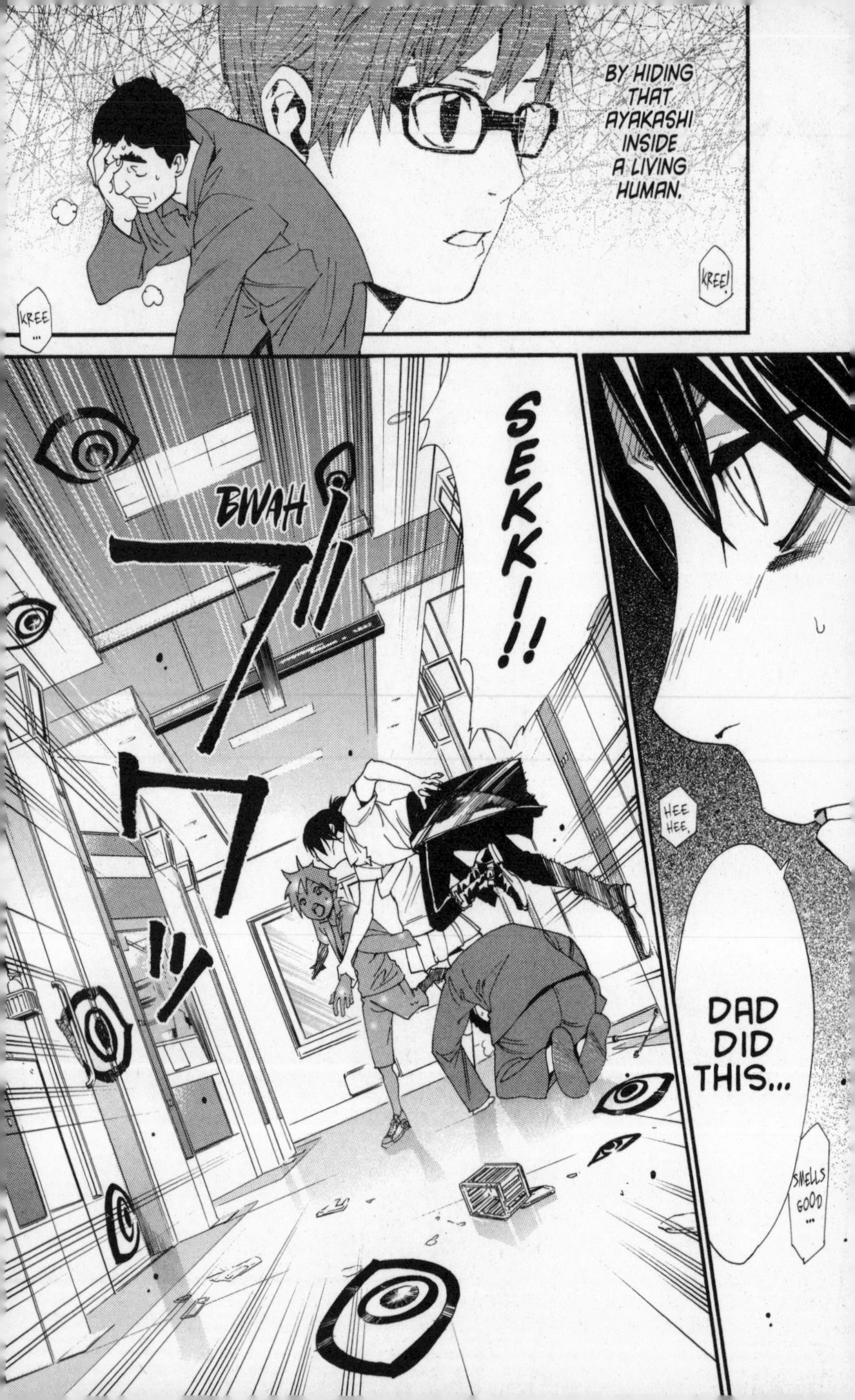

BY HIDING THAT AYAKASHI INSIDE A LIVING HUMAN.
KREE!
KREE ...
HEE HEE.
DAD DID THIS...
SMELLS GOOD ...
SEKKI!!
BWAH
ブワッ

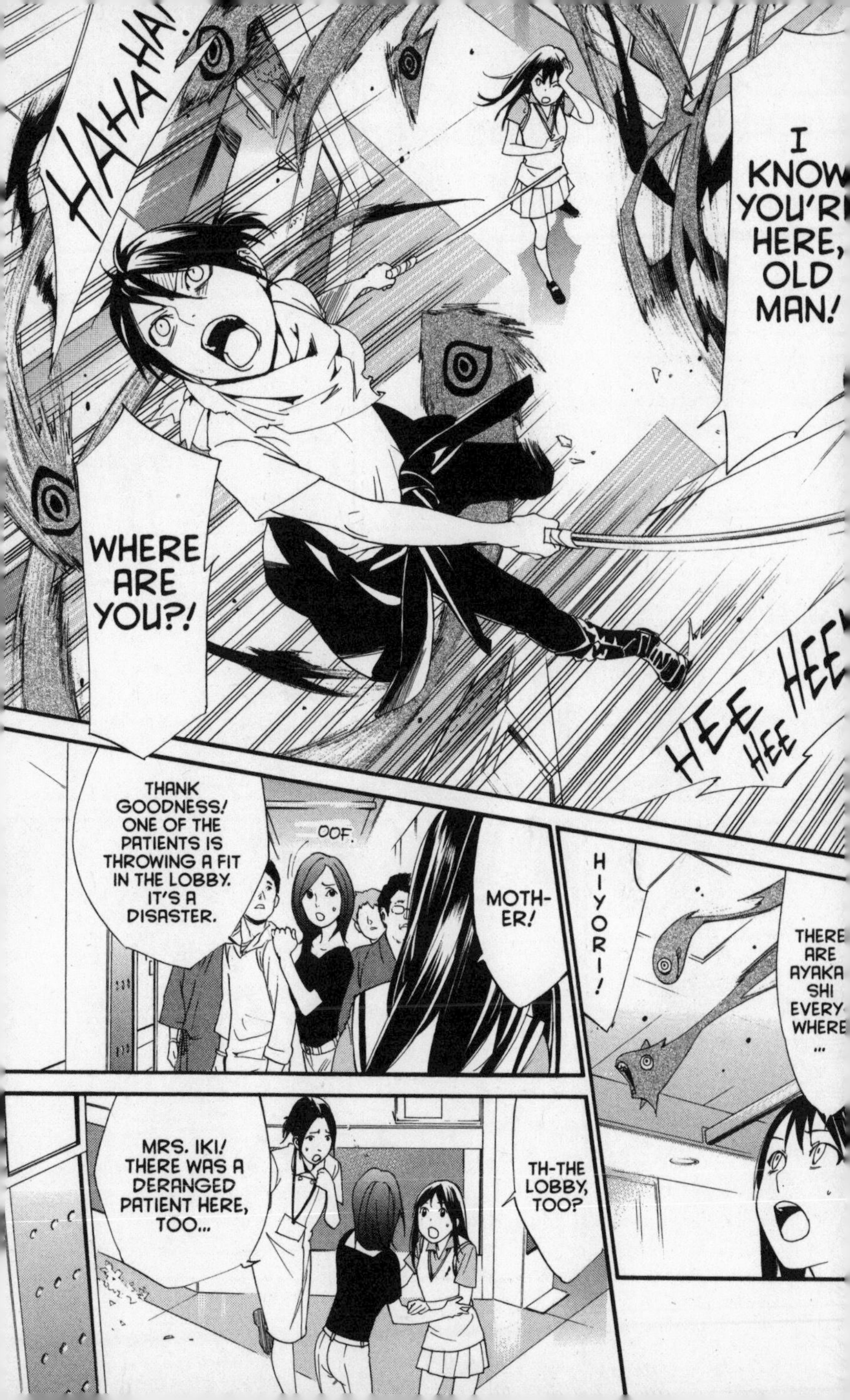

I KNOW YOU'R HERE, OLD MAN!
HAHAHA!
HEE HEE HEE
WHERE ARE YOU?!
THERE ARE AYAKASHI EVERYWHERE...
HIYORI!
MOTH-ER!
OOF.
THANK GOODNESS! ONE OF THE PATIENTS IS THROWING A FIT IN THE LOBBY. IT'S A DISASTER.
TH-THE LOBBY, TOO?
MRS. IKI! THERE WAS A DERANGED PATIENT HERE, TOO...

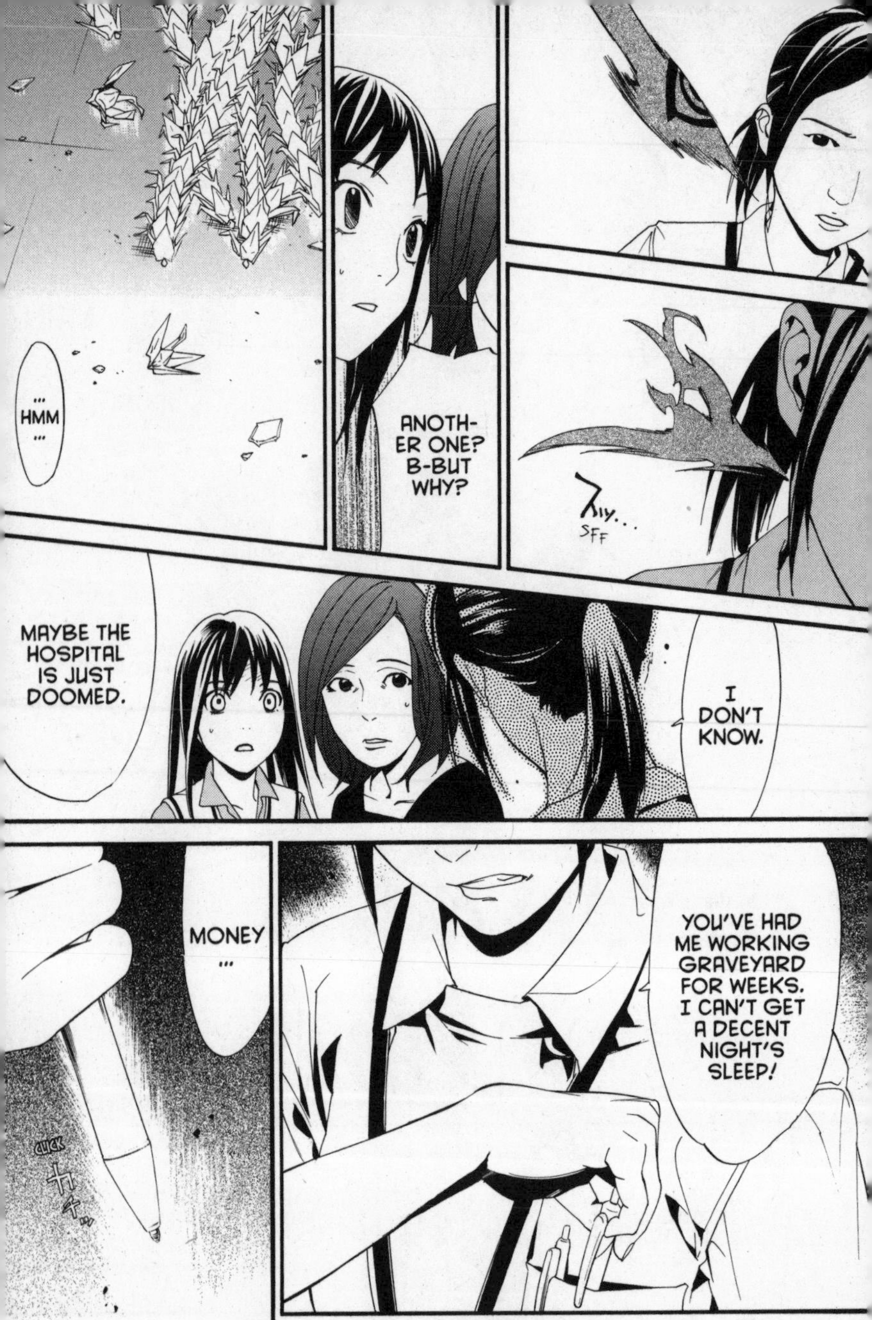
SFF
ANOTH-ER ONE? B-BUT WHY?
... HMM ...
I DON'T KNOW.
MAYBE THE HOSPITAL IS JUST DOOMED.
YOU'VE HAD ME WORKING GRAVEYARD FOR WEEKS. I CAN'T GET A DECENT NIGHT'S SLEEP!
MONEY ...
CLICK

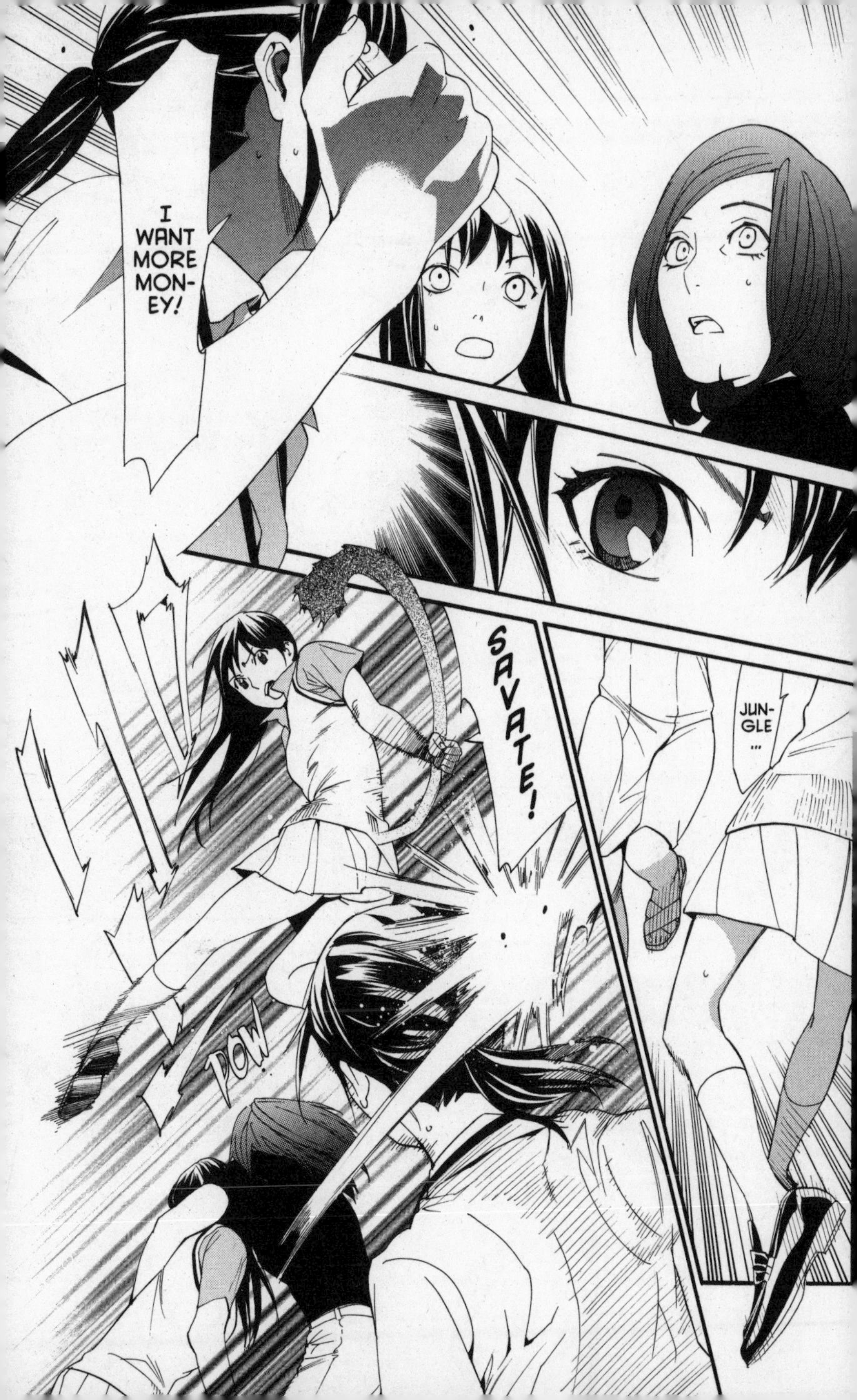
I WANT MORE MON-EY!
JUN-GLE ...
SAVATE!
POW

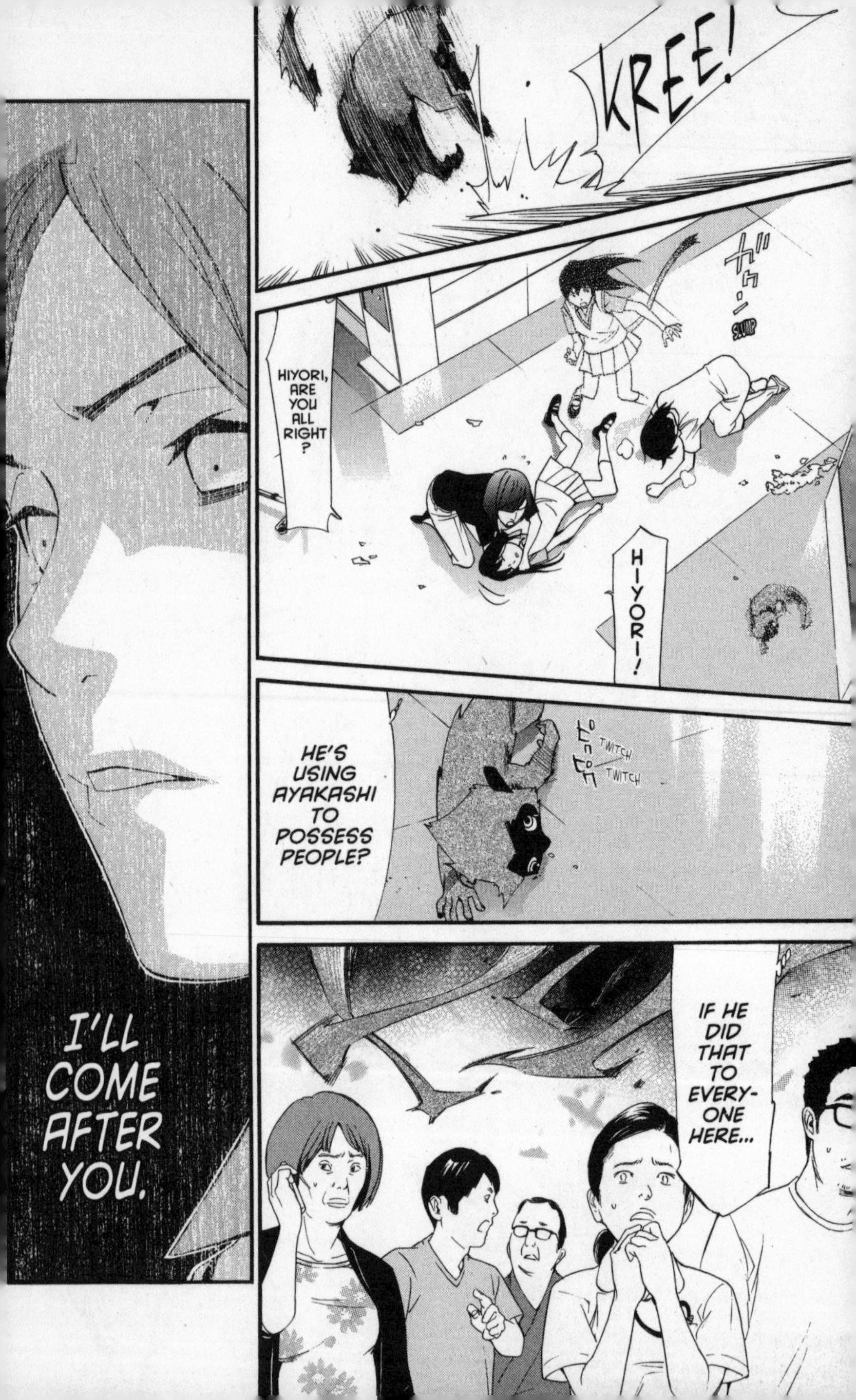

KREE!
SLUMP
HIYORI!
HIYORI, ARE YOU ALL RIGHT?
TWITCH TWITCH
HE'S USING AYAKASHI TO POSSESS PEOPLE?
IF HE DID THAT TO EVERYONE HERE...
I'LL COME AFTER YOU.

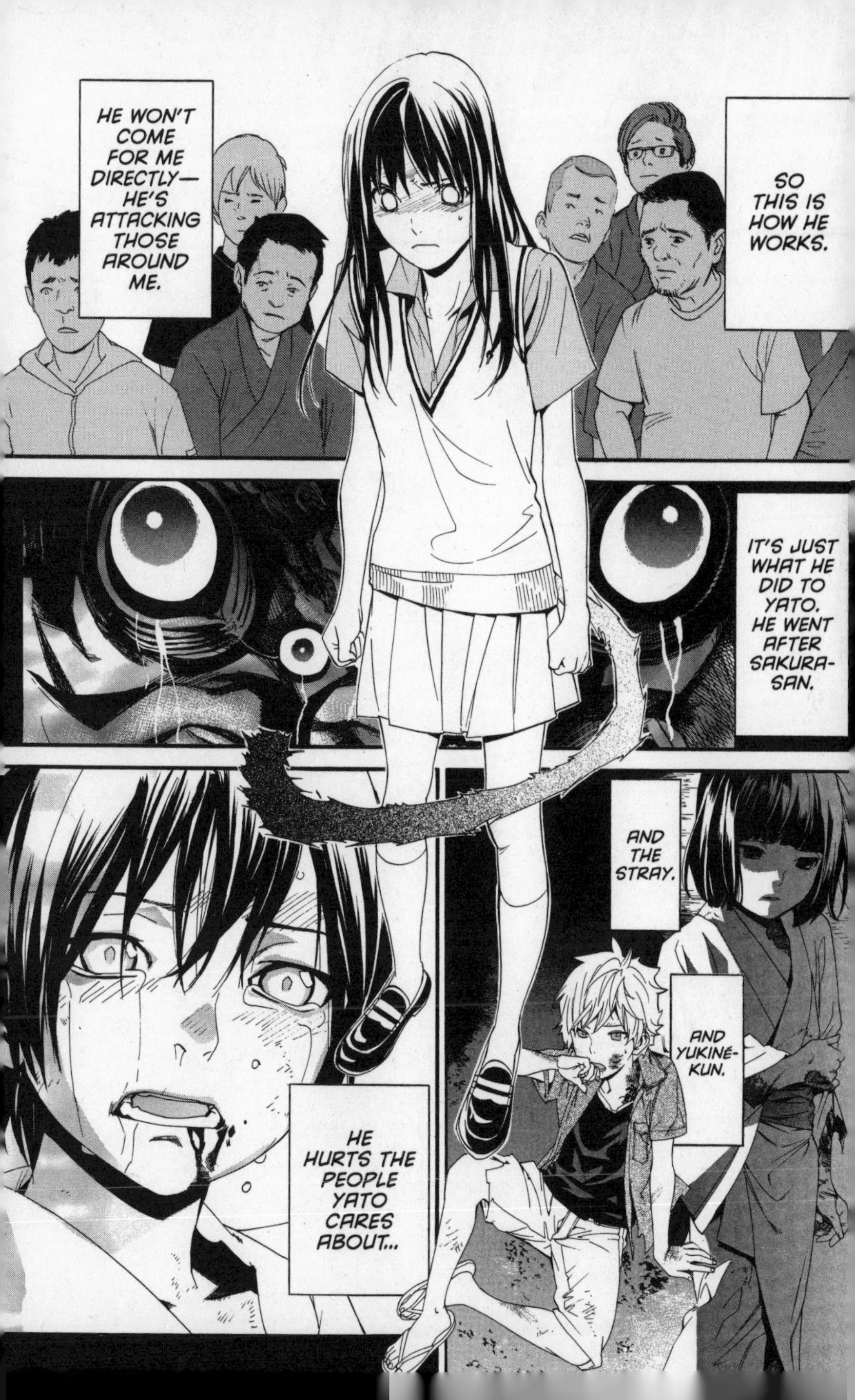
SO THIS IS HOW HE WORKS.
HE WON'T COME FOR ME DIRECTLY— HE'S ATTACKING THOSE AROUND ME.
IT'S JUST WHAT HE DID TO YATO. HE WENT AFTER SAKURA-SAN.
AND THE STRAY.
AND YUKINÉ-KUN.
HE HURTS THE PEOPLE YATO CARES ABOUT...

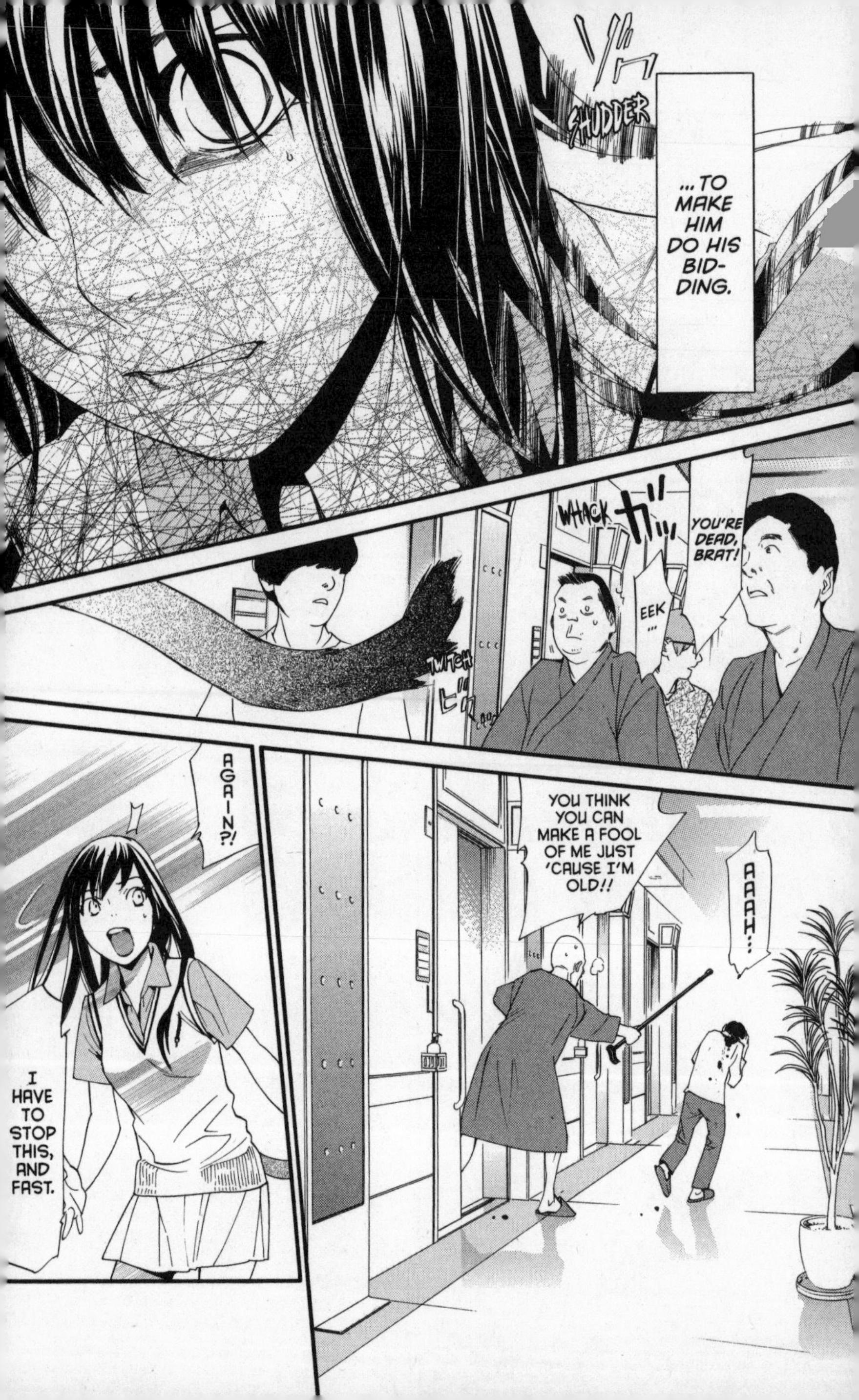
SHUDDER
...TO MAKE HIM DO HIS BID-DING.
YOU'RE DEAD, BRAT!
WHACK
EEK...
TWITCH
AGAIN?!
YOU THINK YOU CAN MAKE A FOOL OF ME JUST 'CAUSE I'M OLD!!
AAAAH...!
I HAVE TO STOP THIS, AND FAST.

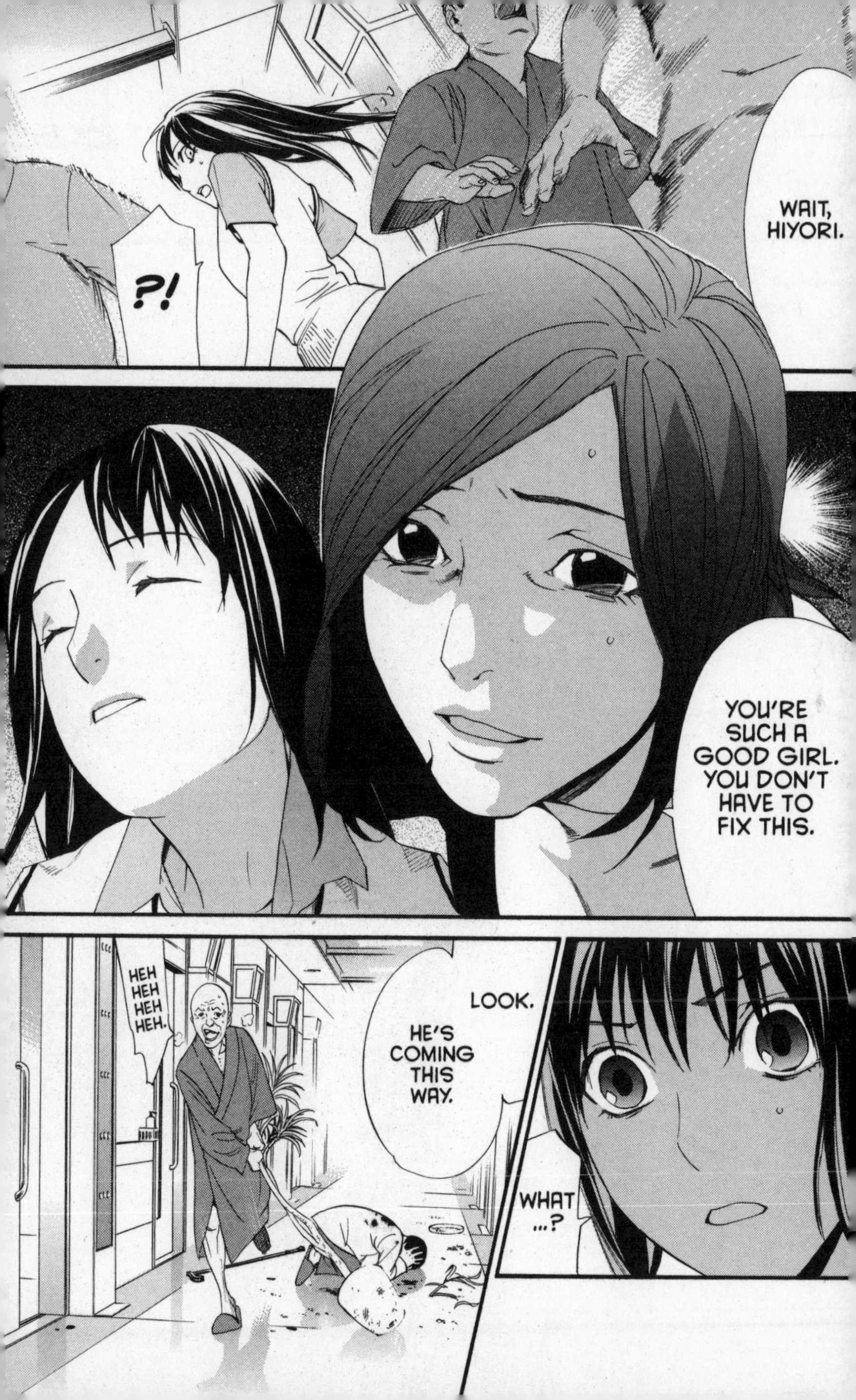
WAIT, HIYORI.
?!
YOU'RE SUCH A GOOD GIRL. YOU DON'T HAVE TO FIX THIS.
WHAT ...?
LOOK.
HE'S COMING THIS WAY.
HEH HEH HEH HEH.

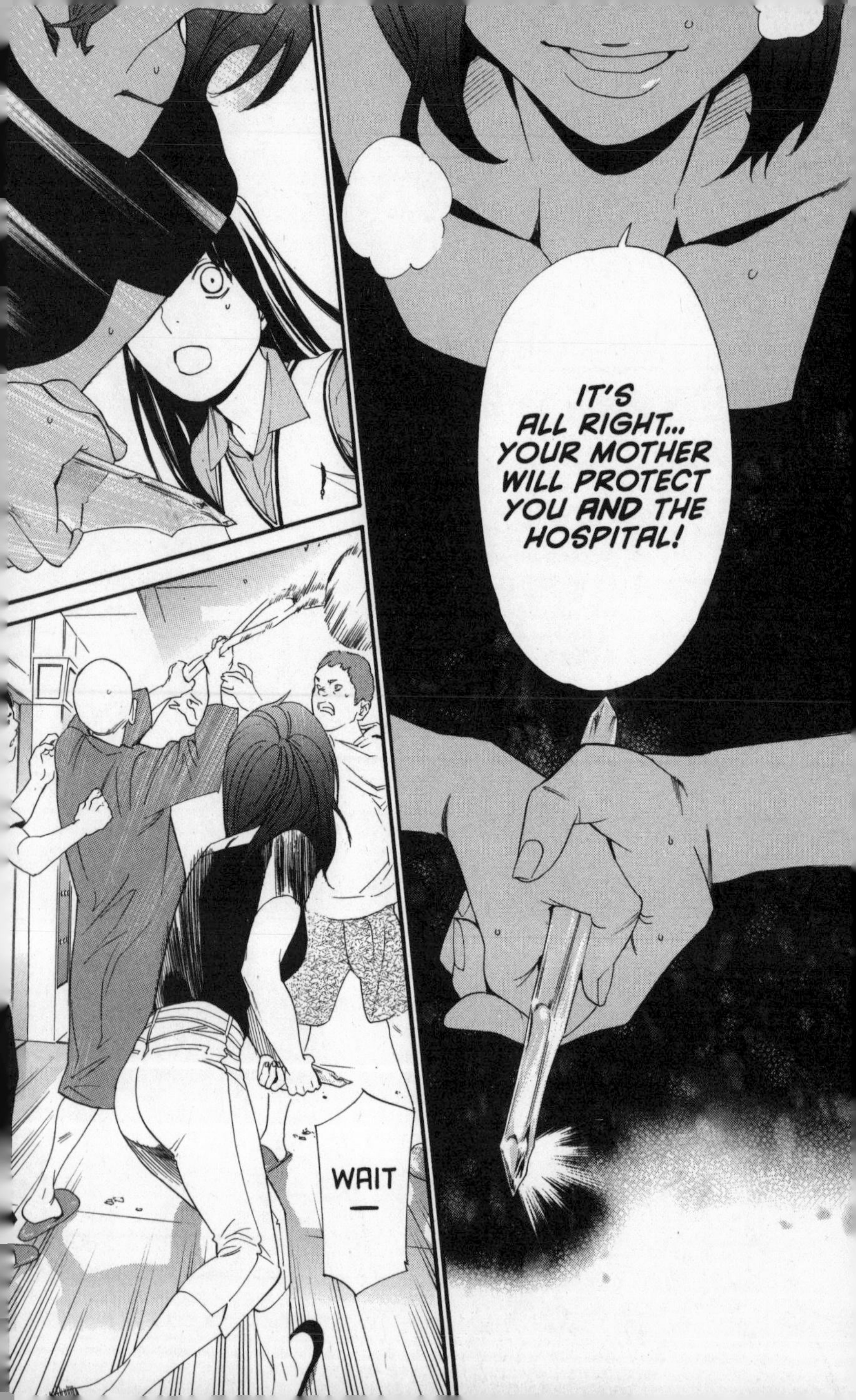
IT'S ALL RIGHT... YOUR MOTHER WILL PROTECT YOU AND THE HOSPITAL!
WAIT —

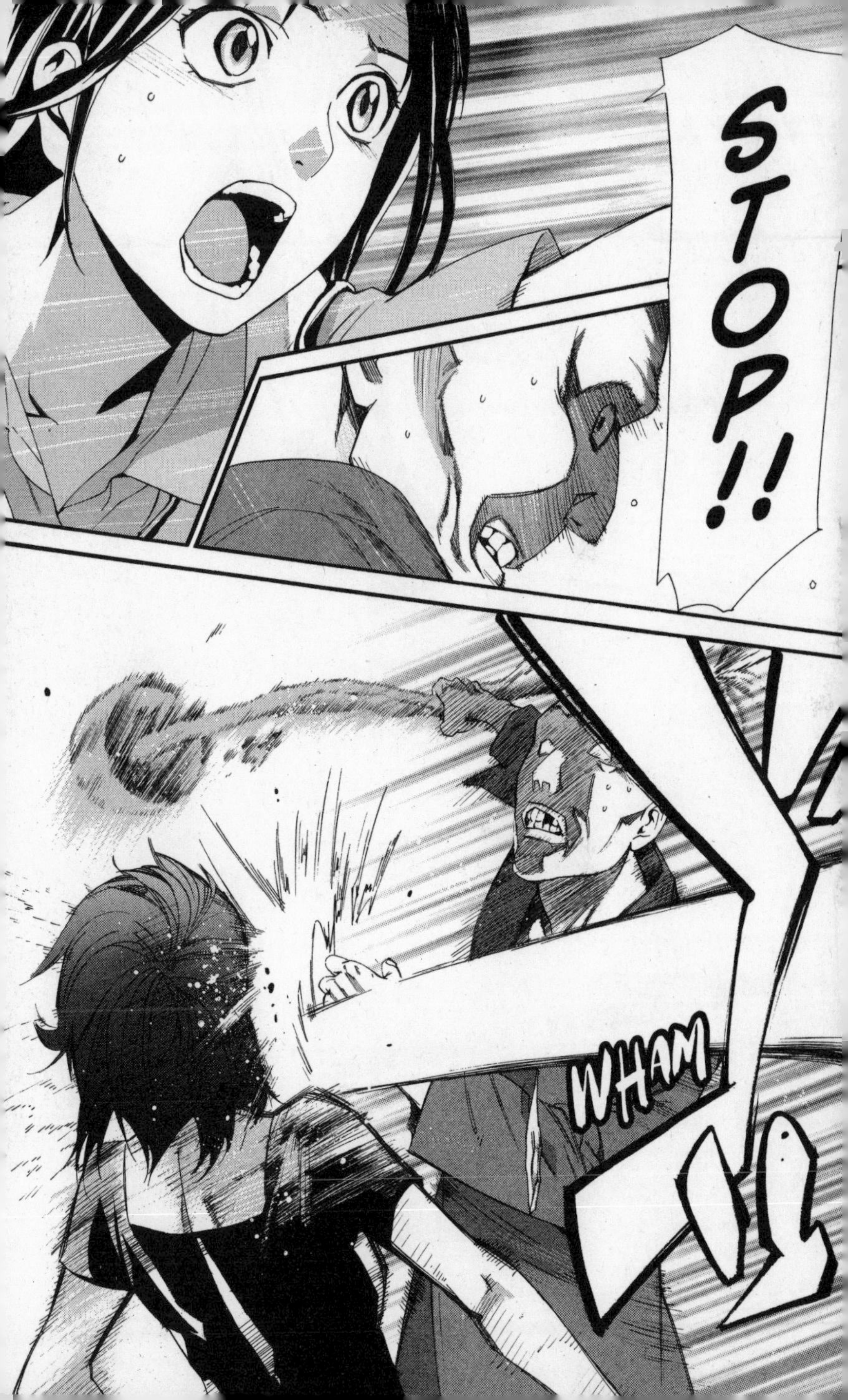
STOP!!
WHAM

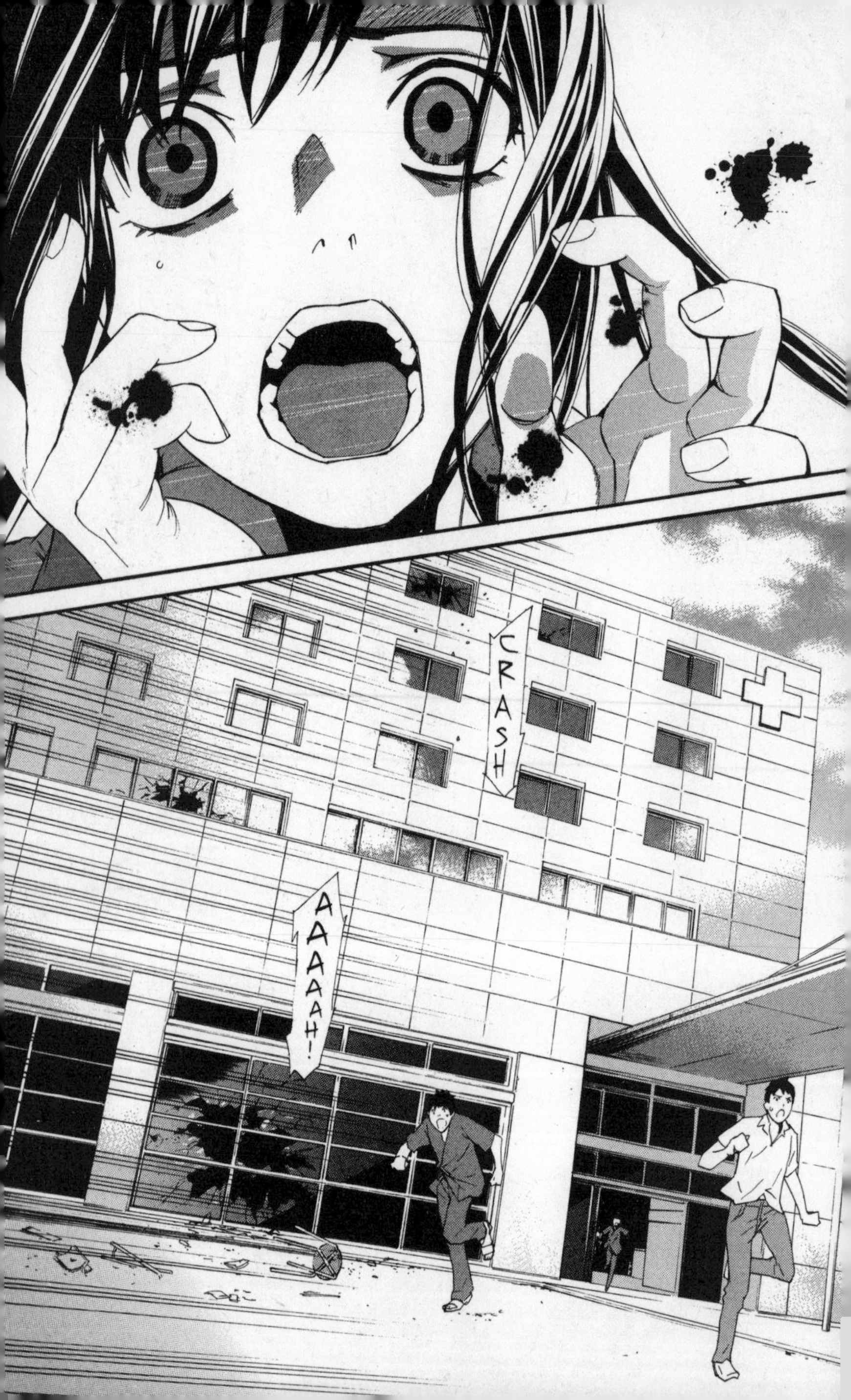
CRASH
AAAAAAH!

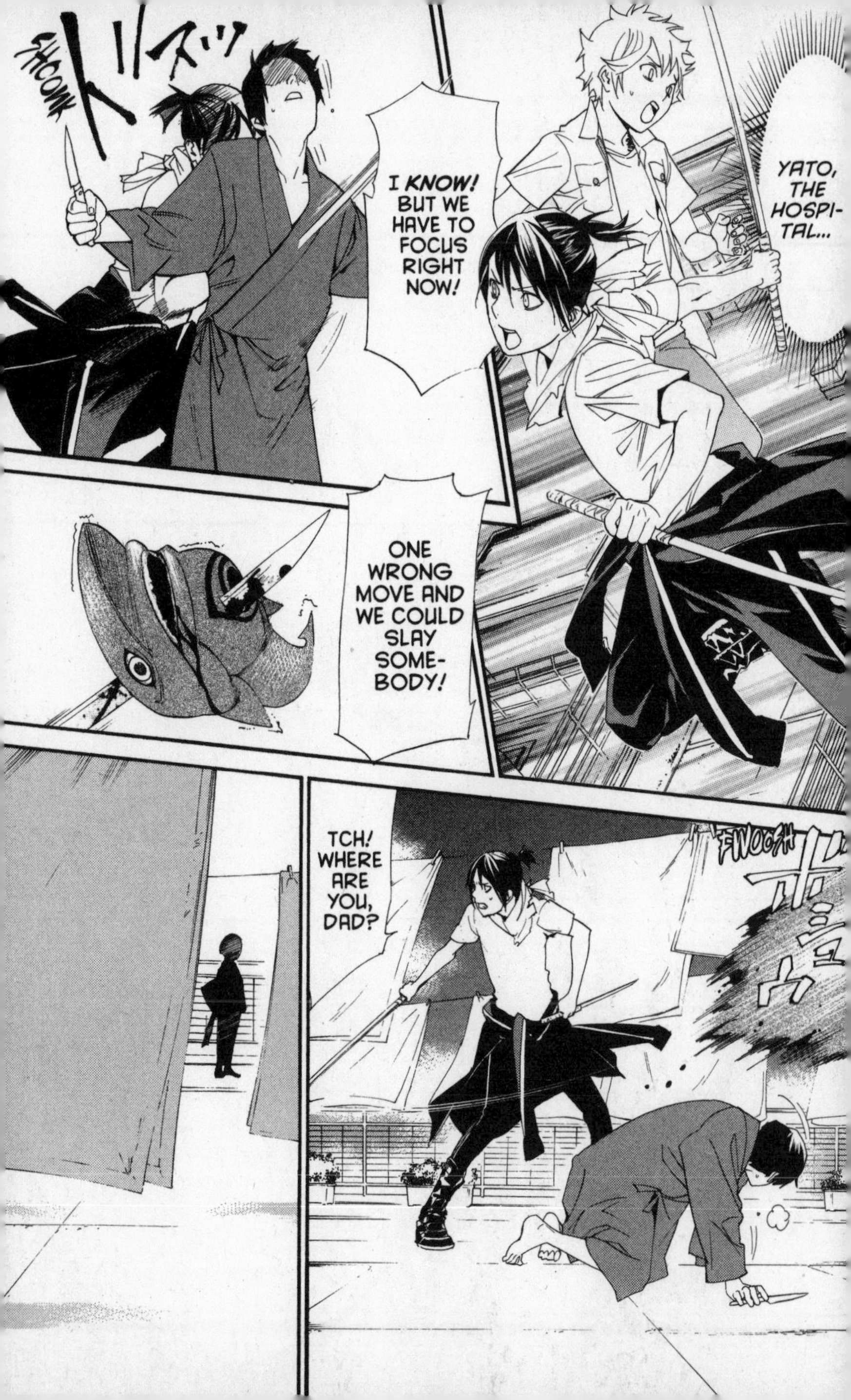
YATO, THE HOSPITAL...
I *KNOW!* BUT WE HAVE TO FOCUS RIGHT NOW!
ONE WRONG MOVE AND WE COULD SLAY SOME-BODY!
SHCONK
FWOOSH
TCH! WHERE ARE YOU, DAD?

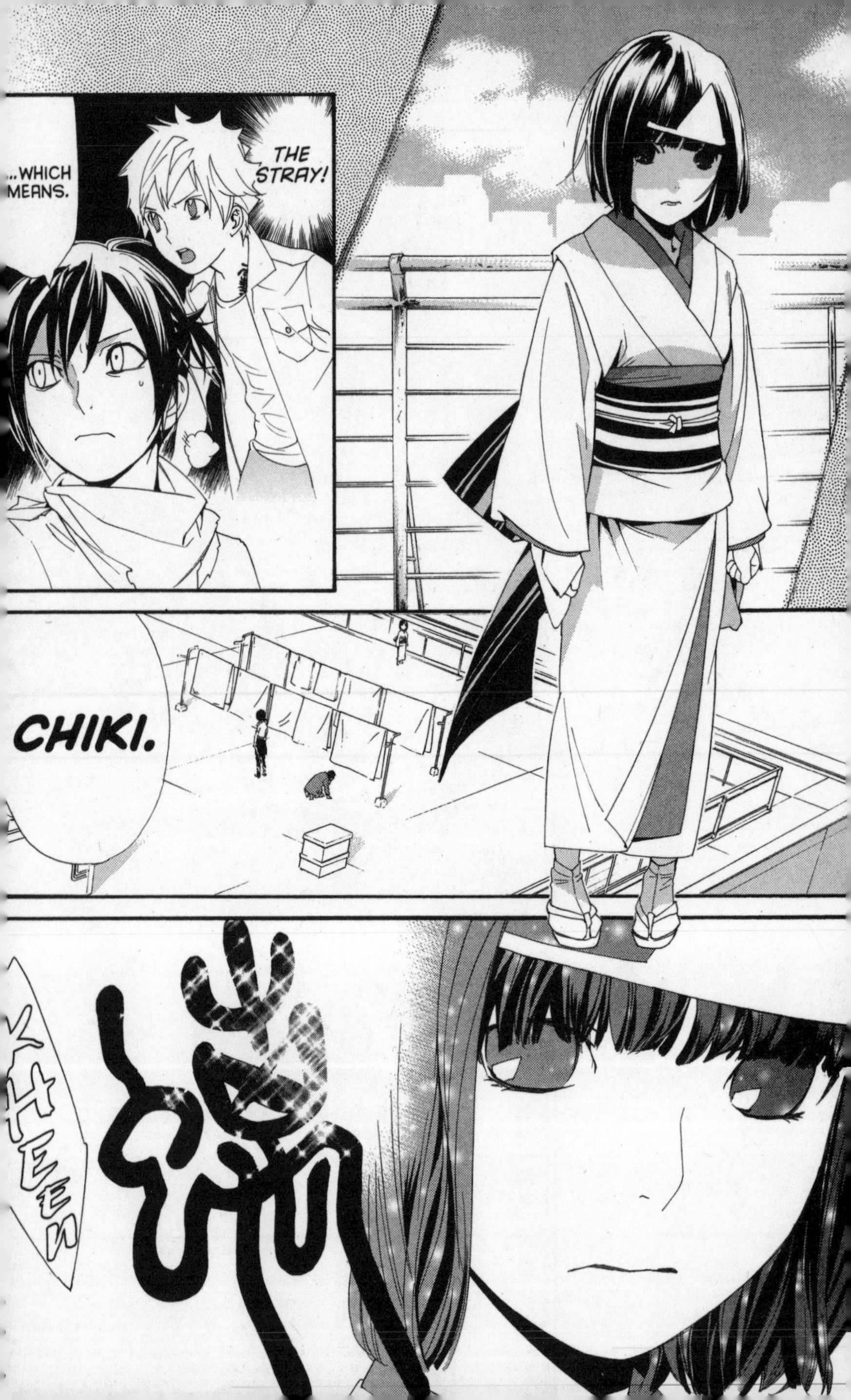
THE STRAY!
...WHICH MEANS.
CHIKI.
KHEEN

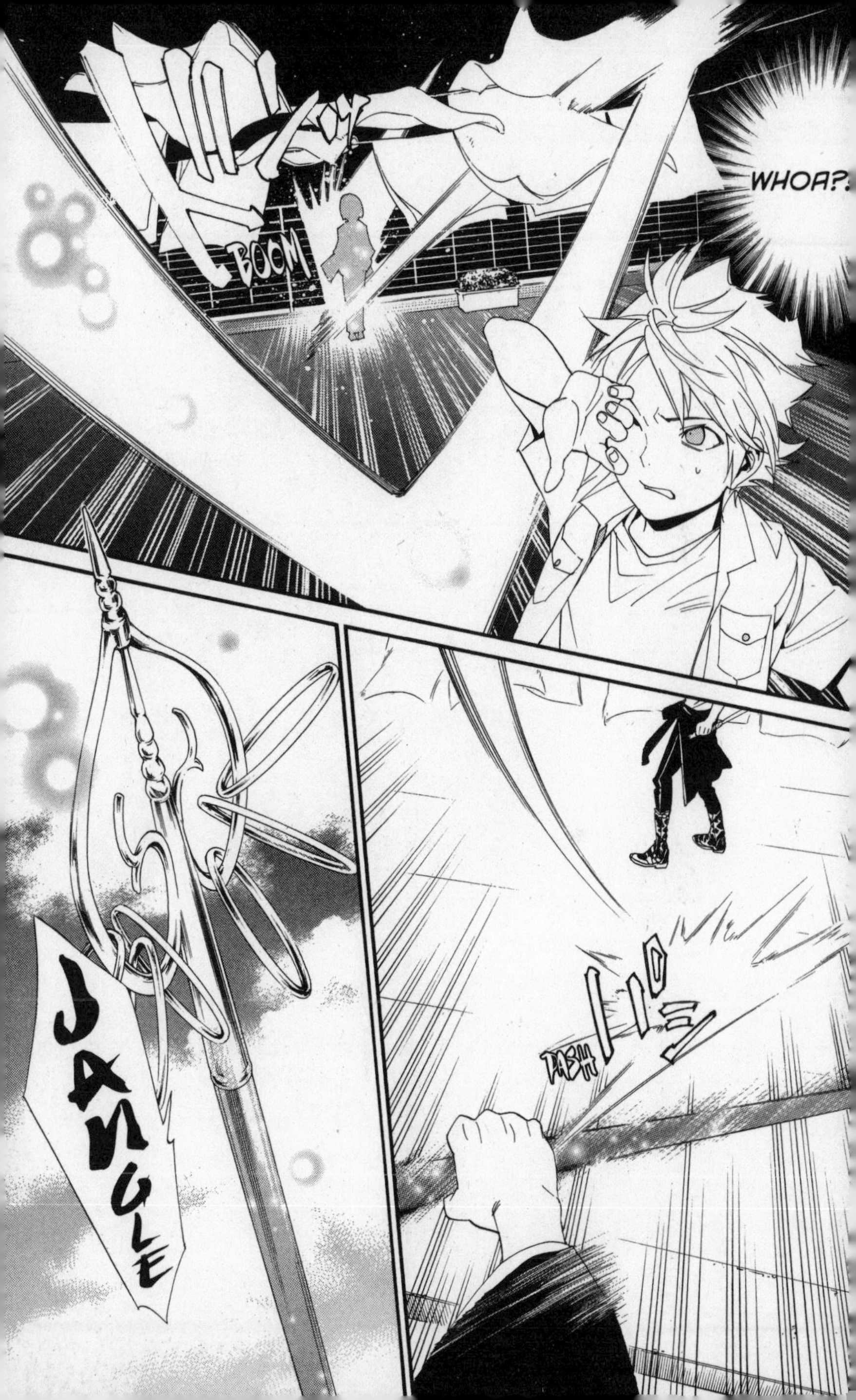
WHOA?!
BOOM
DASH
JANGLE

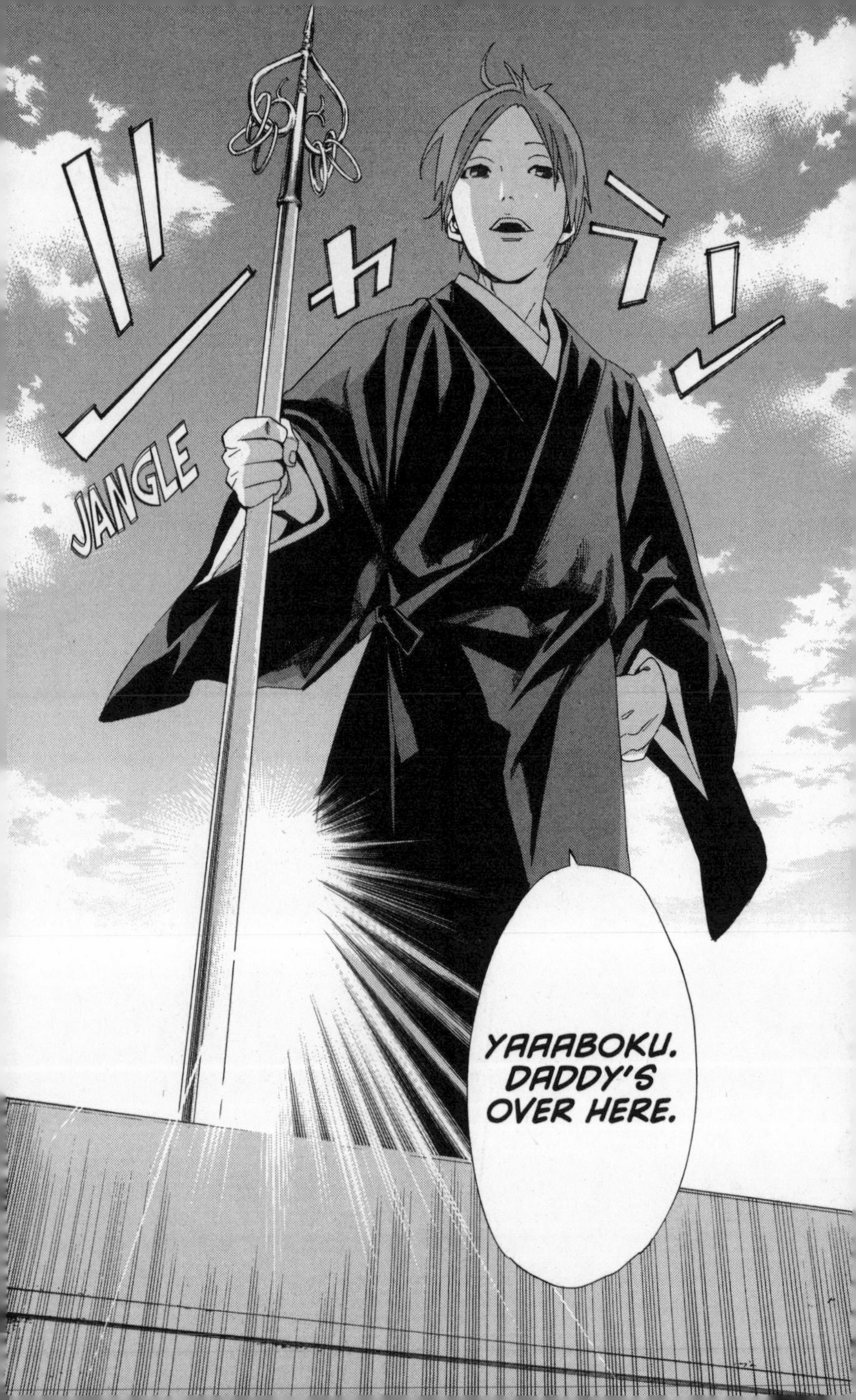
JANGLE
YAAABOKU. DADDY'S OVER HERE.

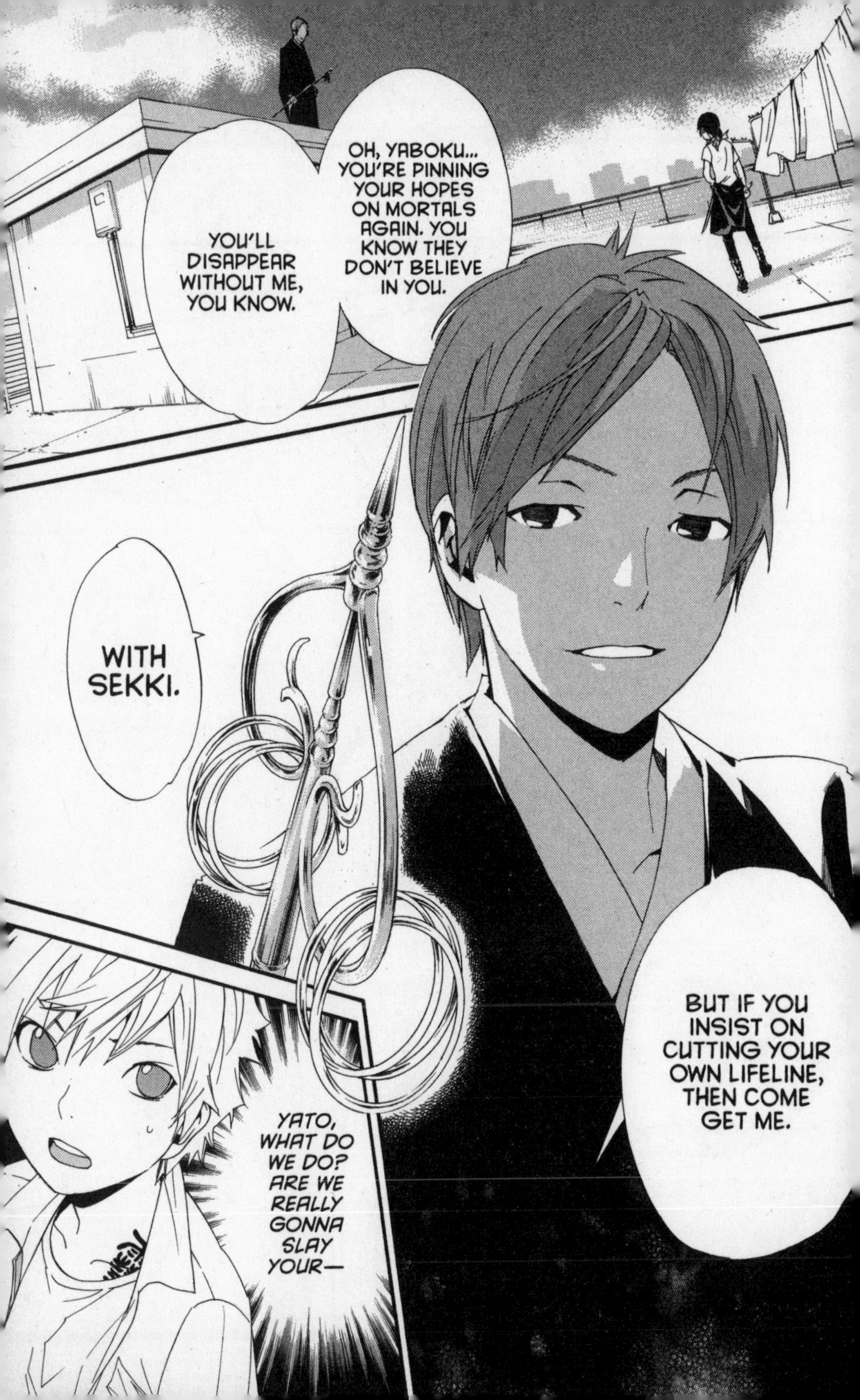
OH, YABOKU... YOU'RE PINNING YOUR HOPES ON MORTALS AGAIN. YOU KNOW THEY DON'T BELIEVE IN YOU.
YOU'LL DISAPPEAR WITHOUT ME, YOU KNOW.
WITH SEKKI.
BUT IF YOU INSIST ON CUTTING YOUR OWN LIFELINE, THEN COME GET ME.
YATO, WHAT DO WE DO? ARE WE REALLY GONNA SLAY YOUR—

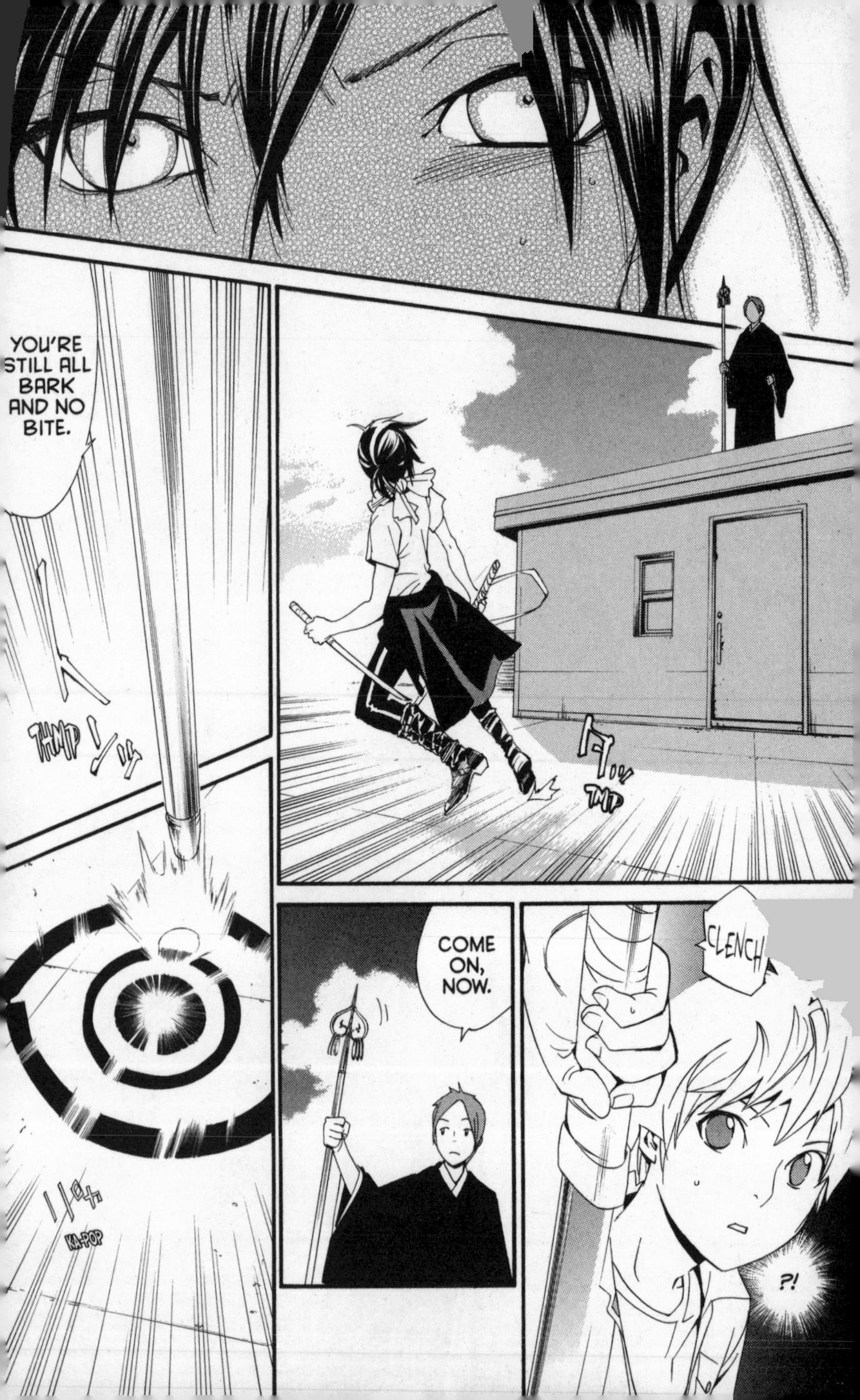
TMP
CLENCH
?!
COME ON, NOW.
YOU'RE STILL ALL BARK AND NO BITE.
THMP
KA-POP

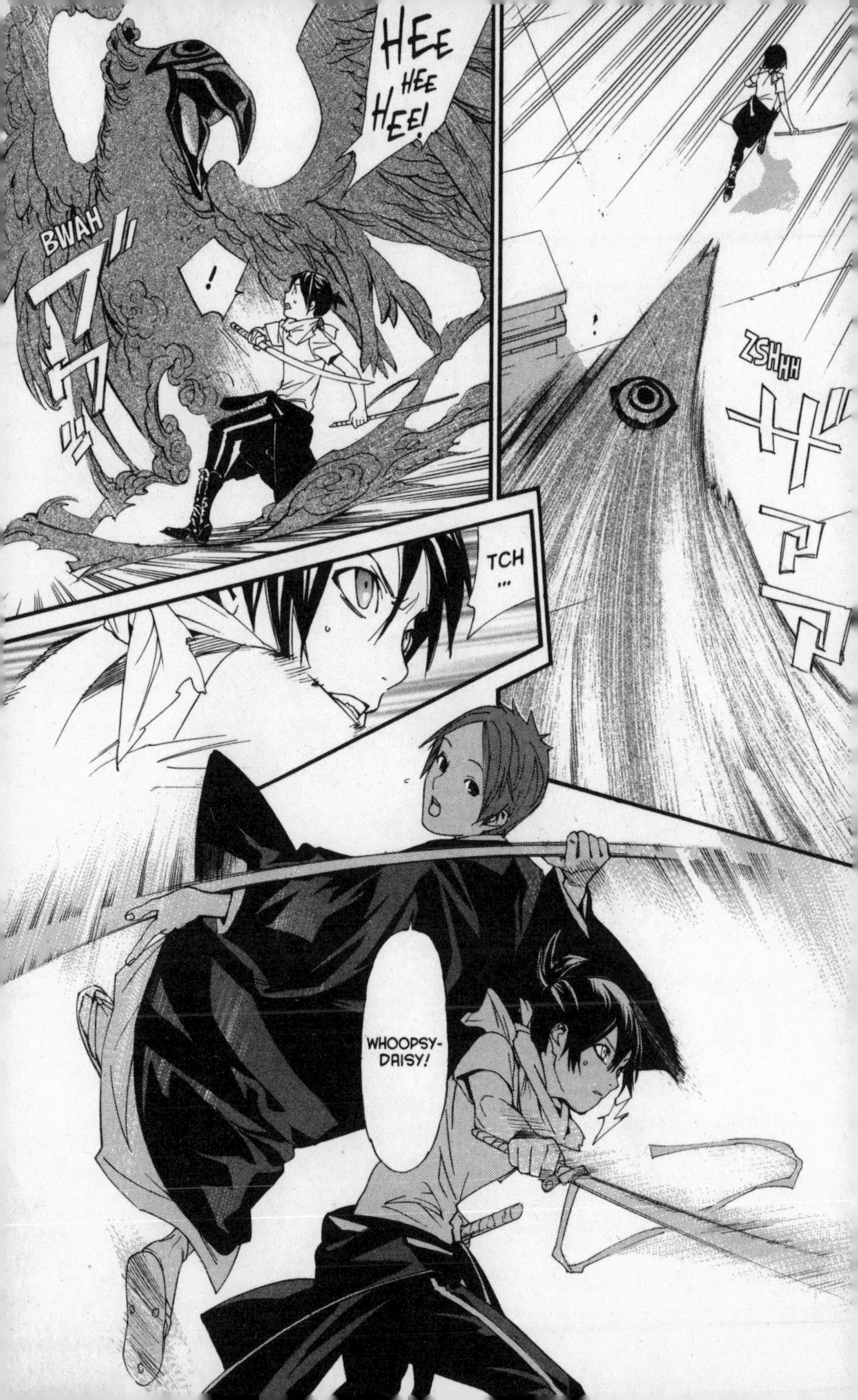
ZSHHH
ザァァ
HEE HEE HEE!
BWAH
ブワッ
!
TCH...
WHOOPSY-DAISY!

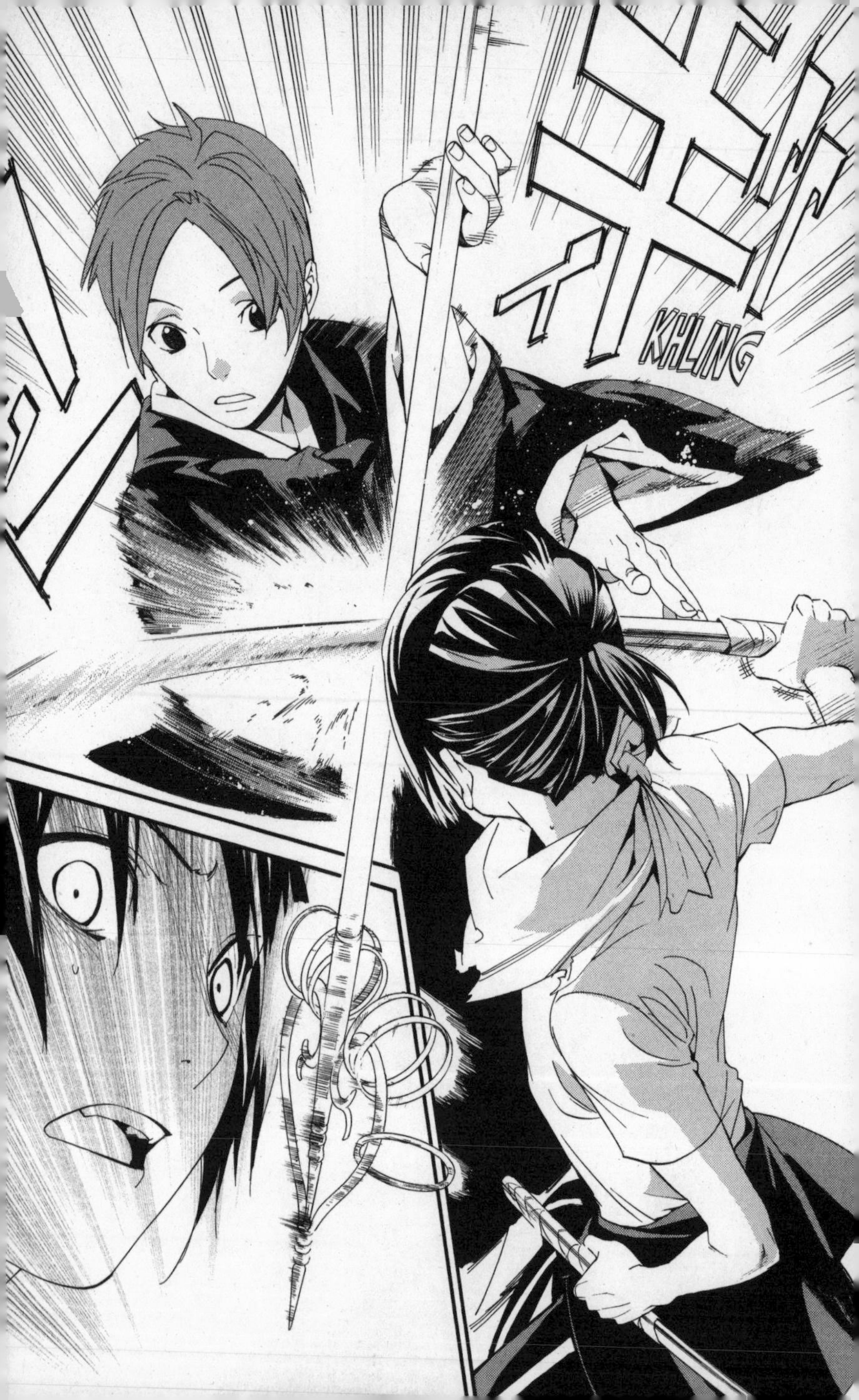
KHLING

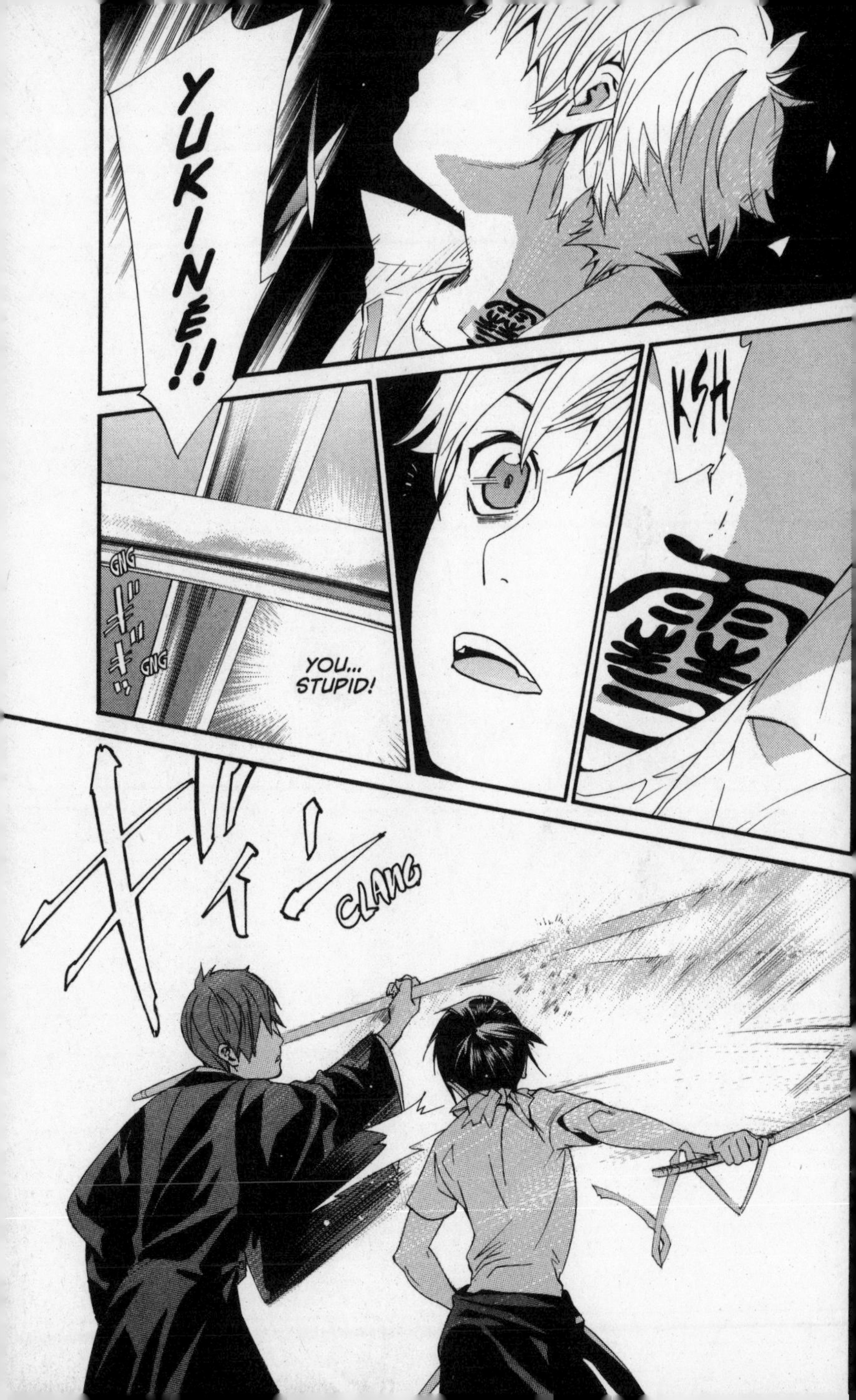
YUKINE!!
KSH
GNG
GNG
YOU... STUPID!
CLANG

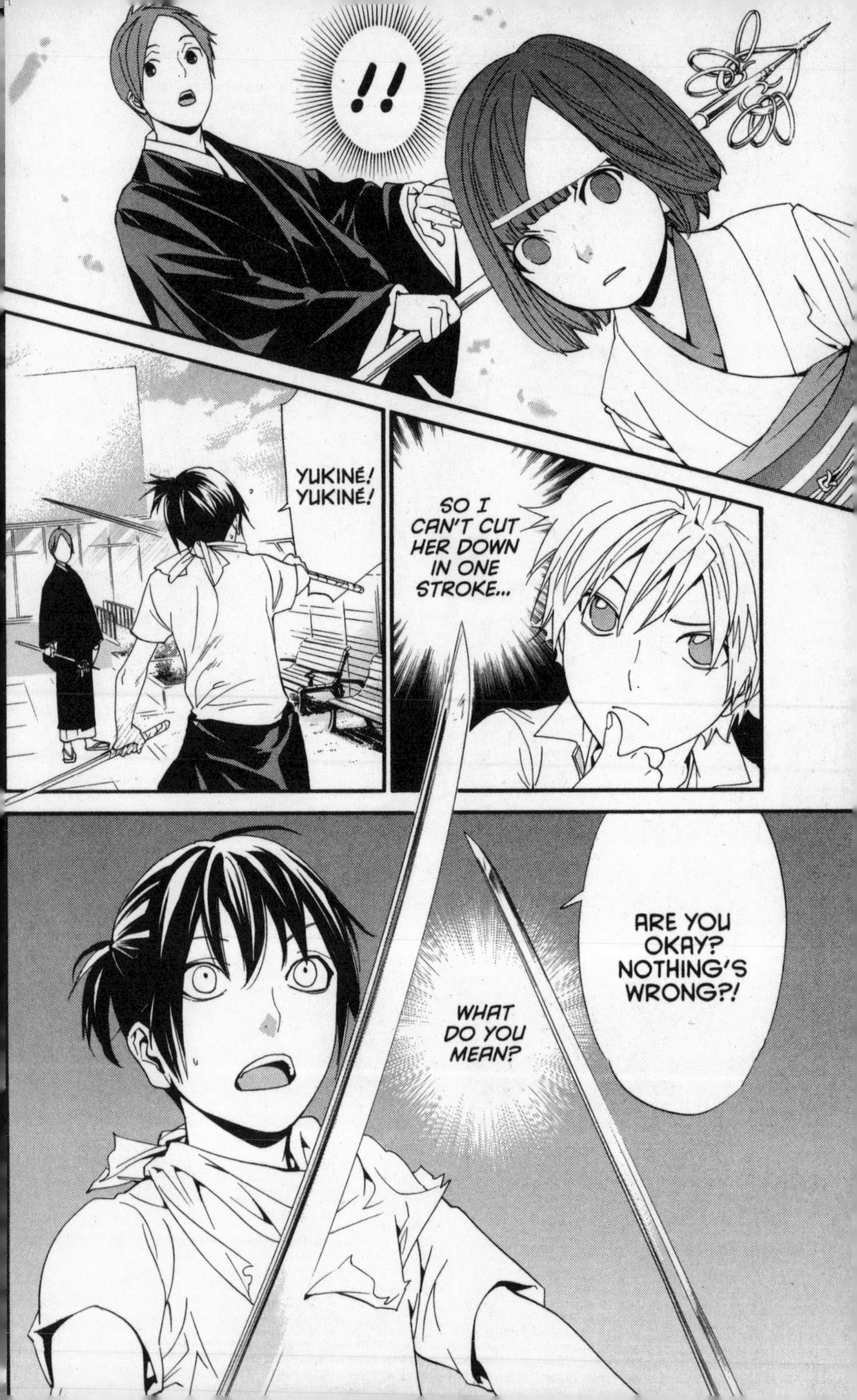
!!
SO I CAN'T CUT HER DOWN IN ONE STROKE...
YUKINÉ! YUKINÉ!
ARE YOU OKAY? NOTHING'S WRONG?!
WHAT DO YOU MEAN?

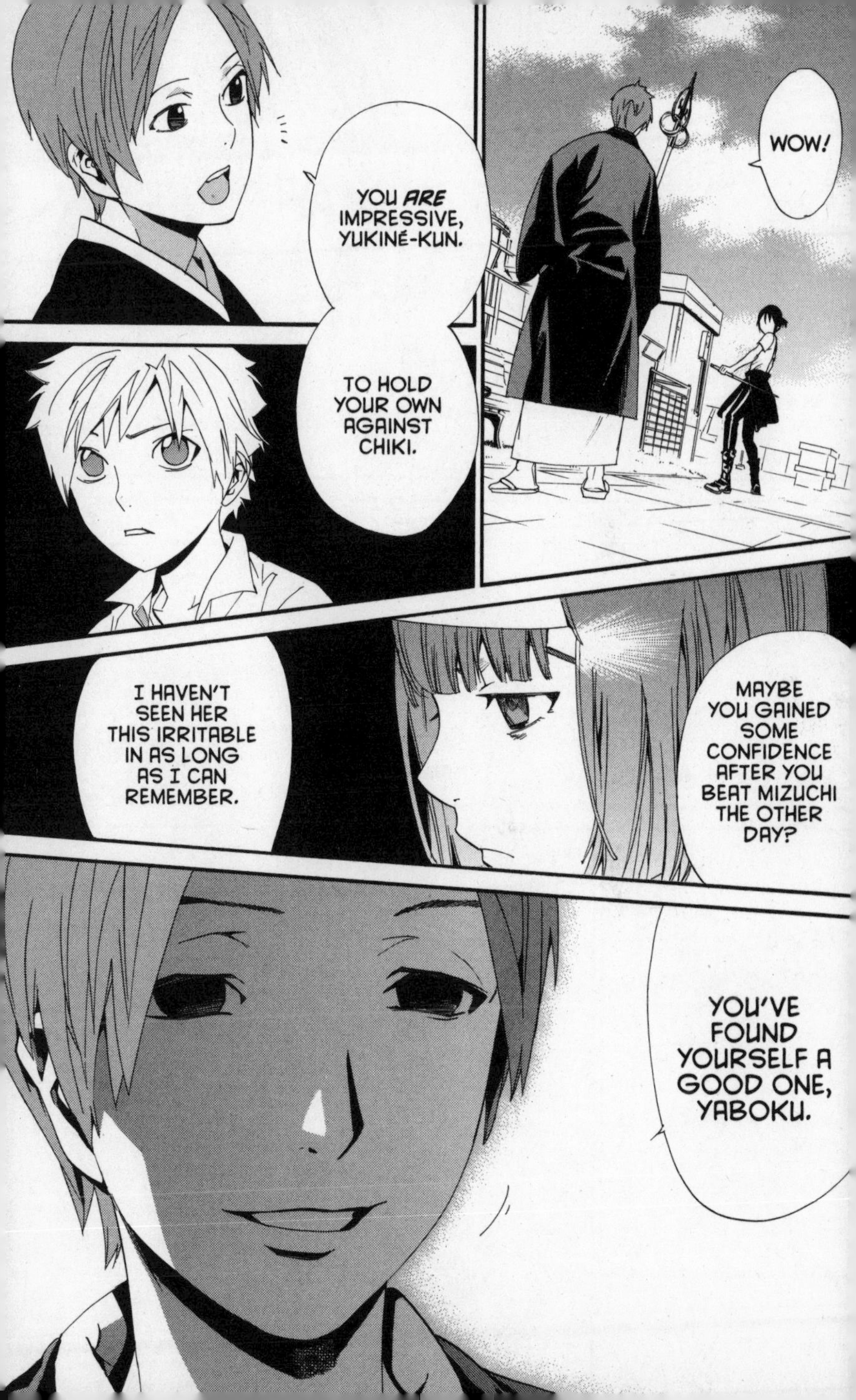
WOW!
YOU ARE IMPRESSIVE, YUKINÉ-KUN.
TO HOLD YOUR OWN AGAINST CHIKI.
MAYBE YOU GAINED SOME CONFIDENCE AFTER YOU BEAT MIZUCHI THE OTHER DAY?
I HAVEN'T SEEN HER THIS IRRITABLE IN AS LONG AS I CAN REMEMBER.
YOU'VE FOUND YOURSELF A GOOD ONE, YABOKU.

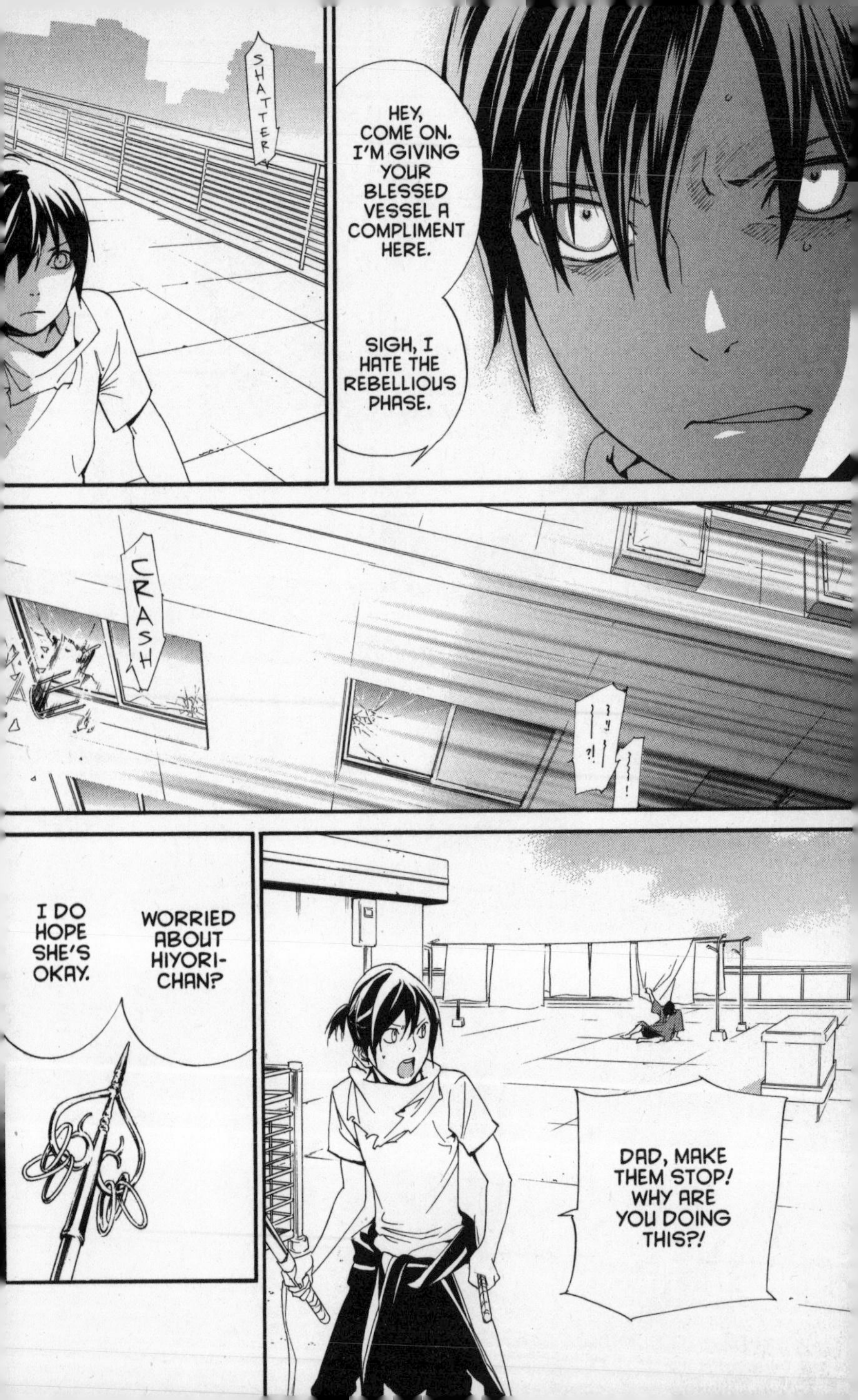
HEY, COME ON. I'M GIVING YOUR BLESSED VESSEL A COMPLIMENT HERE.
SIGH, I HATE THE REBELLIOUS PHASE.
SHATTER
CRASH
DAD, MAKE THEM STOP! WHY ARE YOU DOING THIS?!
WORRIED ABOUT HIYORI-CHAN?
I DO HOPE SHE'S OKAY.

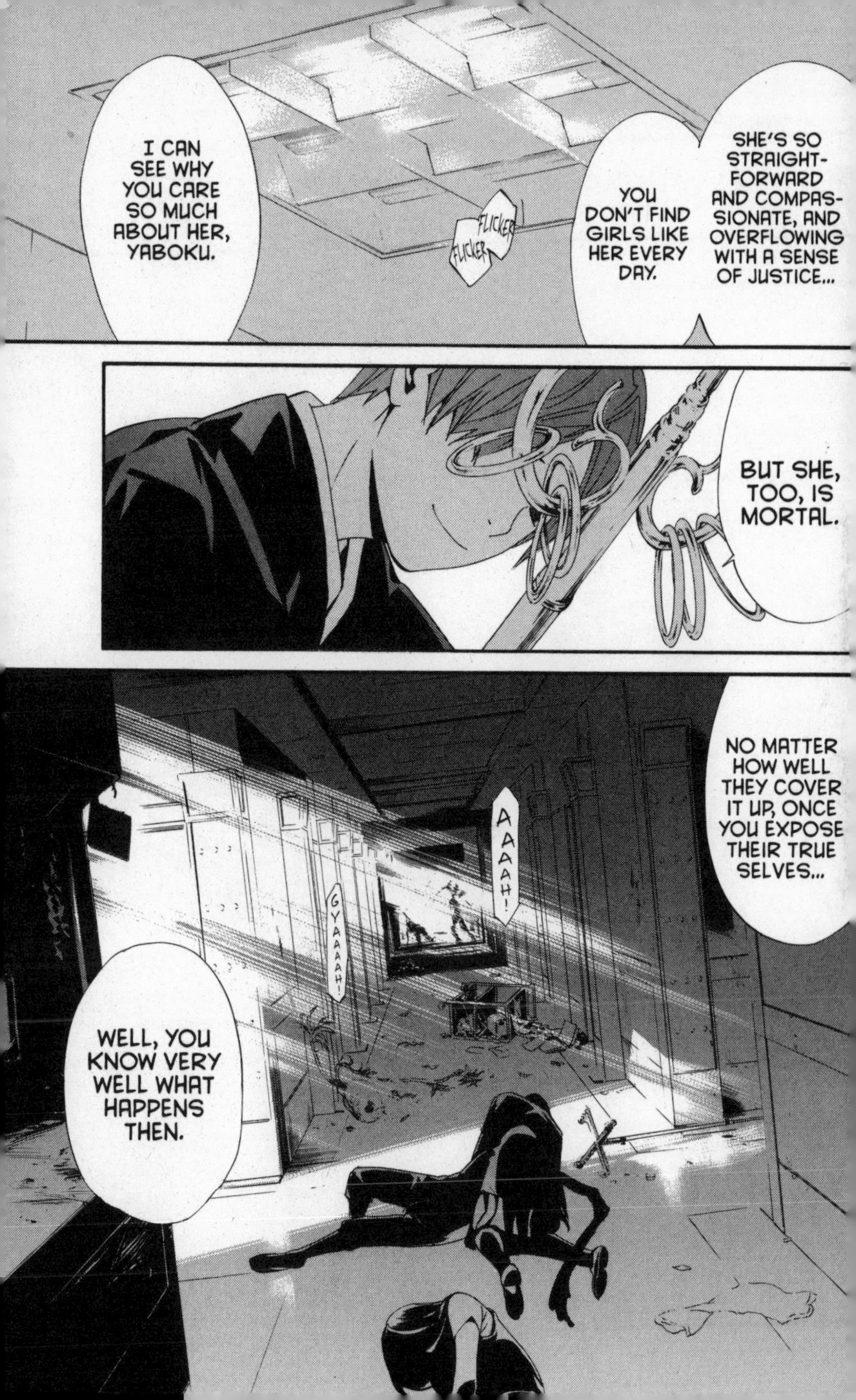
SHE'S SO STRAIGHT-FORWARD AND COMPAS-SIONATE, AND OVERFLOWING WITH A SENSE OF JUSTICE...
YOU DON'T FIND GIRLS LIKE HER EVERY DAY.
FLICKER
FLICKER
I CAN SEE WHY YOU CARE SO MUCH ABOUT HER, YABOKU.
BUT SHE, TOO, IS MORTAL.
NO MATTER HOW WELL THEY COVER IT UP, ONCE YOU EXPOSE THEIR TRUE SELVES...
AAAAAH!
GYAAAAAH!
WELL, YOU KNOW VERY WELL WHAT HAPPENS THEN.

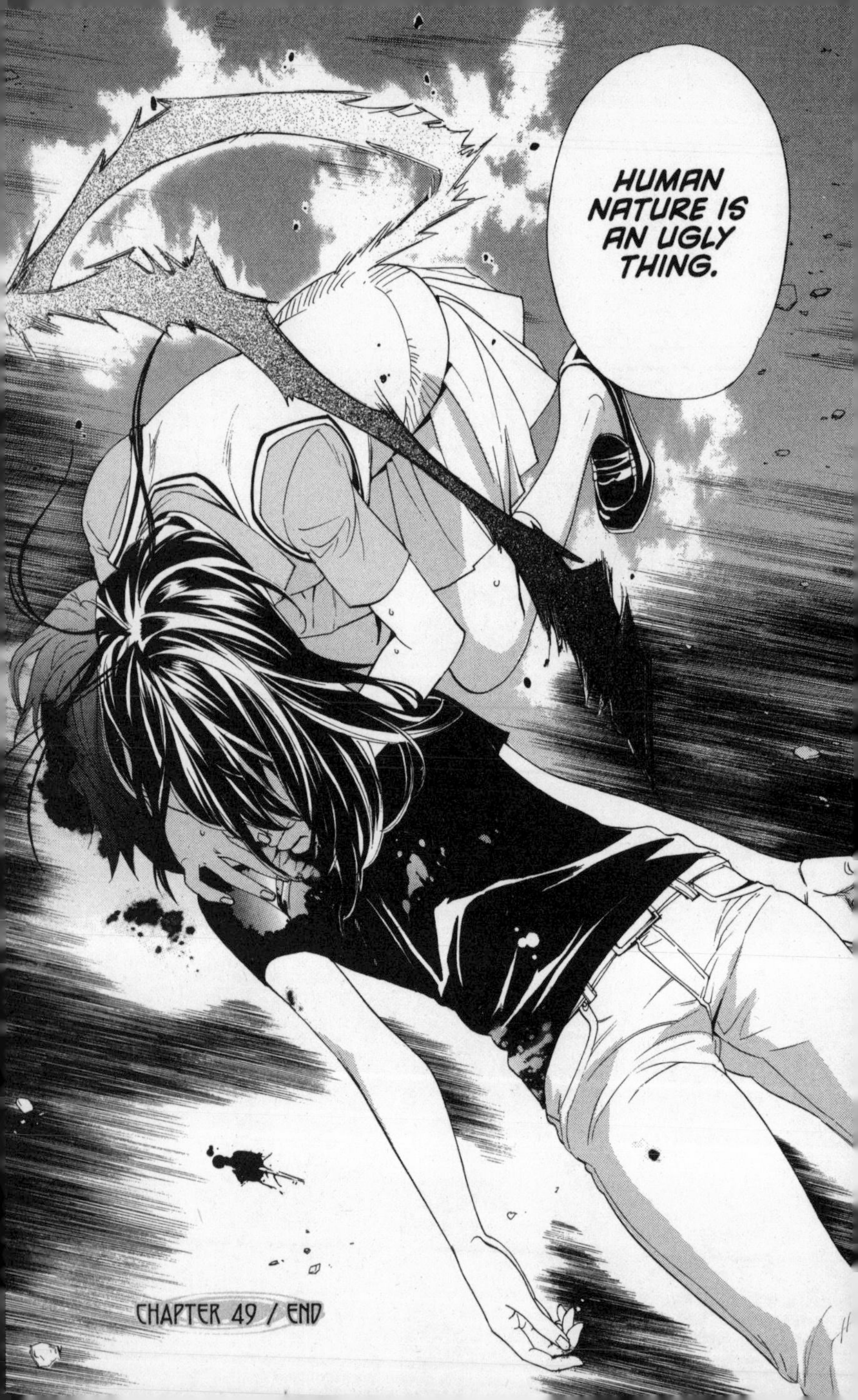
HUMAN NATURE IS AN UGLY THING.
CHAPTER 49 / END

野

兒

神

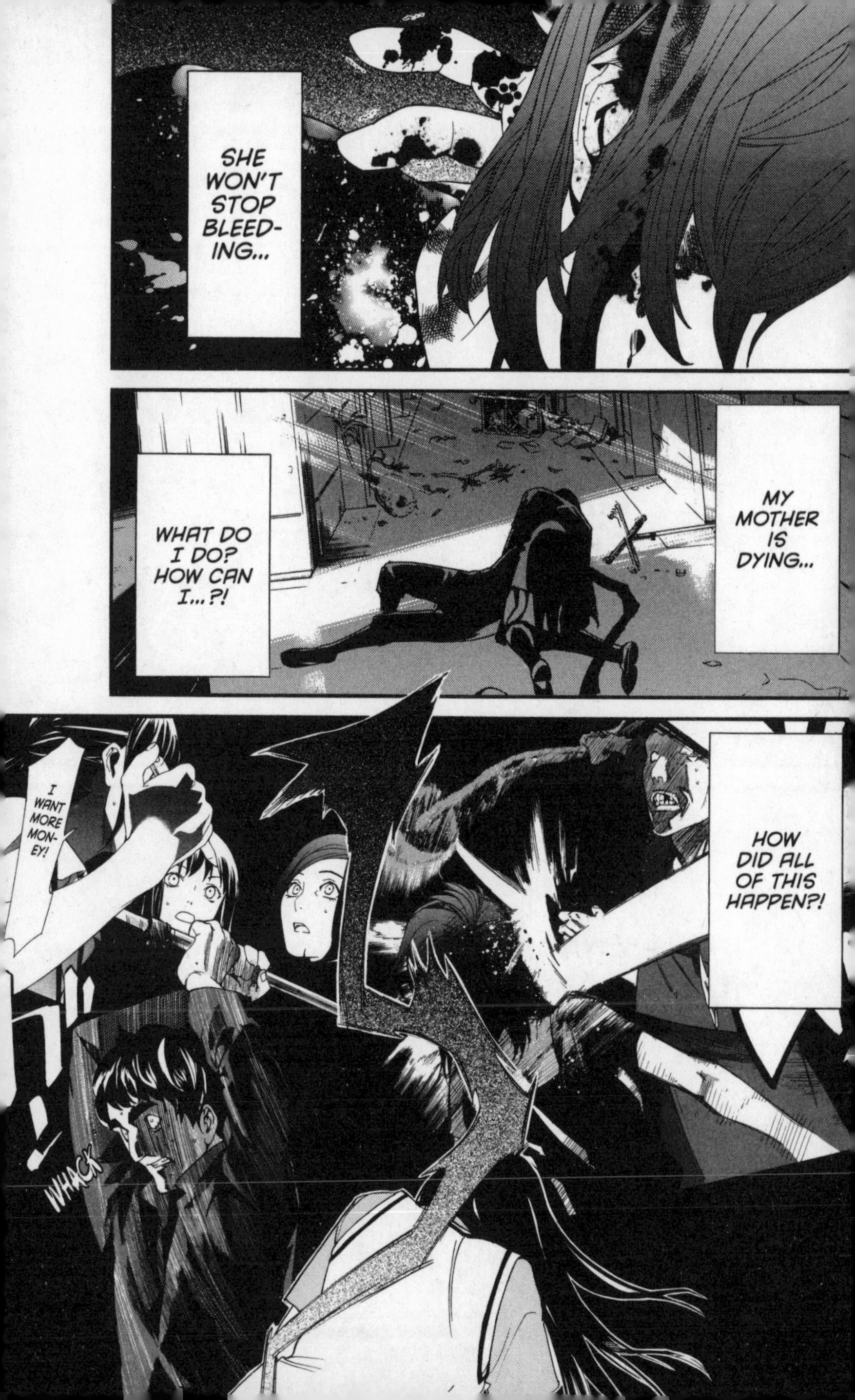
SHE WON'T STOP BLEED-ING...
MY MOTHER IS DYING...
WHAT DO I DO? HOW CAN I...?!
HOW DID ALL OF THIS HAPPEN?!
I WANT MORE MON-EY!
WHACK

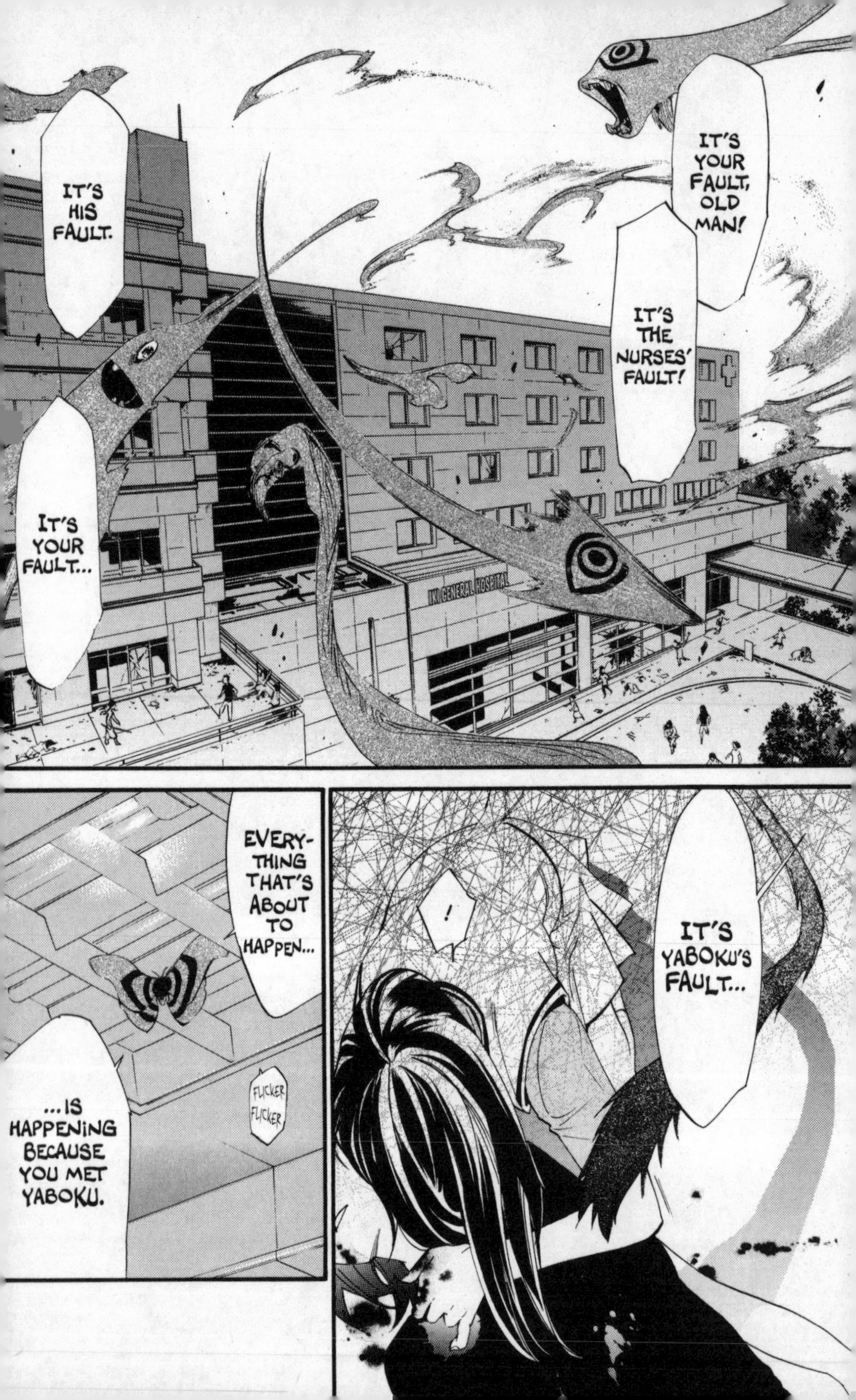
IT'S YOUR FAULT, OLD MAN!
IT'S THE NURSES' FAULT!
IT'S HIS FAULT.
IKI GENERAL HOSPITAL
IT'S YOUR FAULT...
!
IT'S YABOKU'S FAULT...
EVERYTHING THAT'S ABOUT TO HAPPEN...
FLICKER FLICKER
...IS HAPPENING BECAUSE YOU MET YABOKU.

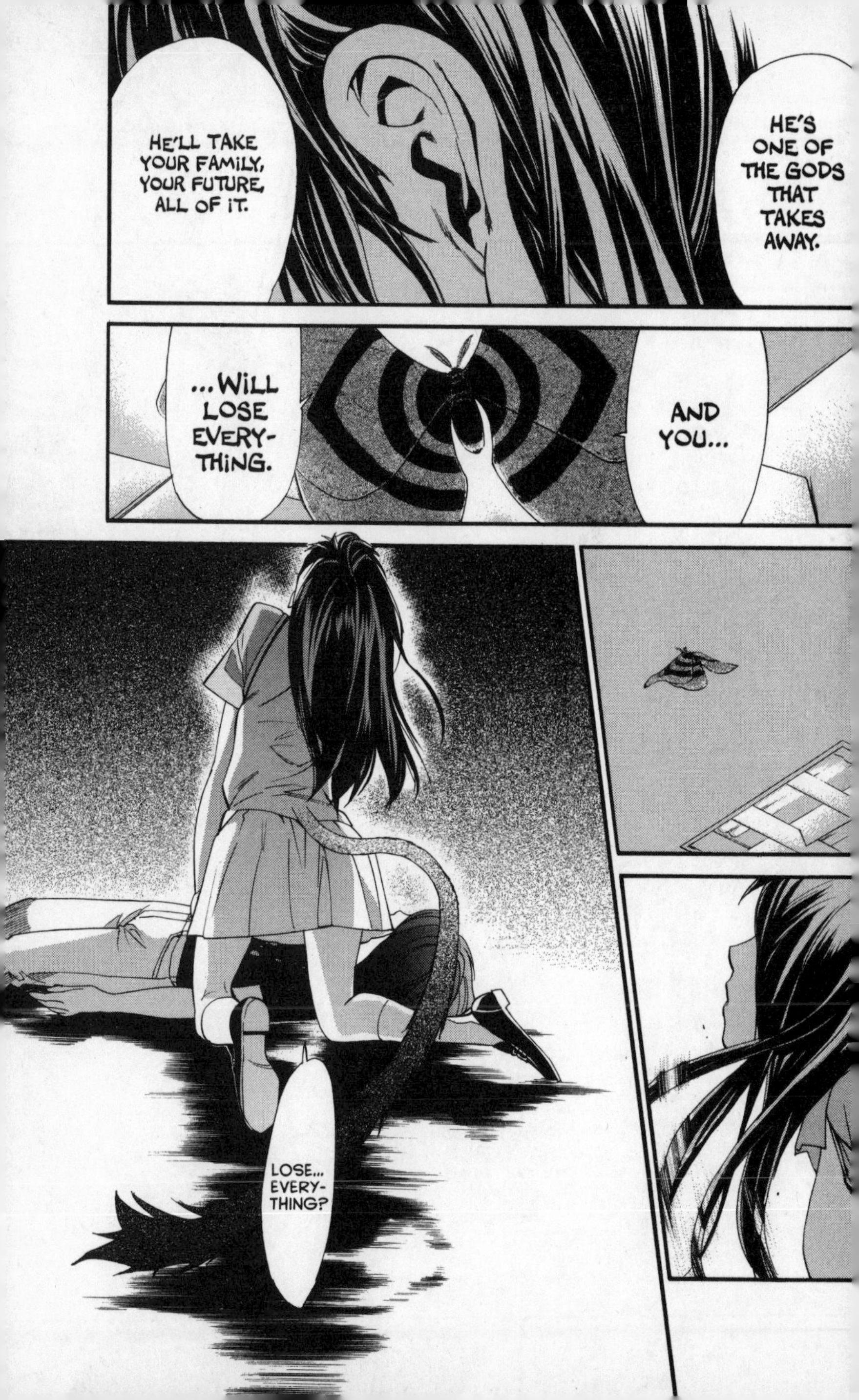
HE'S ONE OF THE GODS THAT TAKES AWAY.
HE'LL TAKE YOUR FAMILY, YOUR FUTURE, ALL OF IT.
AND YOU...
...WILL LOSE EVERY-THING.
LOSE... EVERY-THING?

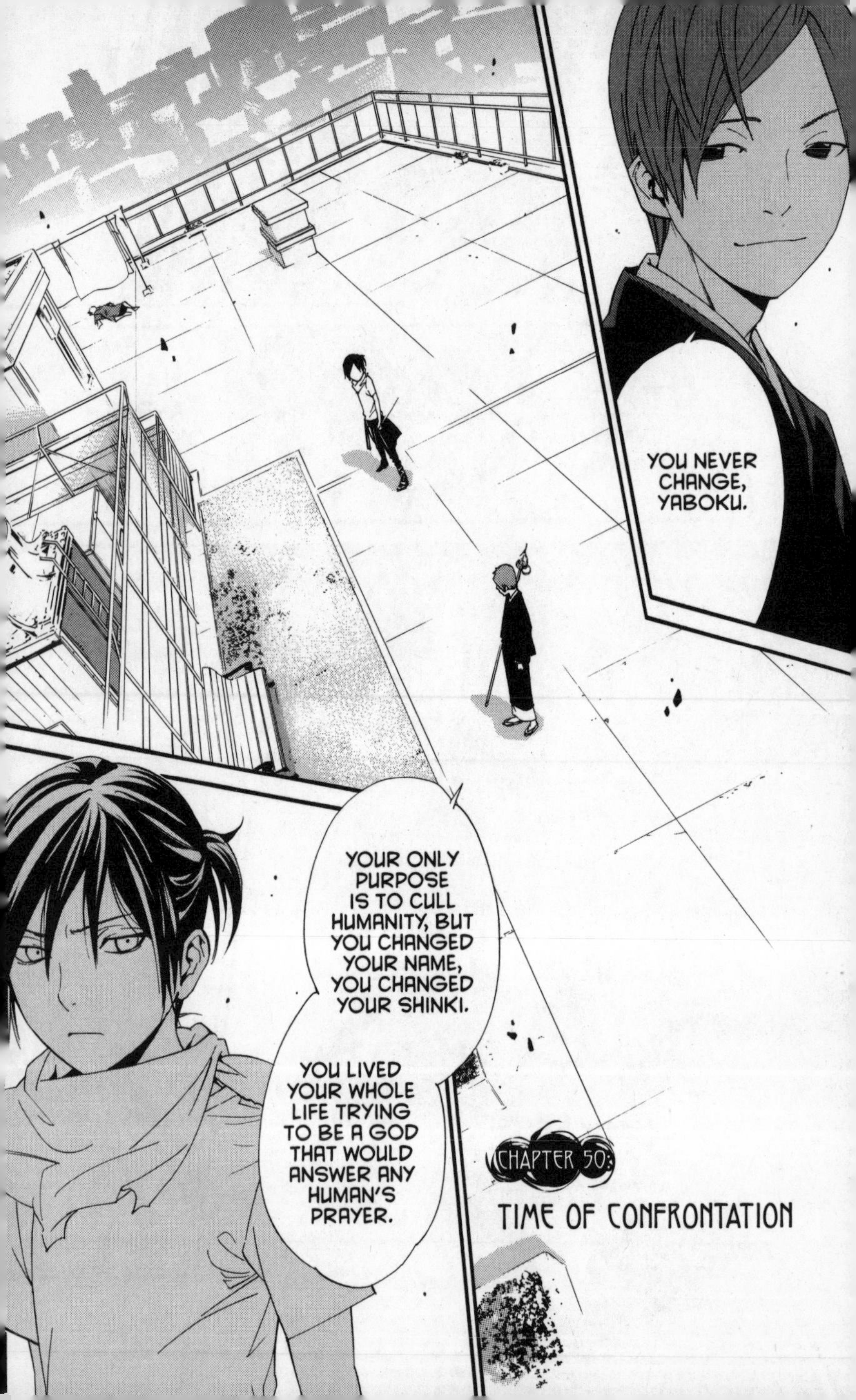
YOU NEVER CHANGE, YABOKU.
CHAPTER 50:
TIME OF CONFRONTATION
YOUR ONLY PURPOSE IS TO CULL HUMANITY, BUT YOU CHANGED YOUR NAME, YOU CHANGED YOUR SHINKI.
YOU LIVED YOUR WHOLE LIFE TRYING TO BE A GOD THAT WOULD ANSWER ANY HUMAN'S PRAYER.

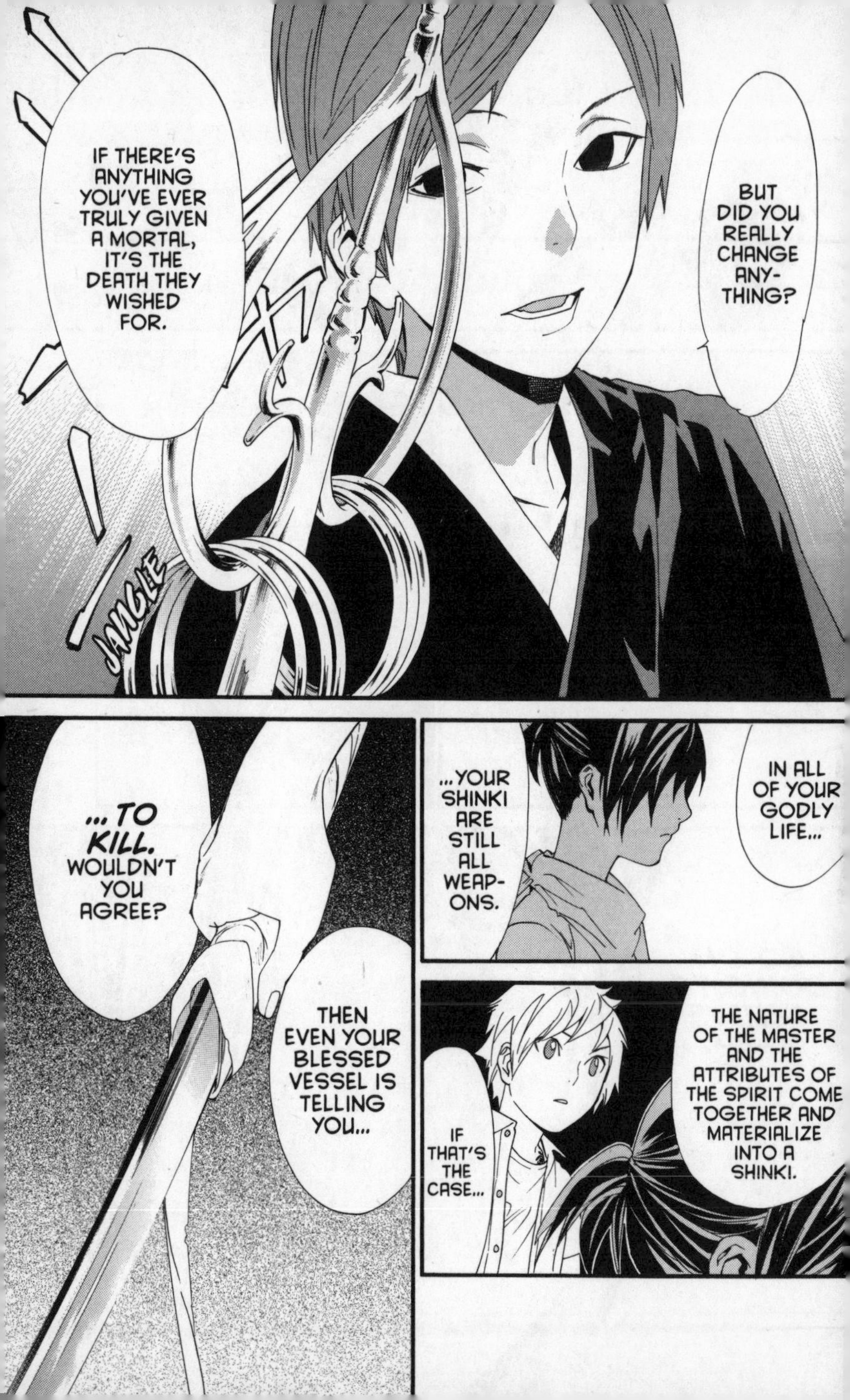
BUT DID YOU REALLY CHANGE ANYTHING?
IF THERE'S ANYTHING YOU'VE EVER TRULY GIVEN A MORTAL, IT'S THE DEATH THEY WISHED FOR.
JANGLE
IN ALL OF YOUR GODLY LIFE...
...YOUR SHINKI ARE STILL ALL WEAPONS.
THE NATURE OF THE MASTER AND THE ATTRIBUTES OF THE SPIRIT COME TOGETHER AND MATERIALIZE INTO A SHINKI.
IF THAT'S THE CASE...
THEN EVEN YOUR BLESSED VESSEL IS TELLING YOU...
...TO *KILL.* WOULDN'T YOU AGREE?

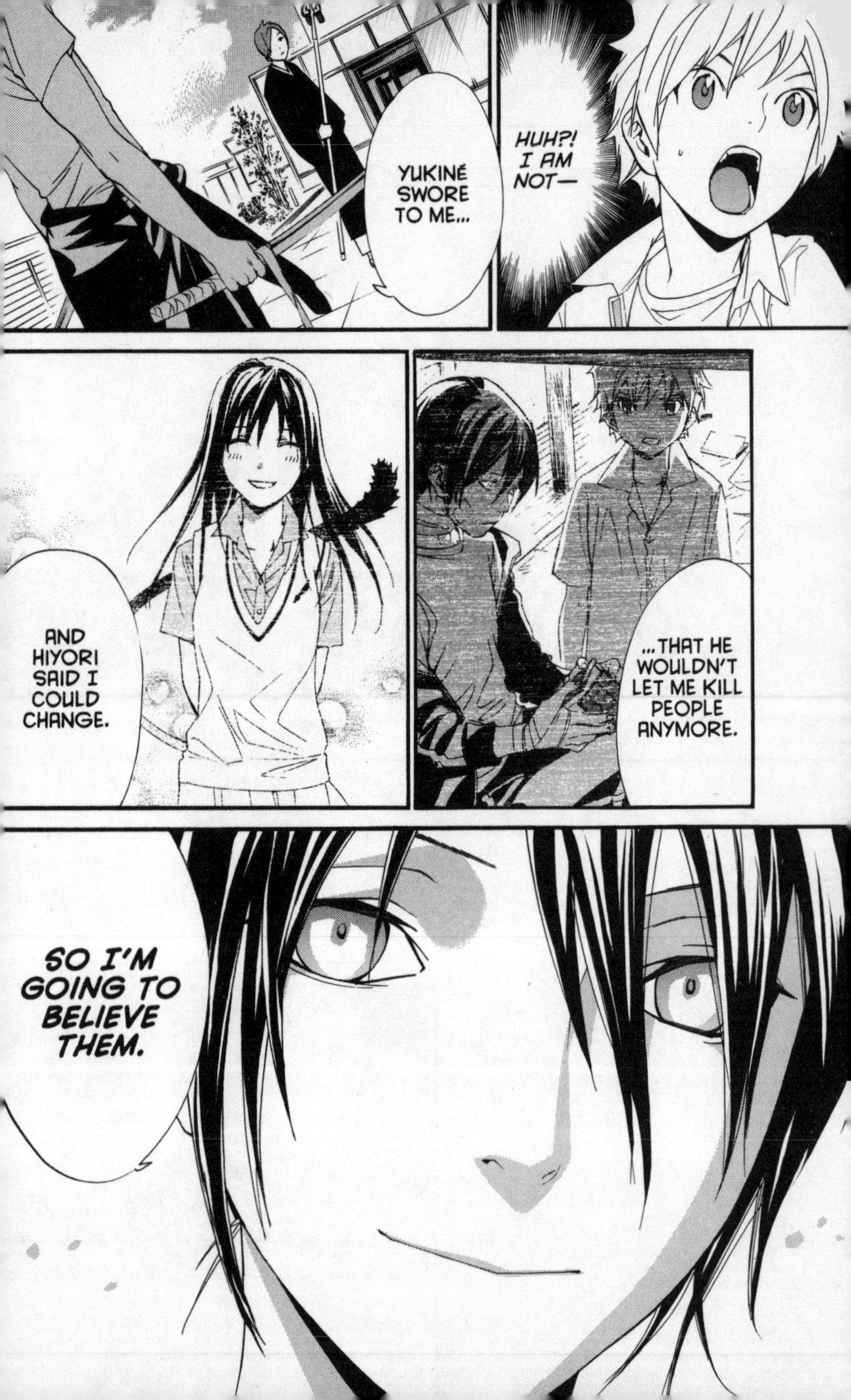
HUH?! I AM NOT—
YUKINÉ SWORE TO ME...
...THAT HE WOULDN'T LET ME KILL PEOPLE ANYMORE.
AND HIYORI SAID I COULD CHANGE.
SO I'M GOING TO BELIEVE THEM.

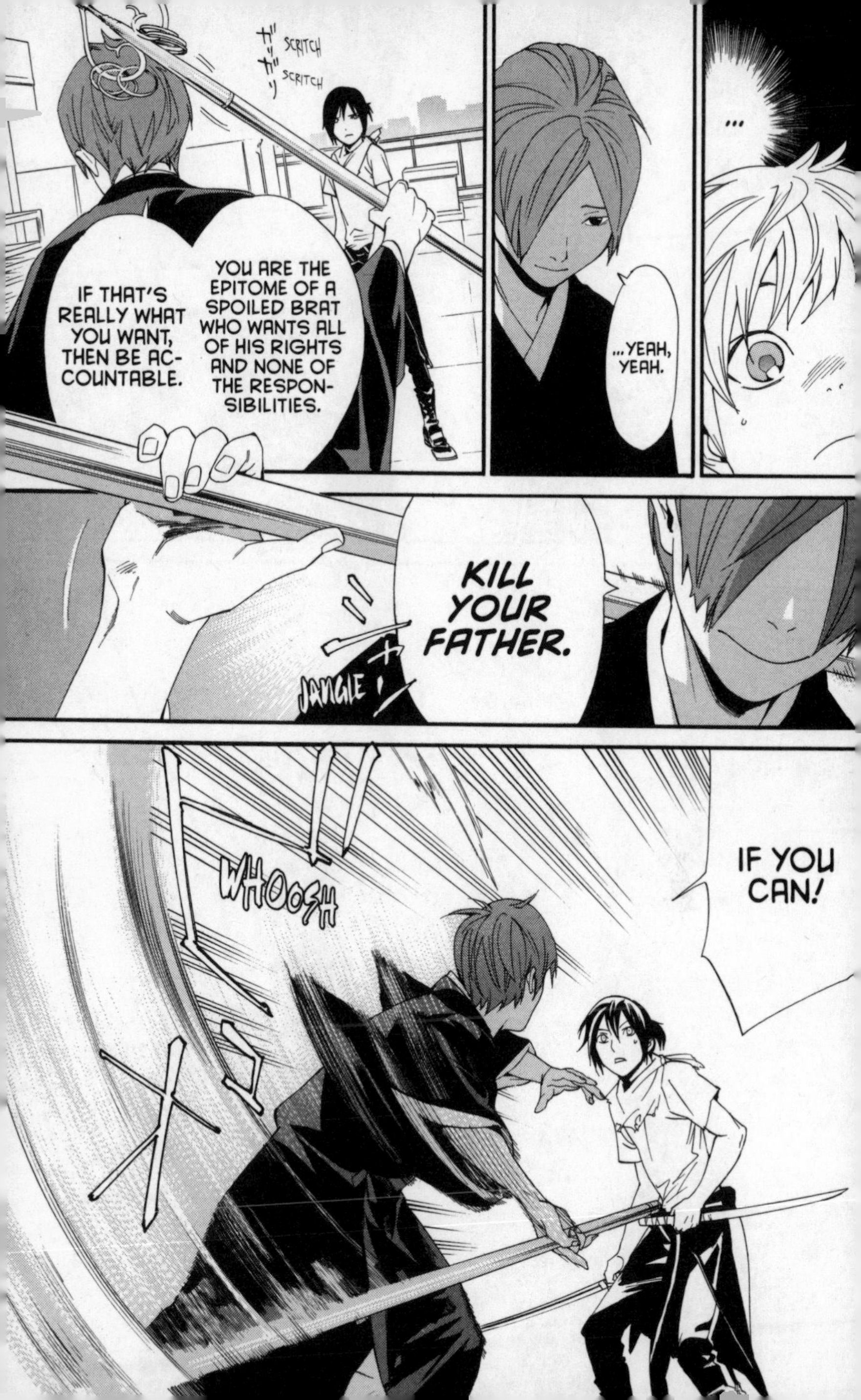
...
...YEAH, YEAH.
SCRITCH
SCRITCH
YOU ARE THE EPITOME OF A SPOILED BRAT WHO WANTS ALL OF HIS RIGHTS AND NONE OF THE RESPONSIBILITIES.
IF THAT'S REALLY WHAT YOU WANT, THEN BE ACCOUNTABLE.
KILL YOUR FATHER.
JANGLE
IF YOU CAN!
WHOOSH

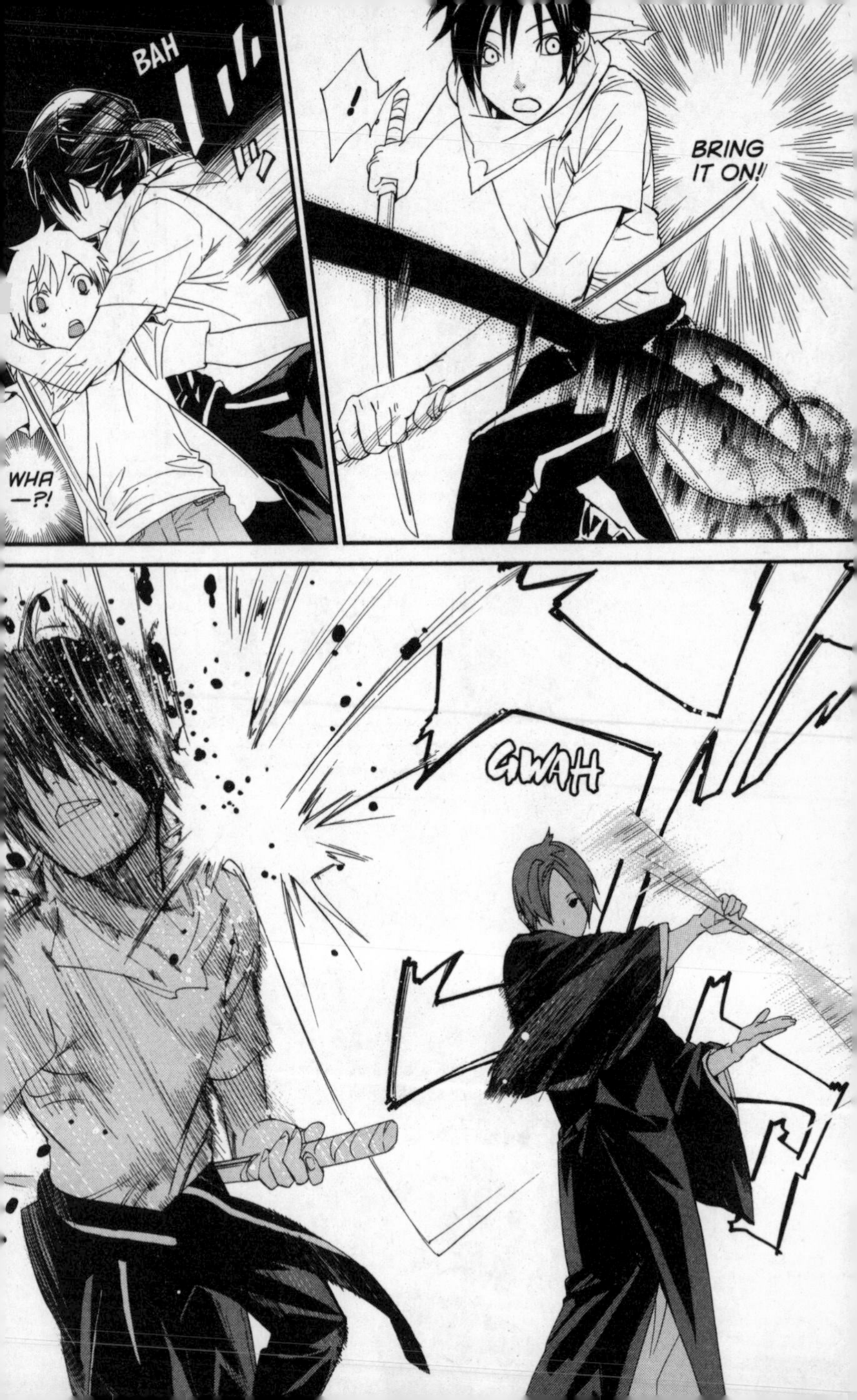
!
BRING IT ON!!
BAH
WHA —?!
GWAH

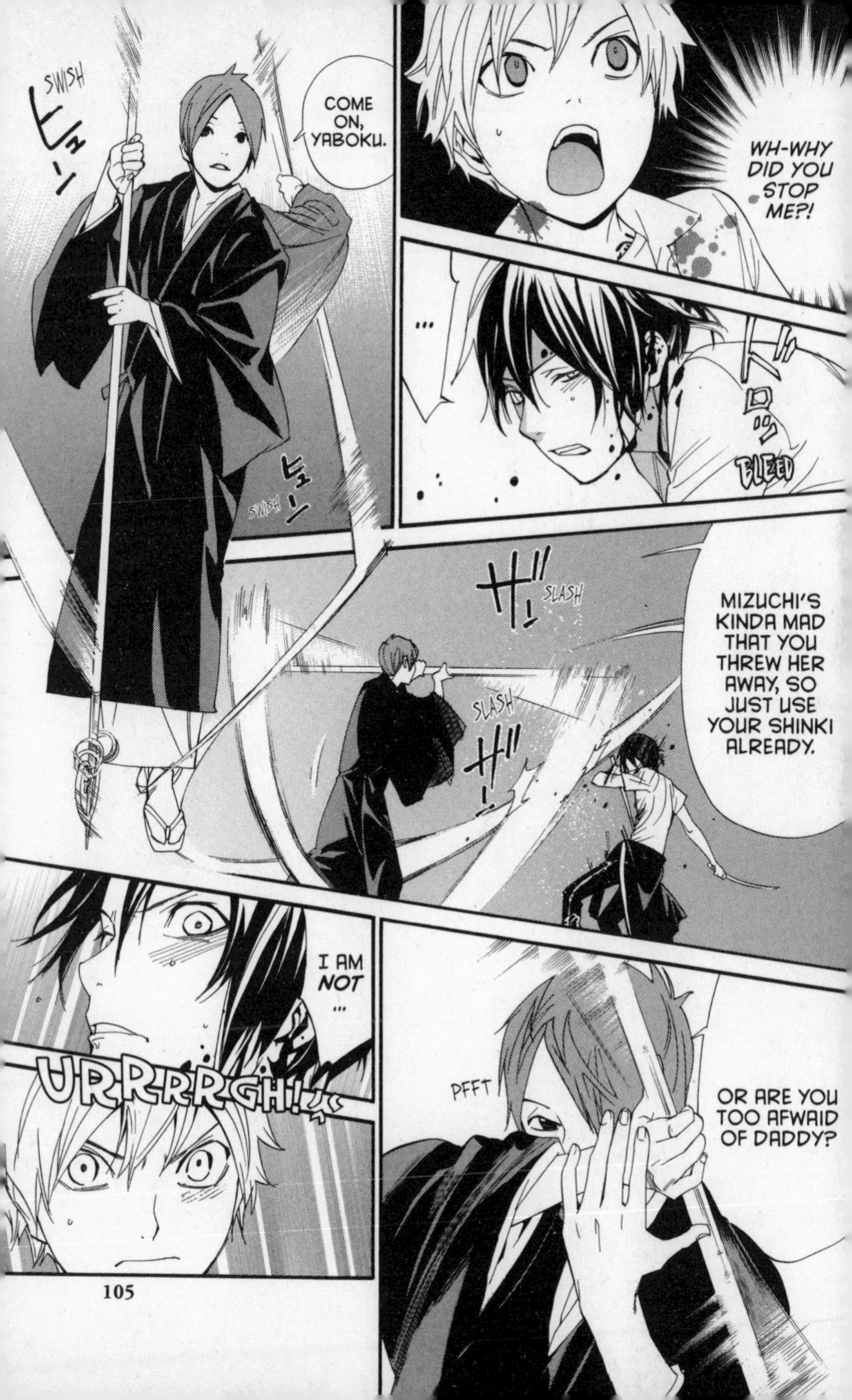
WH-WHY DID YOU STOP ME?!
...
BLEED
COME ON, YABOKU.
SWISH
SWISH
MIZUCHI'S KINDA MAD THAT YOU THREW HER AWAY, SO JUST USE YOUR SHINKI ALREADY.
SLASH
SLASH
OR ARE YOU TOO AFWAID OF DADDY?
PFFT
I AM *NOT* ...
URRRRGH!!

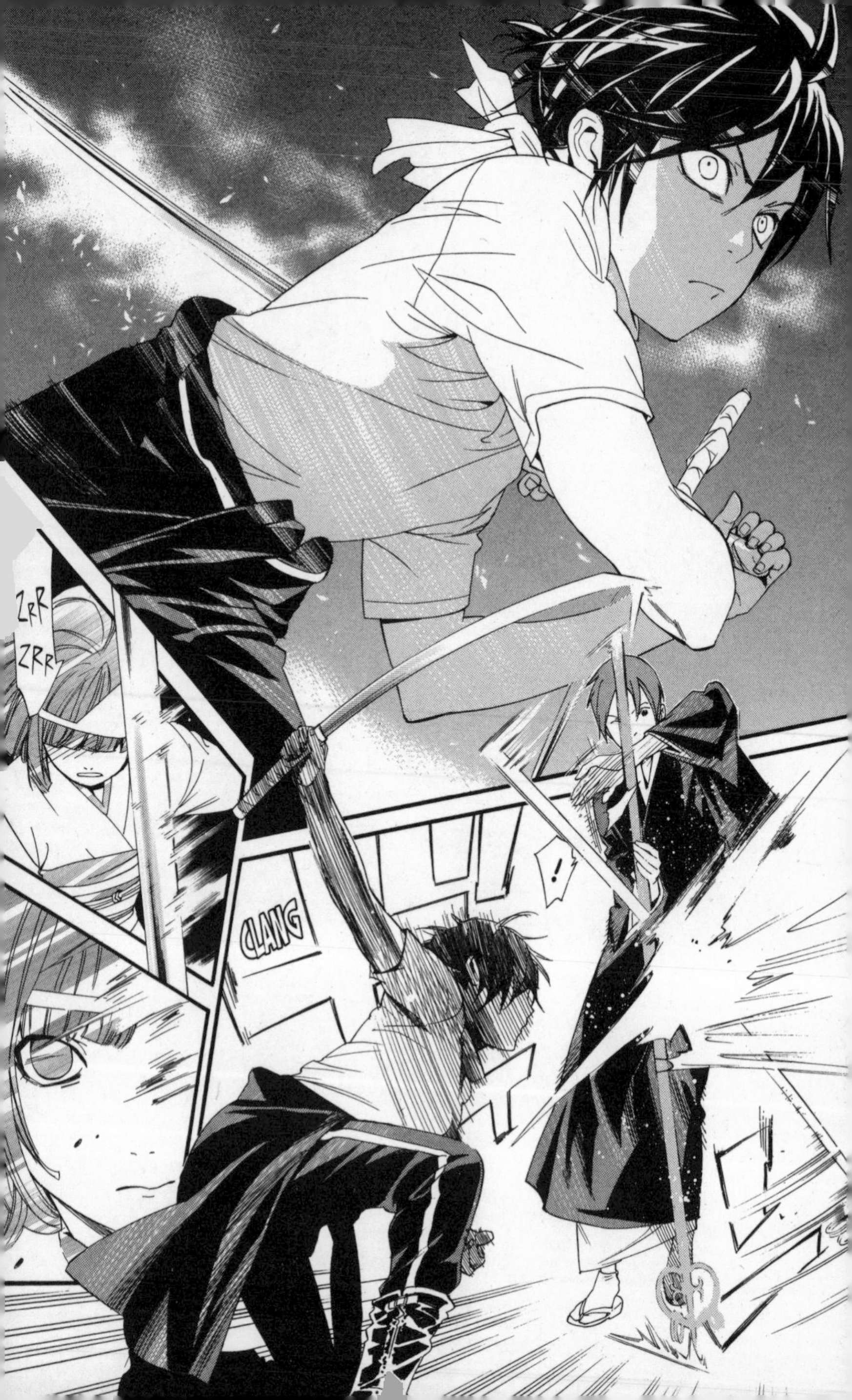

ZRR
ZRR
!
CLANG

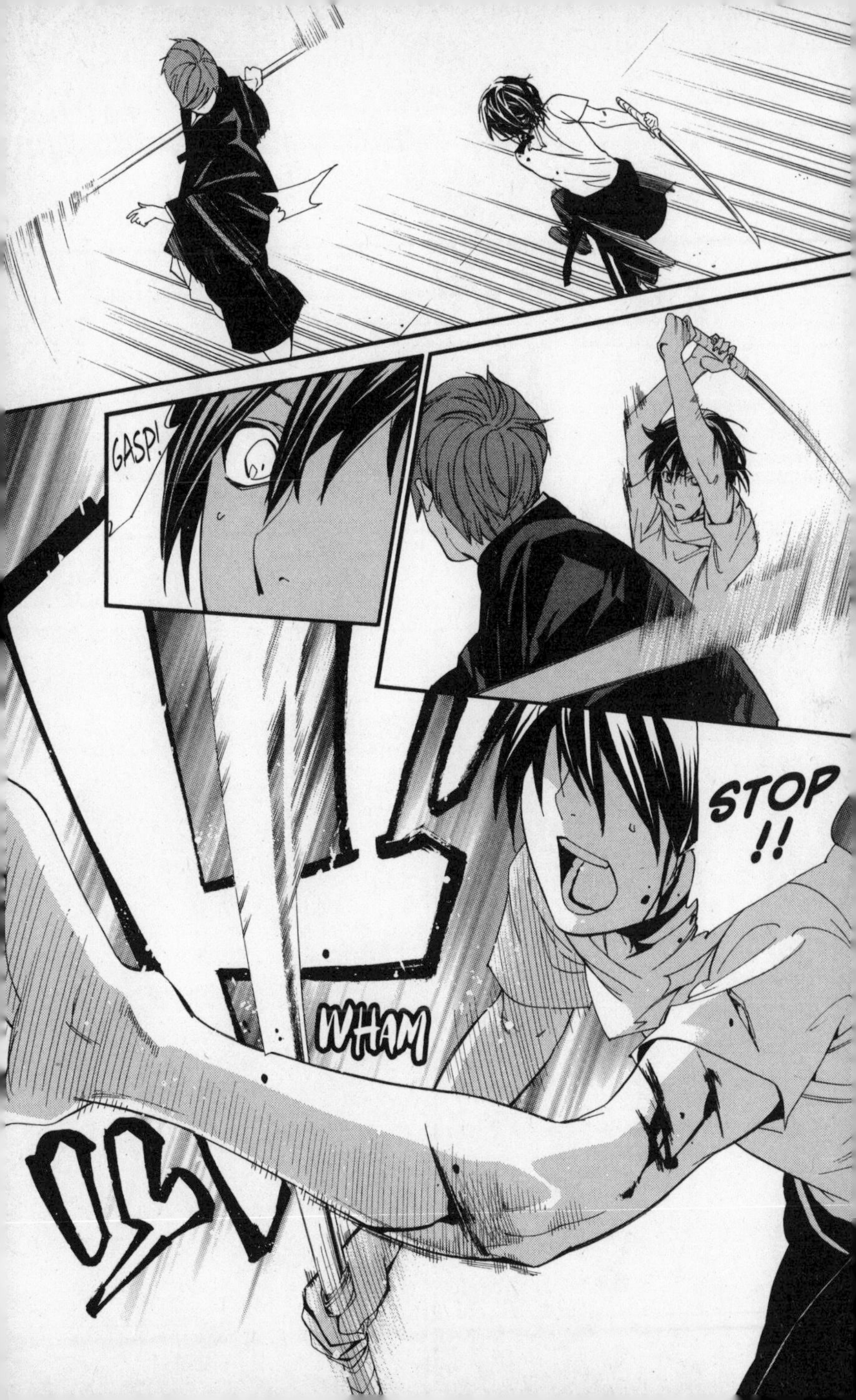
GASP!
STOP !!
WHAM

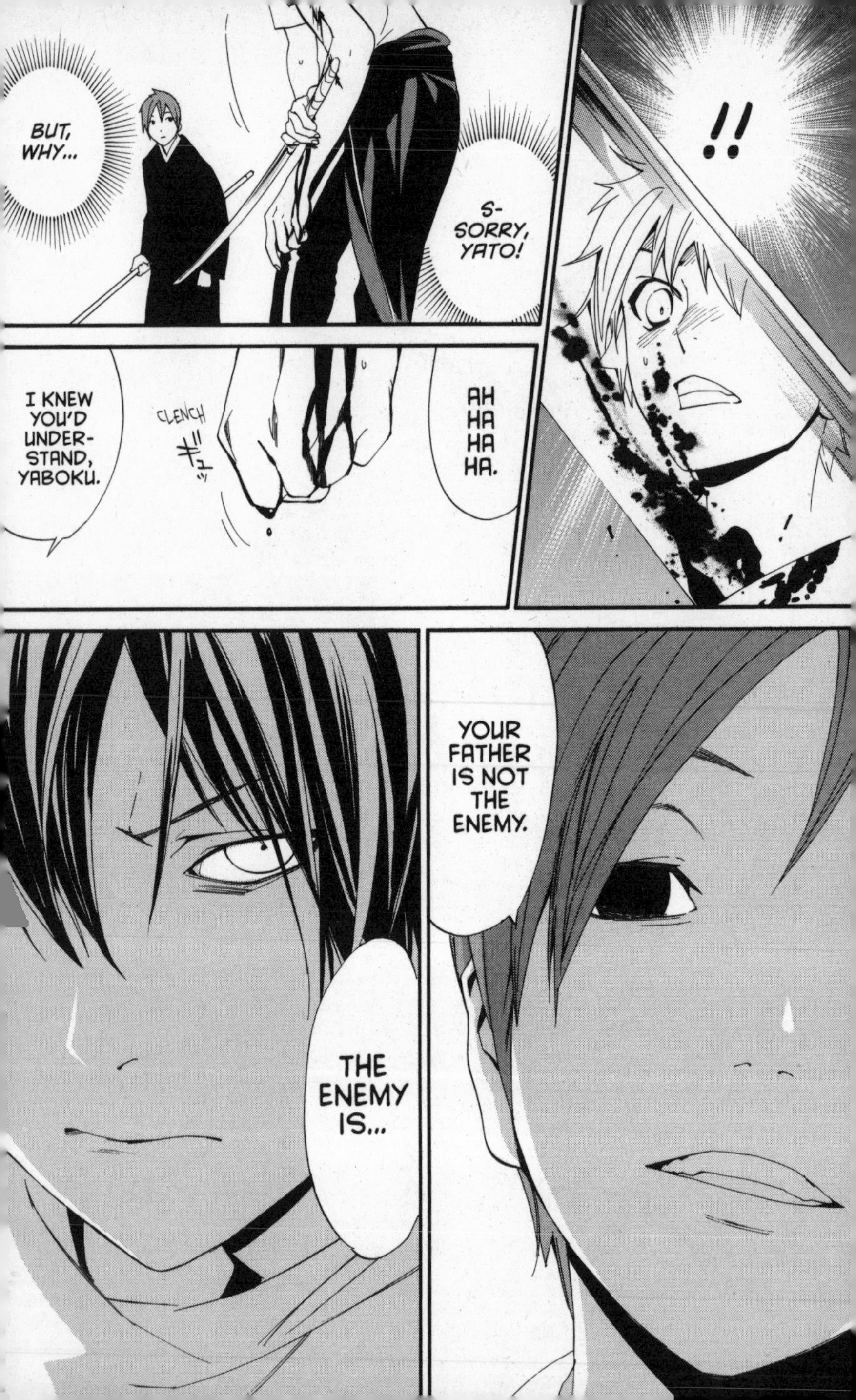
!!
S-SORRY, YATO!
BUT, WHY...
AH HA HA HA.
CLENCH
I KNEW YOU'D UNDER-STAND, YABOKU.
YOUR FATHER IS NOT THE ENEMY.
THE ENEMY IS...

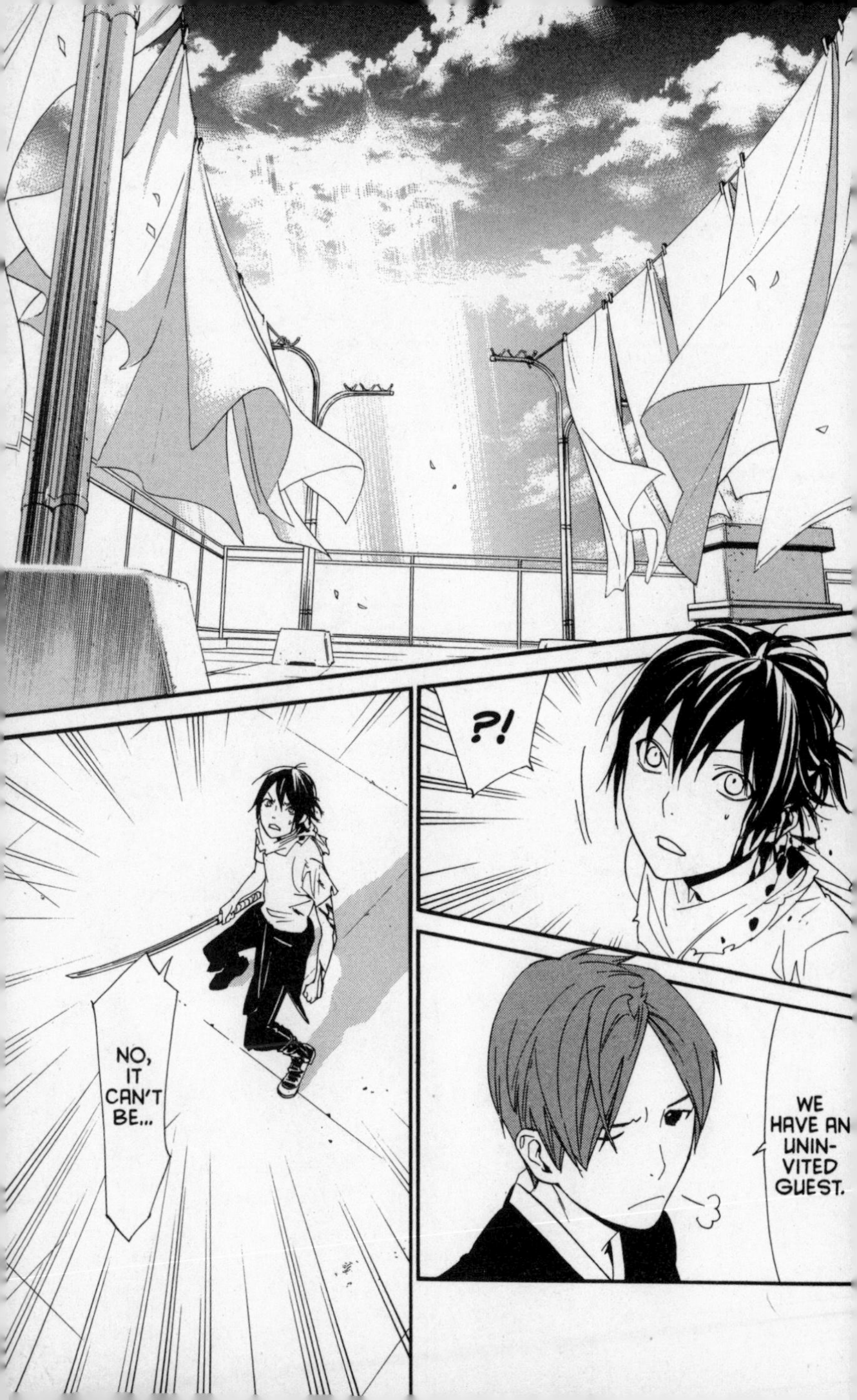
?!
WE HAVE AN UNIN-VITED GUEST.
NO, IT CAN'T BE...

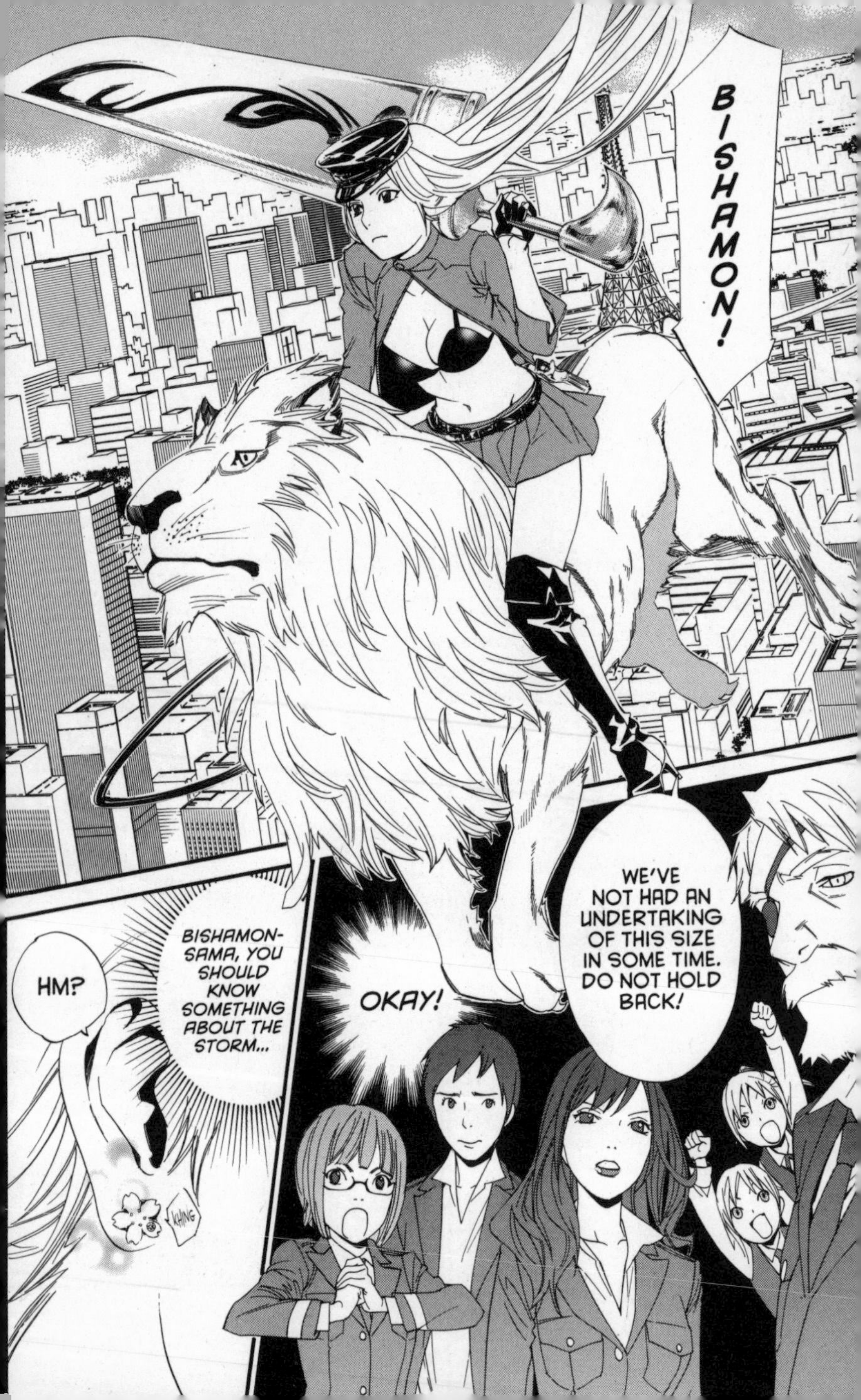
BISHAMON!
WE'VE NOT HAD AN UNDERTAKING OF THIS SIZE IN SOME TIME. DO NOT HOLD BACK!
OKAY!
BISHAMON-SAMA, YOU SHOULD KNOW SOMETHING ABOUT THE STORM...
HM?
KHING

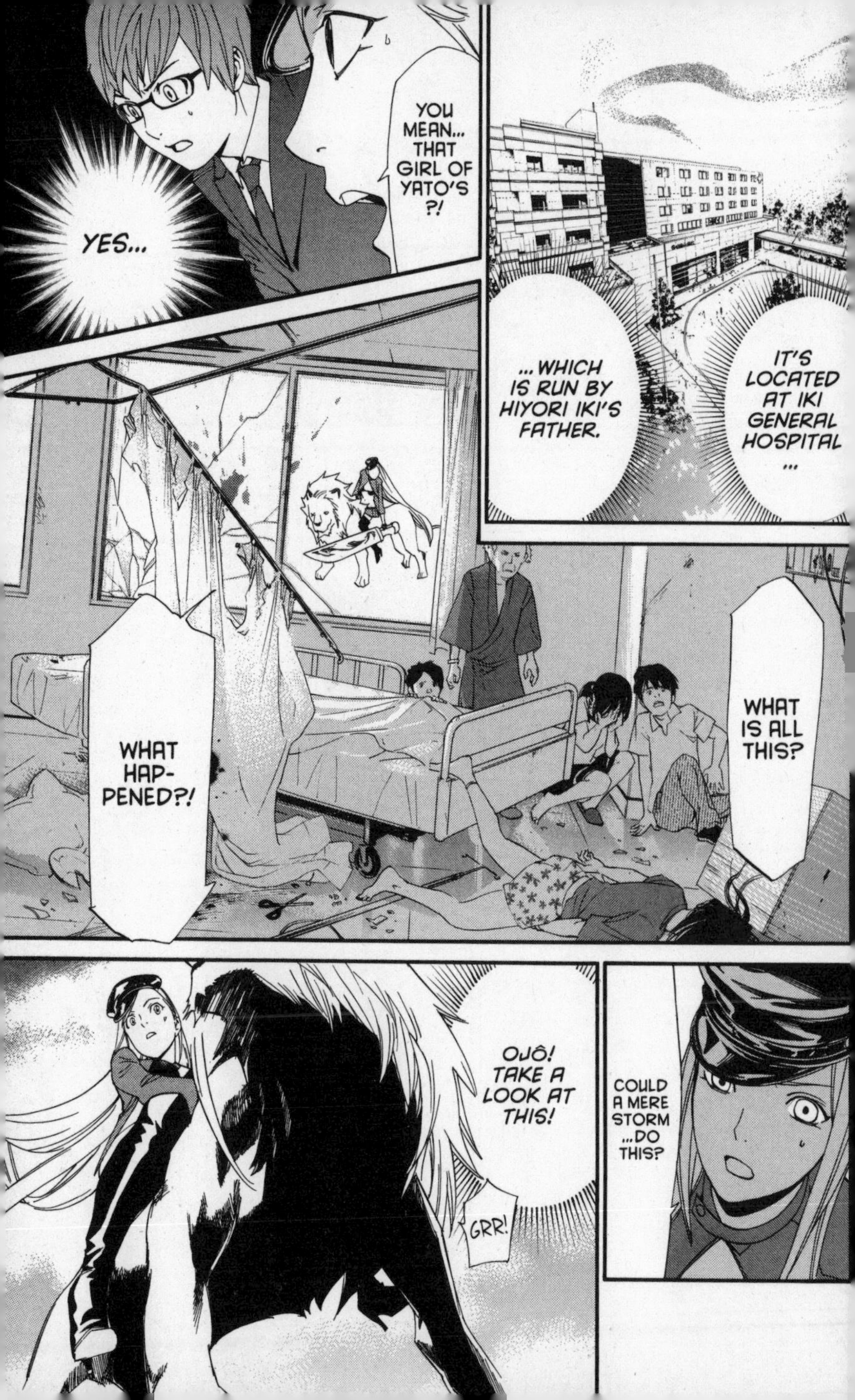
IT'S LOCATED AT IKI GENERAL HOSPITAL ...
...WHICH IS RUN BY HIYORI IKI'S FATHER.
YOU MEAN... THAT GIRL OF YATO'S ?!
YES...
WHAT IS ALL THIS?
WHAT HAP-PENED?!
COULD A MERE STORM ...DO THIS?
OJÔ! TAKE A LOOK AT THIS!
GRR!

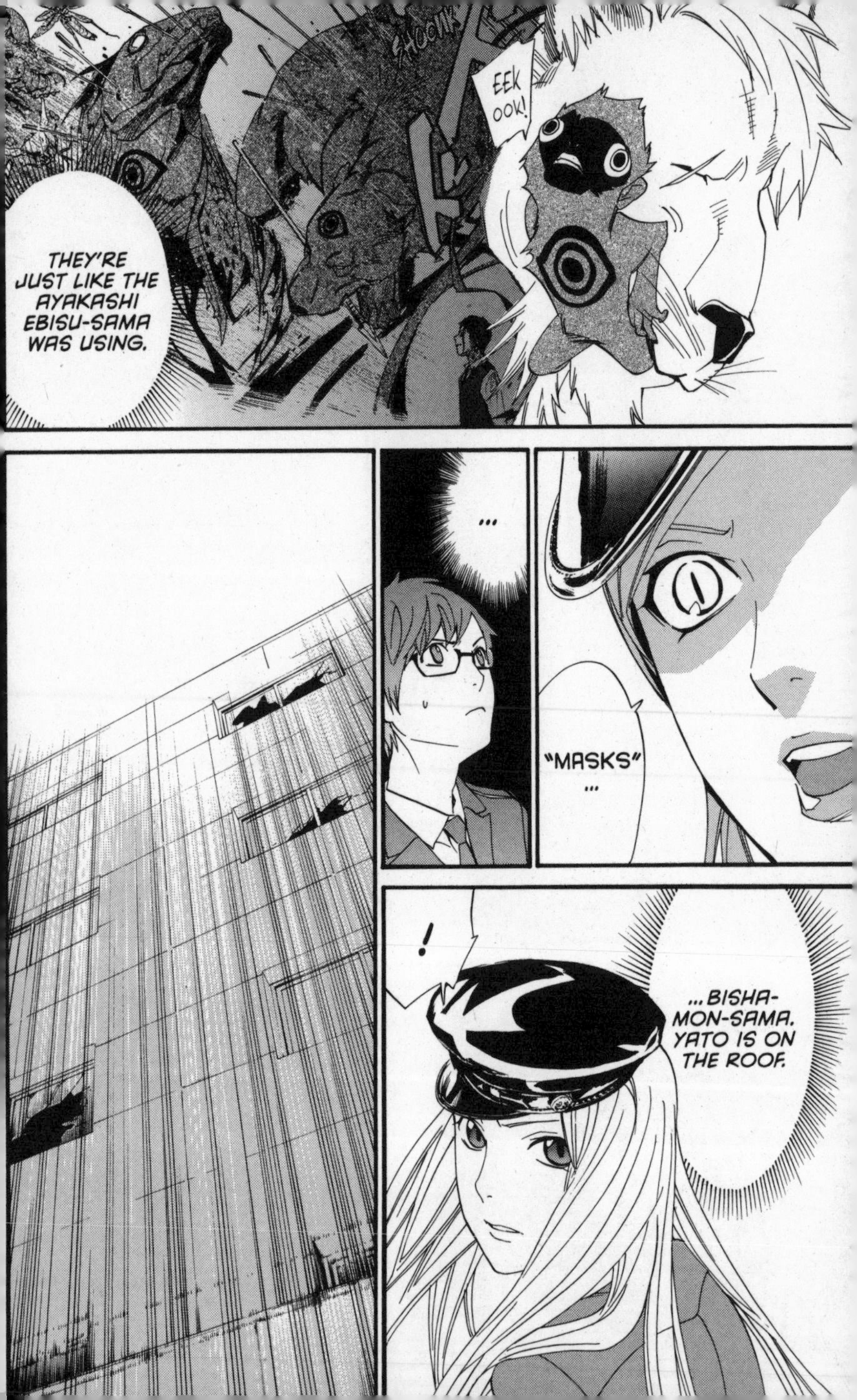
EEK OOK!
THEY'RE JUST LIKE THE AYAKASHI EBISU-SAMA WAS USING.
"MASKS" ...
...
!
...BISHA-MON-SAMA. YATO IS ON THE ROOF.

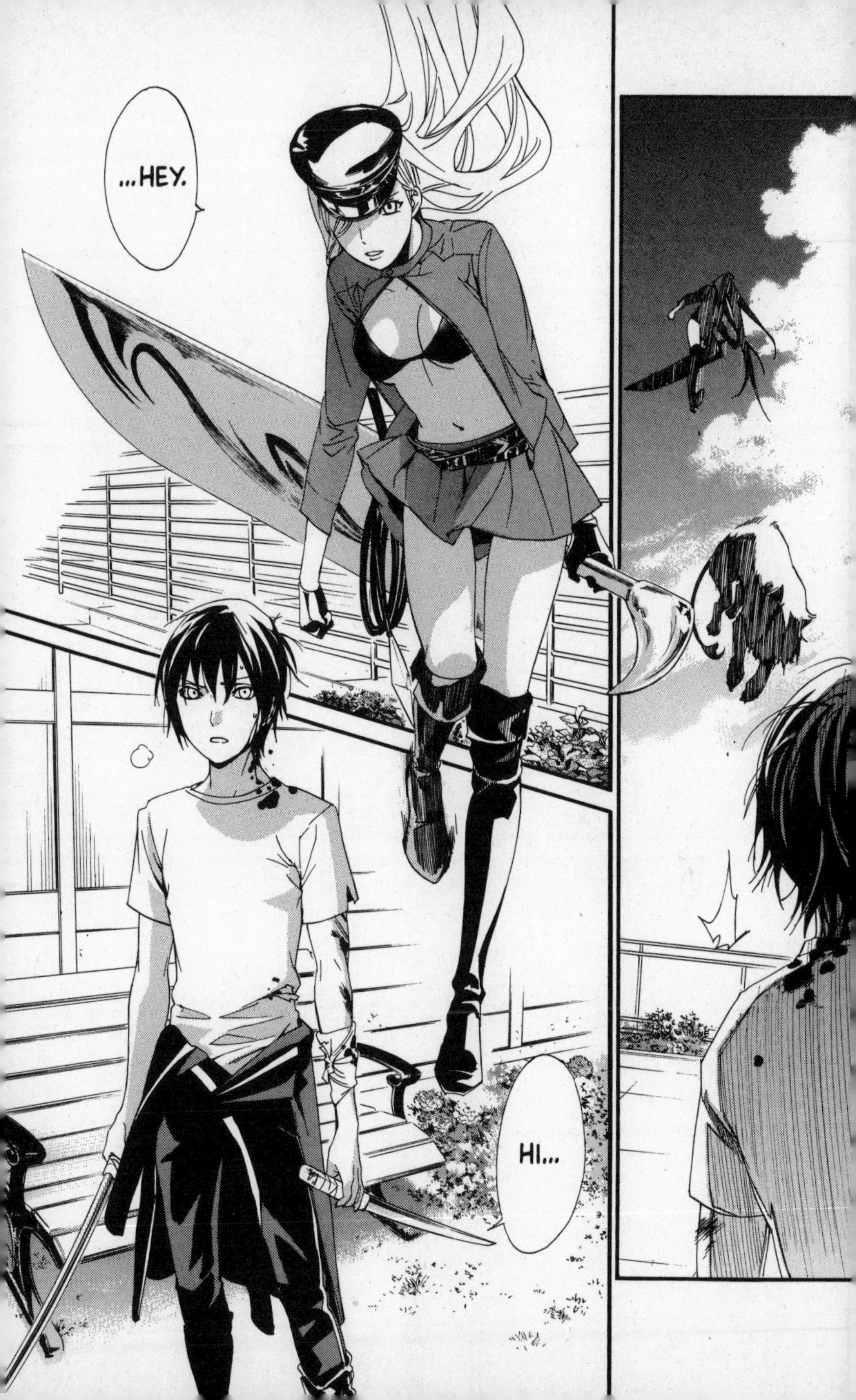
...HEY.
HI...

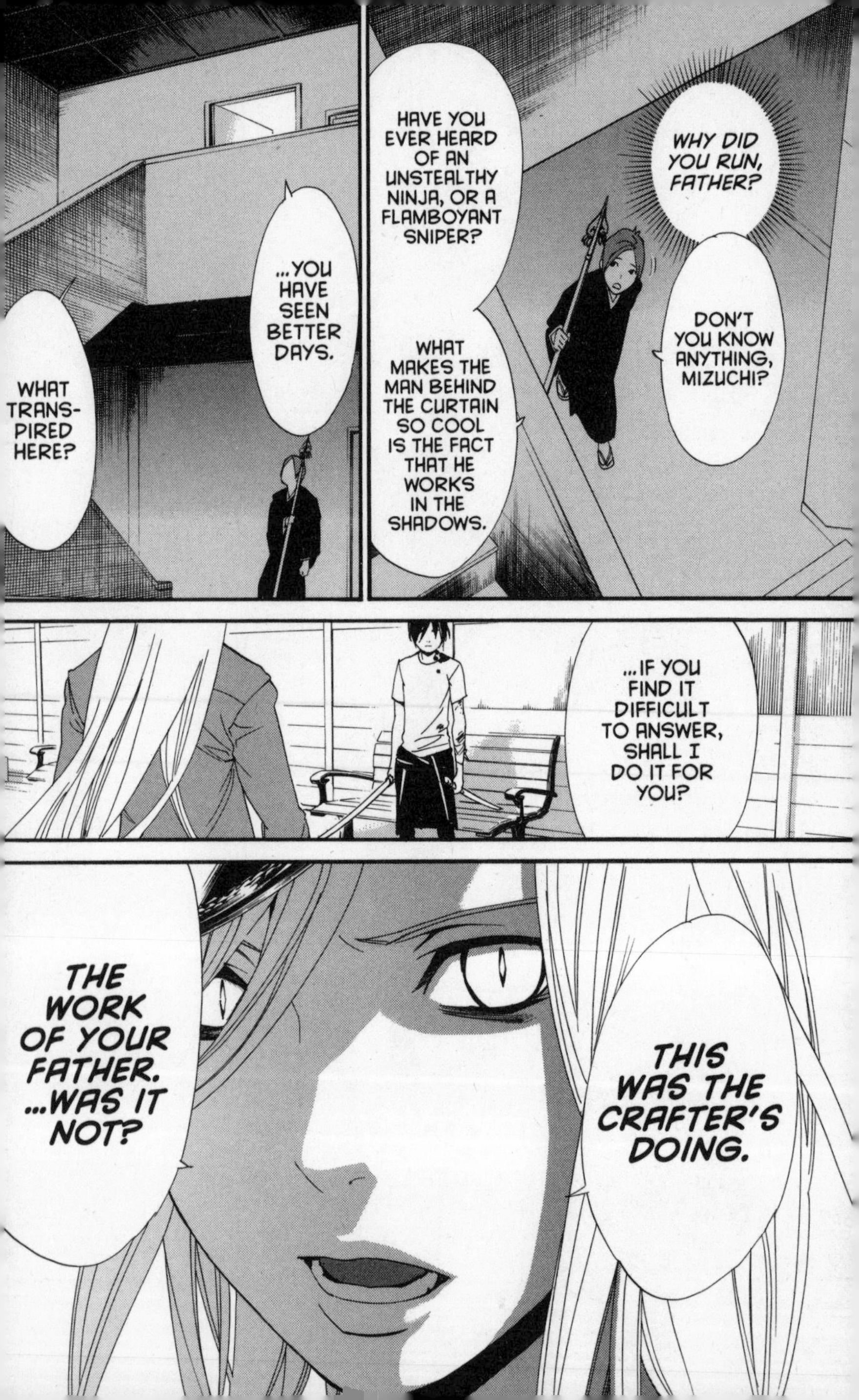
WHY DID YOU RUN, FATHER?
DON'T YOU KNOW ANYTHING, MIZUCHI?
HAVE YOU EVER HEARD OF AN UNSTEALTHY NINJA, OR A FLAMBOYANT SNIPER?
WHAT MAKES THE MAN BEHIND THE CURTAIN SO COOL IS THE FACT THAT HE WORKS IN THE SHADOWS.
...YOU HAVE SEEN BETTER DAYS.
WHAT TRANSPIRED HERE?
...IF YOU FIND IT DIFFICULT TO ANSWER, SHALL I DO IT FOR YOU?
THIS WAS THE CRAFTER'S DOING.
THE WORK OF YOUR FATHER. ...WAS IT NOT?

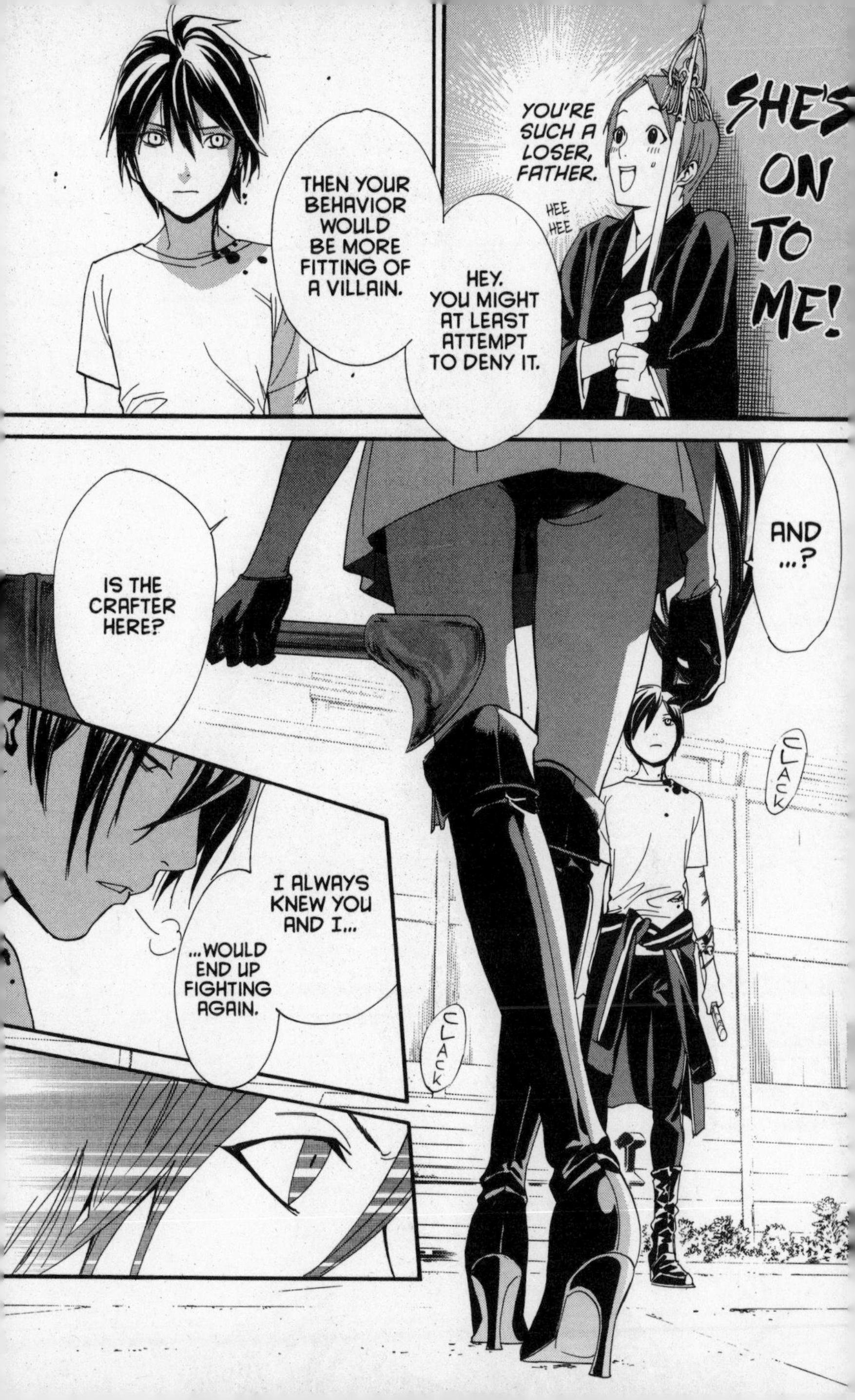
SHE'S ON TO ME!
YOU'RE SUCH A LOSER, FATHER.
HEE HEE
HEY. YOU MIGHT AT LEAST ATTEMPT TO DENY IT.
THEN YOUR BEHAVIOR WOULD BE MORE FITTING OF A VILLAIN.
AND ...?
CLACK
IS THE CRAFTER HERE?
CLACK
I ALWAYS KNEW YOU AND I...
...WOULD END UP FIGHTING AGAIN.

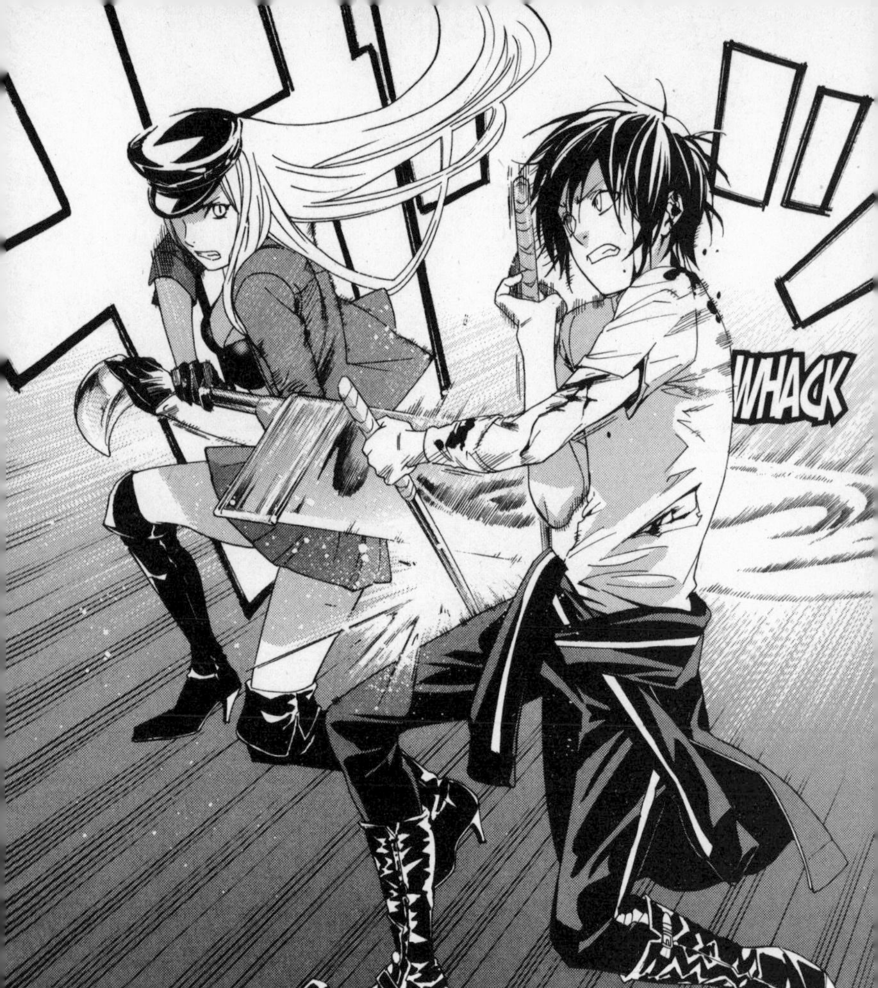
WHACK
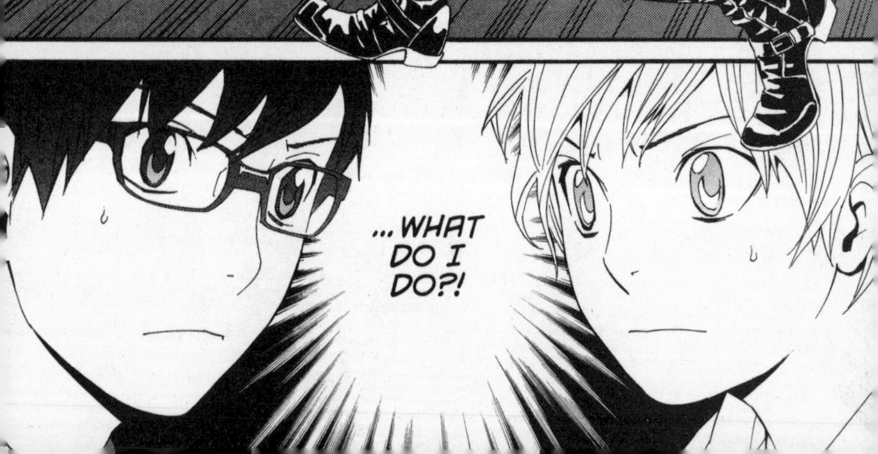
...WHAT DO I DO?!

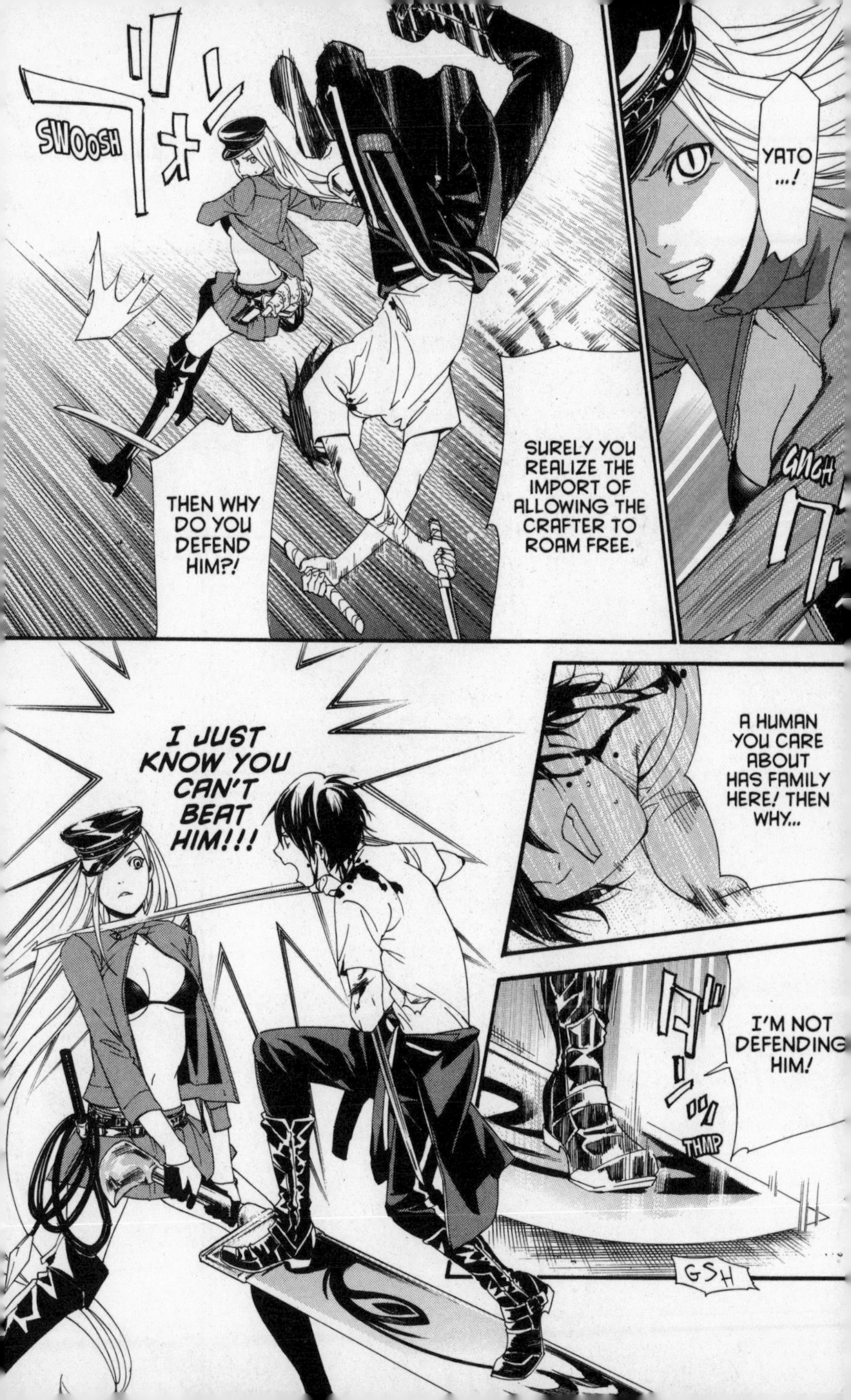
YATO ...!
GNCH
SURELY YOU REALIZE THE IMPORT OF ALLOWING THE CRAFTER TO ROAM FREE.
THEN WHY DO YOU DEFEND HIM?!
SWOOSH
A HUMAN YOU CARE ABOUT HAS FAMILY HERE! THEN WHY...
I'M NOT DEFENDING HIM!
THMP
GSH
I JUST KNOW YOU CAN'T BEAT HIM!!!

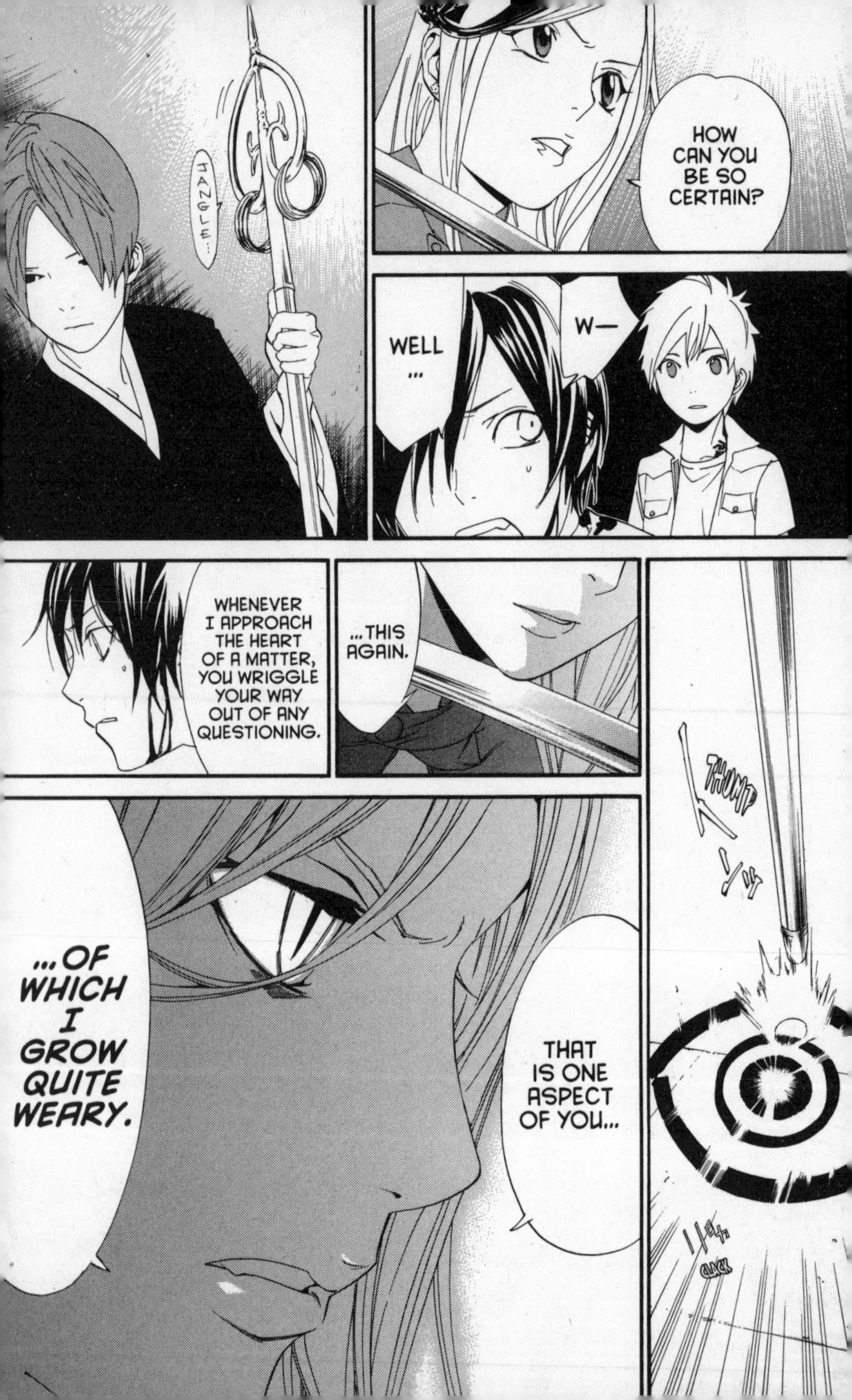
HOW CAN YOU BE SO CERTAIN?
W—
WELL ...
JANGLE...
THUMP
CLICK
...THIS AGAIN.
WHENEVER I APPROACH THE HEART OF A MATTER, YOU WRIGGLE YOUR WAY OUT OF ANY QUESTIONING.
THAT IS ONE ASPECT OF YOU...
...OF WHICH I GROW QUITE WEARY.

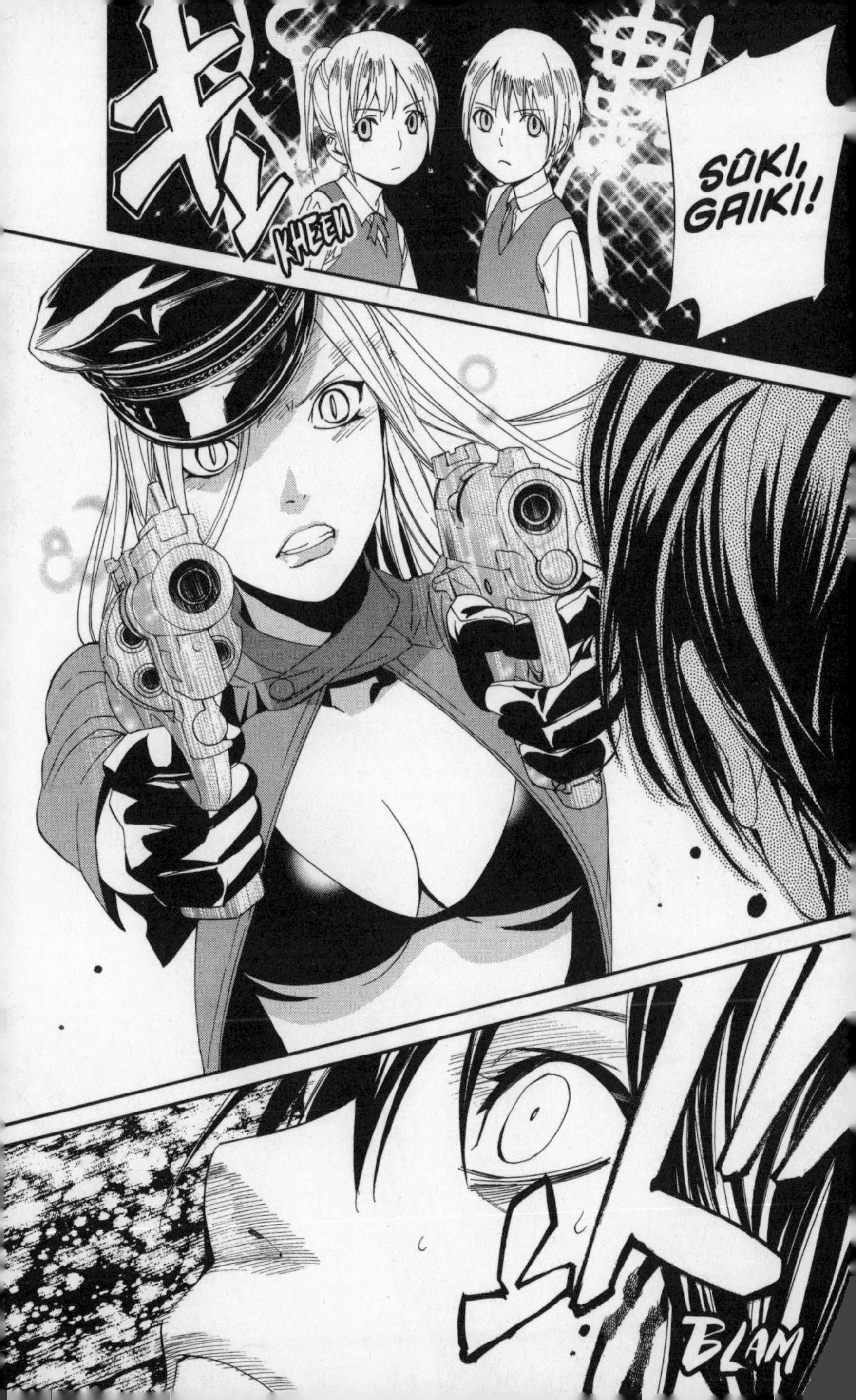
SÔKI, GAIKI!
KHEEN
BLAM

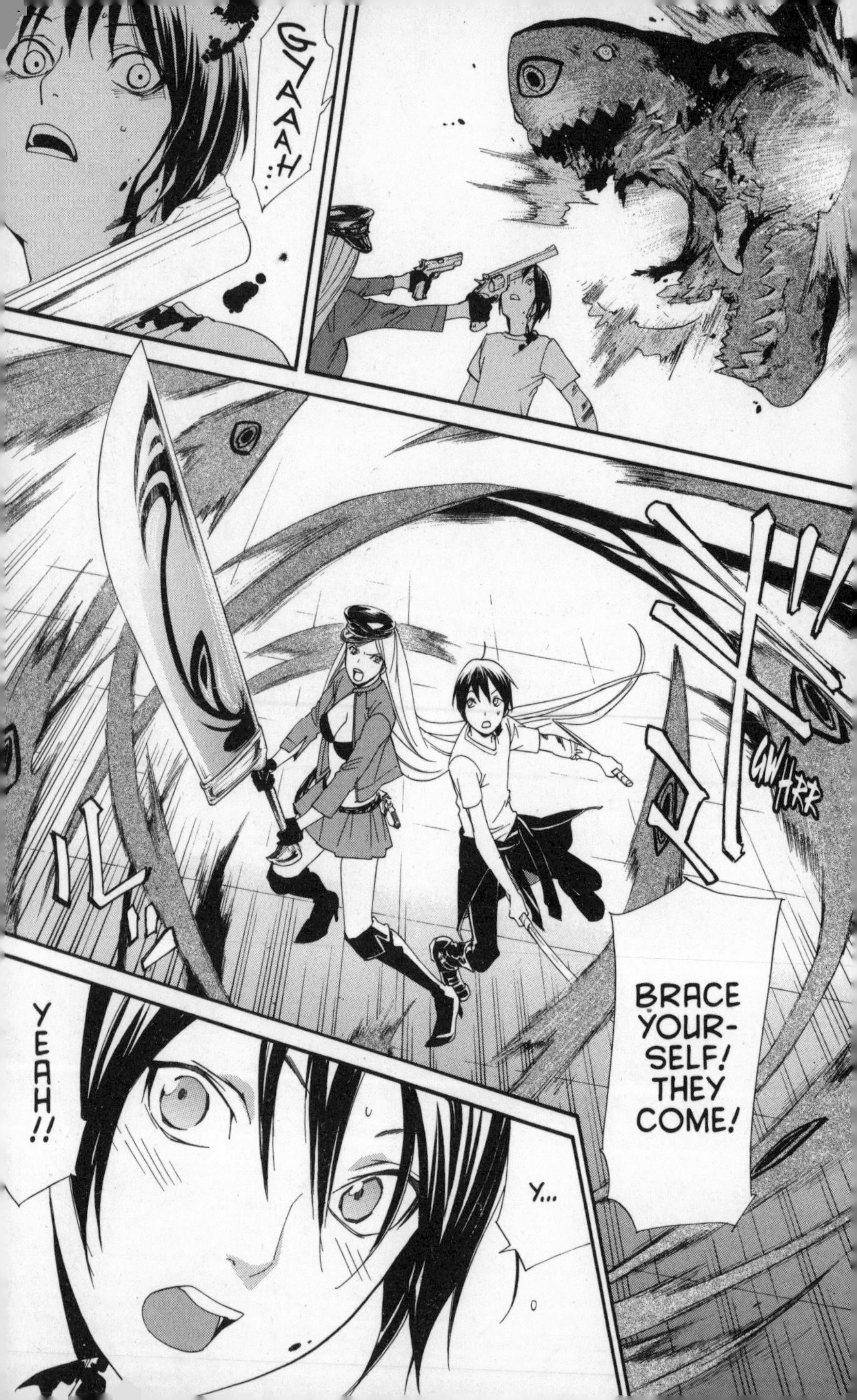
GYAAAH...!!
BRACE YOURSELF! THEY COME!
GWARR
Y...
YEAH!!

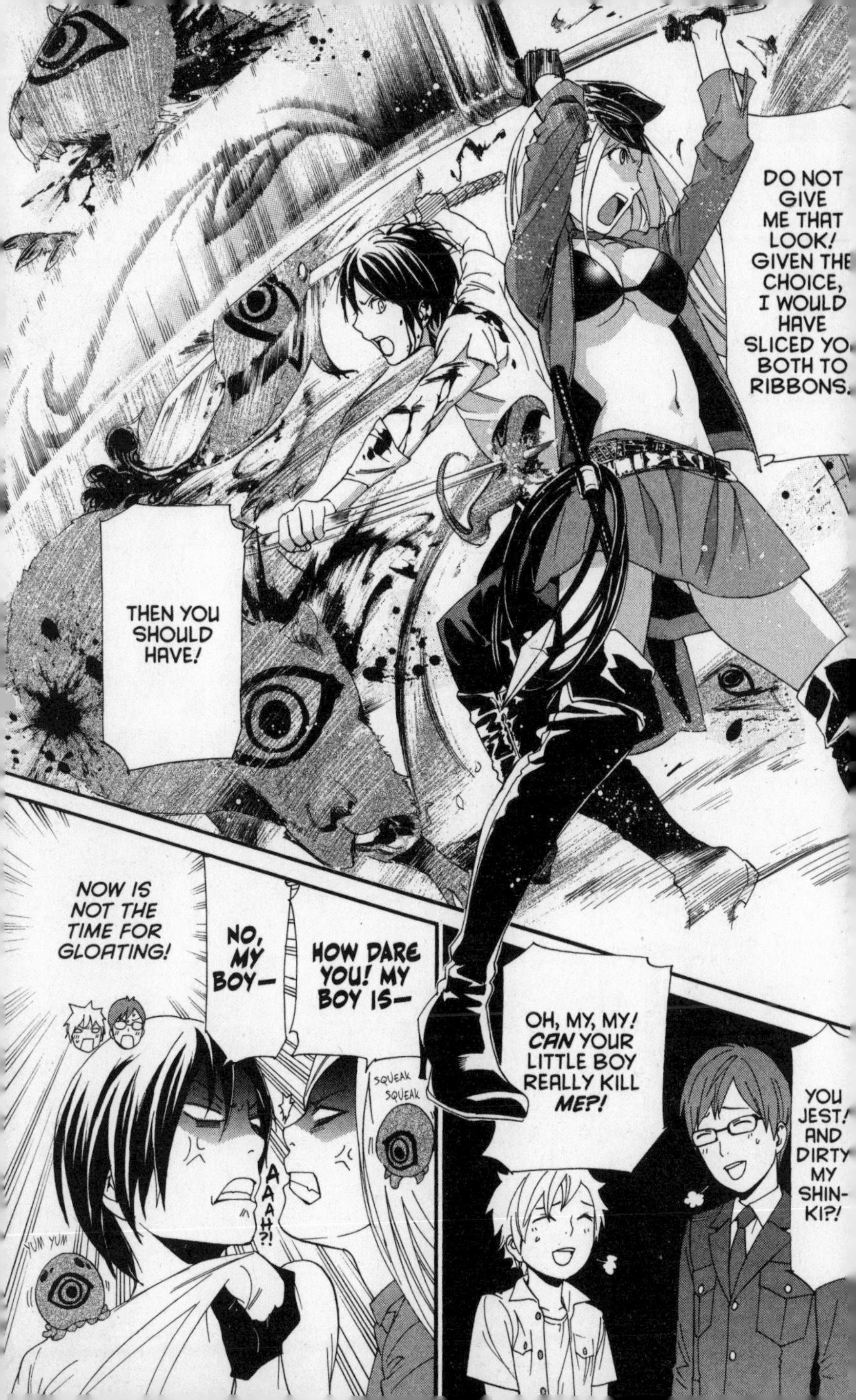
DO NOT GIVE ME THAT LOOK! GIVEN THE CHOICE, I WOULD HAVE SLICED YO BOTH TO RIBBONS.
THEN YOU SHOULD HAVE!
OH, MY, MY! *CAN* YOUR LITTLE BOY REALLY KILL *ME?!*
YOU JEST! AND DIRTY MY SHINKI?!
HOW DARE YOU! MY BOY IS—
NO, MY BOY—
NOW IS NOT THE TIME FOR GLOATING!
SQUEAK SQUEAK
AAAH?!
YUM YUM

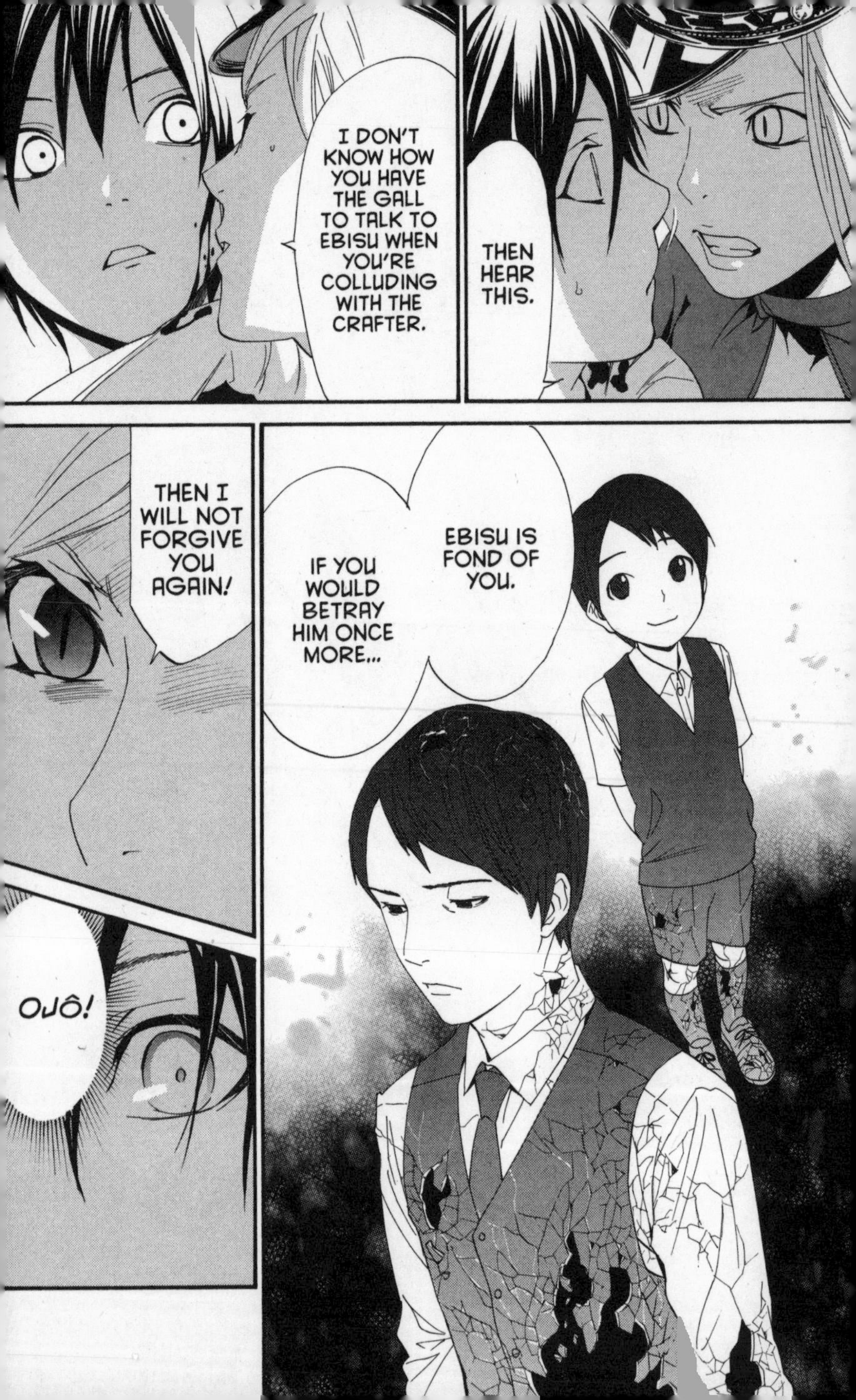
THEN HEAR THIS.
I DON'T KNOW HOW YOU HAVE THE GALL TO TALK TO EBISU WHEN YOU'RE COLLUDING WITH THE CRAFTER.
EBISU IS FOND OF YOU.
IF YOU WOULD BETRAY HIM ONCE MORE...
THEN I WILL NOT FORGIVE YOU AGAIN!
OJÔ!

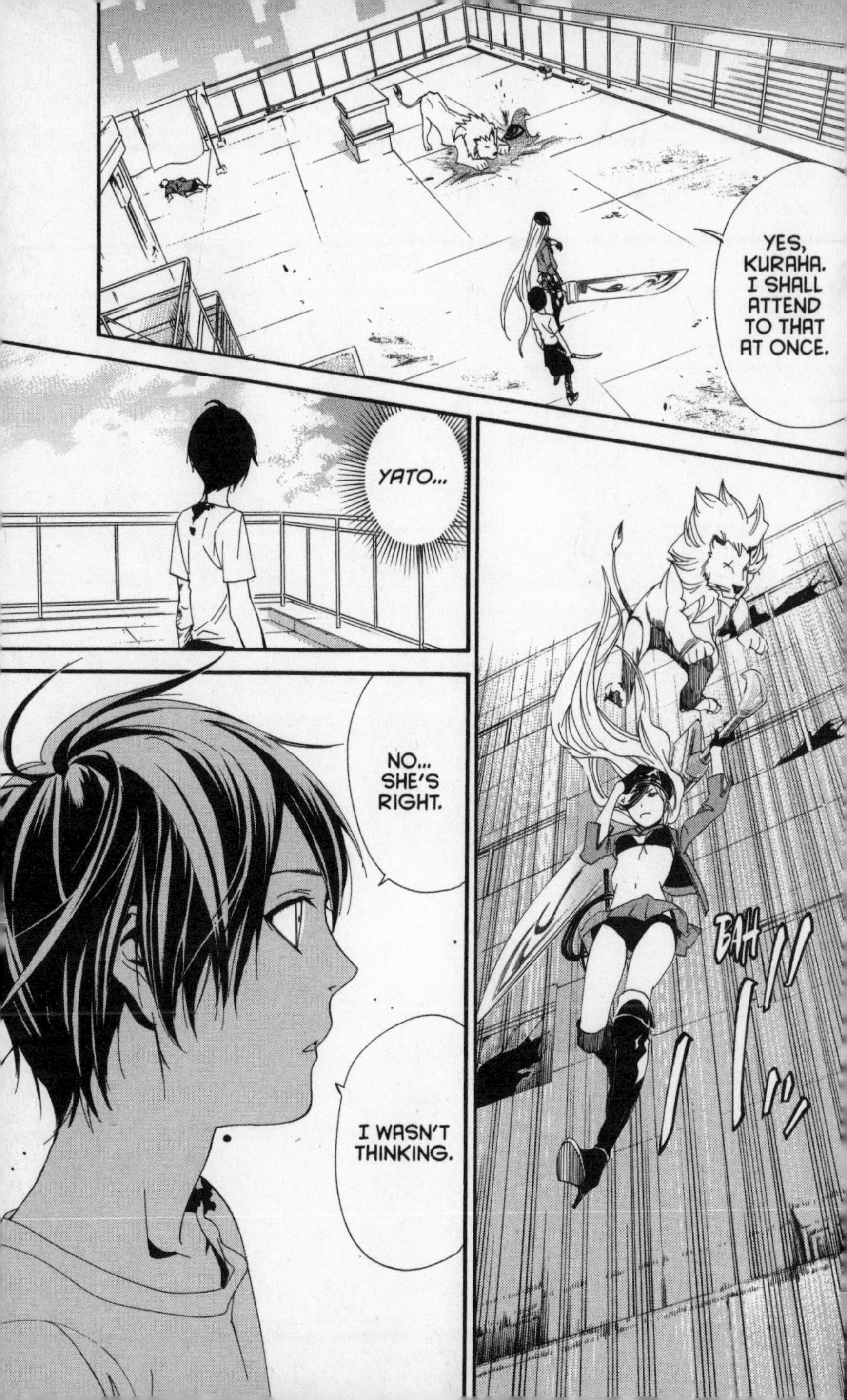
YES, KURAHA. I SHALL ATTEND TO THAT AT ONCE.
BAH
YATO...
NO... SHE'S RIGHT.
I WASN'T THINKING.

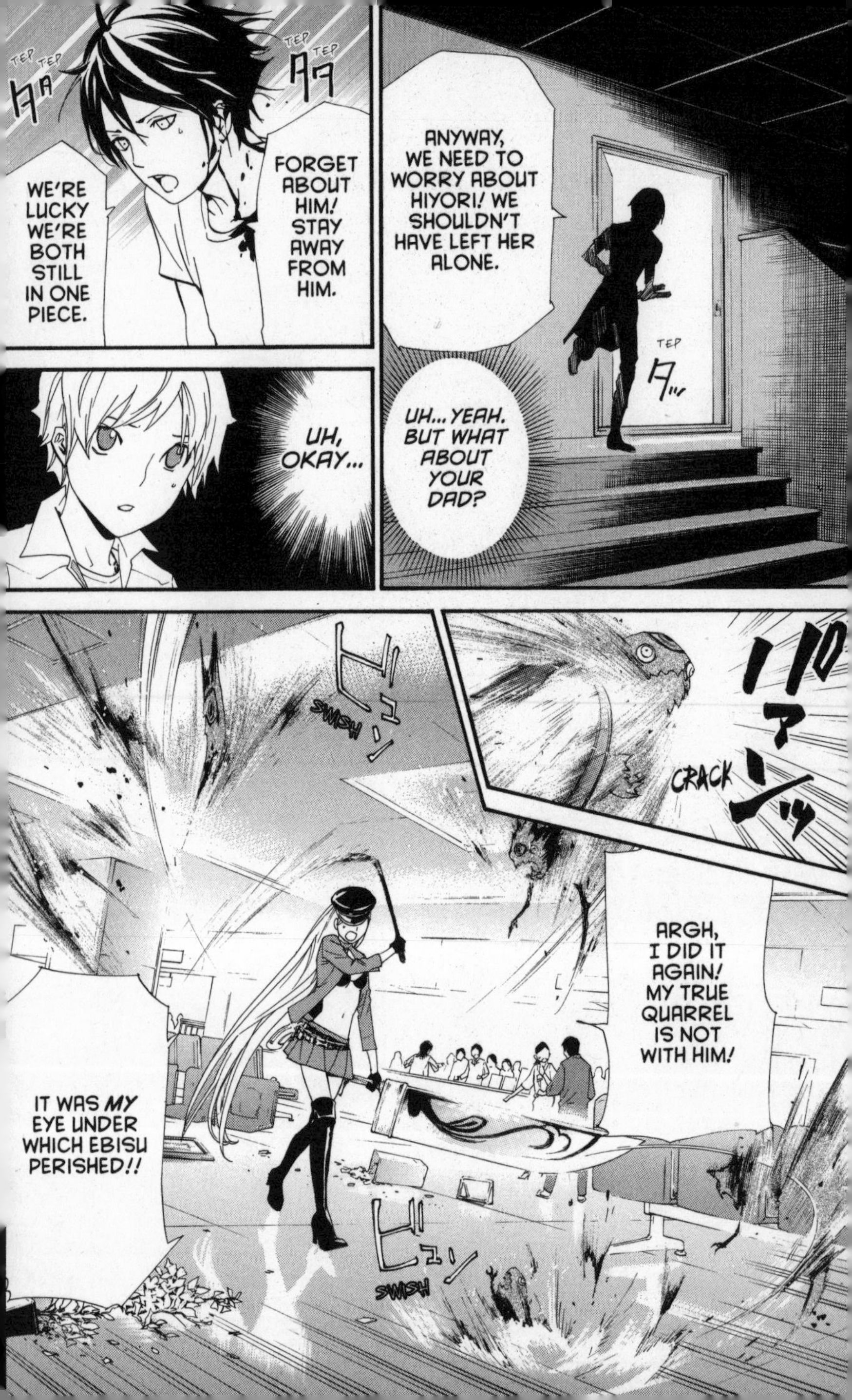
ANYWAY, WE NEED TO WORRY ABOUT HIYORI! WE SHOULDN'T HAVE LEFT HER ALONE.
TEP
UH... YEAH. BUT WHAT ABOUT YOUR DAD?
TEP TEP
FORGET ABOUT HIM! STAY AWAY FROM HIM.
WE'RE LUCKY WE'RE BOTH STILL IN ONE PIECE.
TEP TEP
UH, OKAY...
CRACK
SWISH
ARGH, I DID IT AGAIN! MY TRUE QUARREL IS NOT WITH HIM!
IT WAS *MY* EYE UNDER WHICH EBISU PERISHED!!
SWISH

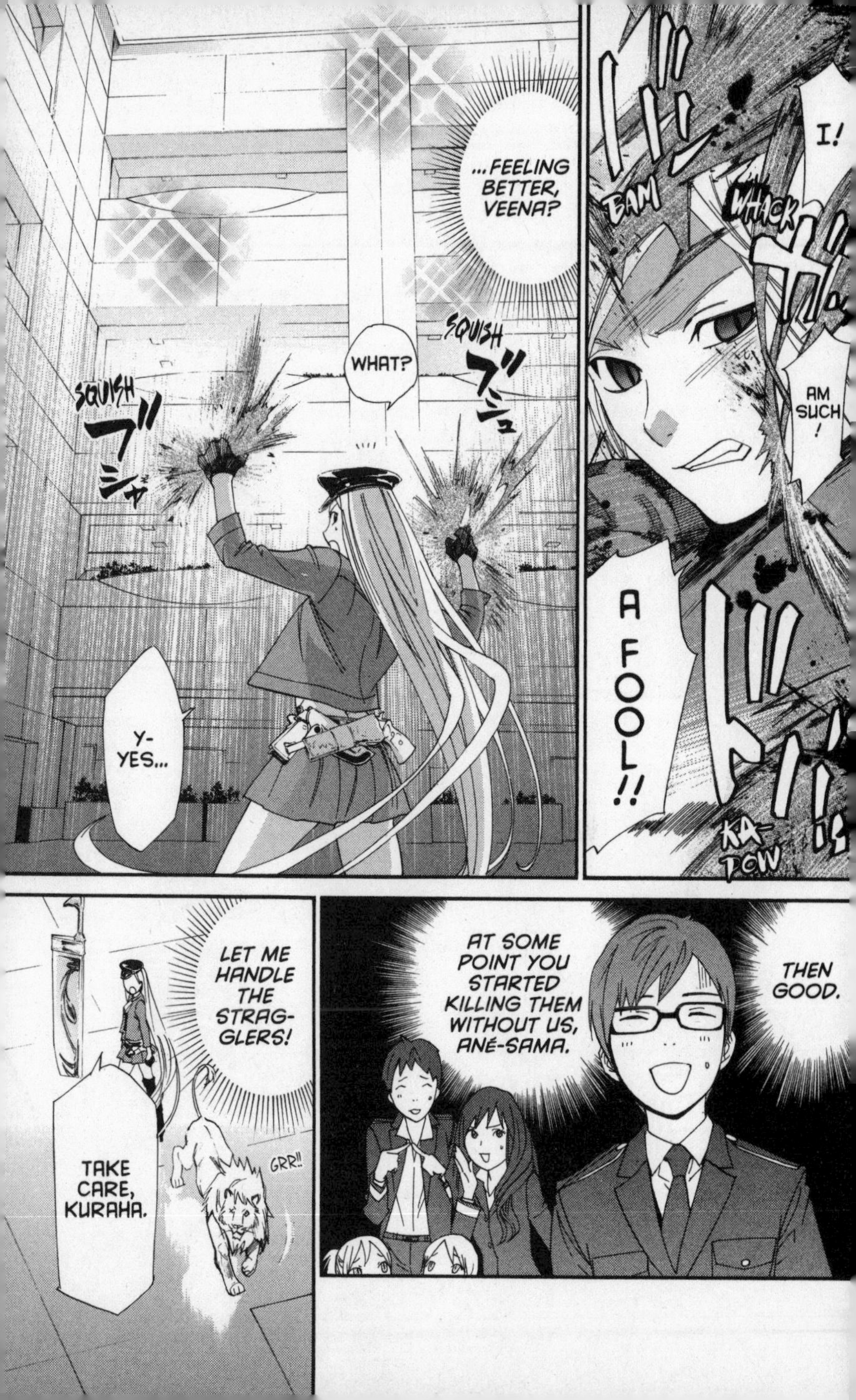
I!
BAM
WHACK
AM SUCH!
A FOOL!!
KA-DOW
...FEELING BETTER, VEENA?
SQUISH
WHAT?
SQUISH
Y-YES...
THEN GOOD.
AT SOME POINT YOU STARTED KILLING THEM WITHOUT US, ANÉ-SAMA.
LET ME HANDLE THE STRAGGLERS!
GRR!!
TAKE CARE, KURAHA.

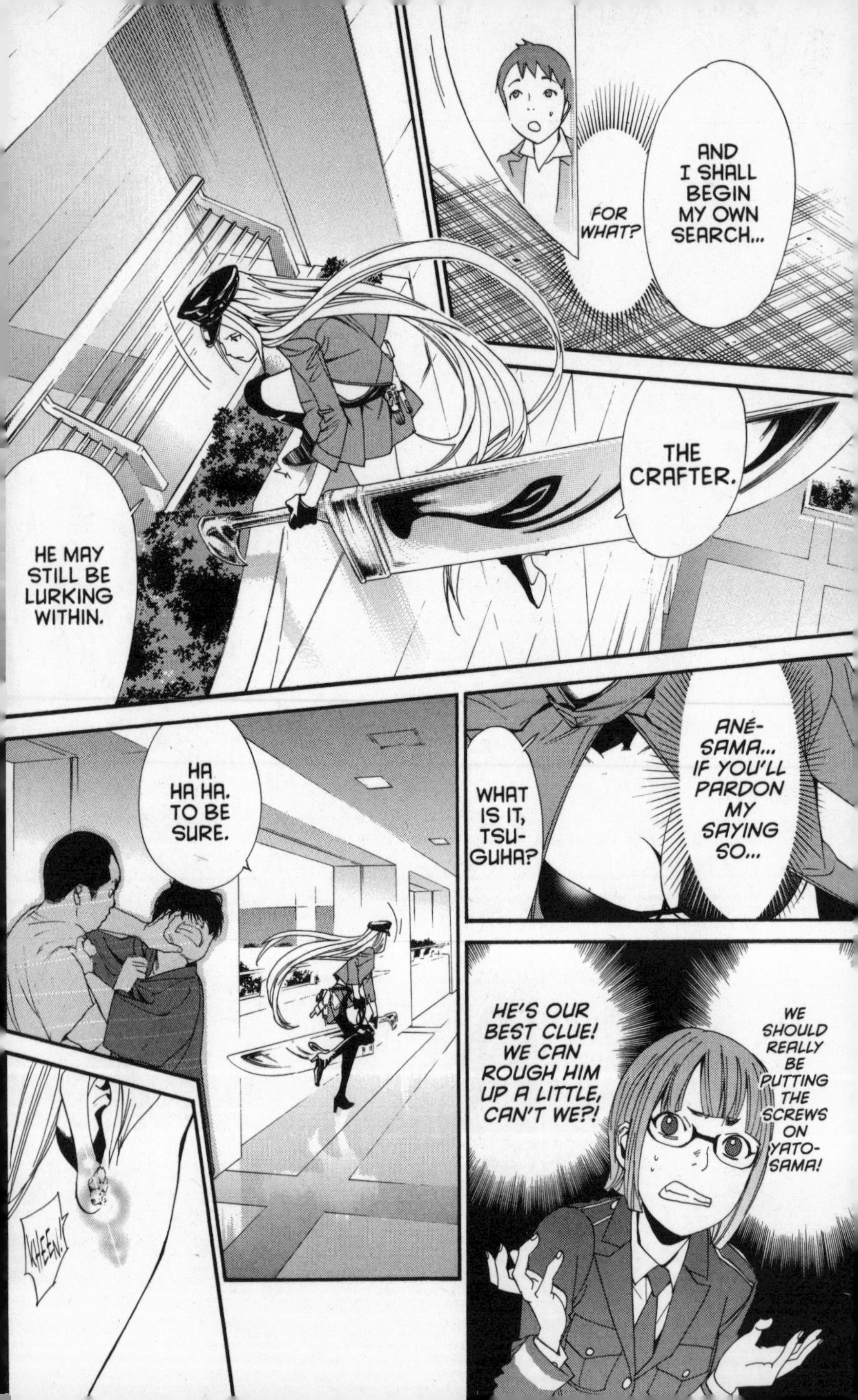
AND I SHALL BEGIN MY OWN SEARCH...
FOR WHAT?
THE CRAFTER.
HE MAY STILL BE LURKING WITHIN.
ANÉ-SAMA... IF YOU'LL PARDON MY SAYING SO...
WHAT IS IT, TSUGUHA?
WE SHOULD REALLY BE PUTTING THE SCREWS ON YATO-SAMA!
HE'S OUR BEST CLUE! WE CAN ROUGH HIM UP A LITTLE, CAN'T WE?!
HA HA HA. TO BE SURE.
KHEEN!

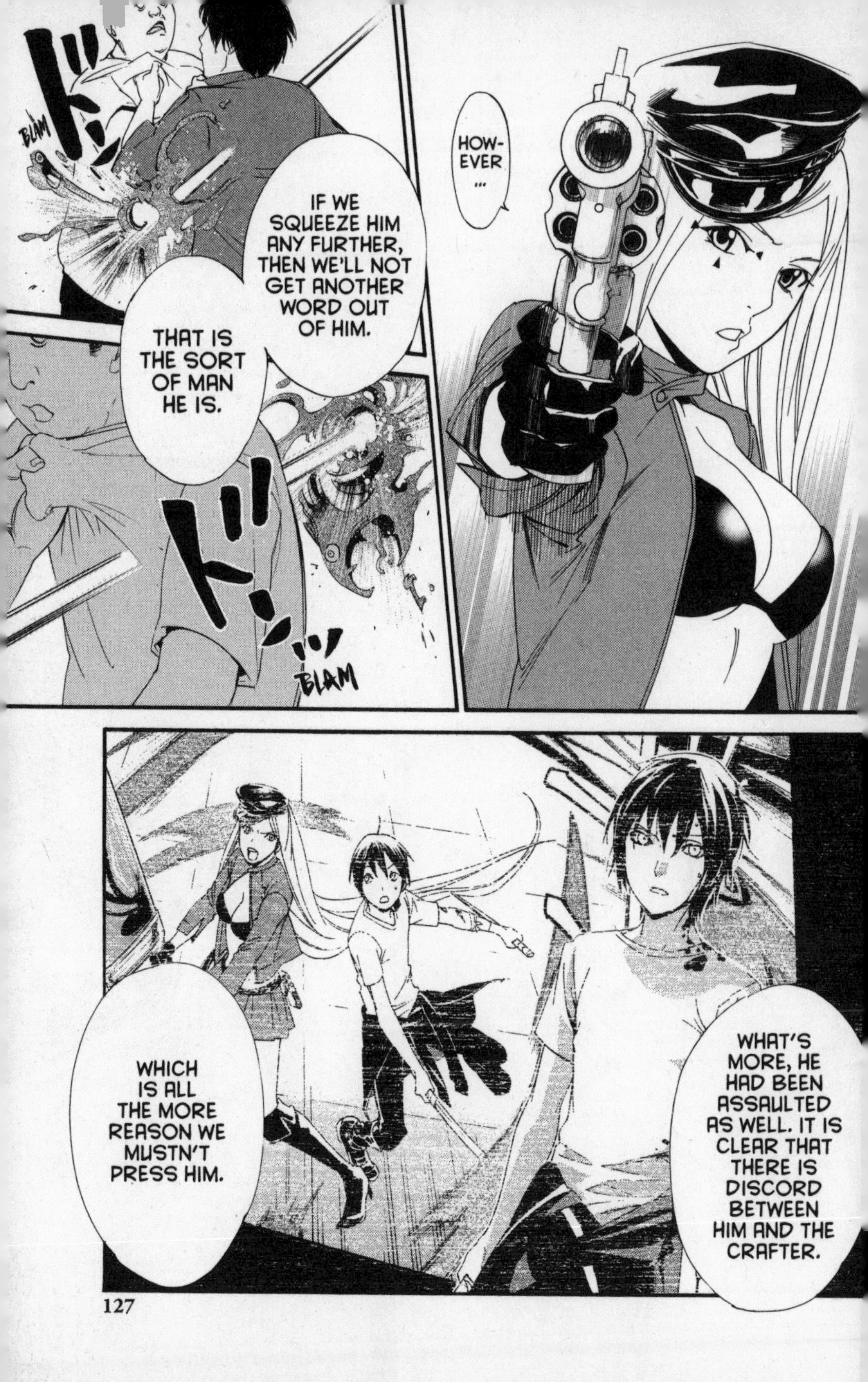
HOW-EVER ...
IF WE SQUEEZE HIM ANY FURTHER, THEN WE'LL NOT GET ANOTHER WORD OUT OF HIM.
BLAM
THAT IS THE SORT OF MAN HE IS.
BLAM
WHAT'S MORE, HE HAD BEEN ASSAULTED AS WELL. IT IS CLEAR THAT THERE IS DISCORD BETWEEN HIM AND THE CRAFTER.
WHICH IS ALL THE MORE REASON WE MUSTN'T PRESS HIM.

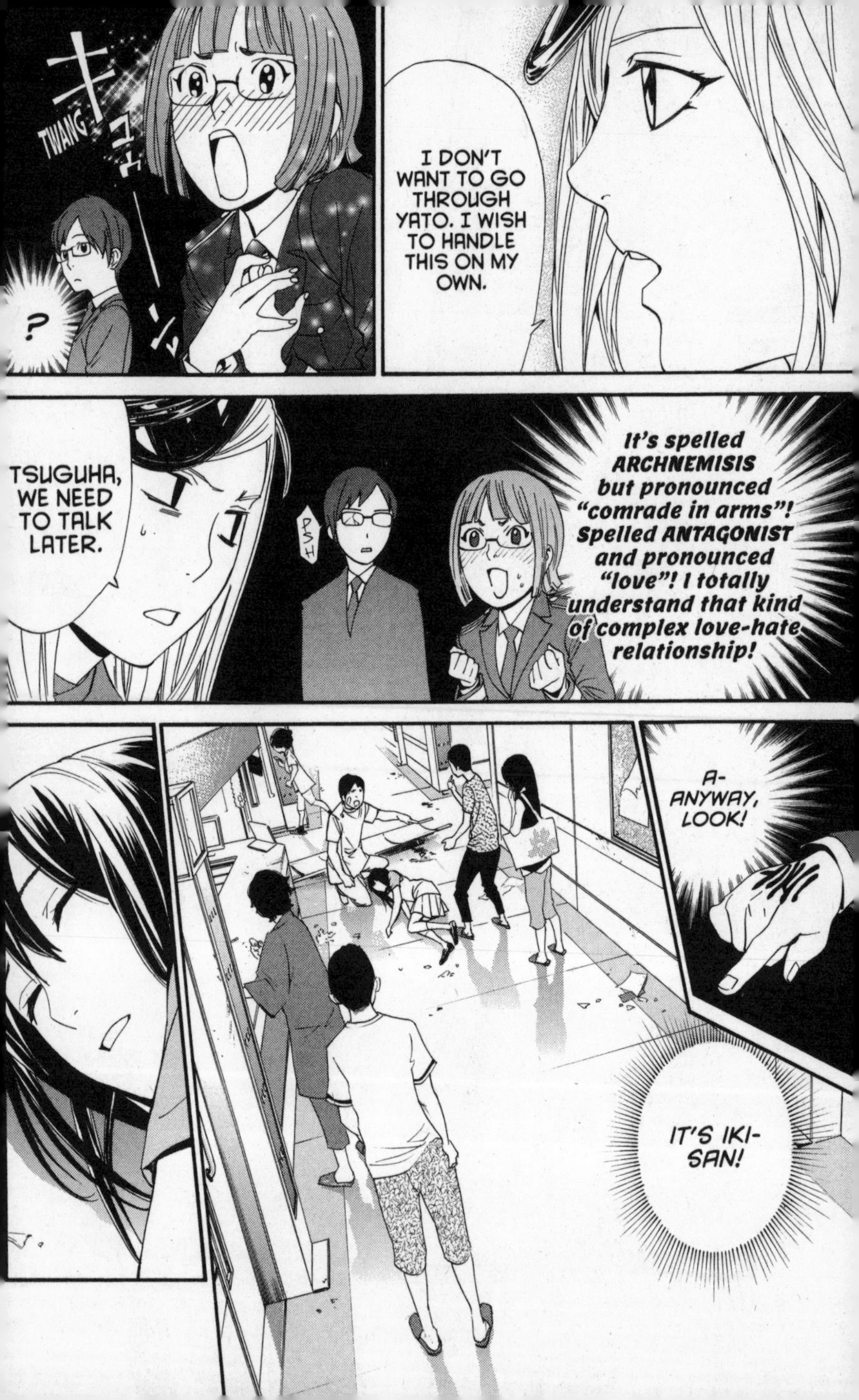
I DON'T WANT TO GO THROUGH YATO. I WISH TO HANDLE THIS ON MY OWN.
TWANG
?
It's spelled ARCHNEMISIS but pronounced "comrade in arms"! Spelled ANTAGONIST and pronounced "love"! I totally understand that kind of complex love-hate relationship!
PSH
TSUGUHA, WE NEED TO TALK LATER.
A- ANYWAY, LOOK!
IT'S IKI-SAN!

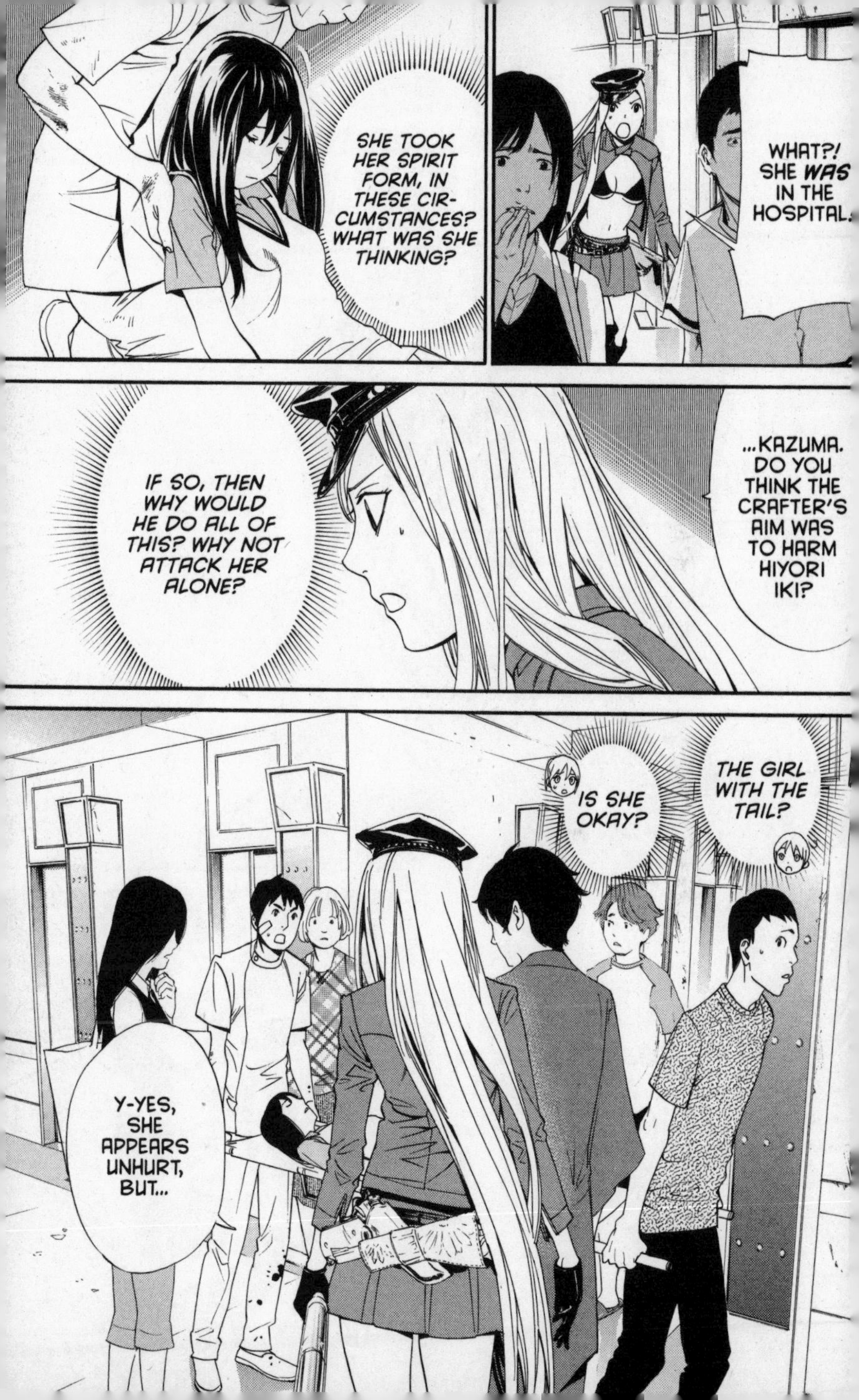
WHAT?! SHE WAS IN THE HOSPITAL.
SHE TOOK HER SPIRIT FORM, IN THESE CIR-CUMSTANCES? WHAT WAS SHE THINKING?
...KAZUMA. DO YOU THINK THE CRAFTER'S AIM WAS TO HARM HIYORI IKI?
IF SO, THEN WHY WOULD HE DO ALL OF THIS? WHY NOT ATTACK HER ALONE?
THE GIRL WITH THE TAIL?
IS SHE OKAY?
Y-YES, SHE APPEARS UNHURT, BUT...

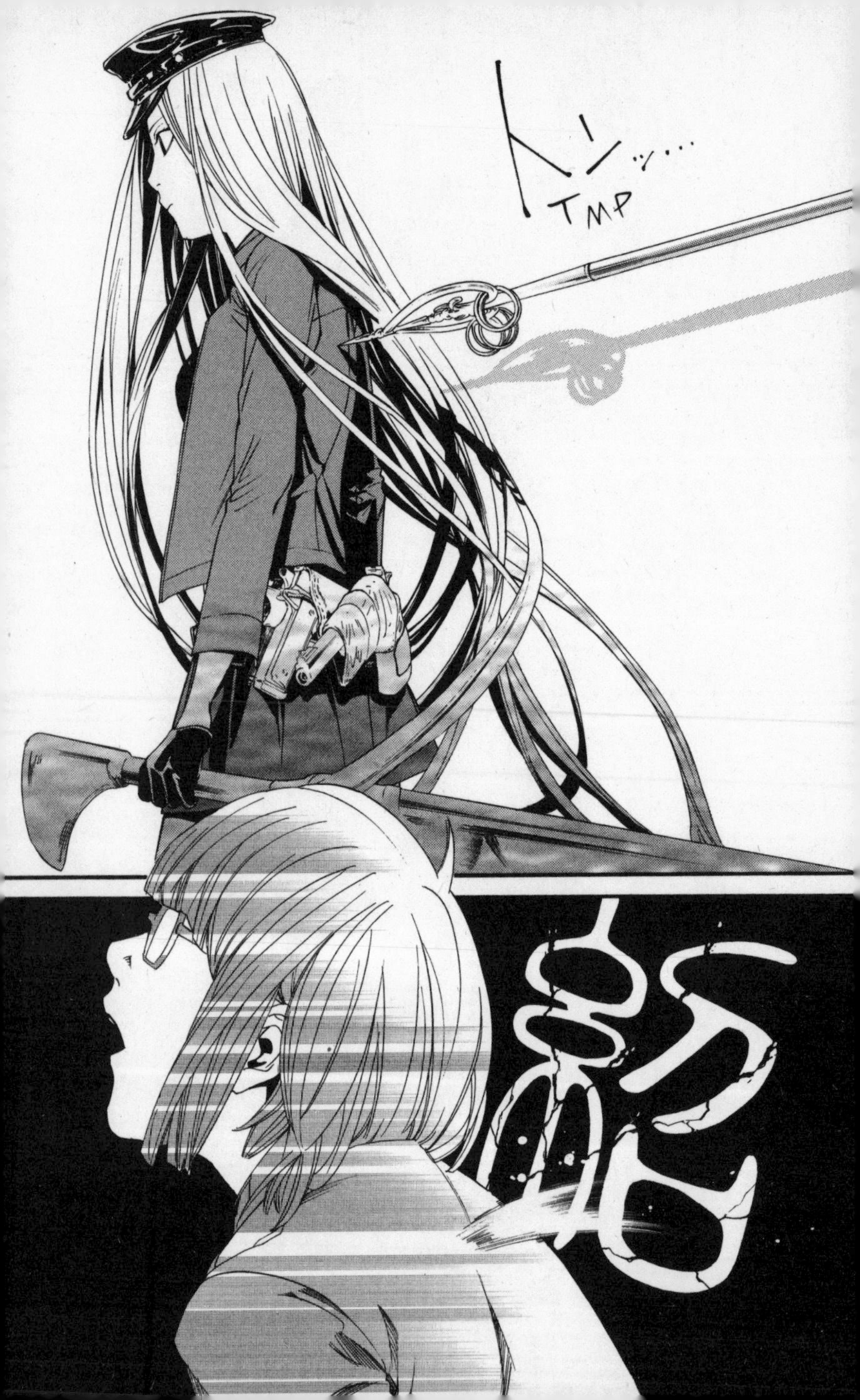
トンッ…
TMP

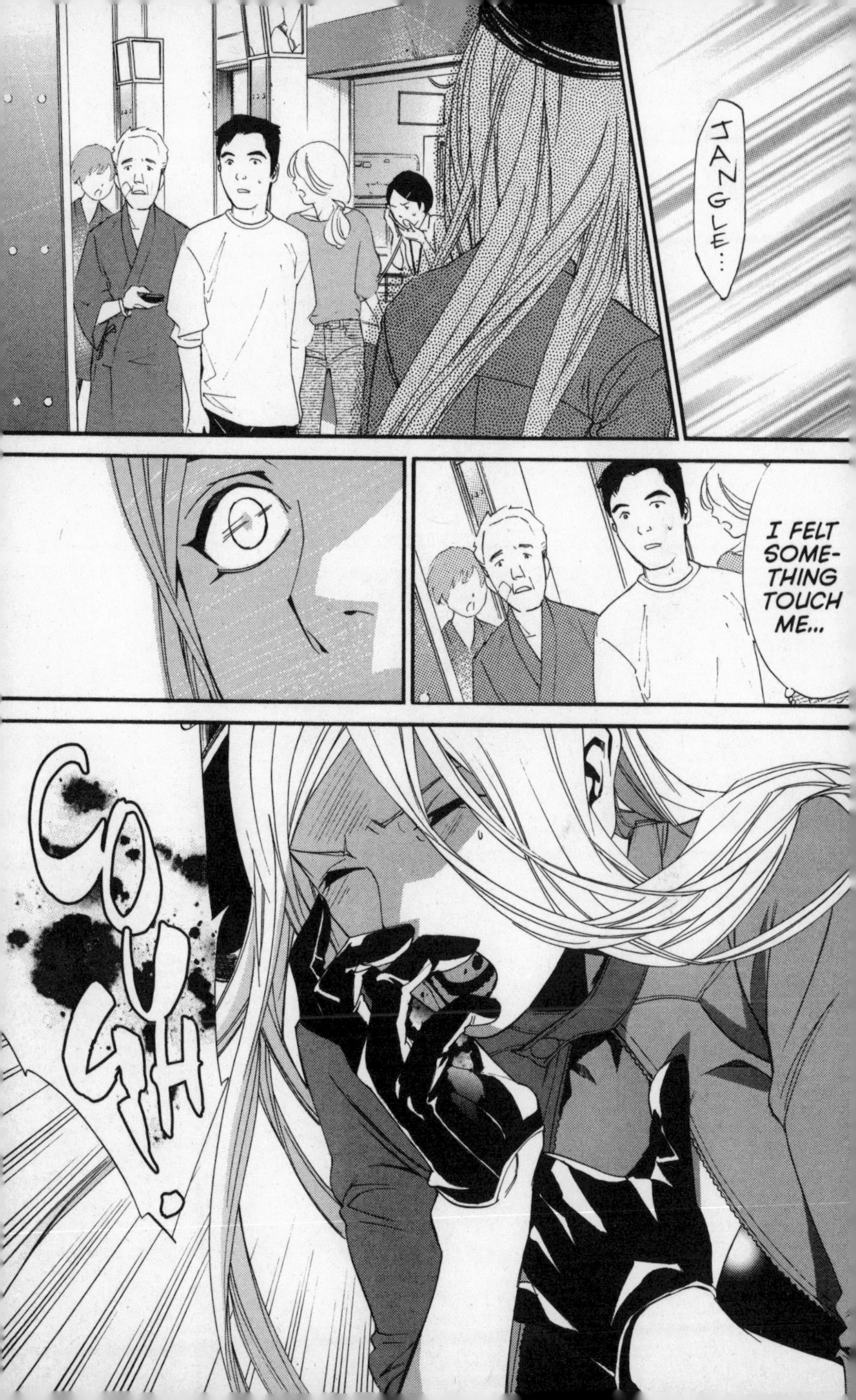
JANGLE...
I FELT SOME-THING TOUCH ME...
COUGH

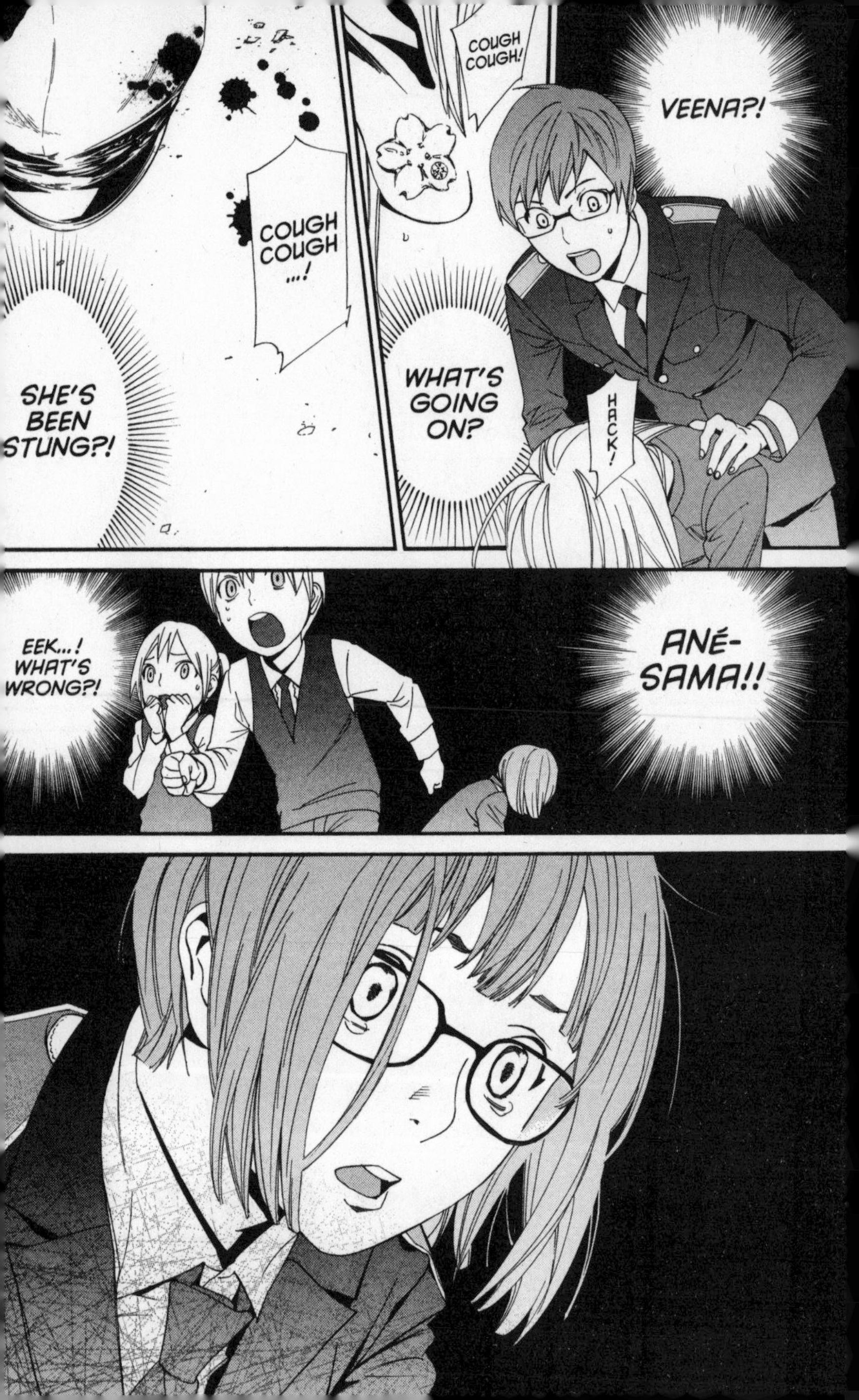
VEENA?!
COUGH COUGH!
HACK!
WHAT'S GOING ON?
COUGH COUGH ...!
SHE'S BEEN STUNG?!
ANÉ-SAMA!!
EEK...! WHAT'S WRONG?!

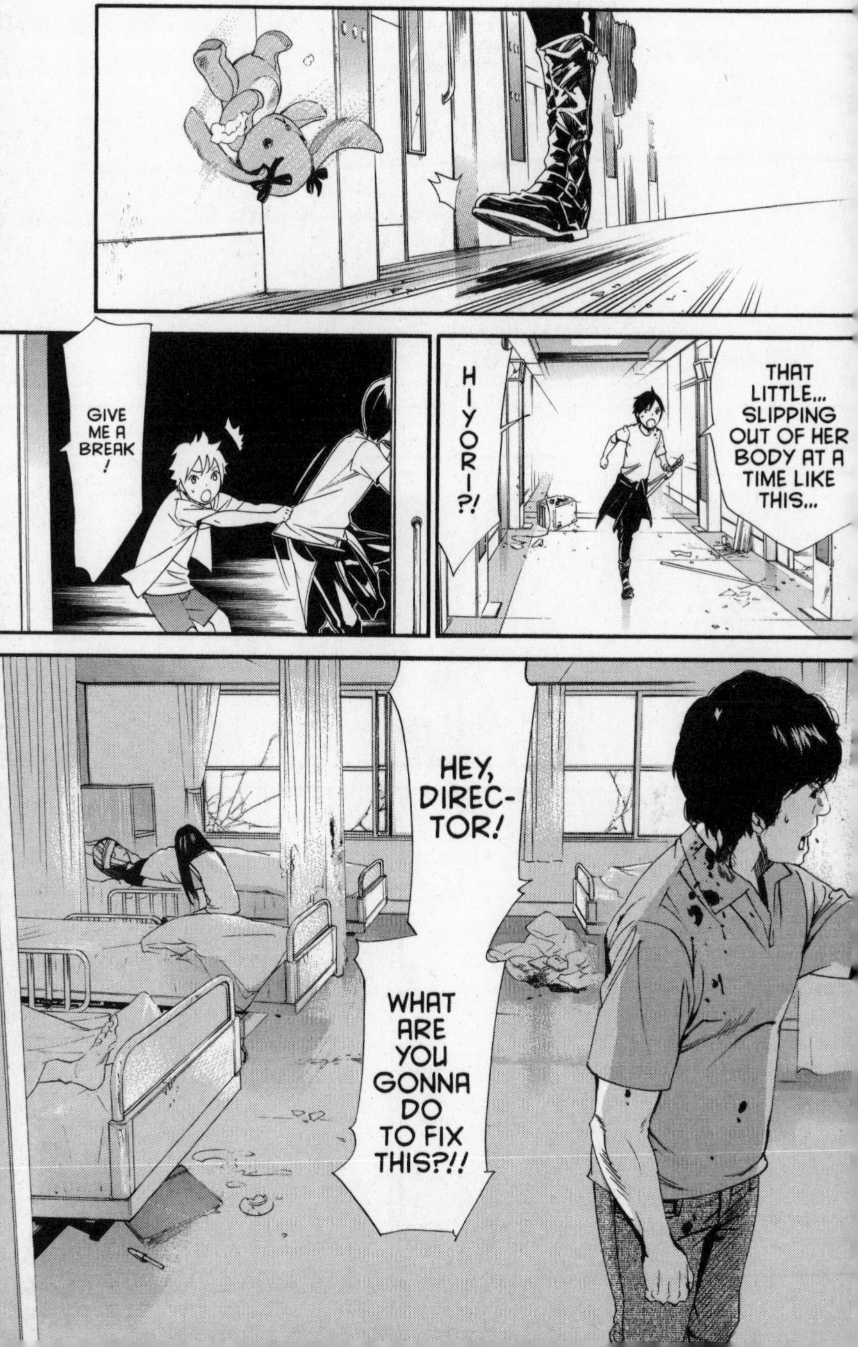
THAT LITTLE... SLIPPING OUT OF HER BODY AT A TIME LIKE THIS...
HIYORI?!
GIVE ME A BREAK!
HEY, DIRECTOR!
WHAT ARE YOU GONNA DO TO FIX THIS?!!

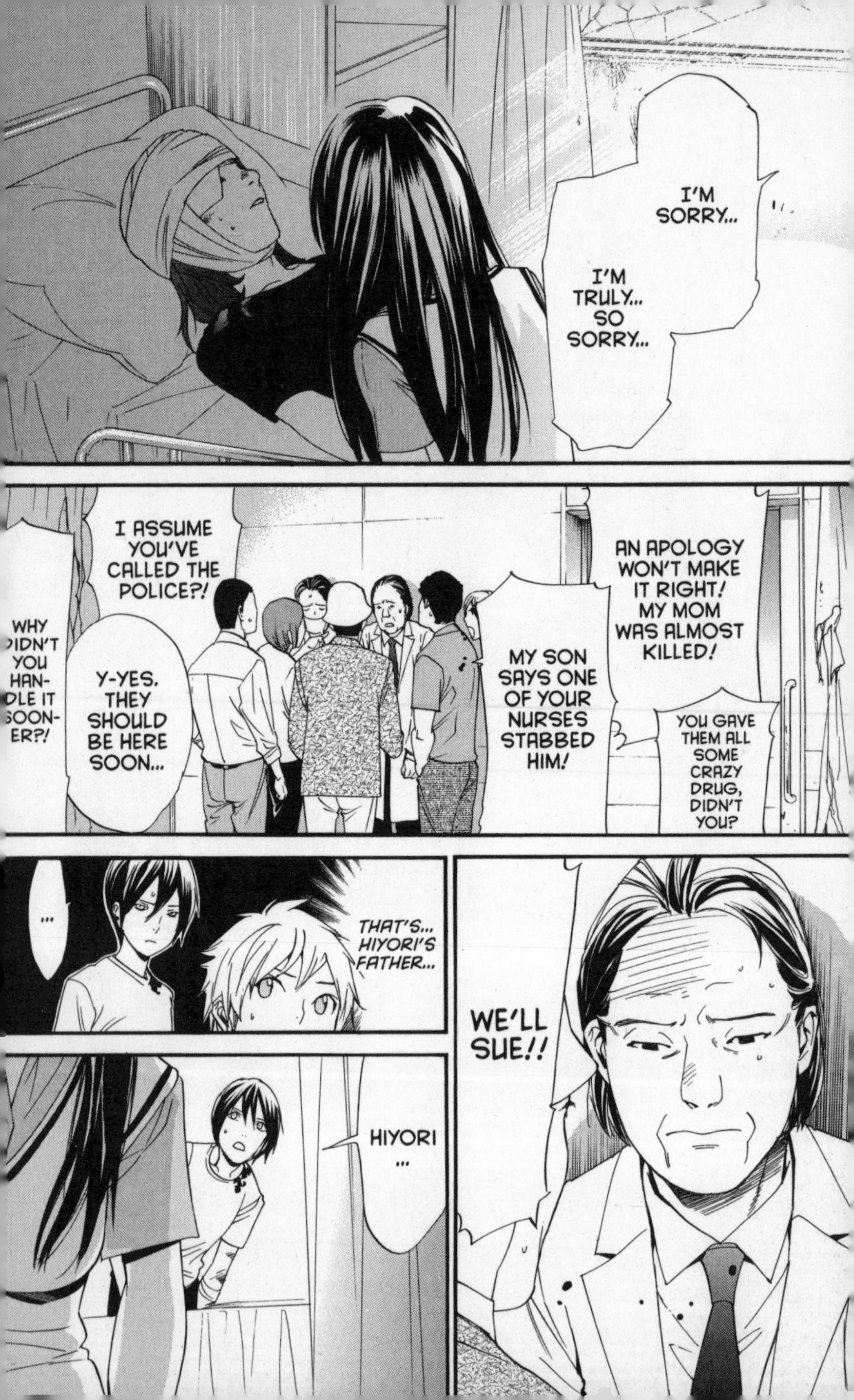
I'M SORRY...
I'M TRULY... SO SORRY...
AN APOLOGY WON'T MAKE IT RIGHT! MY MOM WAS ALMOST KILLED!
YOU GAVE THEM ALL SOME CRAZY DRUG, DIDN'T YOU?
MY SON SAYS ONE OF YOUR NURSES STABBED HIM!
I ASSUME YOU'VE CALLED THE POLICE?!
Y-YES. THEY SHOULD BE HERE SOON...
WHY DIDN'T YOU HAN-DLE IT SOON-ER?!
WE'LL SUE!!
THAT'S... HIYORI'S FATHER...
...
HIYORI ...

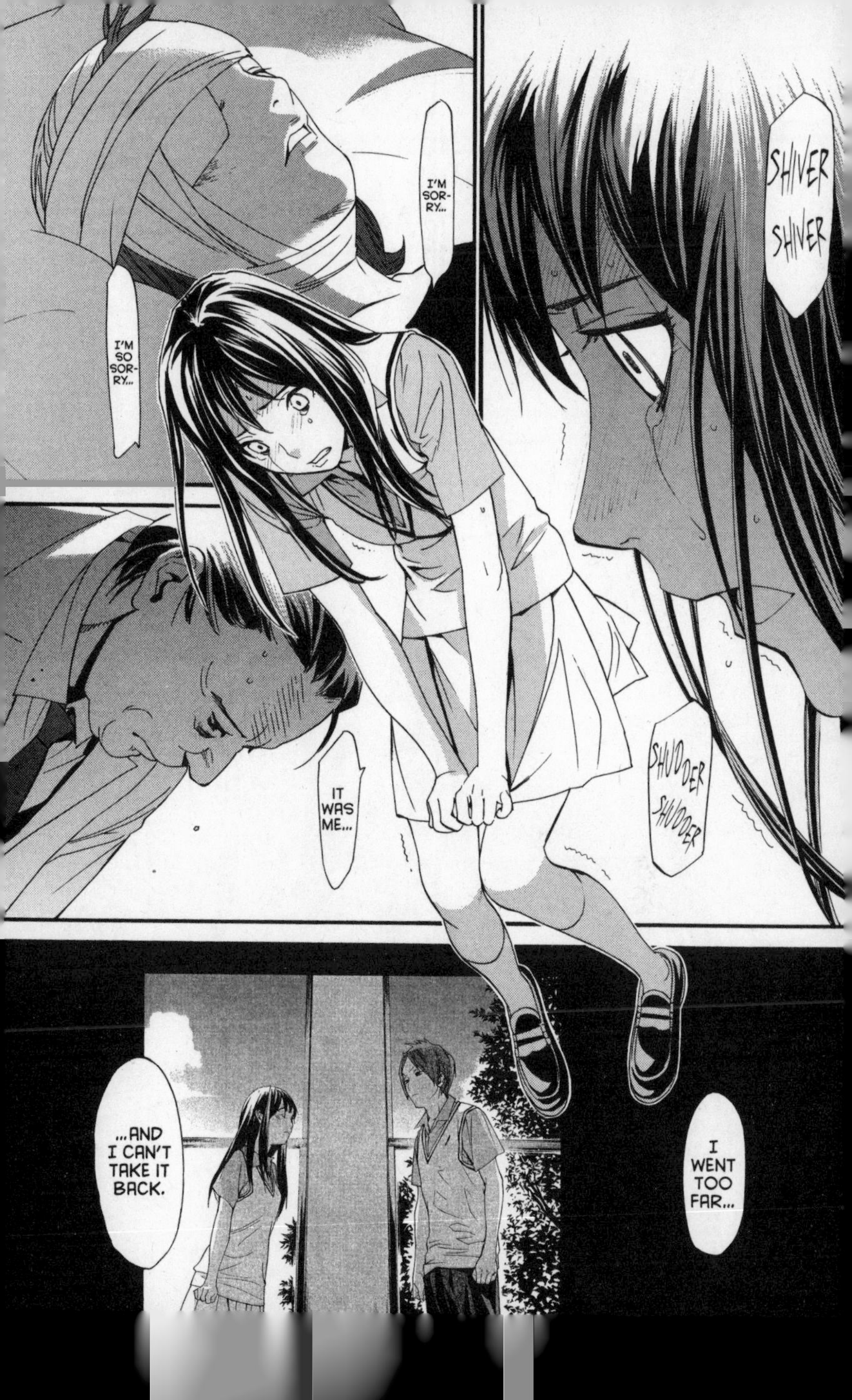
SHIVER SHIVER
SHUDDER SHUDDER
I'M SORRY...
I'M SO SORRY...
IT WAS ME...
I WENT TOO FAR...
...AND I CAN'T TAKE IT BACK.

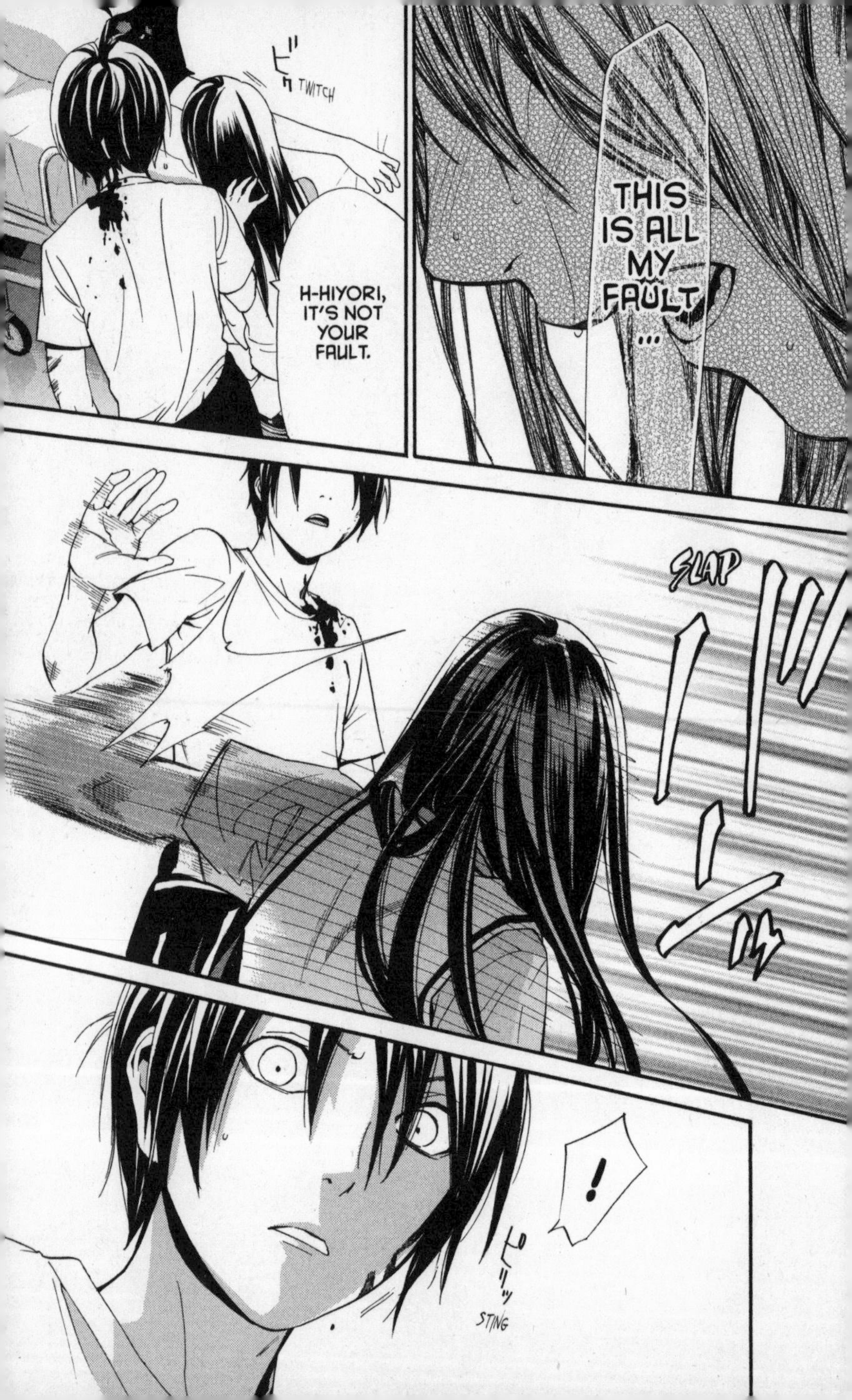
THIS IS ALL MY FAULT...
ビク TWITCH
H-HIYORI, IT'S NOT YOUR FAULT.
SLAP
!
ピリッ STING

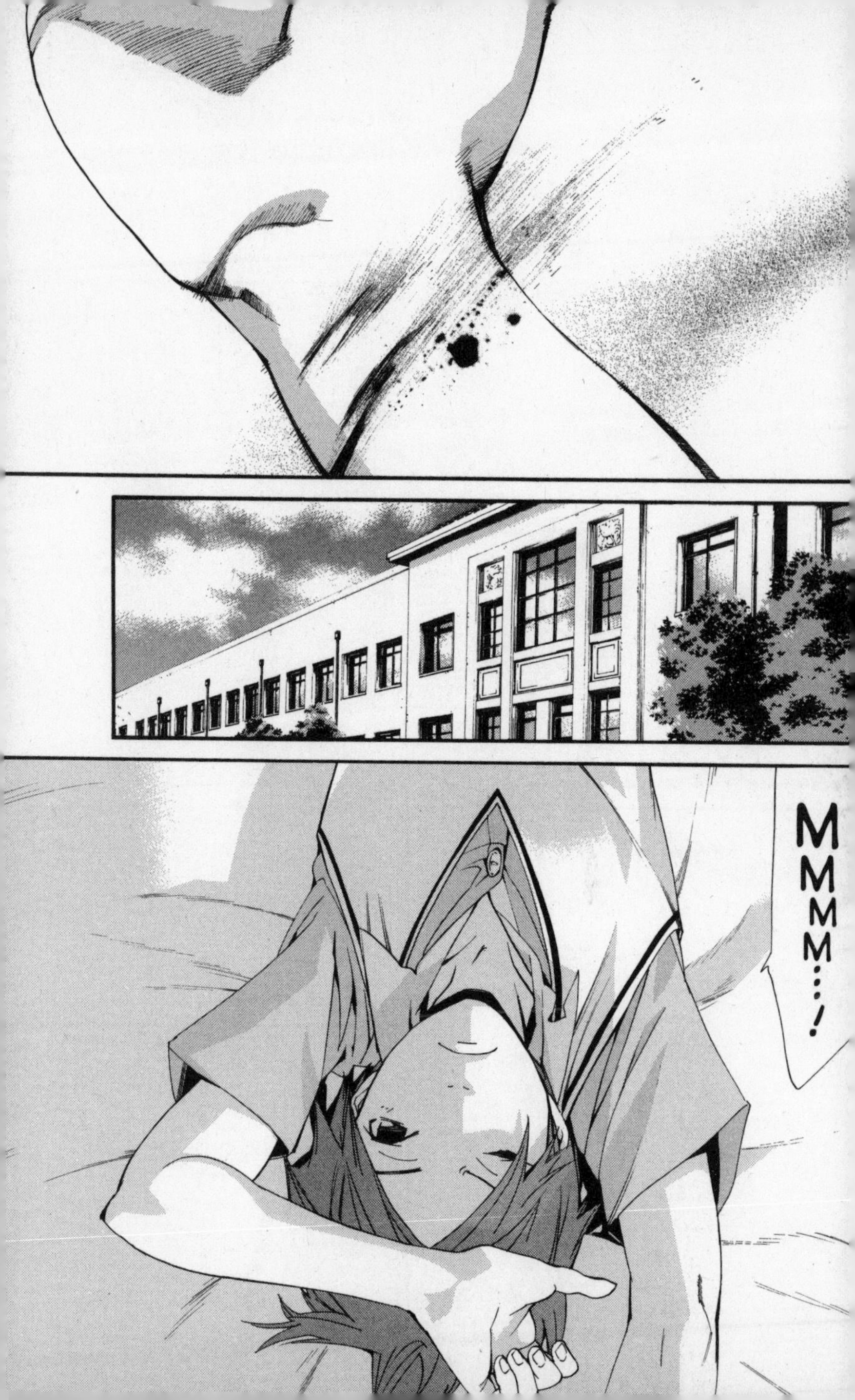
MMMM...!

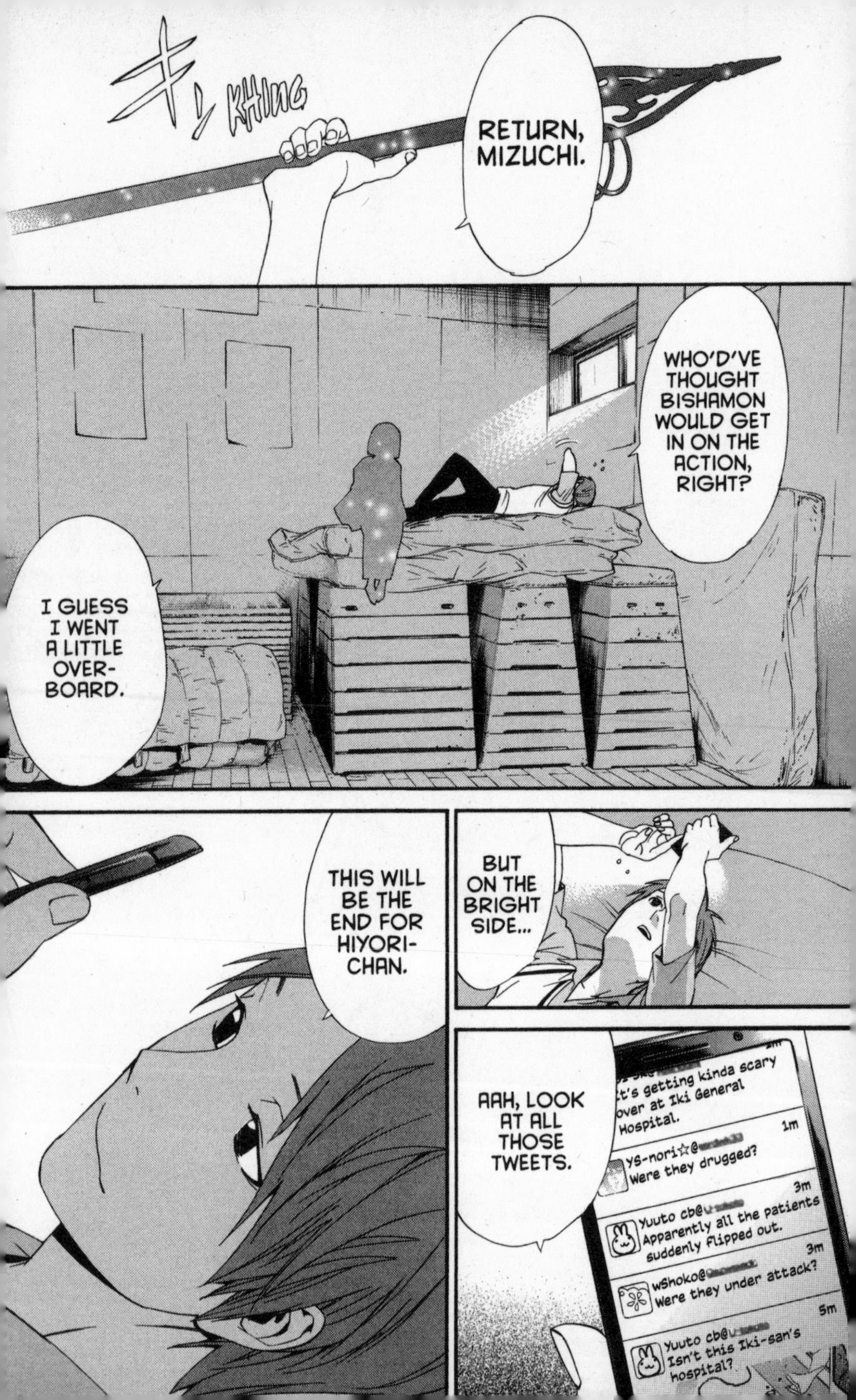
RETURN, MIZUCHI.
KHING
WHO'D'VE THOUGHT BISHAMON WOULD GET IN ON THE ACTION, RIGHT?
I GUESS I WENT A LITTLE OVER-BOARD.
BUT ON THE BRIGHT SIDE...
AAH, LOOK AT ALL THOSE TWEETS.
It's getting kinda scary over at Iki General Hospital.
1m
YS-nori☆@
Were they drugged?
3m
Yuuto cb@
Apparently all the patients suddenly flipped out.
3m
wShoko@
Were they under attack?
5m
Yuuto cb@
Isn't this Iki-san's hospital?
THIS WILL BE THE END FOR HIYORI-CHAN.

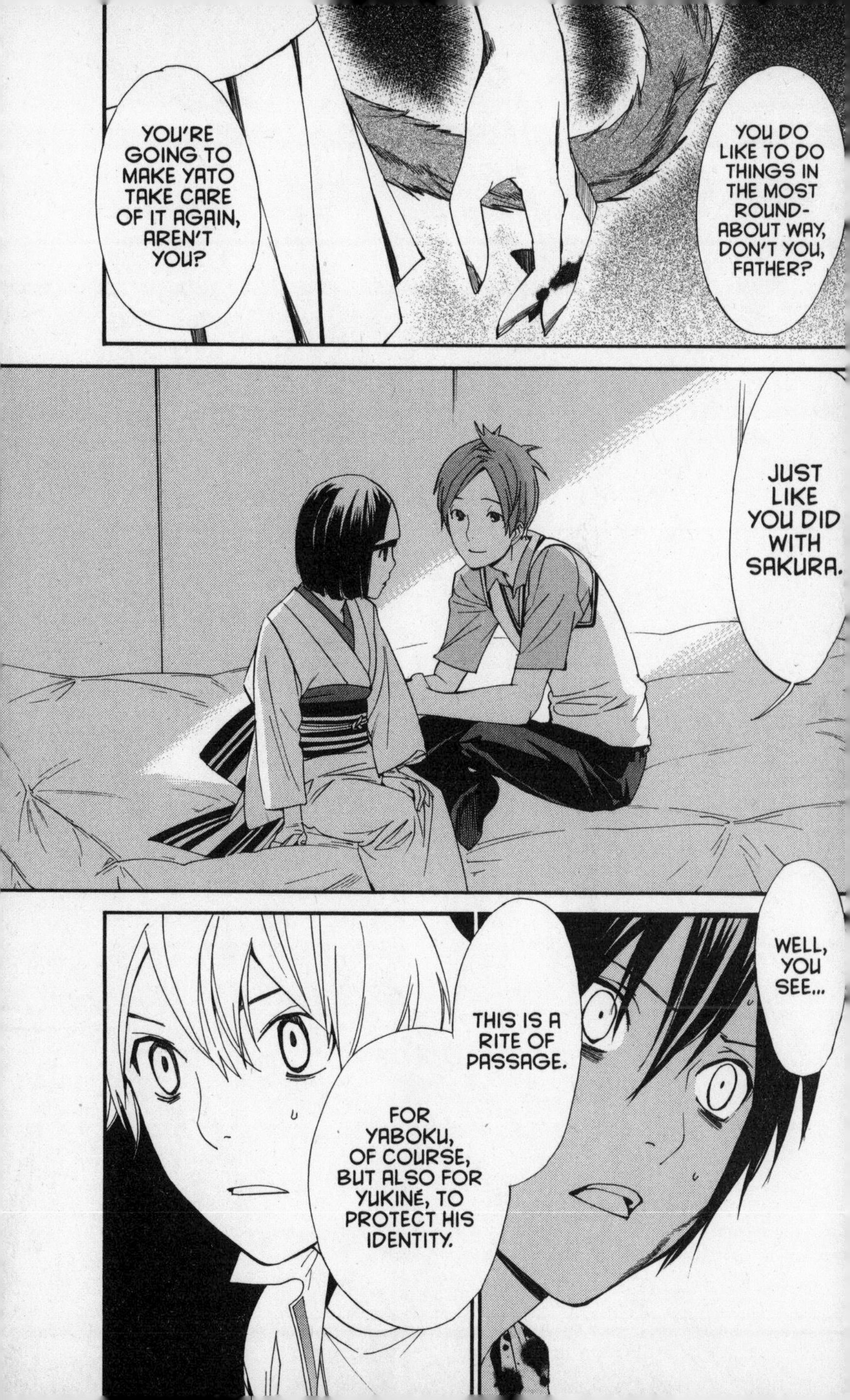
YOU DO LIKE TO DO THINGS IN THE MOST ROUND-ABOUT WAY, DON'T YOU, FATHER?
YOU'RE GOING TO MAKE YATO TAKE CARE OF IT AGAIN, AREN'T YOU?
JUST LIKE YOU DID WITH SAKURA.
WELL, YOU SEE...
THIS IS A RITE OF PASSAGE.
FOR YABOKU, OF COURSE, BUT ALSO FOR YUKINÉ, TO PROTECT HIS IDENTITY.

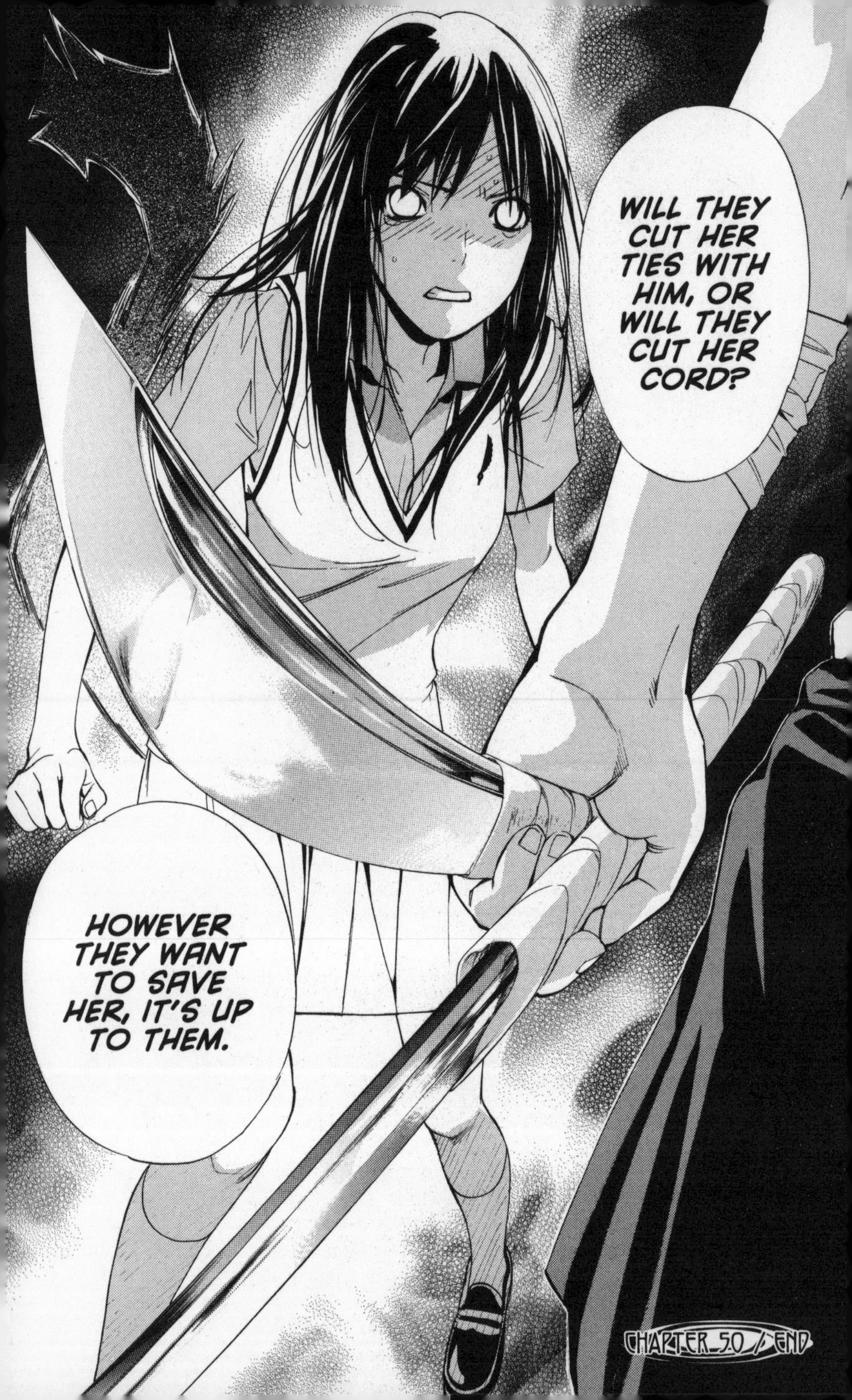
WILL THEY CUT HER TIES WITH HIM, OR WILL THEY CUT HER CORD?
HOWEVER THEY WANT TO SAVE HER, IT'S UP TO THEM.
CHAPTER 50 / END

野

皀

神

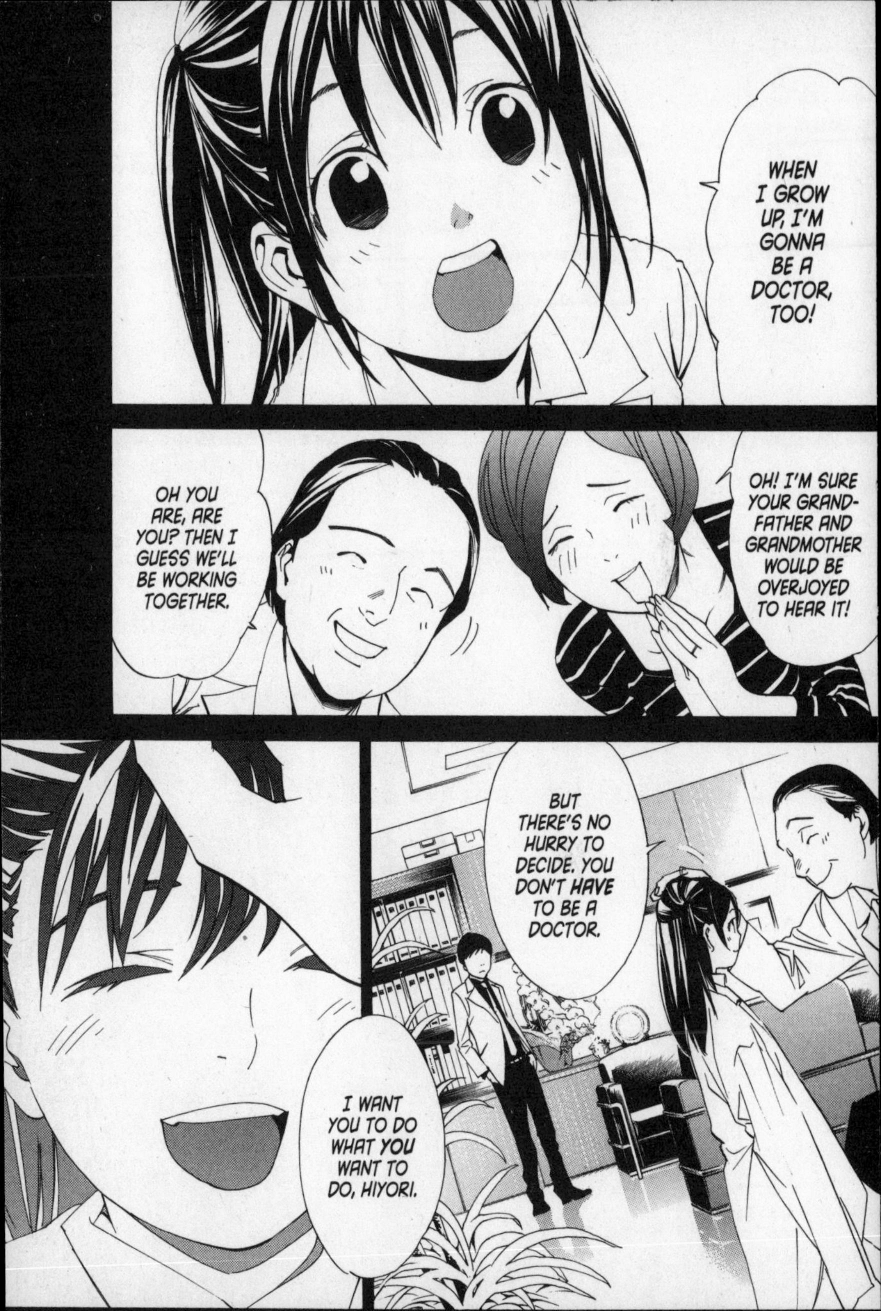
WHEN I GROW UP, I'M GONNA BE A DOCTOR, TOO!
OH! I'M SURE YOUR GRAND-FATHER AND GRANDMOTHER WOULD BE OVERJOYED TO HEAR IT!
OH YOU ARE, ARE YOU? THEN I GUESS WE'LL BE WORKING TOGETHER.
BUT THERE'S NO HURRY TO DECIDE. YOU DON'T *HAVE* TO BE A DOCTOR.
I WANT YOU TO DO WHAT *YOU* WANT TO DO, HIYORI.

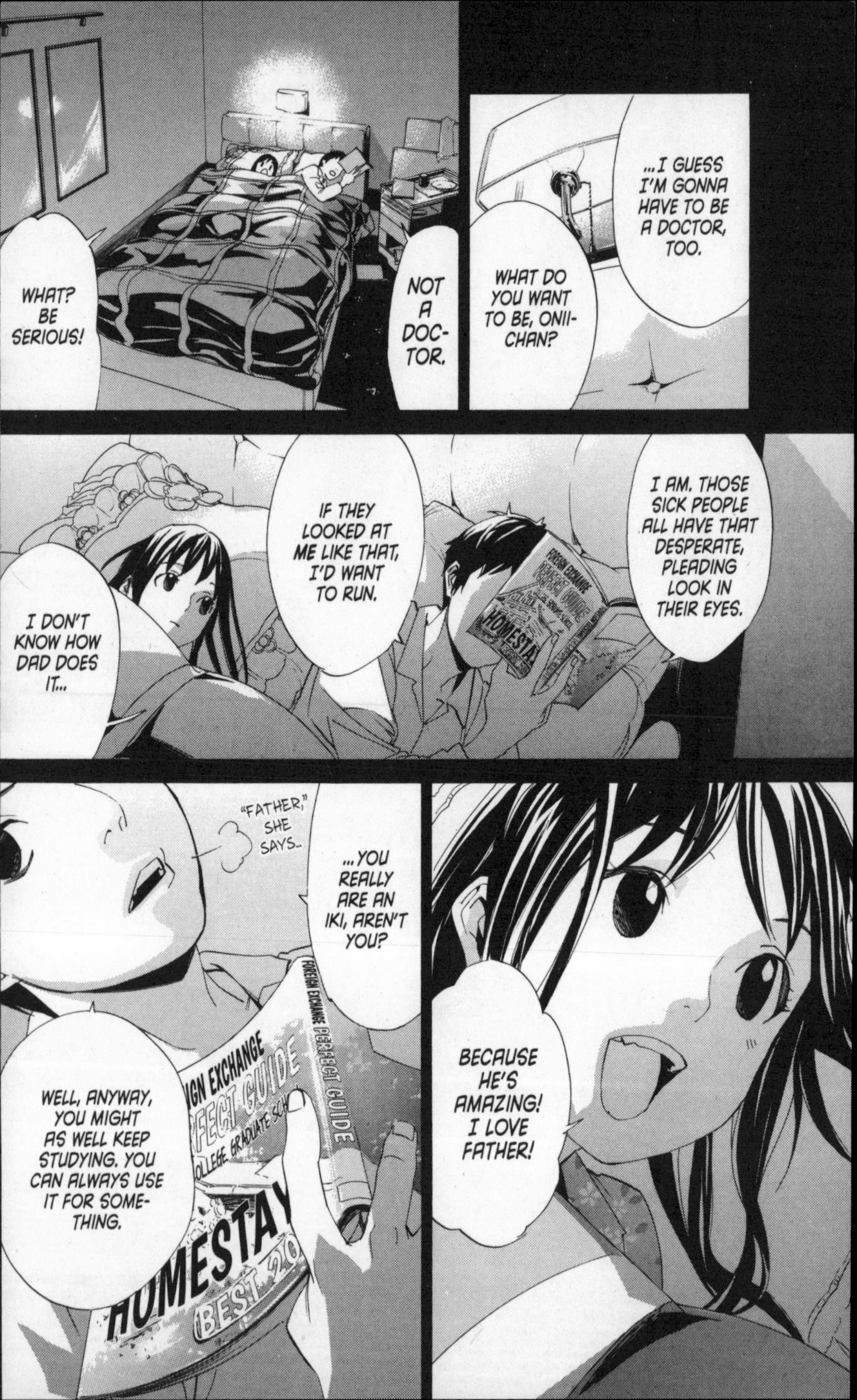
...I GUESS I'M GONNA HAVE TO BE A DOCTOR, TOO.
WHAT DO YOU WANT TO BE, ONII-CHAN?
NOT A DOCTOR.
WHAT? BE SERIOUS!
I AM. THOSE SICK PEOPLE ALL HAVE THAT DESPERATE, PLEADING LOOK IN THEIR EYES.
IF THEY LOOKED AT ME LIKE THAT, I'D WANT TO RUN.
I DON'T KNOW HOW DAD DOES IT...
BECAUSE HE'S AMAZING! I LOVE FATHER!
"FATHER," SHE SAYS...
...YOU REALLY ARE AN IKI, AREN'T YOU?
FOREIGN EXCHANGE PERFECT GUIDE
WELL, ANYWAY, YOU MIGHT AS WELL KEEP STUDYING. YOU CAN ALWAYS USE IT FOR SOMETHING.
HOMESTAY
BEST 20

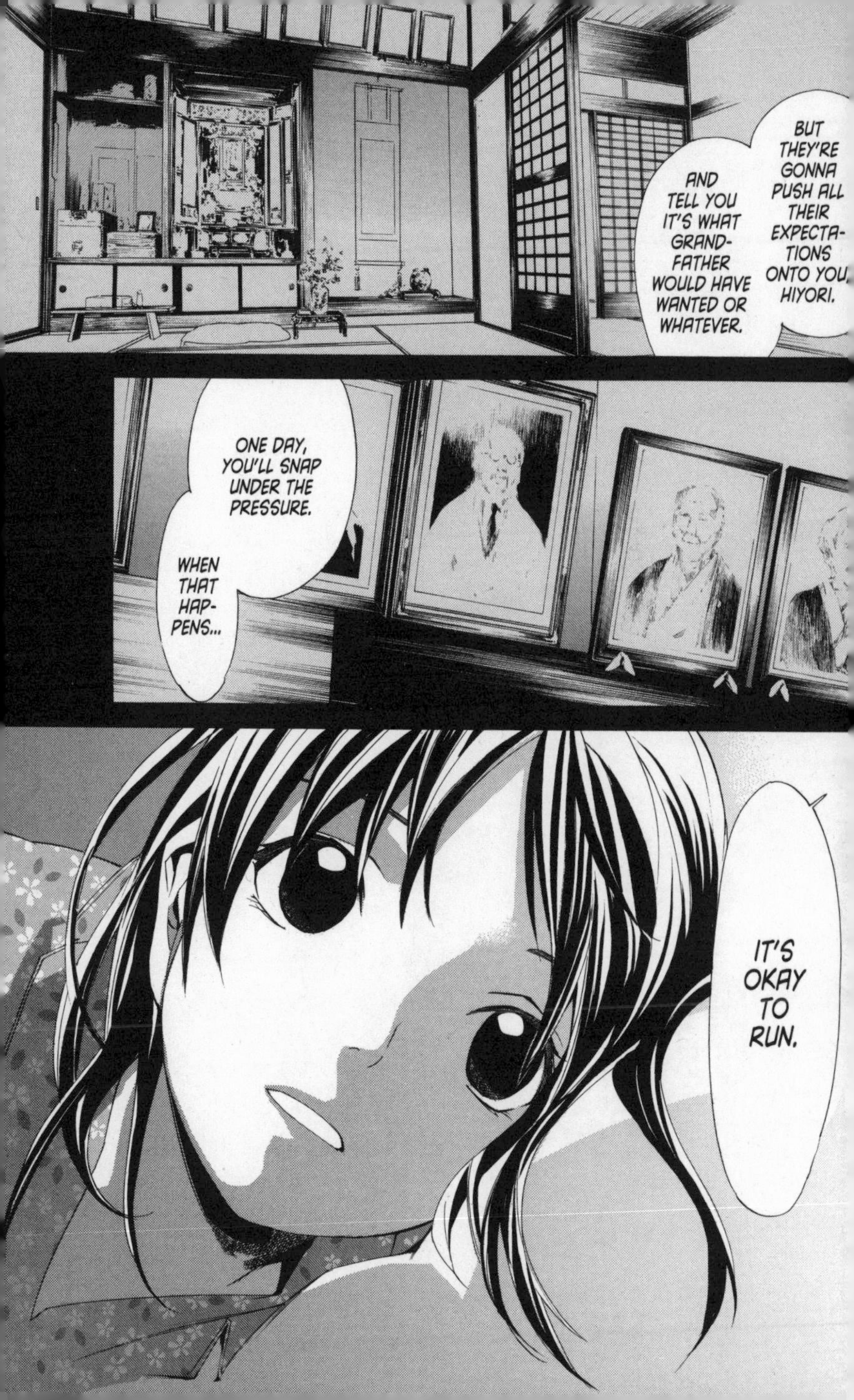
BUT THEY'RE GONNA PUSH ALL THEIR EXPECTATIONS ONTO YOU, HIYORI.
AND TELL YOU IT'S WHAT GRANDFATHER WOULD HAVE WANTED OR WHATEVER.
ONE DAY, YOU'LL SNAP UNDER THE PRESSURE.
WHEN THAT HAPPENS...
IT'S OKAY TO RUN.

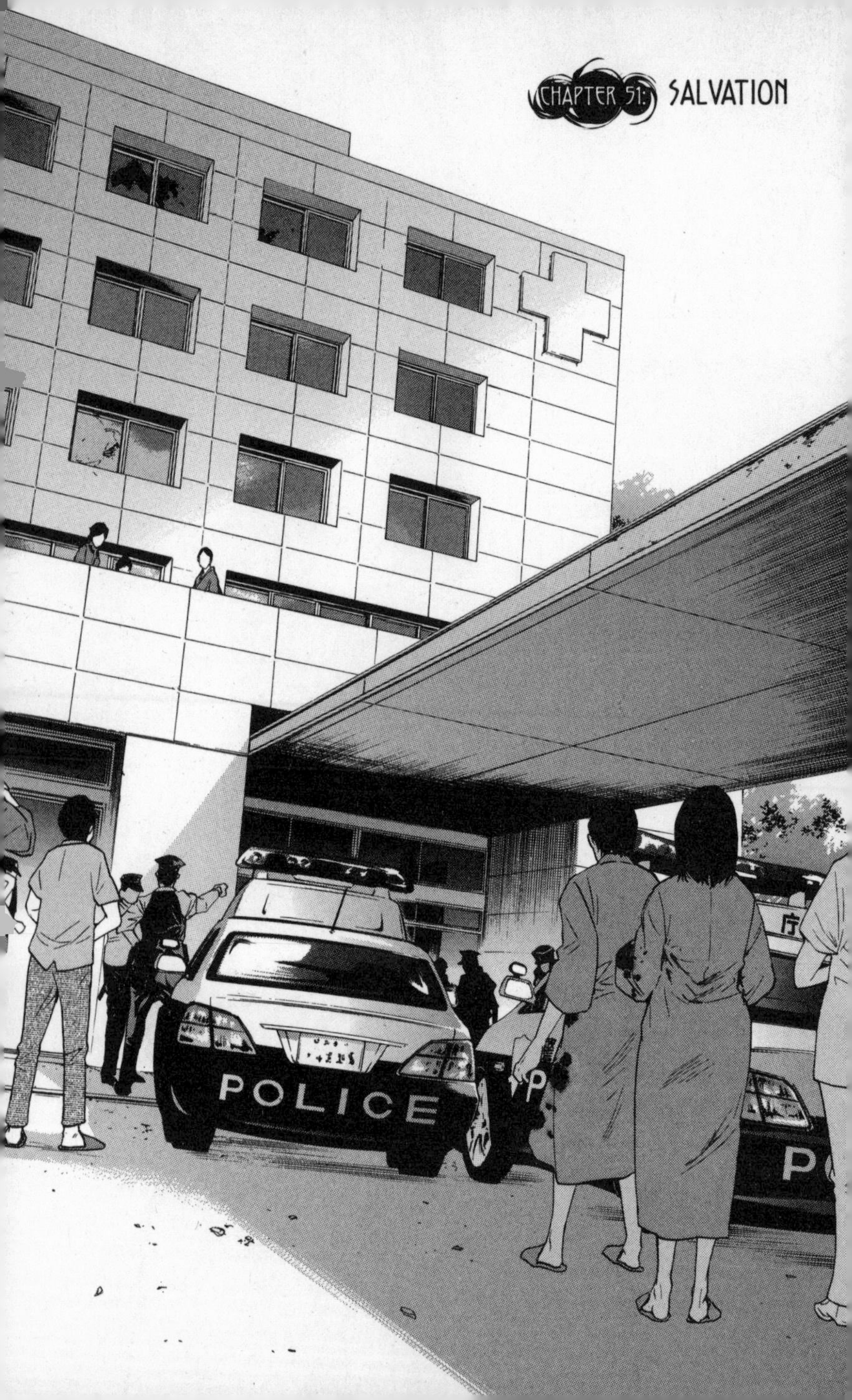
CHAPTER 51: SALVATION
POLICE

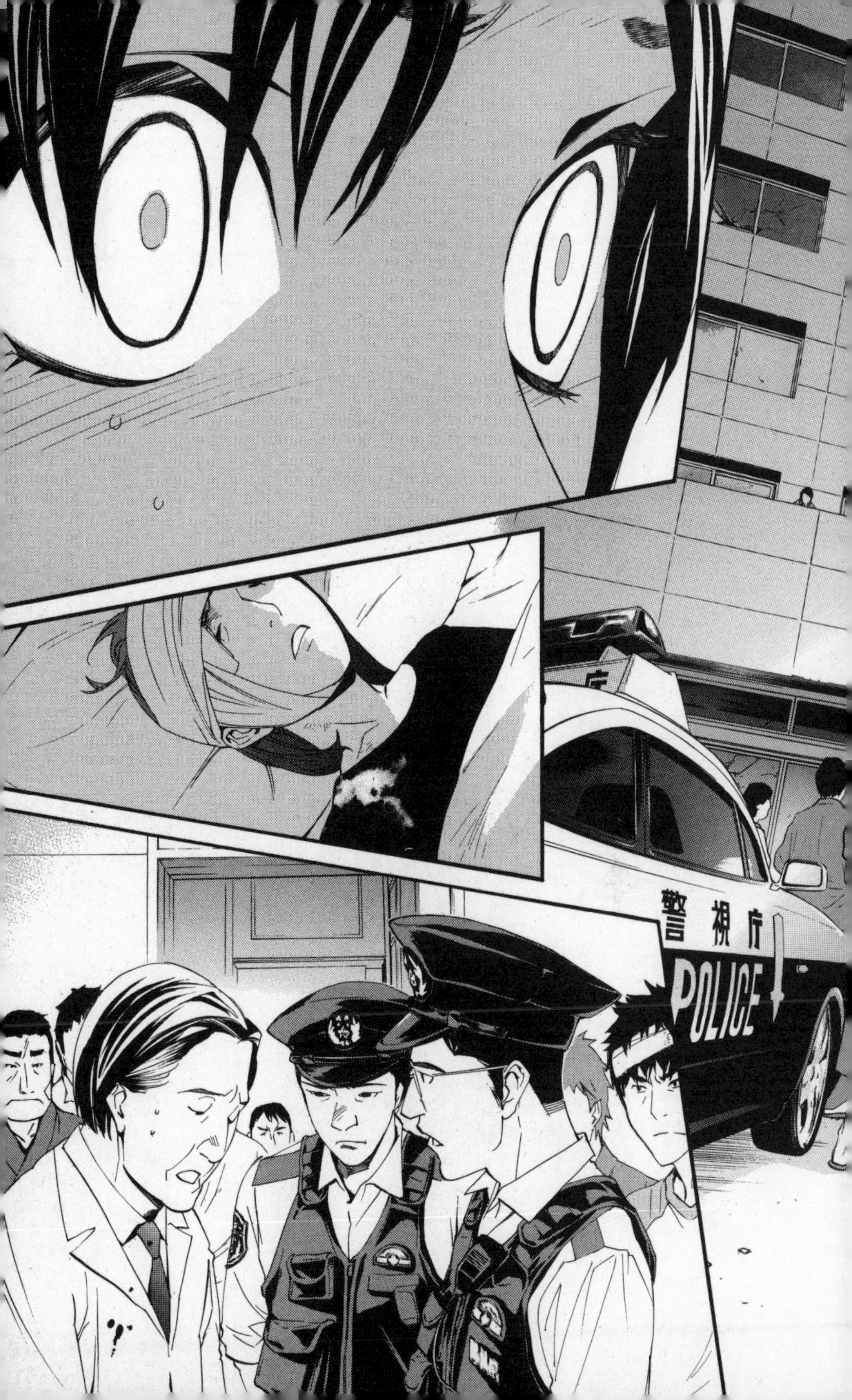
警視庁
POLICE

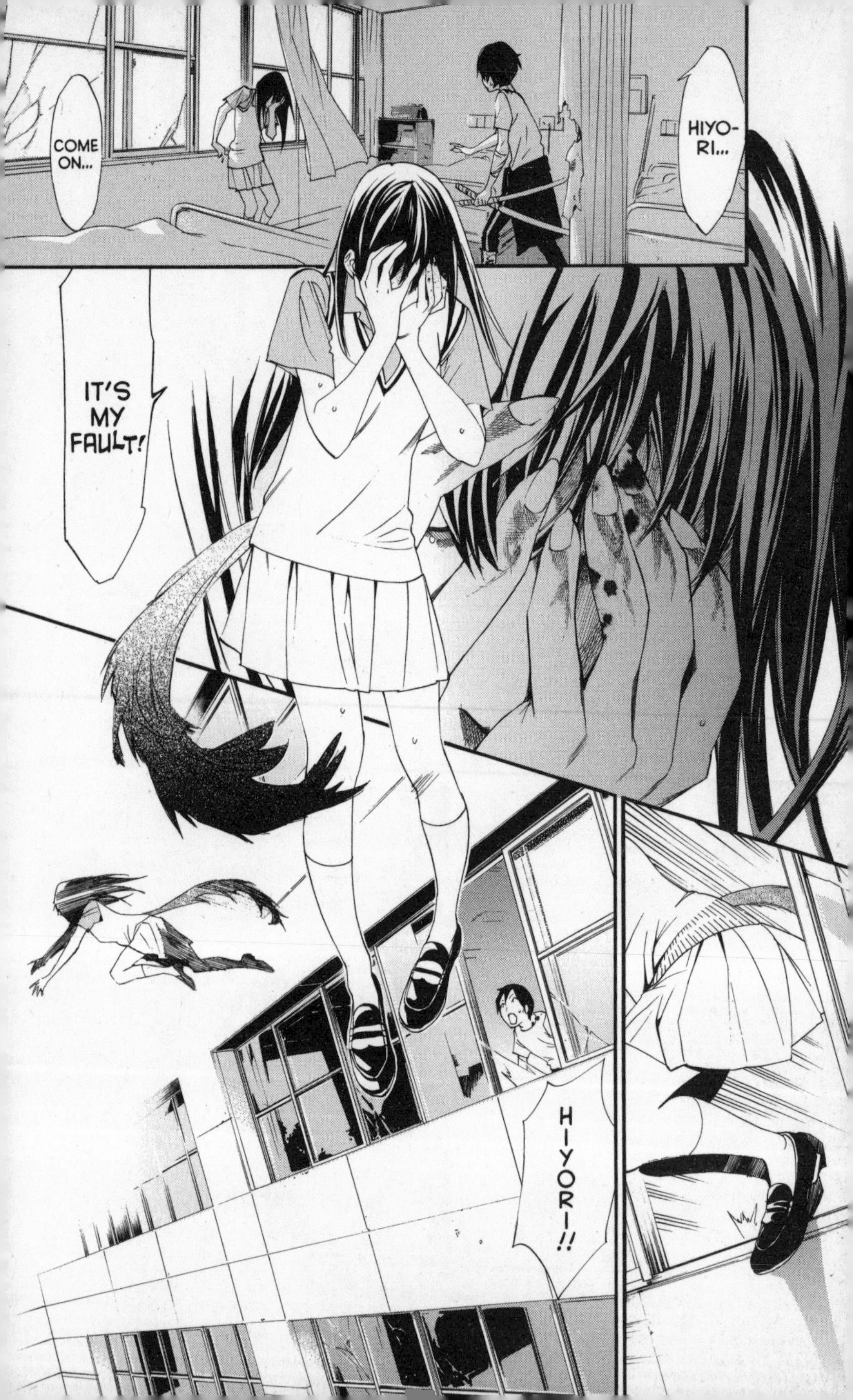
HIYO-RI...
COME ON...
IT'S MY FAULT!
HIYORI!!

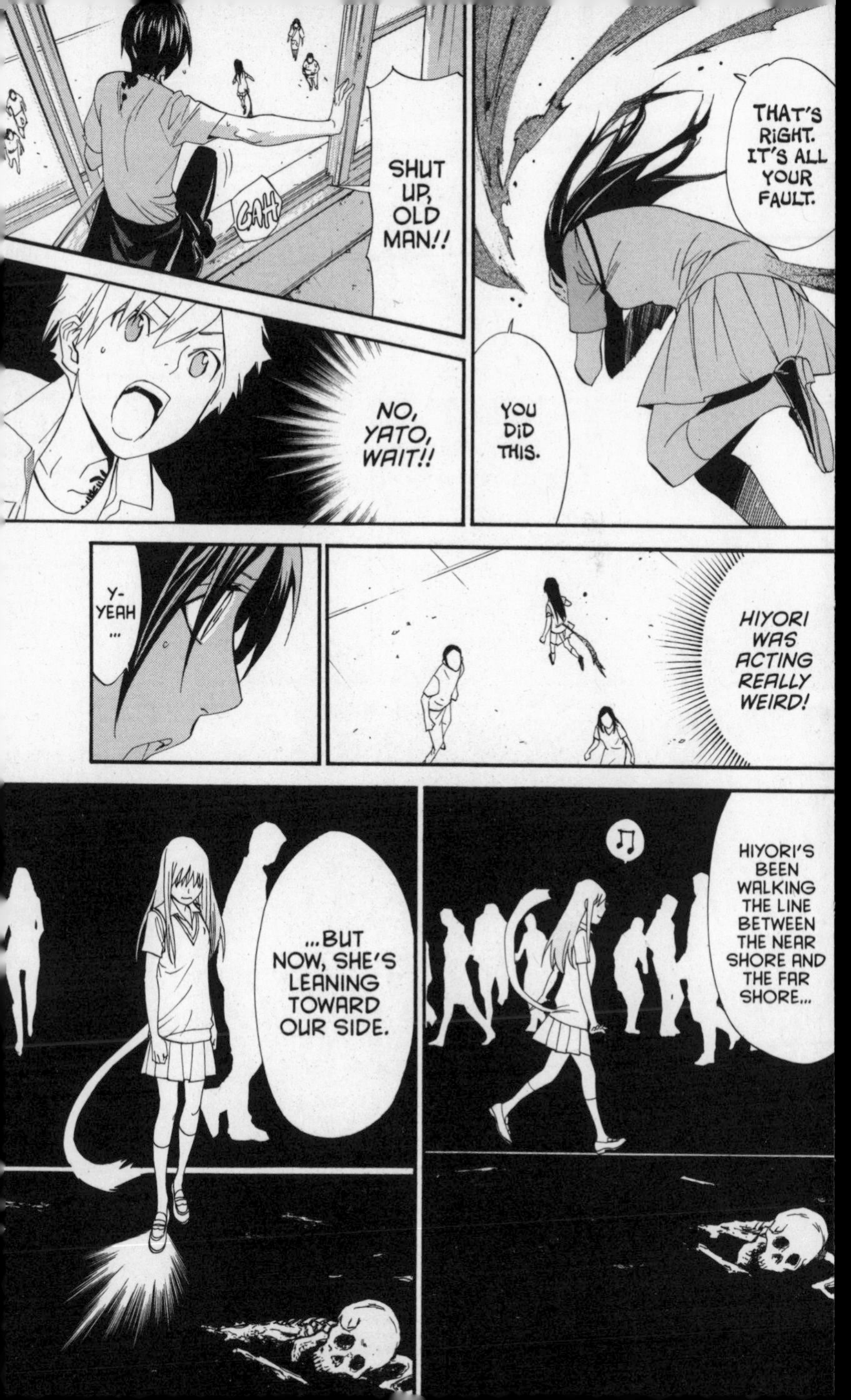
THAT'S RIGHT. IT'S ALL YOUR FAULT.
YOU DID THIS.
SHUT UP, OLD MAN!!
GAH
NO, YATO, WAIT!!
HIYORI WAS ACTING REALLY WEIRD!
Y-YEAH ...
HIYORI'S BEEN WALKING THE LINE BETWEEN THE NEAR SHORE AND THE FAR SHORE...
♫
...BUT NOW, SHE'S LEANING TOWARD OUR SIDE.

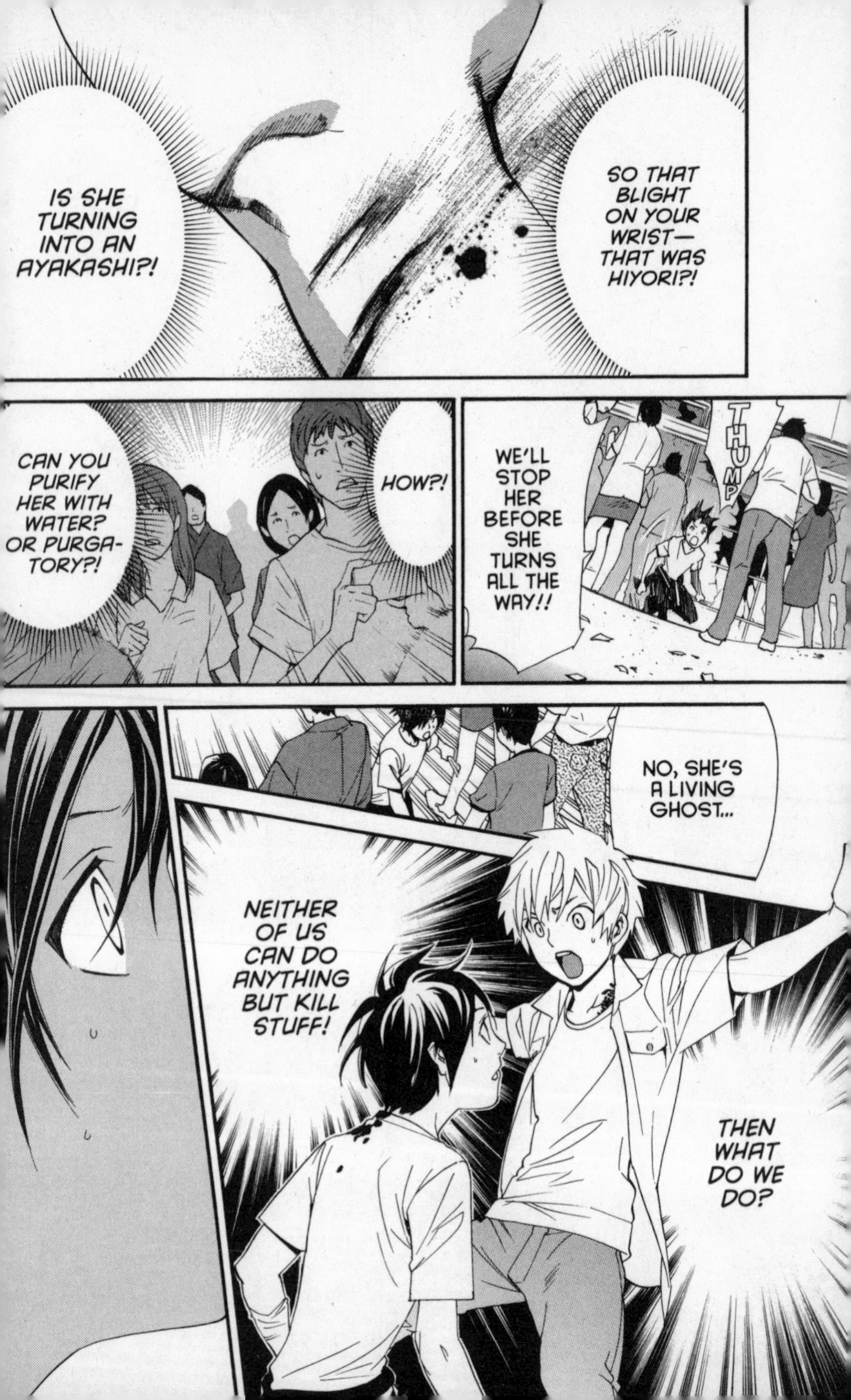
SO THAT BLIGHT ON YOUR WRIST— THAT WAS HIYORI?!
IS SHE TURNING INTO AN AYAKASHI?!
THUMP
WE'LL STOP HER BEFORE SHE TURNS ALL THE WAY!!
HOW?!
CAN YOU PURIFY HER WITH WATER? OR PURGA-TORY?!
NO, SHE'S A LIVING GHOST...
NEITHER OF US CAN DO ANYTHING BUT KILL STUFF!
THEN WHAT DO WE DO?

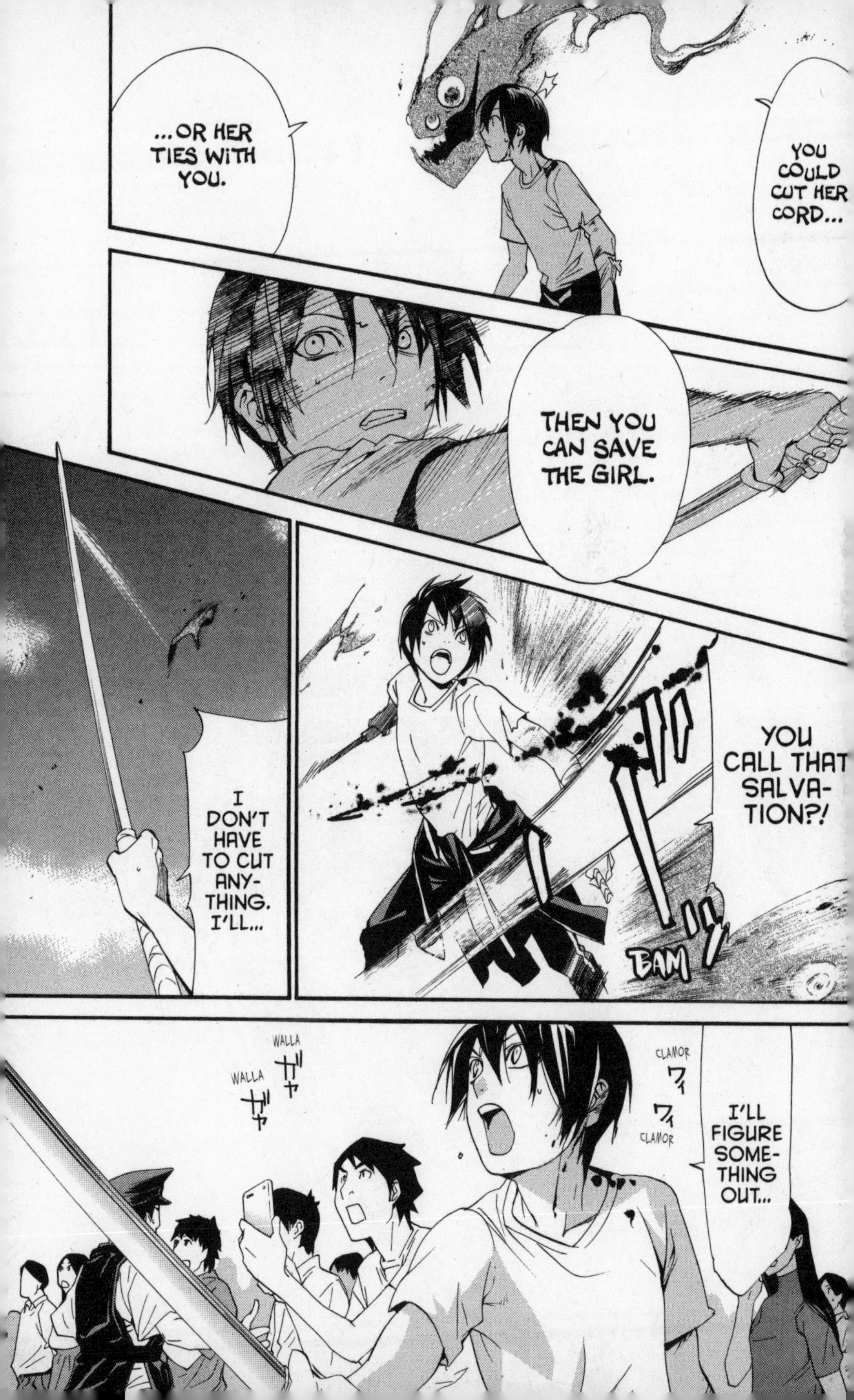
YOU COULD CUT HER CORD...
...OR HER TIES WITH YOU.
THEN YOU CAN SAVE THE GIRL.
YOU CALL THAT SALVATION?!
BAM
I DON'T HAVE TO CUT ANYTHING. I'LL...
CLAMOR ワィ
ワィ CLAMOR
I'LL FIGURE SOMETHING OUT...
WALLA ガヤ
WALLA ガヤ

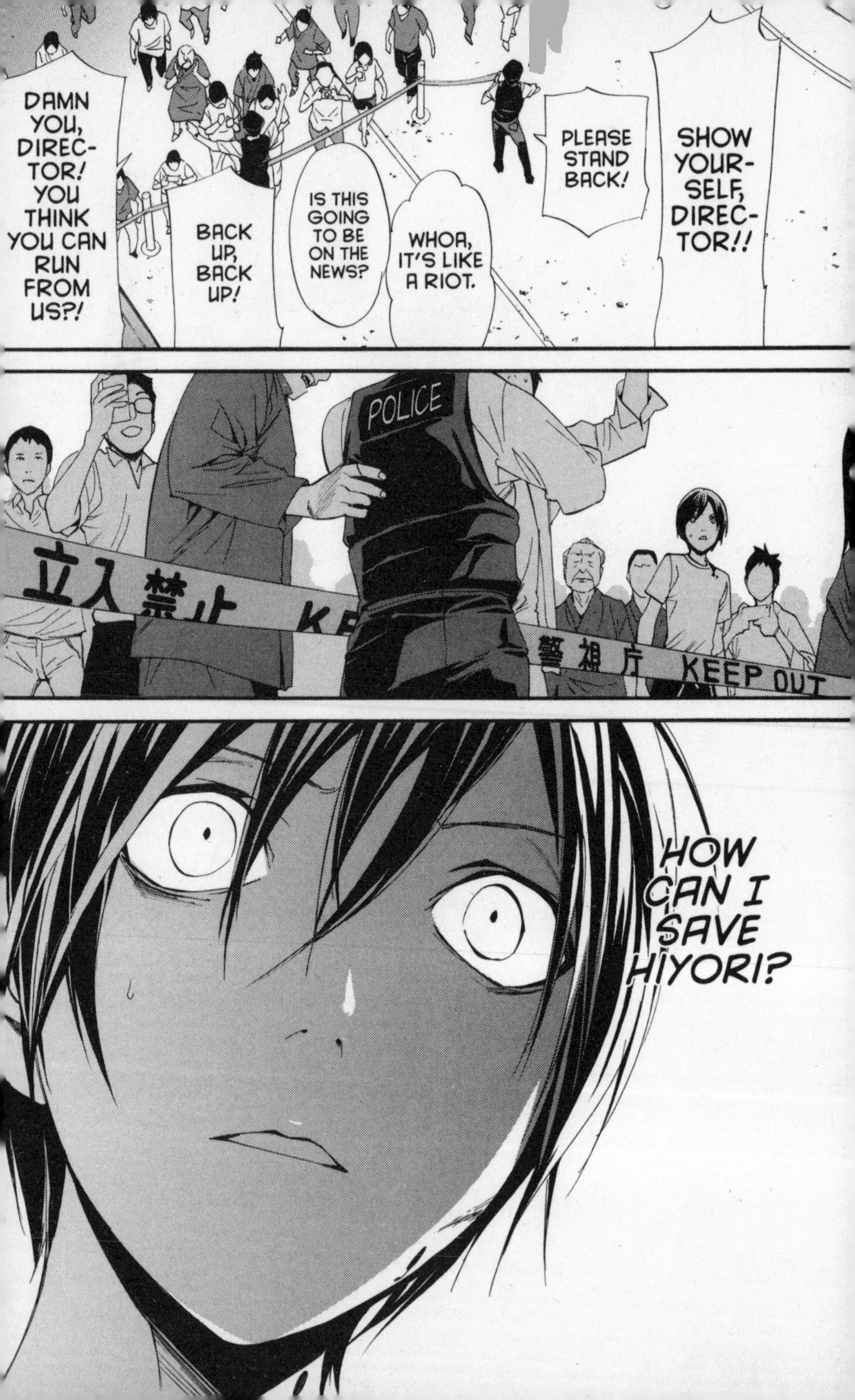
SHOW YOURSELF, DIRECTOR!!
PLEASE STAND BACK!
WHOA, IT'S LIKE A RIOT.
IS THIS GOING TO BE ON THE NEWS?
BACK UP, BACK UP!
DAMN YOU, DIRECTOR! YOU THINK YOU CAN RUN FROM US?!
POLICE
立入禁止
警視庁 KEEP OUT
HOW CAN I SAVE HIYORI?

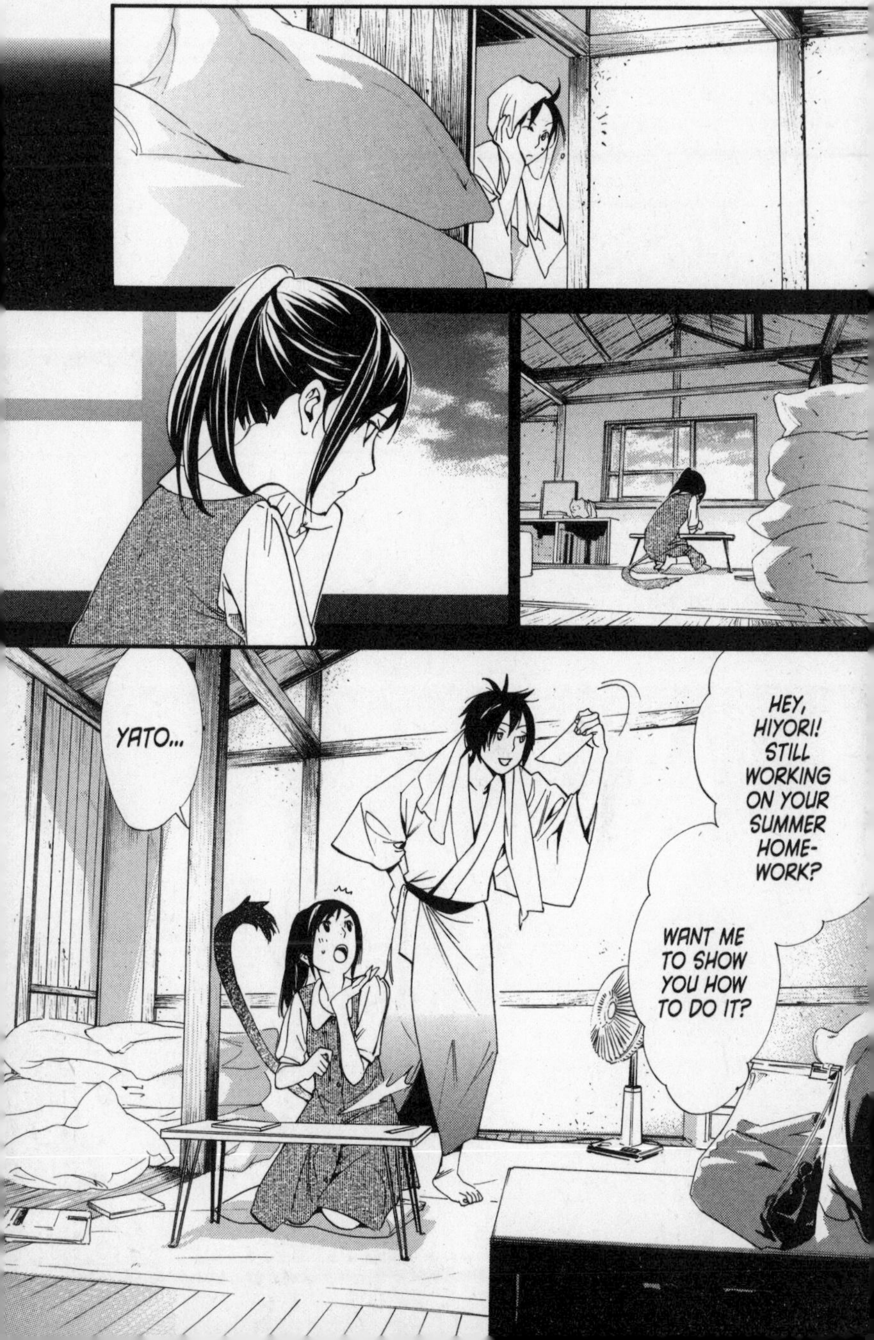
HEY, HIYORI! STILL WORKING ON YOUR SUMMER HOME-WORK?
WANT ME TO SHOW YOU HOW TO DO IT?
YATO...

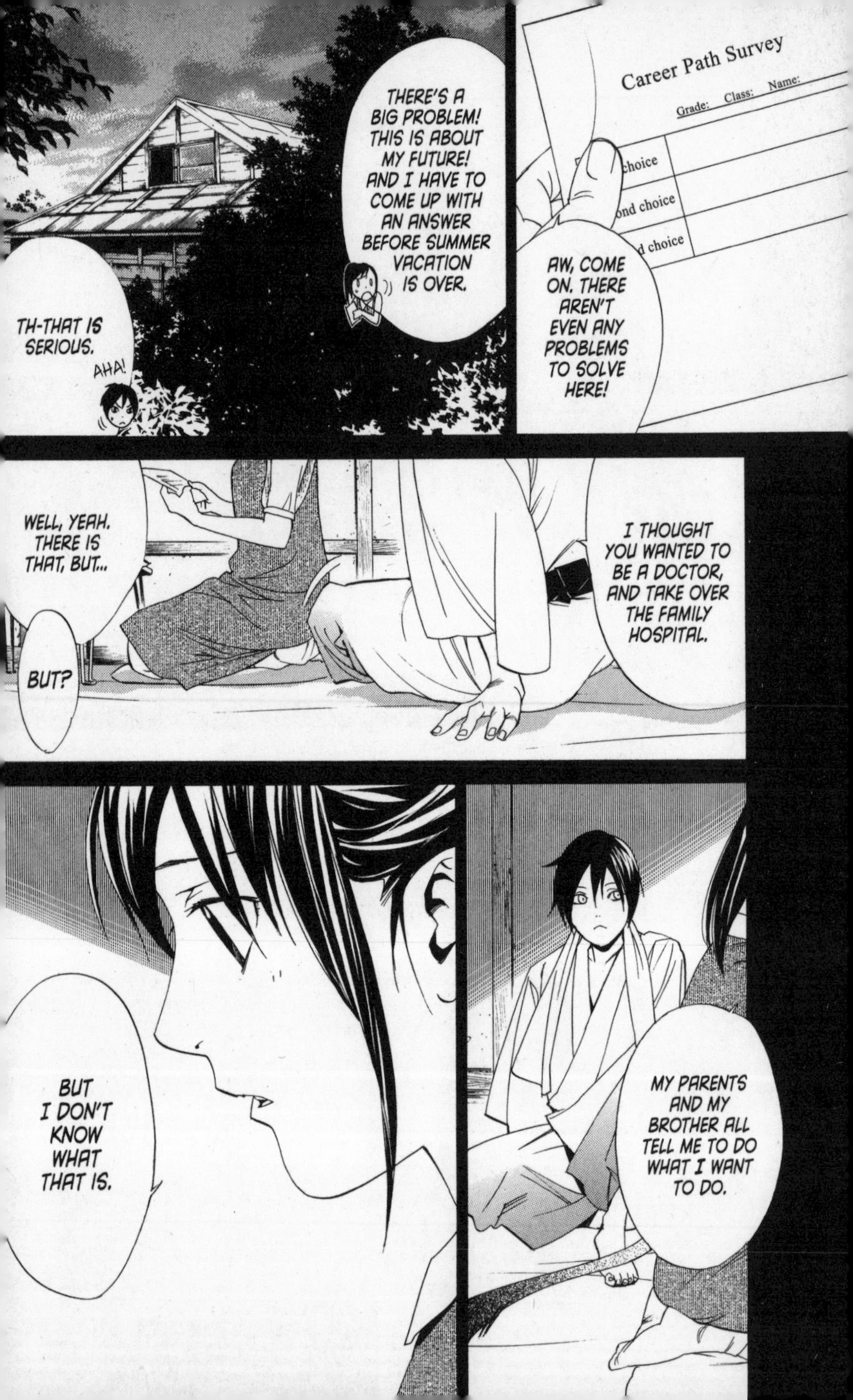
Career Path Survey
Grade: Class: Name:
choice
ond choice
d choice
AW, COME ON. THERE AREN'T EVEN ANY PROBLEMS TO SOLVE HERE!
THERE'S A BIG PROBLEM! THIS IS ABOUT MY FUTURE! AND I HAVE TO COME UP WITH AN ANSWER BEFORE SUMMER VACATION IS OVER.
TH-THAT IS SERIOUS.
AHA!
I THOUGHT YOU WANTED TO BE A DOCTOR, AND TAKE OVER THE FAMILY HOSPITAL.
WELL, YEAH. THERE IS THAT, BUT...
BUT?
MY PARENTS AND MY BROTHER ALL TELL ME TO DO WHAT I WANT TO DO.
BUT I DON'T KNOW WHAT THAT IS.

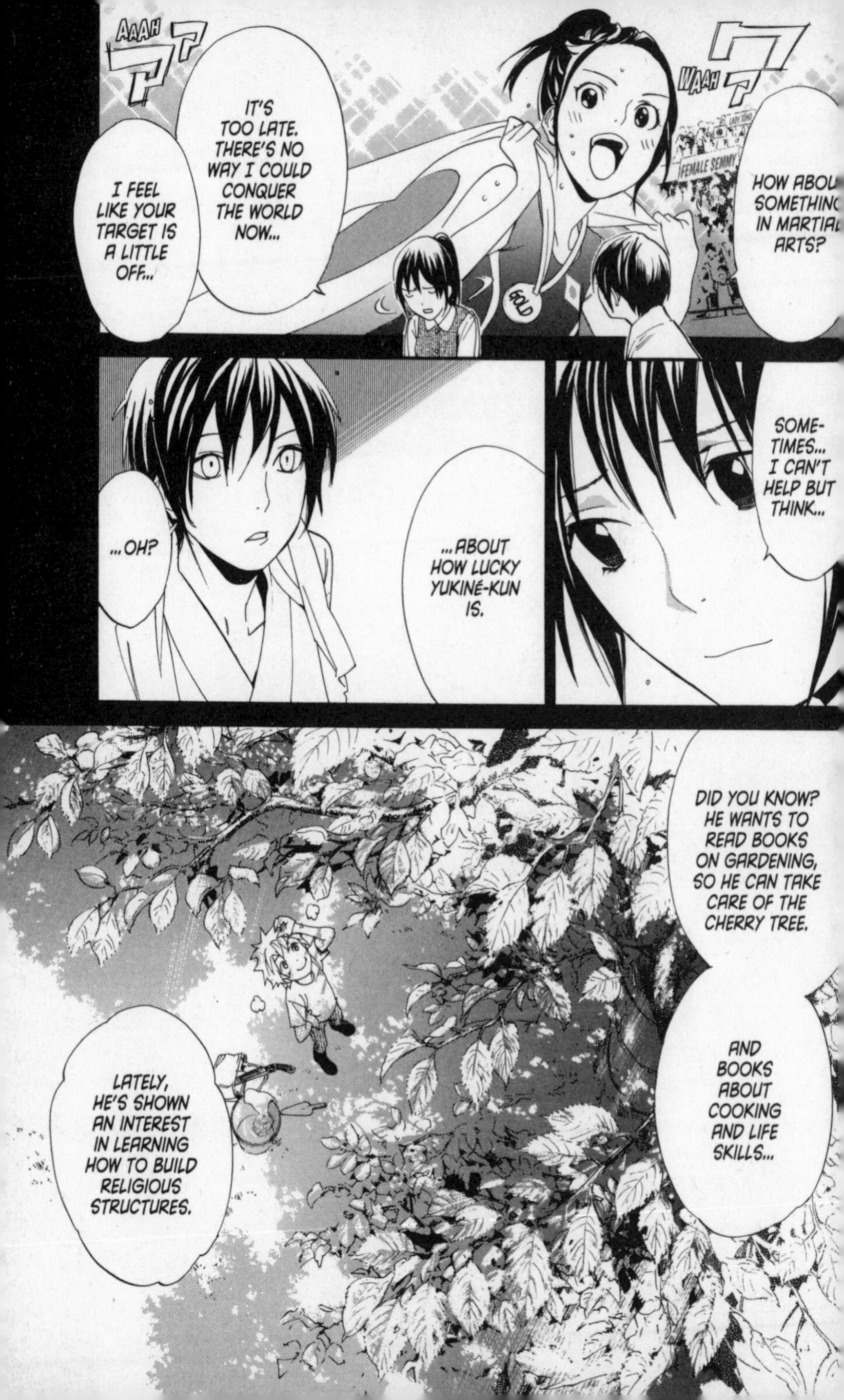
WAAH
HOW ABOU SOMETHING IN MARTIAL ARTS?
FEMALE SEMMY
GOLD
IT'S TOO LATE. THERE'S NO WAY I COULD CONQUER THE WORLD NOW...
I FEEL LIKE YOUR TARGET IS A LITTLE OFF...
AAAH
SOME-TIMES... I CAN'T HELP BUT THINK...
...ABOUT HOW LUCKY YUKINÉ-KUN IS.
...OH?
DID YOU KNOW? HE WANTS TO READ BOOKS ON GARDENING, SO HE CAN TAKE CARE OF THE CHERRY TREE.
AND BOOKS ABOUT COOKING AND LIFE SKILLS...
LATELY, HE'S SHOWN AN INTEREST IN LEARNING HOW TO BUILD RELIGIOUS STRUCTURES.

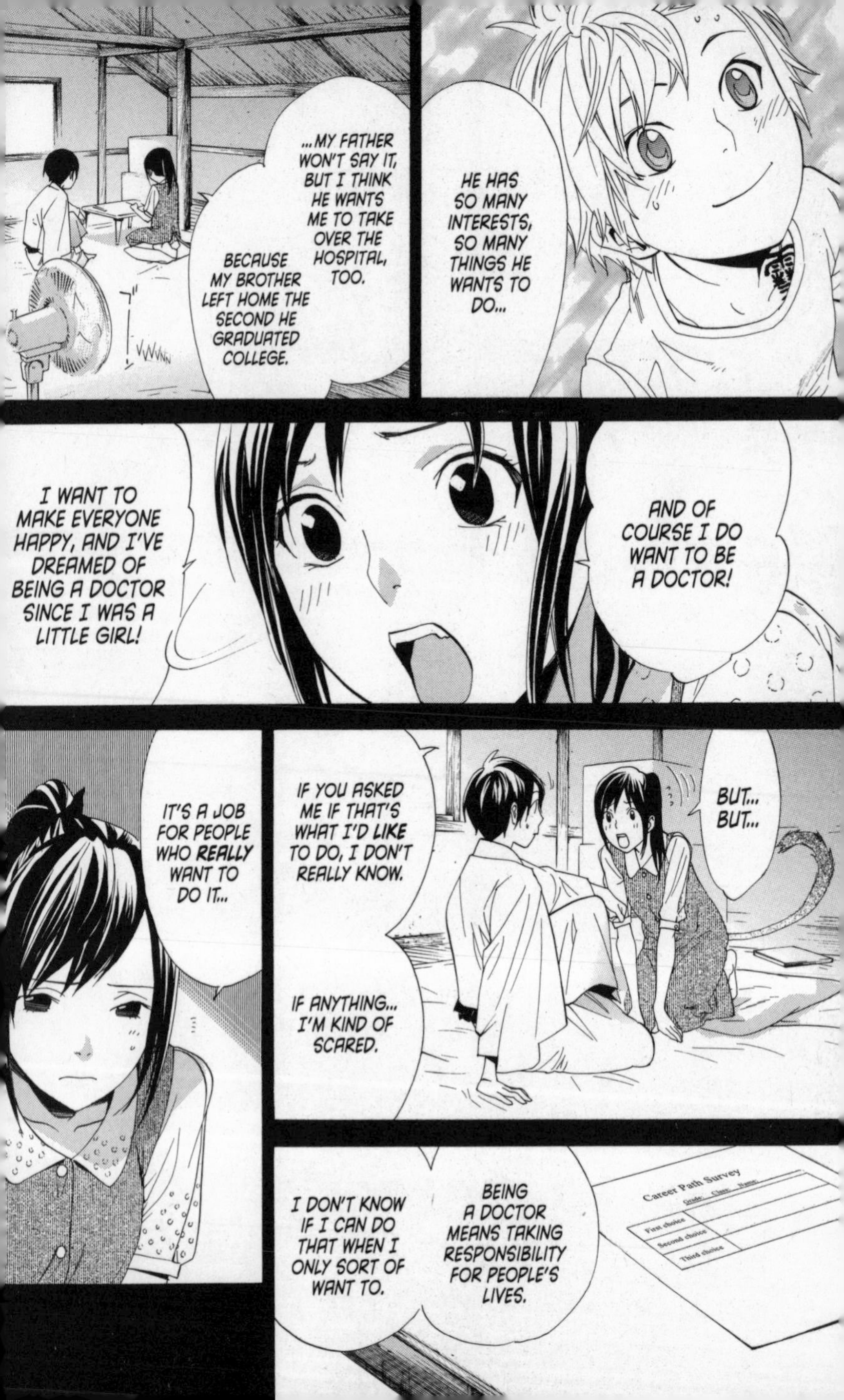
HE HAS SO MANY INTERESTS, SO MANY THINGS HE WANTS TO DO...
...MY FATHER WON'T SAY IT, BUT I THINK HE WANTS ME TO TAKE OVER THE HOSPITAL, TOO.
BECAUSE MY BROTHER LEFT HOME THE SECOND HE GRADUATED COLLEGE.
VWVNN
AND OF COURSE I DO WANT TO BE A DOCTOR!
I WANT TO MAKE EVERYONE HAPPY, AND I'VE DREAMED OF BEING A DOCTOR SINCE I WAS A LITTLE GIRL!
BUT... BUT...
IF YOU ASKED ME IF THAT'S WHAT I'D **LIKE** TO DO, I DON'T REALLY KNOW.
IF ANYTHING... I'M KIND OF SCARED.
BEING A DOCTOR MEANS TAKING RESPONSIBILITY FOR PEOPLE'S LIVES.
I DON'T KNOW IF I CAN DO THAT WHEN I ONLY SORT OF WANT TO.
Career Path Survey
Grade: Class: Name:
First choice
Second choice
Third choice
IT'S A JOB FOR PEOPLE WHO **REALLY** WANT TO DO IT...

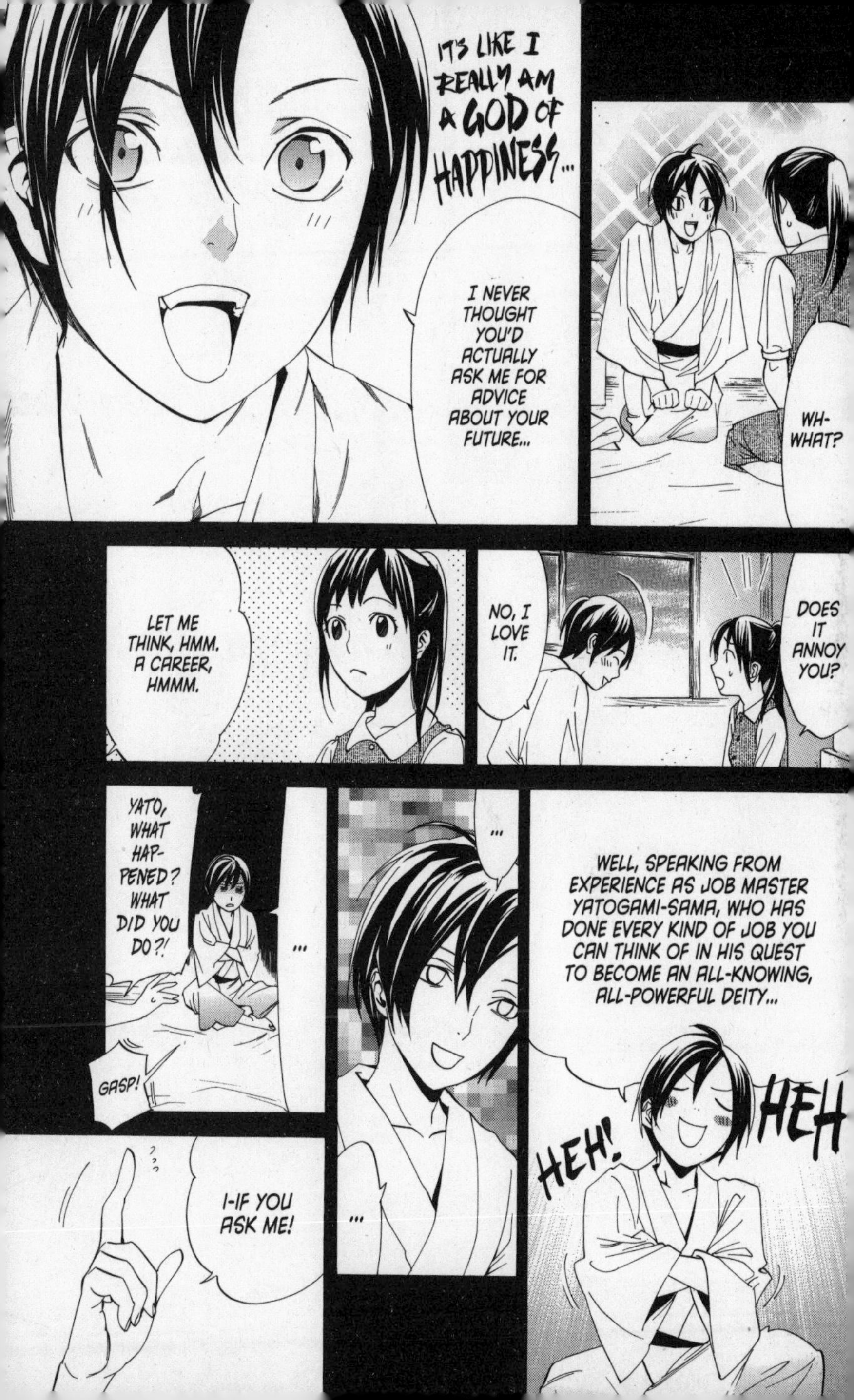
WH-WHAT?
IT'S LIKE I REALLY AM A GOD OF HAPPINESS...
I NEVER THOUGHT YOU'D ACTUALLY ASK ME FOR ADVICE ABOUT YOUR FUTURE...
DOES IT ANNOY YOU?
NO, I LOVE IT.
LET ME THINK, HMM. A CAREER, HMMM.
WELL, SPEAKING FROM EXPERIENCE AS JOB MASTER YATOGAMI-SAMA, WHO HAS DONE EVERY KIND OF JOB YOU CAN THINK OF IN HIS QUEST TO BECOME AN ALL-KNOWING, ALL-POWERFUL DEITY...
HEH
HEH!
...
...
YATO, WHAT HAP-PENED? WHAT DID YOU DO?!
...
GASP!
I-IF YOU ASK ME!

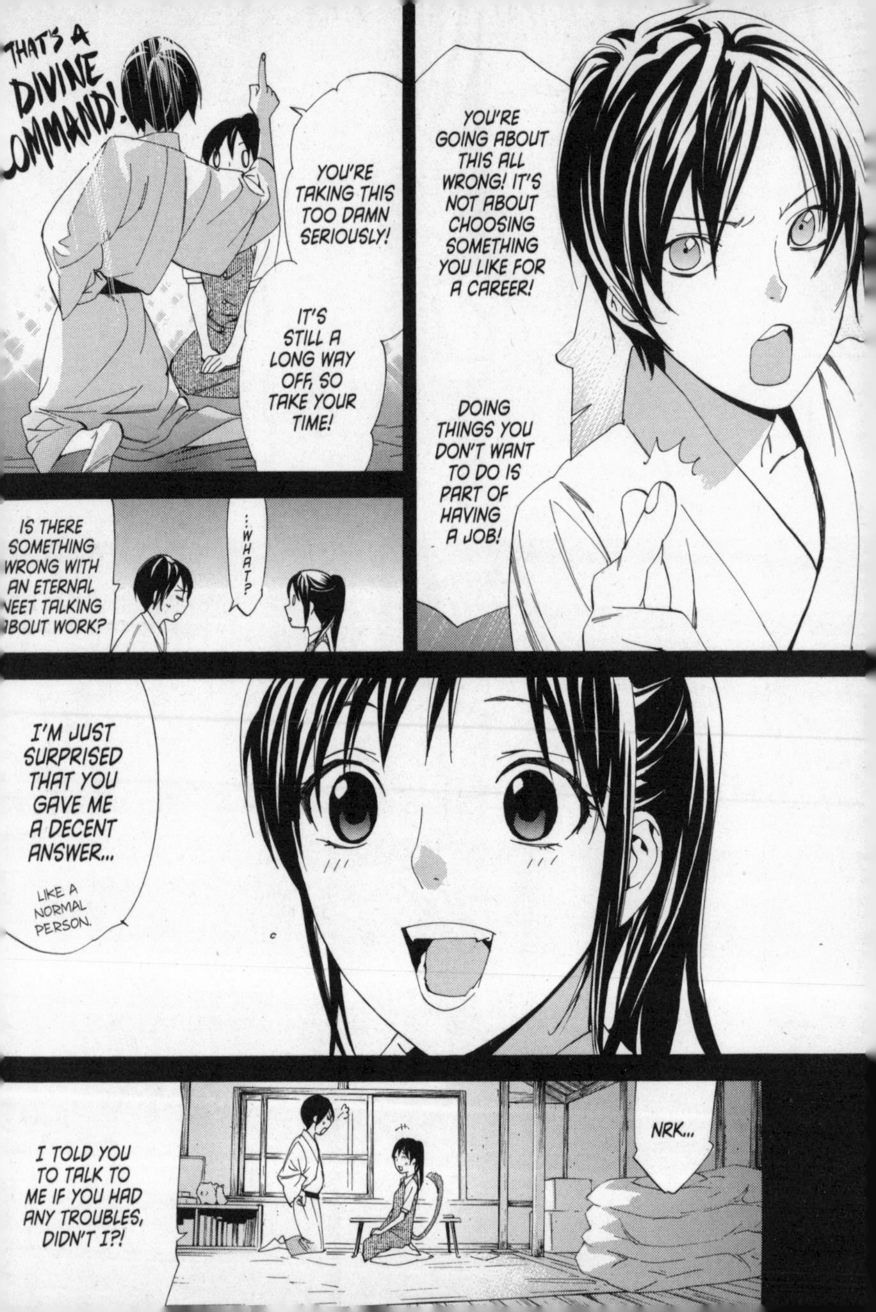
YOU'RE GOING ABOUT THIS ALL WRONG! IT'S NOT ABOUT CHOOSING SOMETHING YOU LIKE FOR A CAREER!
DOING THINGS YOU DON'T WANT TO DO IS PART OF HAVING A JOB!
YOU'RE TAKING THIS TOO DAMN SERIOUSLY!
IT'S STILL A LONG WAY OFF, SO TAKE YOUR TIME!
THAT'S A DIVINE COMMAND!
...WHAT?
IS THERE SOMETHING WRONG WITH AN ETERNAL NEET TALKING ABOUT WORK?
I'M JUST SURPRISED THAT YOU GAVE ME A DECENT ANSWER...
LIKE A NORMAL PERSON.
NRK...
I TOLD YOU TO TALK TO ME IF YOU HAD ANY TROUBLES, DIDN'T I?!

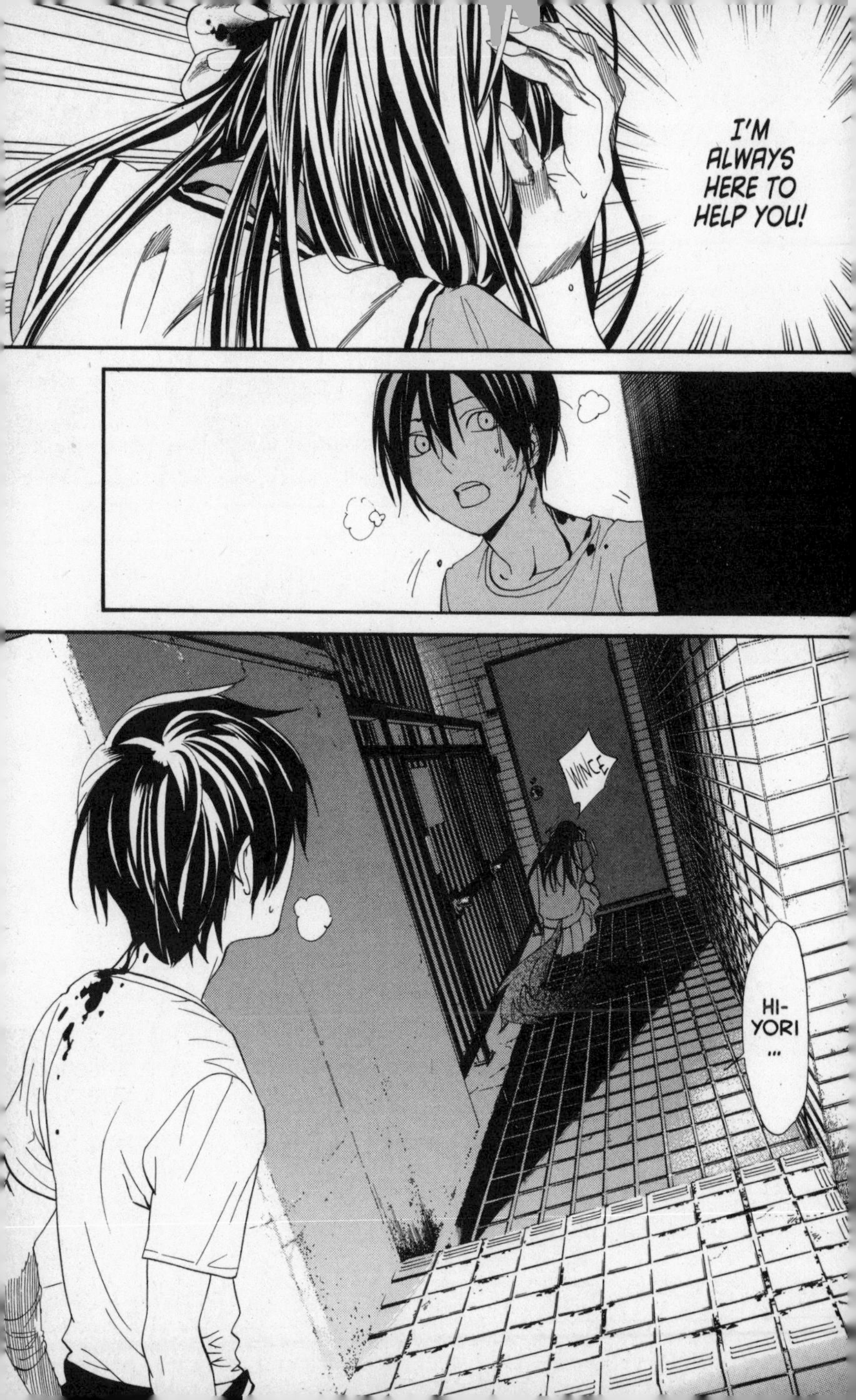
I'M ALWAYS HERE TO HELP YOU!
HI-YORI ...
WINCE

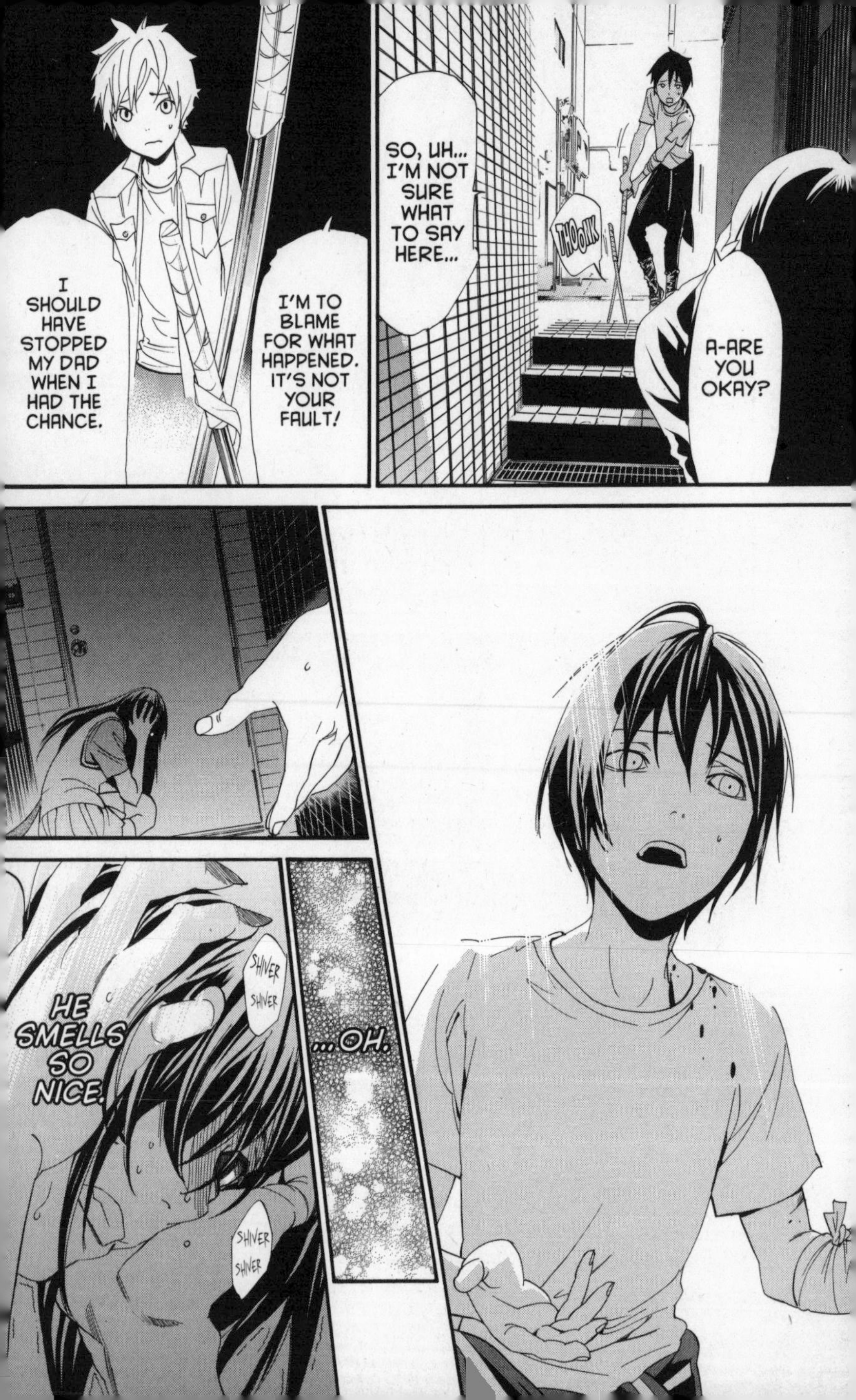
A-ARE YOU OKAY?
THOOK
SO, UH... I'M NOT SURE WHAT TO SAY HERE...
I'M TO BLAME FOR WHAT HAPPENED. IT'S NOT YOUR FAULT!
I SHOULD HAVE STOPPED MY DAD WHEN I HAD THE CHANCE.
...OH.
SHIVER SHIVER
HE SMELLS SO NICE.
SHIVER SHIVER

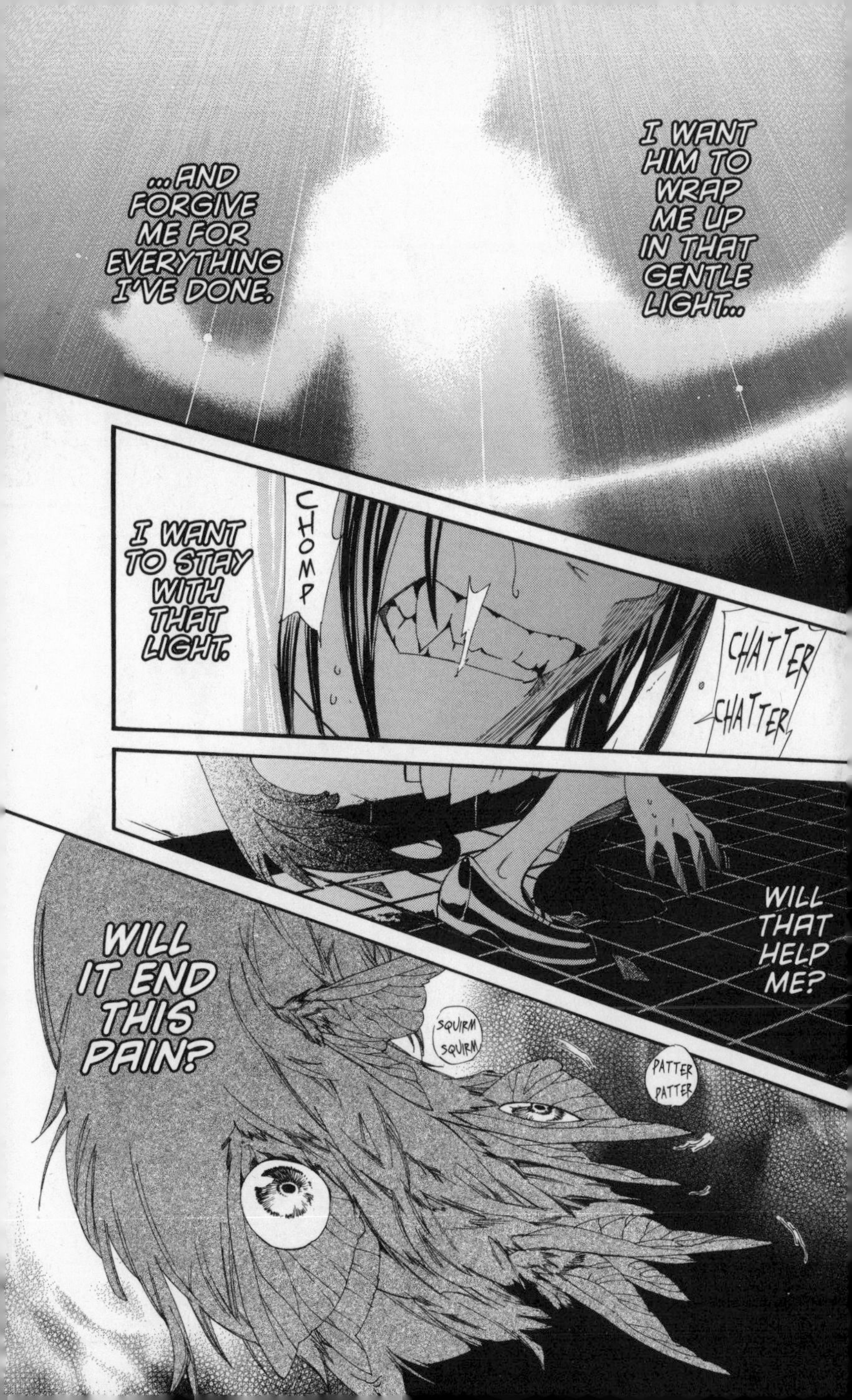
I WANT HIM TO WRAP ME UP IN THAT GENTLE LIGHT...
...AND FORGIVE ME FOR EVERYTHING I'VE DONE.
CHATTER CHATTER
CHOMP
I WANT TO STAY WITH THAT LIGHT.
WILL THAT HELP ME?
WILL IT END THIS PAIN?
PATTER PATTER
SQUIRM SQUIRM

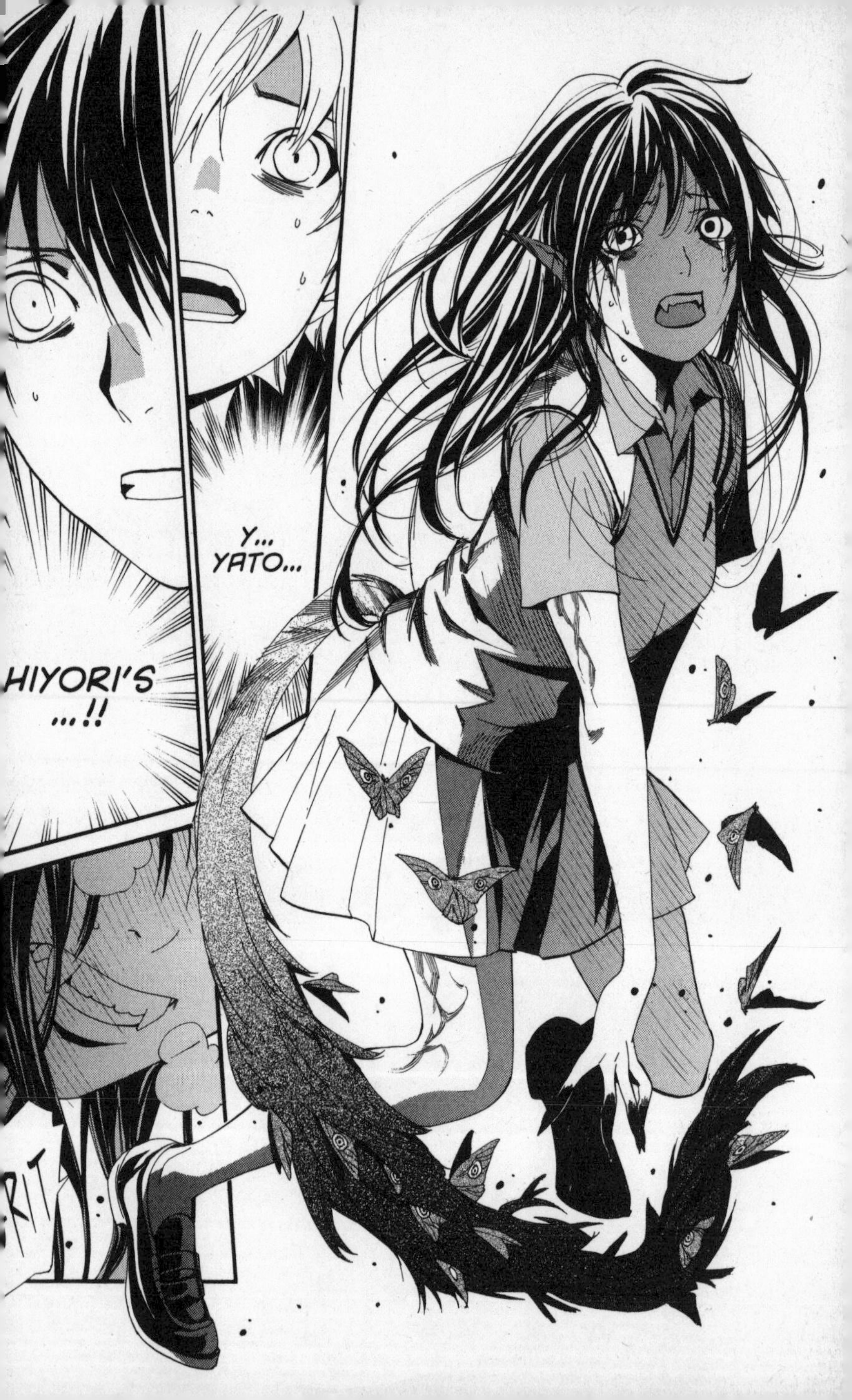
Y... YATO...
HIYORI'S ...!!
RIT

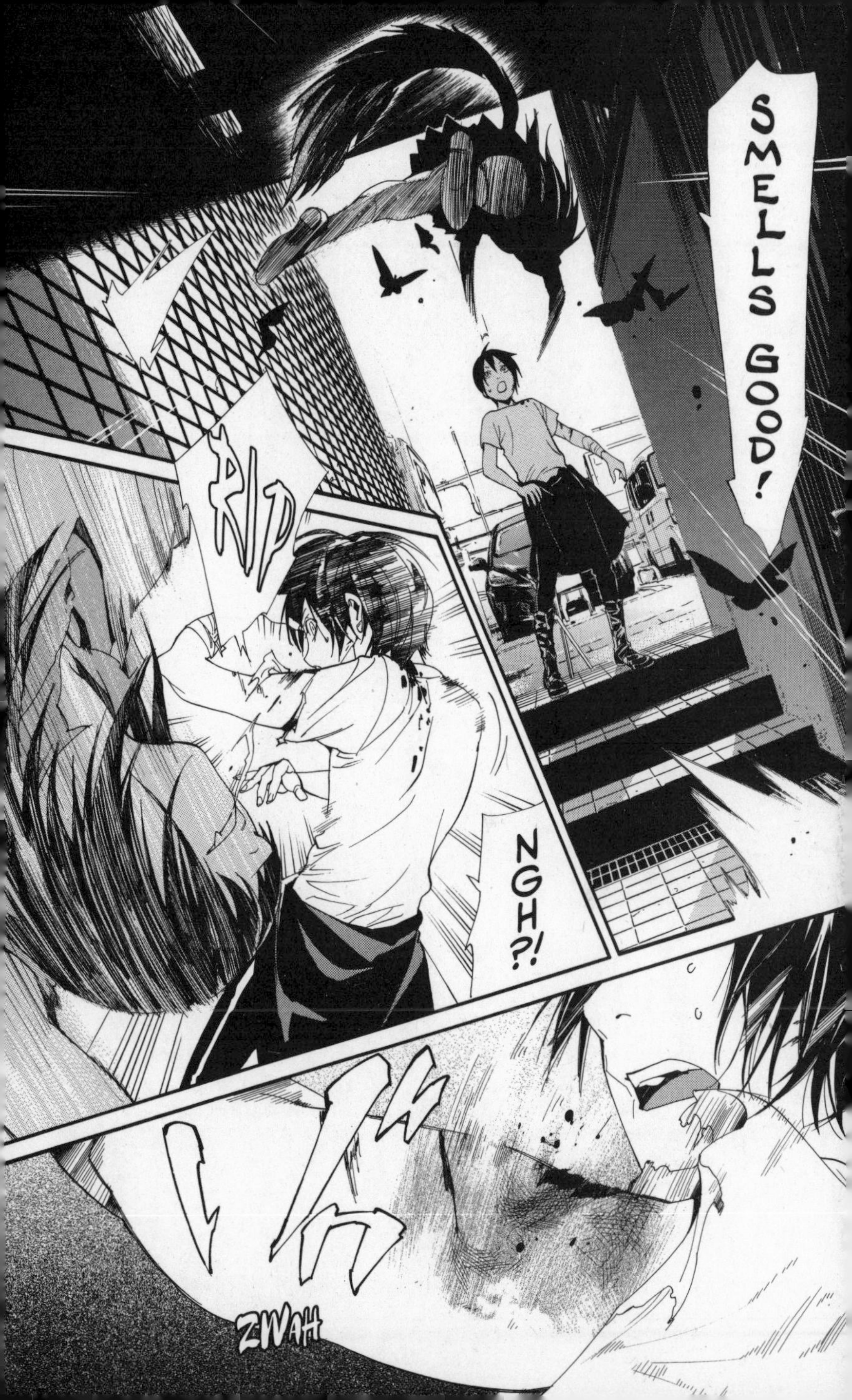
SMELLS GOOD!
RIP
NGH?!
ZWAH

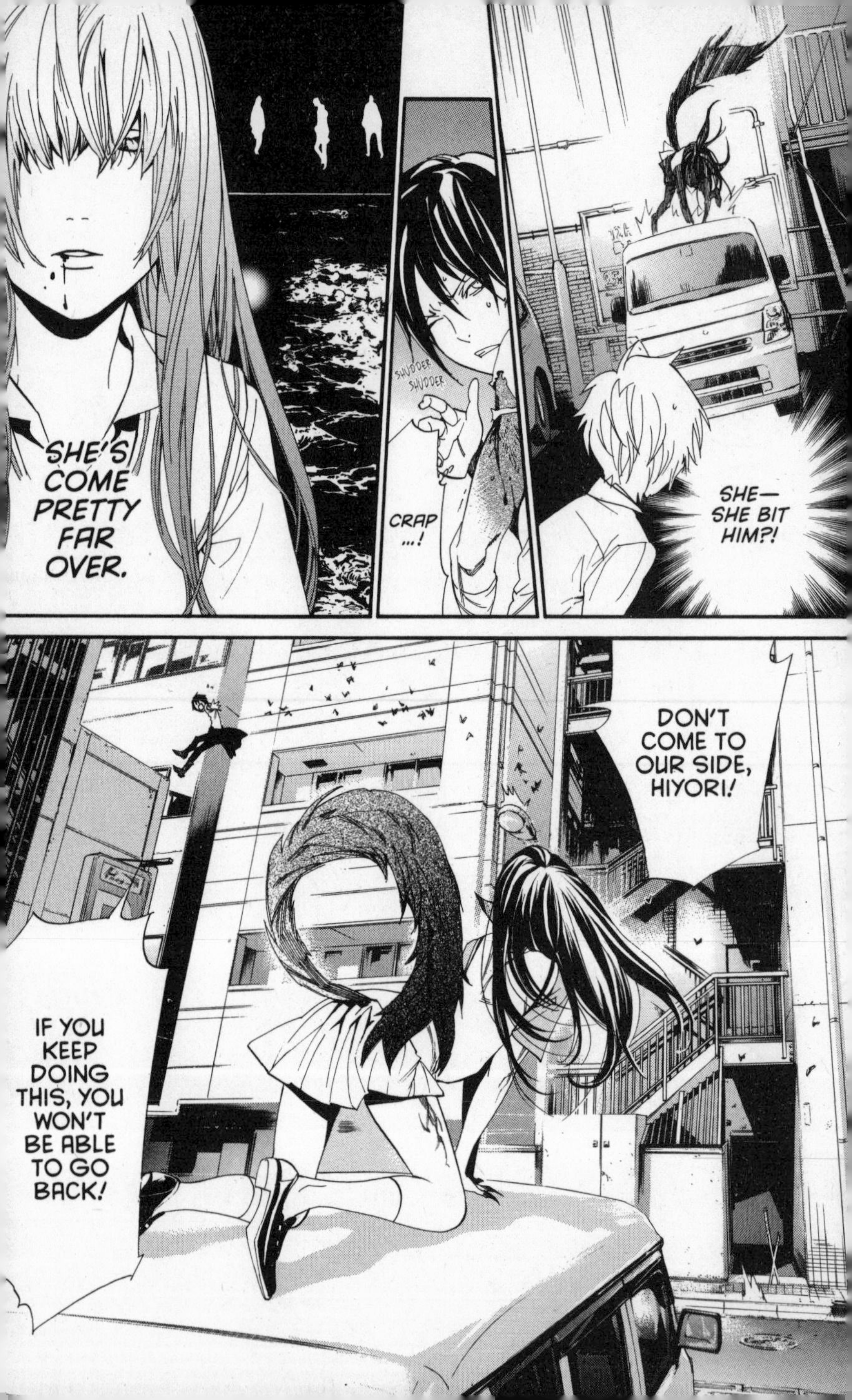
SHE— SHE BIT HIM?!
SHUDDER SHUDDER
CRAP ...!
SHE'S COME PRETTY FAR OVER.
DON'T COME TO OUR SIDE, HIYORI!
IF YOU KEEP DOING THIS, YOU WON'T BE ABLE TO GO BACK!

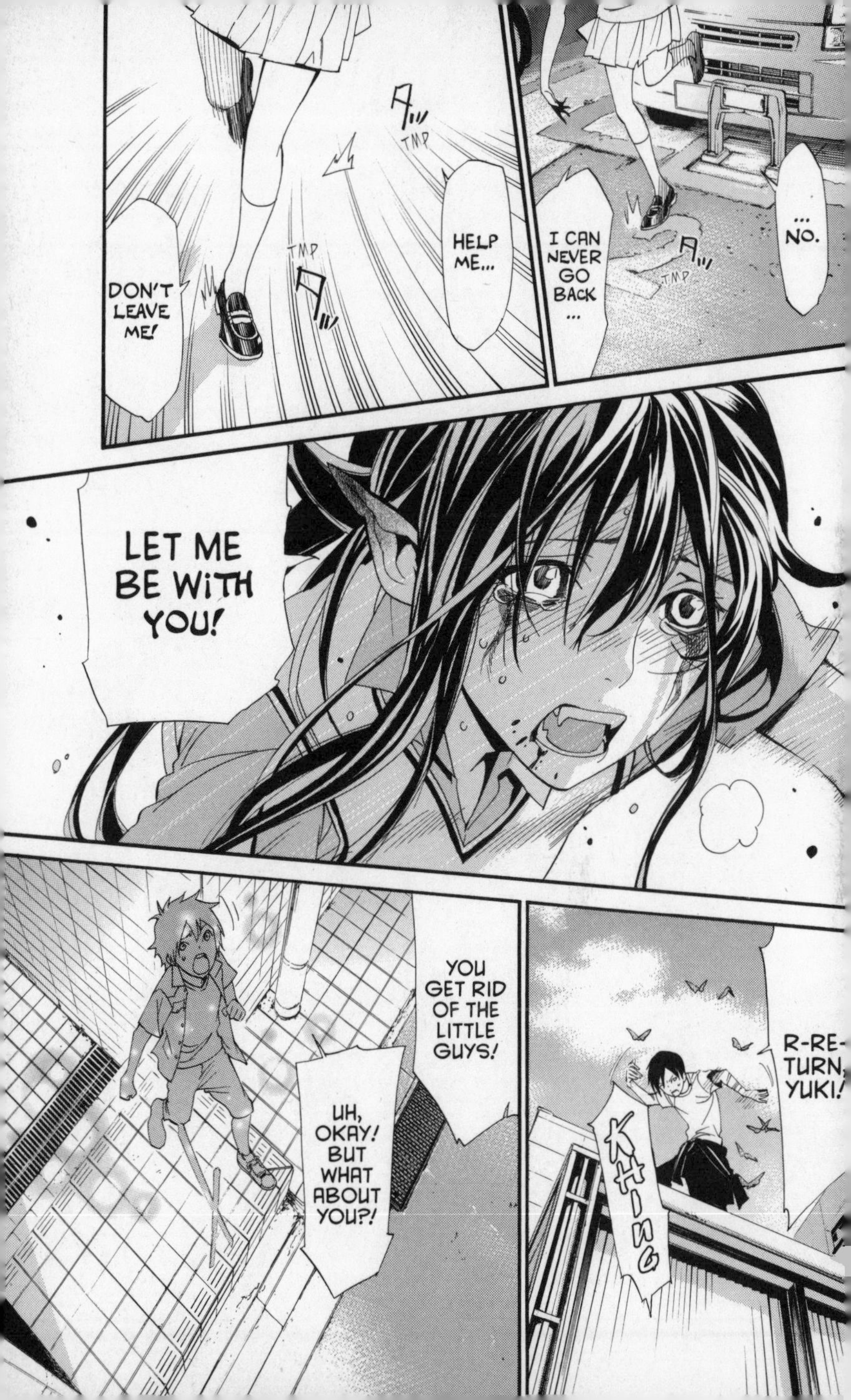
...NO.
TMP
I CAN NEVER GO BACK...
HELP ME...
TMP
TMP
DON'T LEAVE ME!
LET ME BE WITH YOU!
R-RE-TURN, YUKI!
KHING
YOU GET RID OF THE LITTLE GUYS!
UH, OKAY! BUT WHAT ABOUT YOU?!

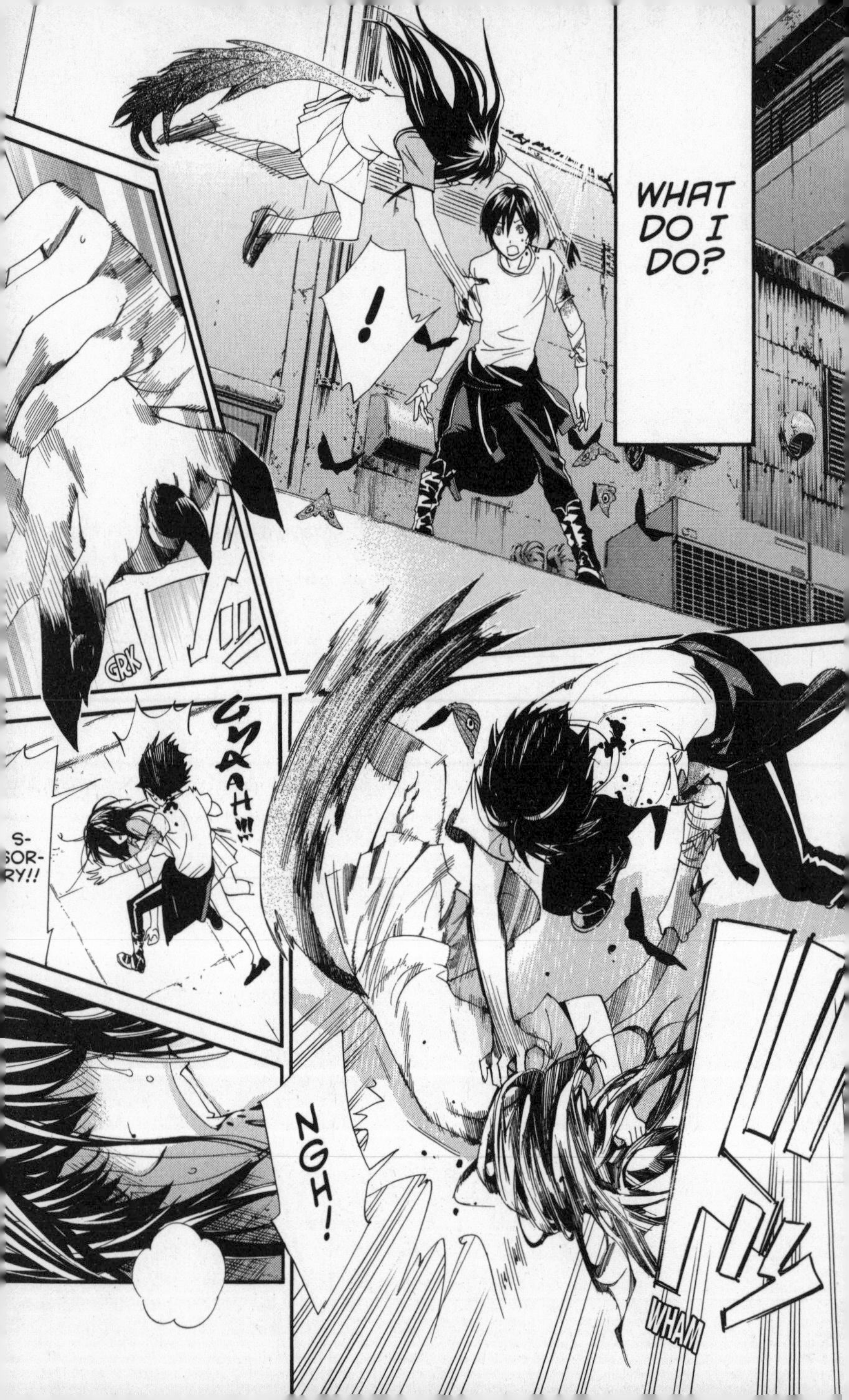
WHAT DO I DO?
!
GRK
NGH!
WHAM
GYAAH!!!
S-SORRY!!

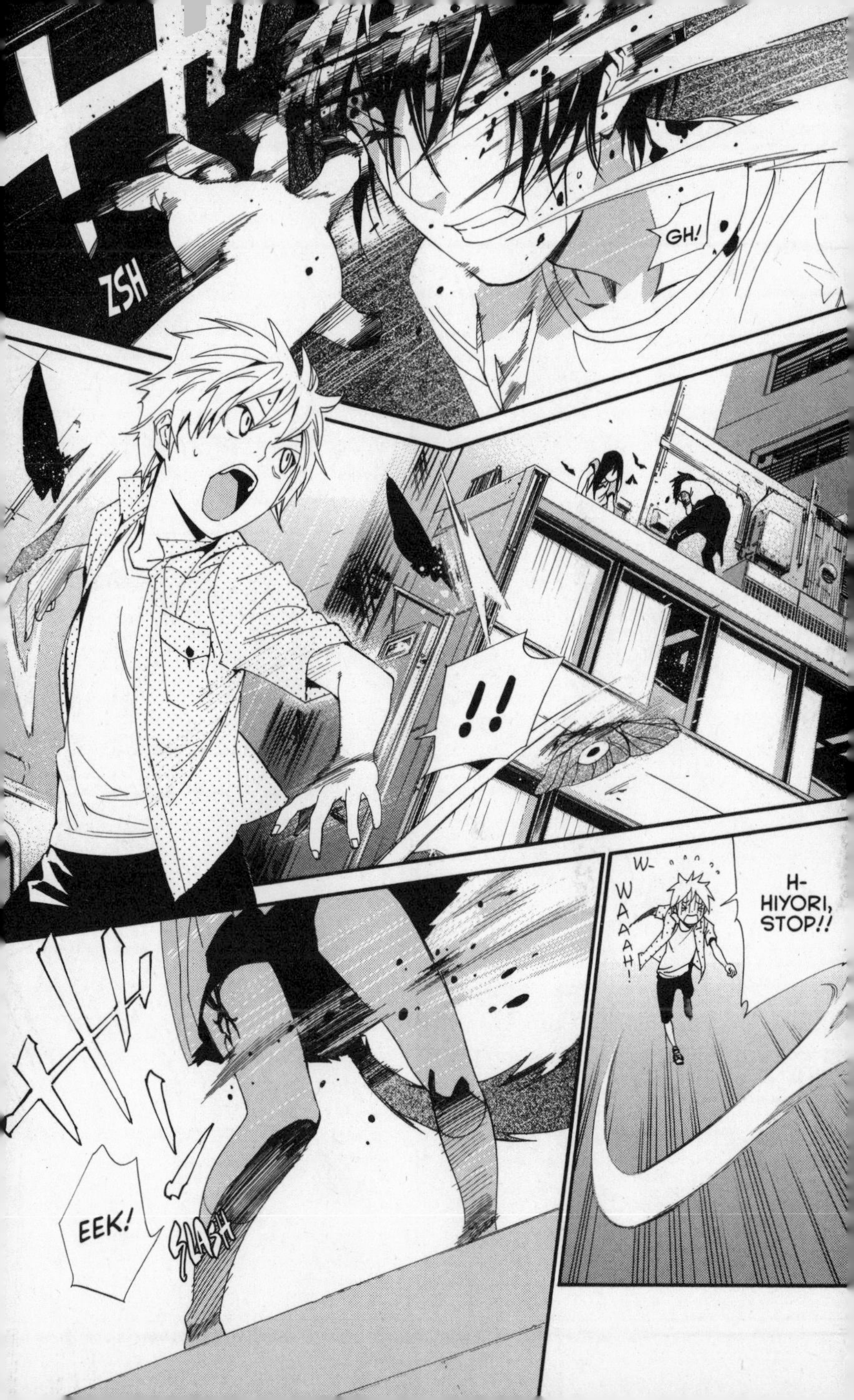
GH!
ZSH
!!
H- HIYORI, STOP!!
W- WAAAH!
SLASH
EEK!

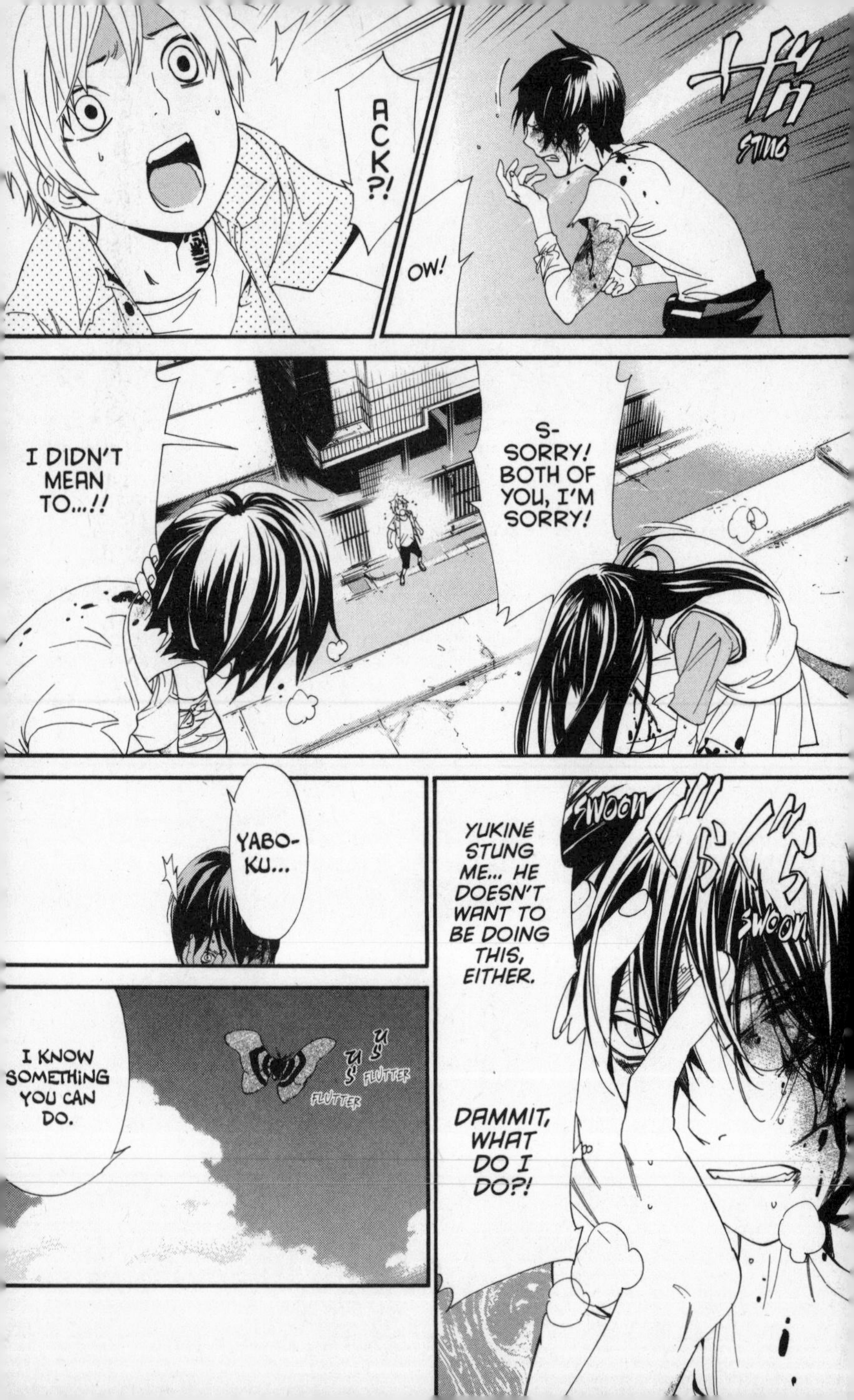
STING
OW!
ACK?!
S-SORRY! BOTH OF YOU, I'M SORRY!
I DIDN'T MEAN TO...!!
SWOON
SWOON
YUKINÉ STUNG ME... HE DOESN'T WANT TO BE DOING THIS, EITHER.
DAMMIT, WHAT DO I DO?!
YABO-KU...
FLUTTER
FLUTTER
I KNOW SOMETHING YOU CAN DO.

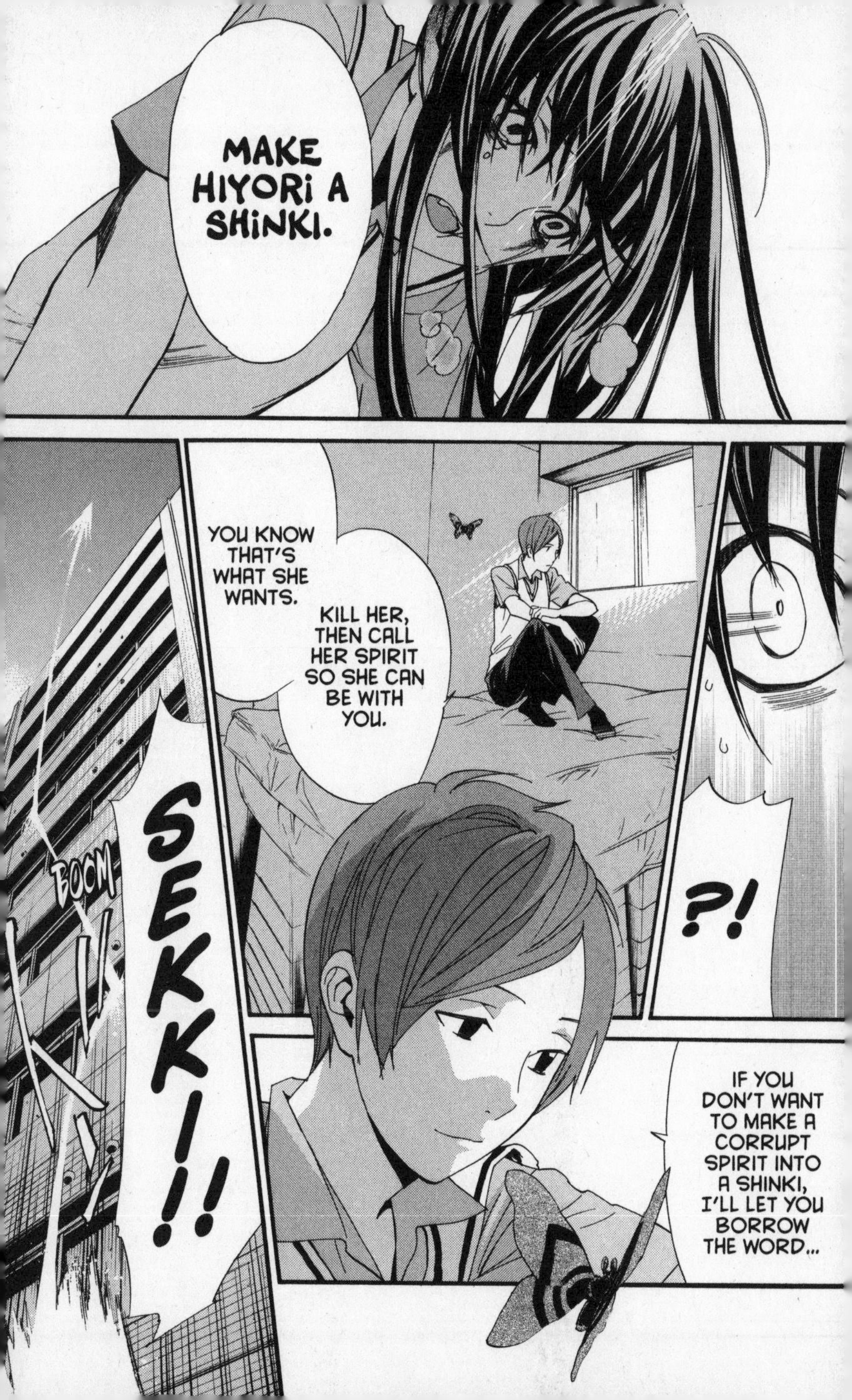
MAKE HIYORI A SHINKI.
?!
YOU KNOW THAT'S WHAT SHE WANTS.
KILL HER, THEN CALL HER SPIRIT SO SHE CAN BE WITH YOU.
IF YOU DON'T WANT TO MAKE A CORRUPT SPIRIT INTO A SHINKI, I'LL LET YOU BORROW THE WORD...
SEKKI!!
BOOM

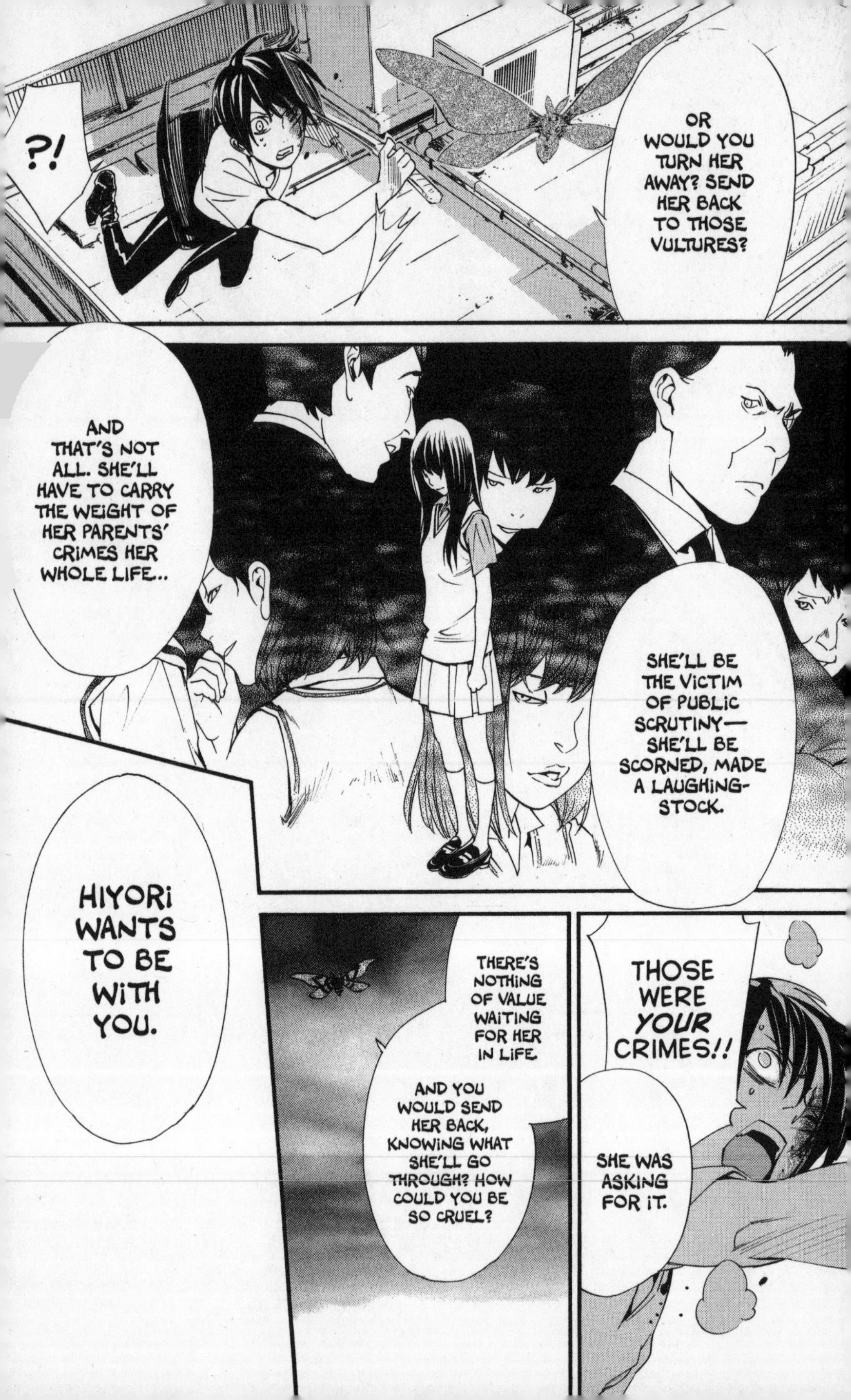
OR WOULD YOU TURN HER AWAY? SEND HER BACK TO THOSE VULTURES?
?!
SHE'LL BE THE VICTIM OF PUBLIC SCRUTINY—SHE'LL BE SCORNED, MADE A LAUGHING-STOCK.
AND THAT'S NOT ALL. SHE'LL HAVE TO CARRY THE WEIGHT OF HER PARENTS' CRIMES HER WHOLE LIFE..
HIYORI WANTS TO BE WITH YOU.
THERE'S NOTHING OF VALUE WAITING FOR HER IN LIFE.
AND YOU WOULD SEND HER BACK, KNOWING WHAT SHE'LL GO THROUGH? HOW COULD YOU BE SO CRUEL?
THOSE WERE *YOUR* CRIMES!!
SHE WAS ASKING FOR IT.

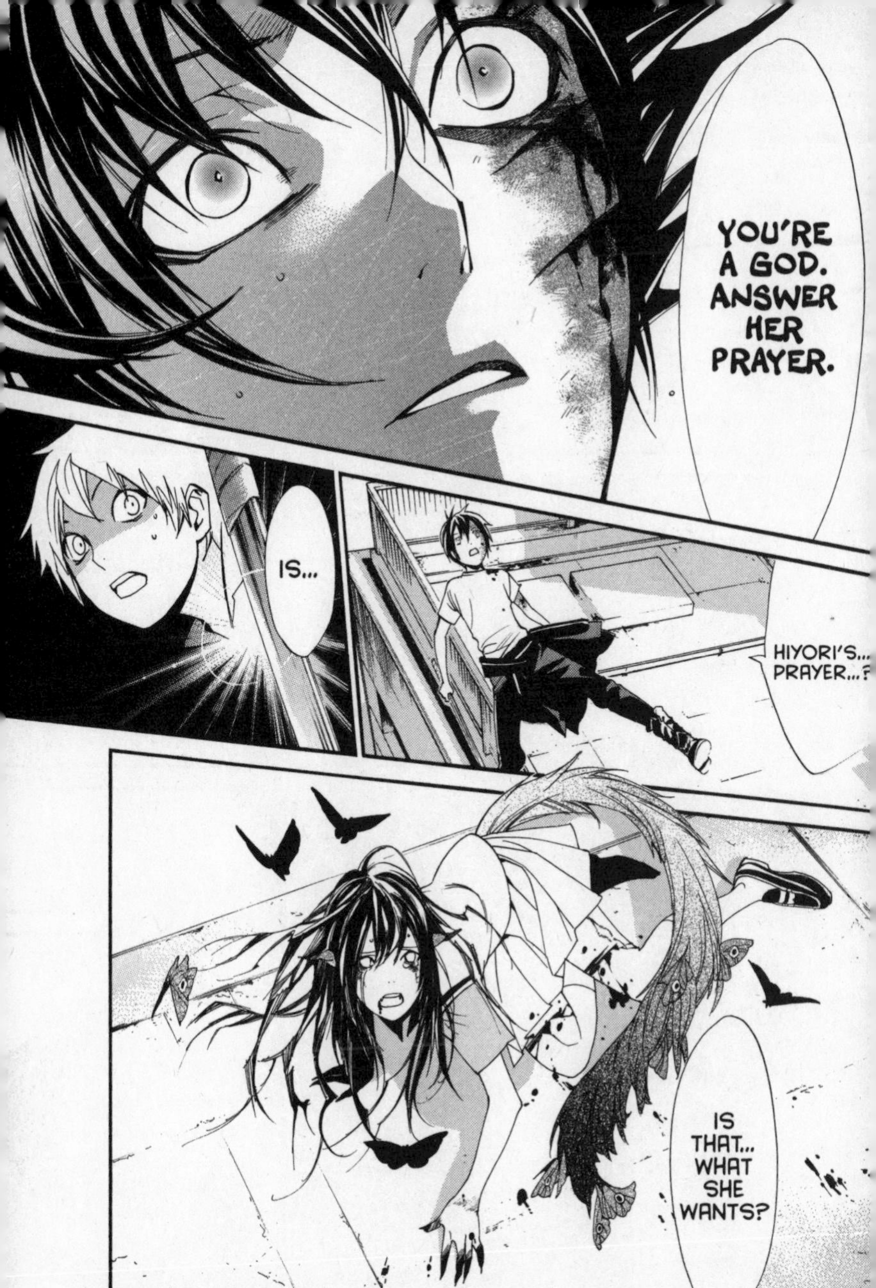
YOU'RE A GOD. ANSWER HER PRAYER.
HIYORI'S... PRAYER...?
IS...
IS THAT... WHAT SHE WANTS?

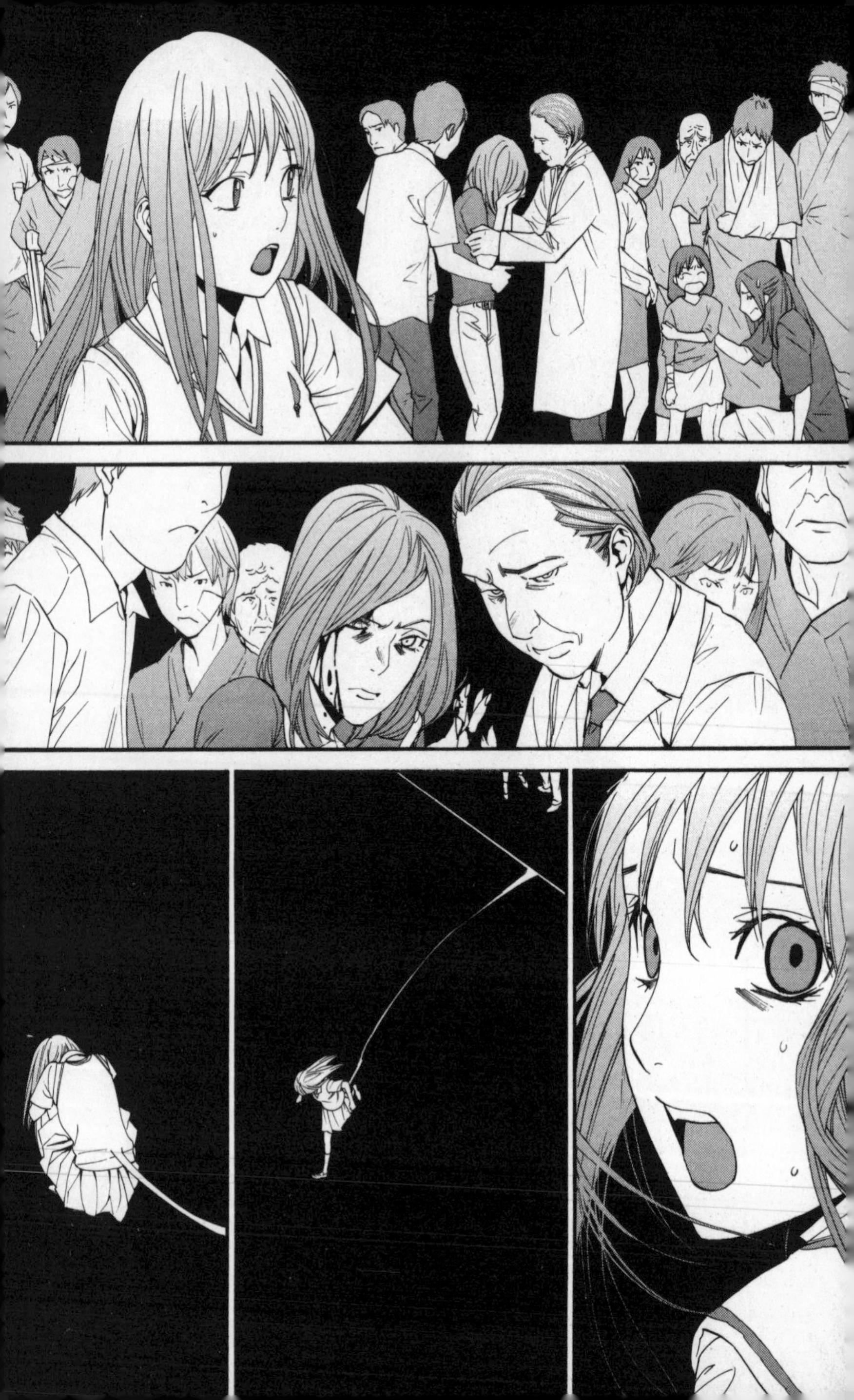

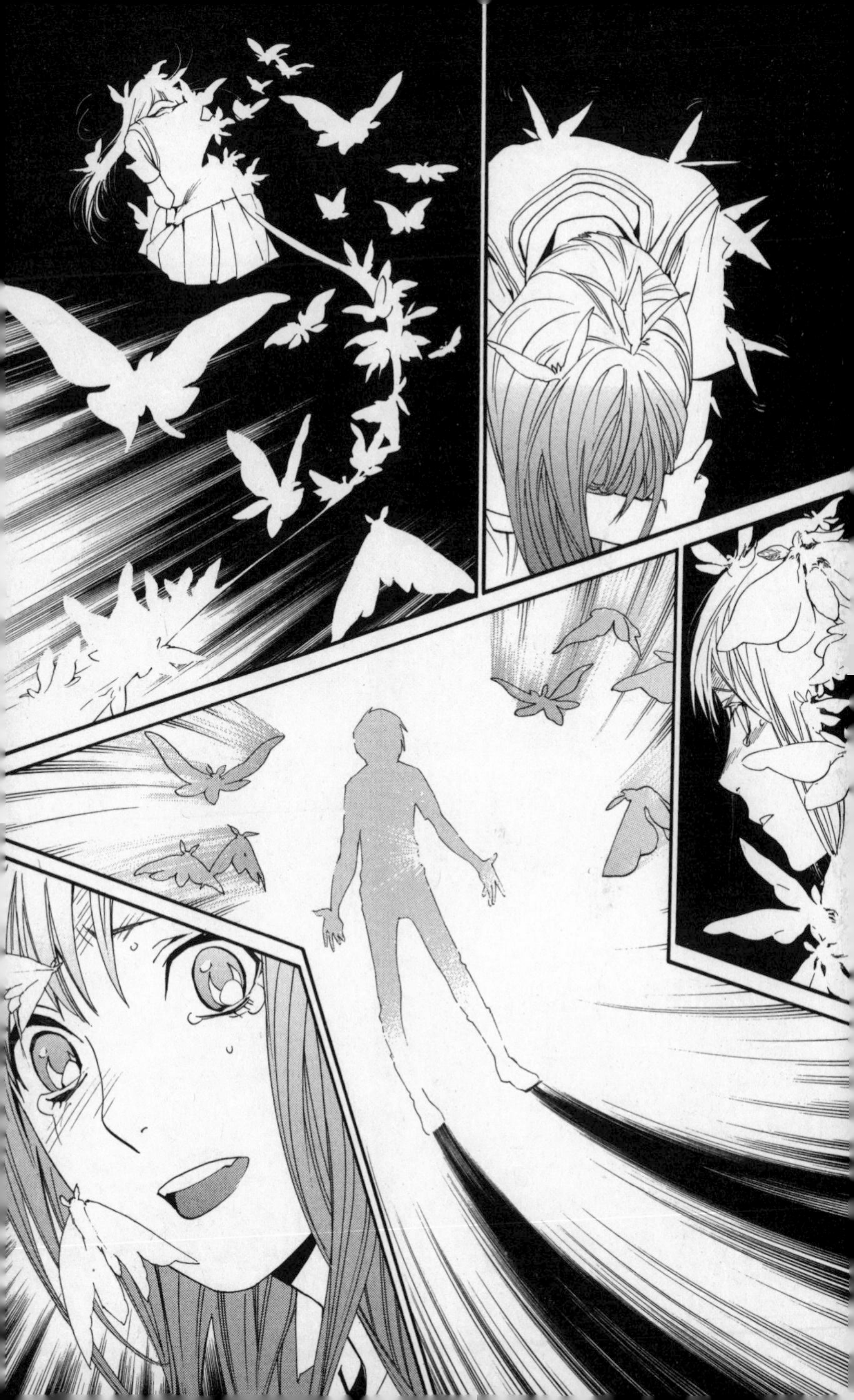

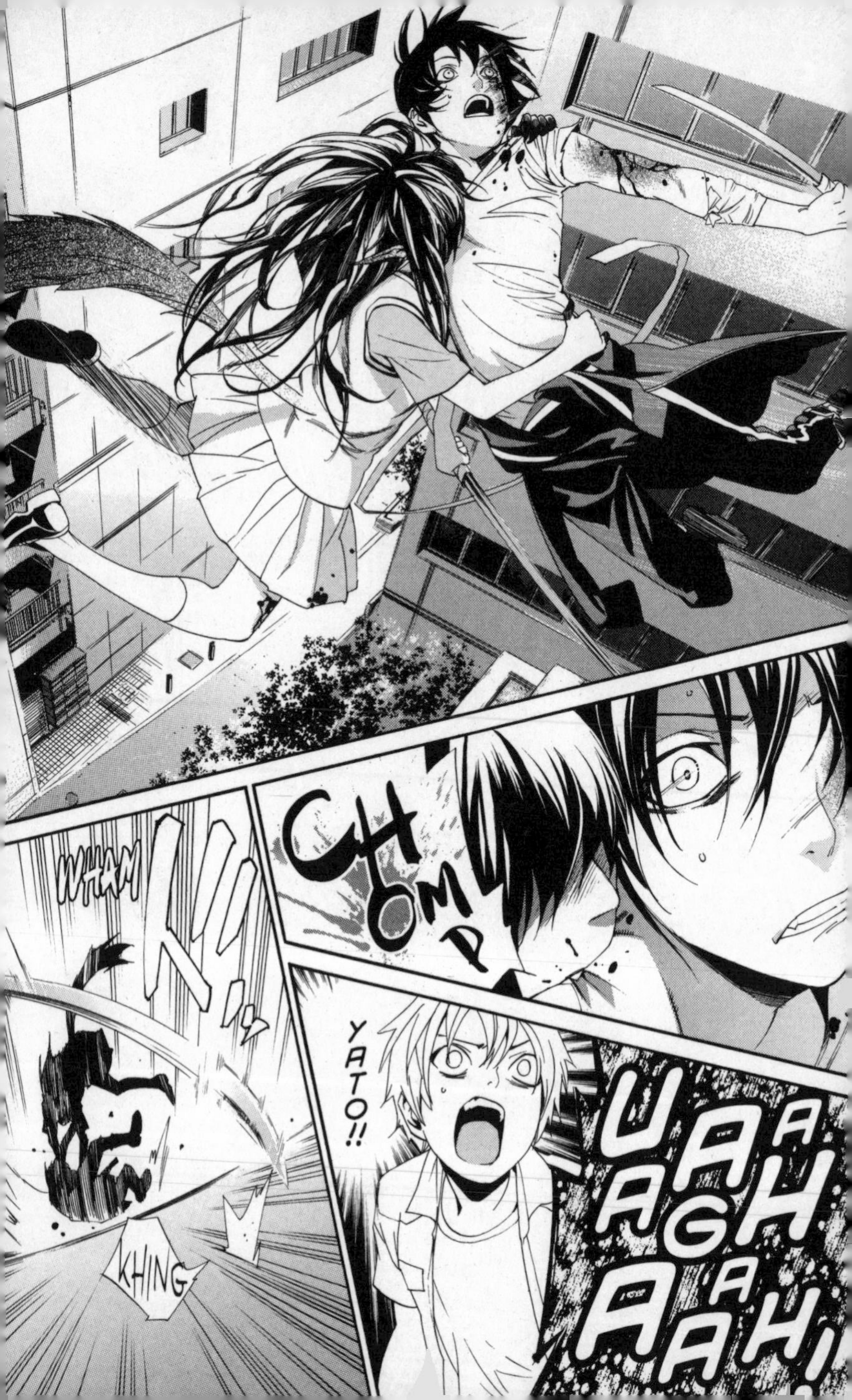
CHOMP
YATO!!
UAAAAGHAAAAH!
WHAM
KHING

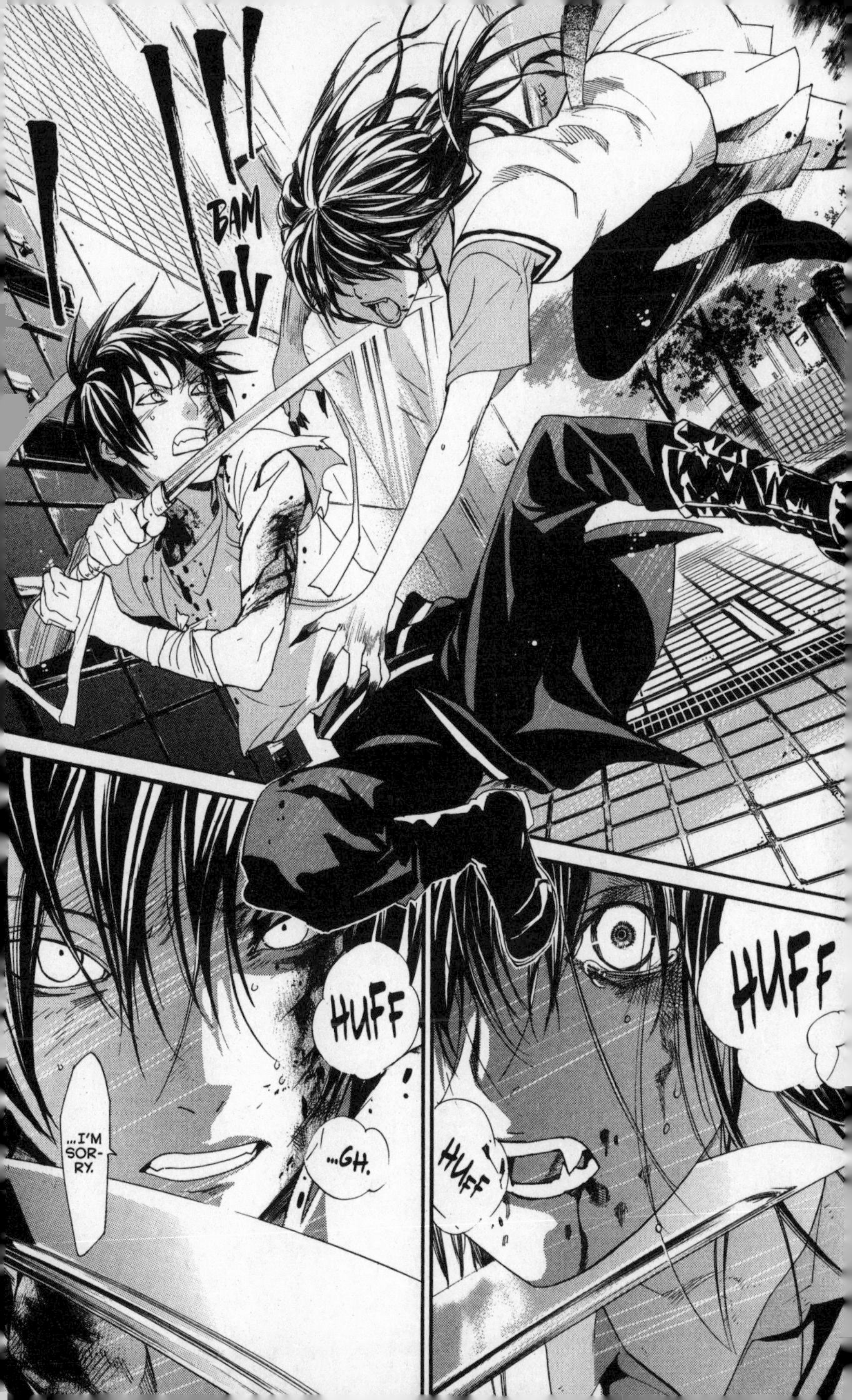
BAM
HUFF
HUFF
HUFF
...GH.
...I'M SORRY.

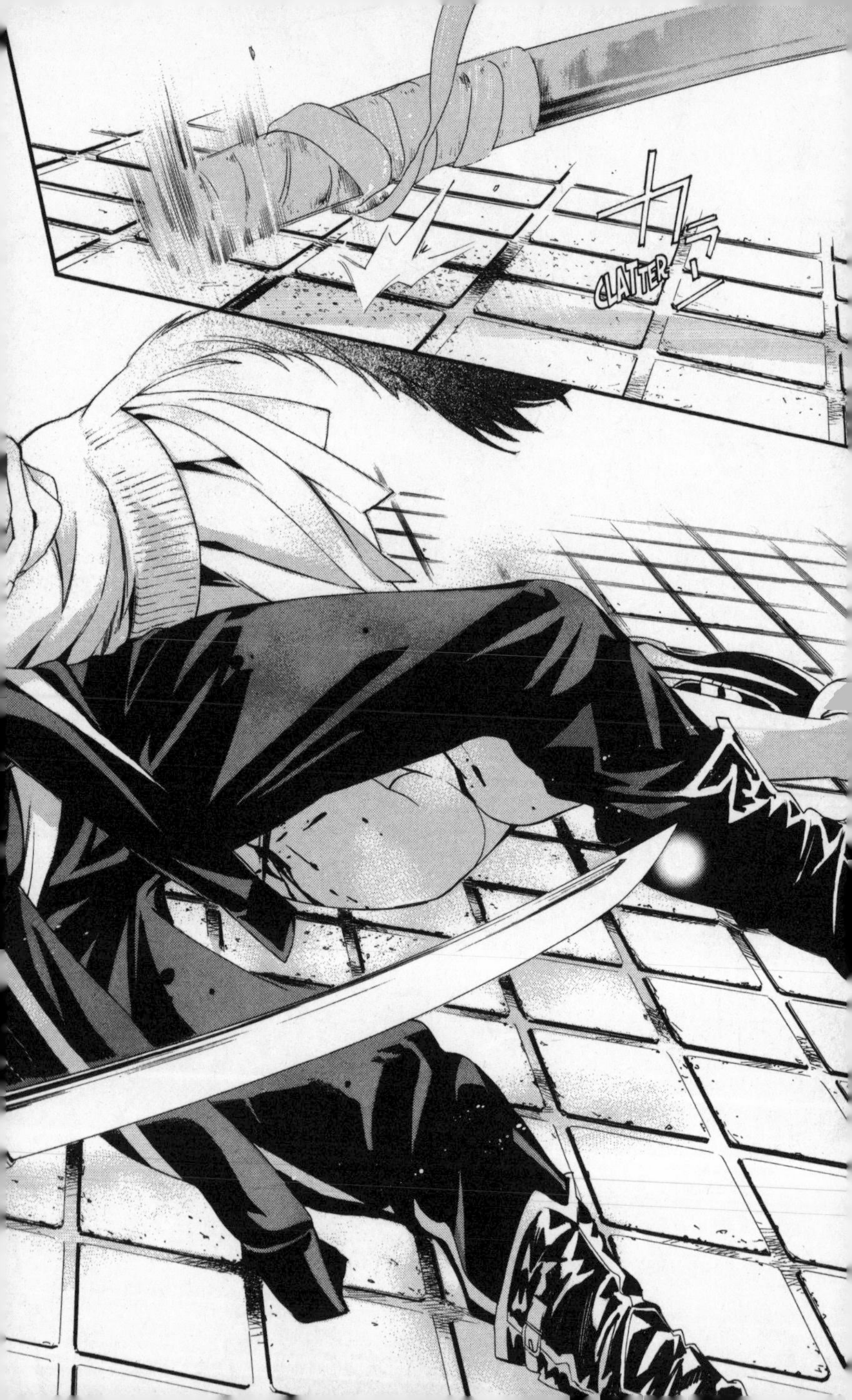
CLATTER

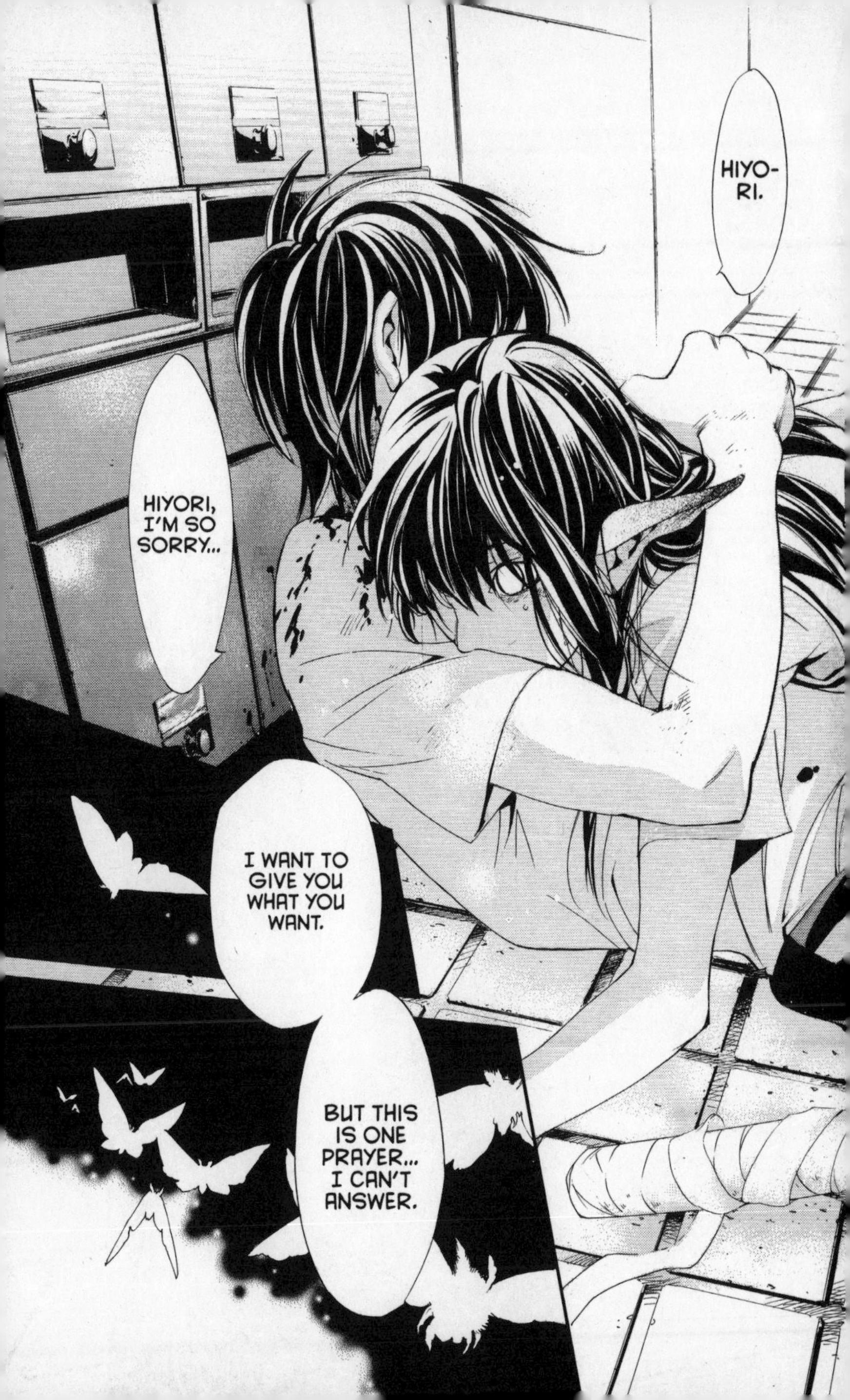
HIYO-RI.
HIYORI, I'M SO SORRY...
I WANT TO GIVE YOU WHAT YOU WANT.
BUT THIS IS ONE PRAYER... I CAN'T ANSWER.

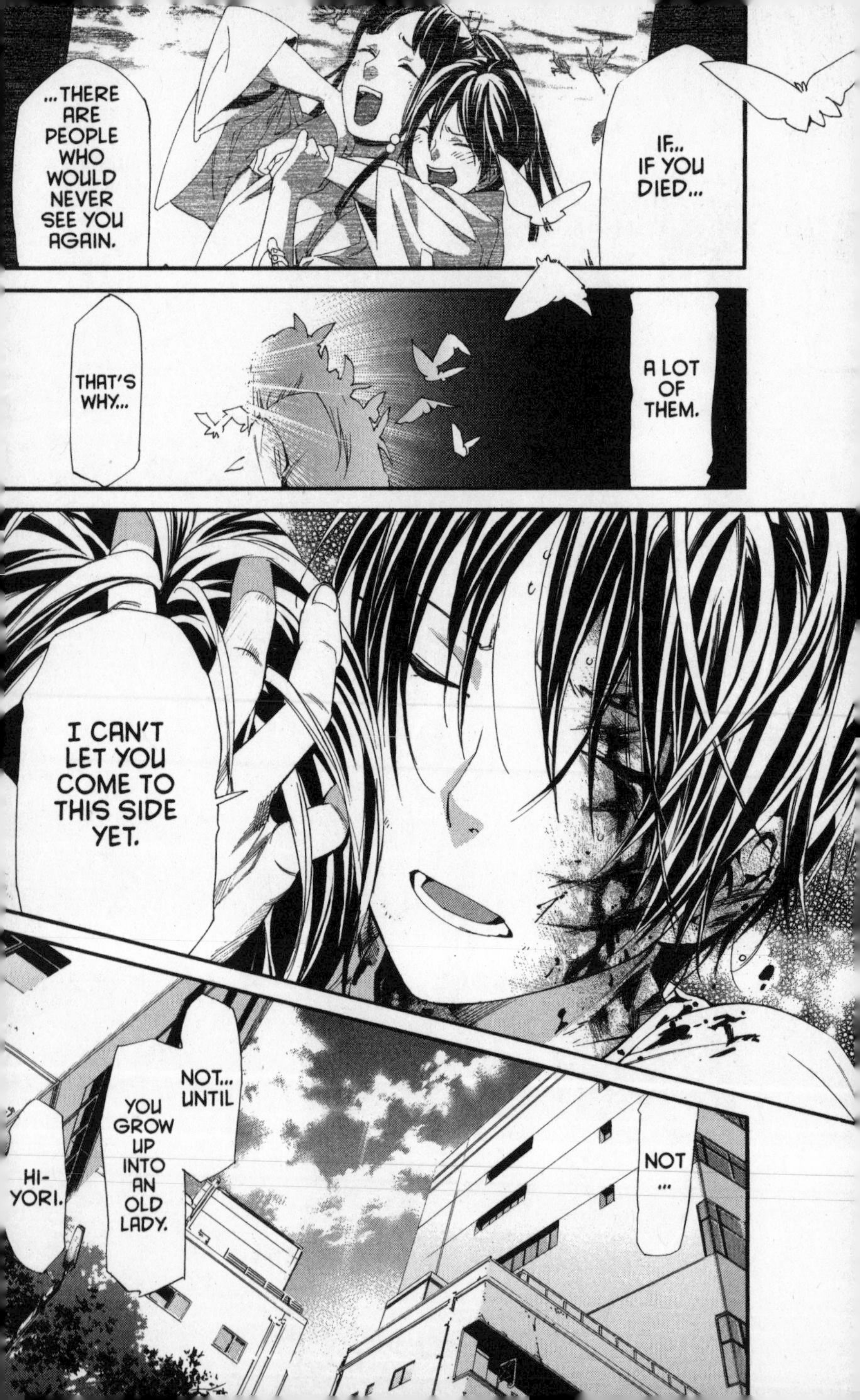
IF... IF YOU DIED...
...THERE ARE PEOPLE WHO WOULD NEVER SEE YOU AGAIN.
A LOT OF THEM.
THAT'S WHY...
I CAN'T LET YOU COME TO THIS SIDE YET.
NOT...
NOT... UNTIL YOU GROW UP INTO AN OLD LADY.
HI-YORI.

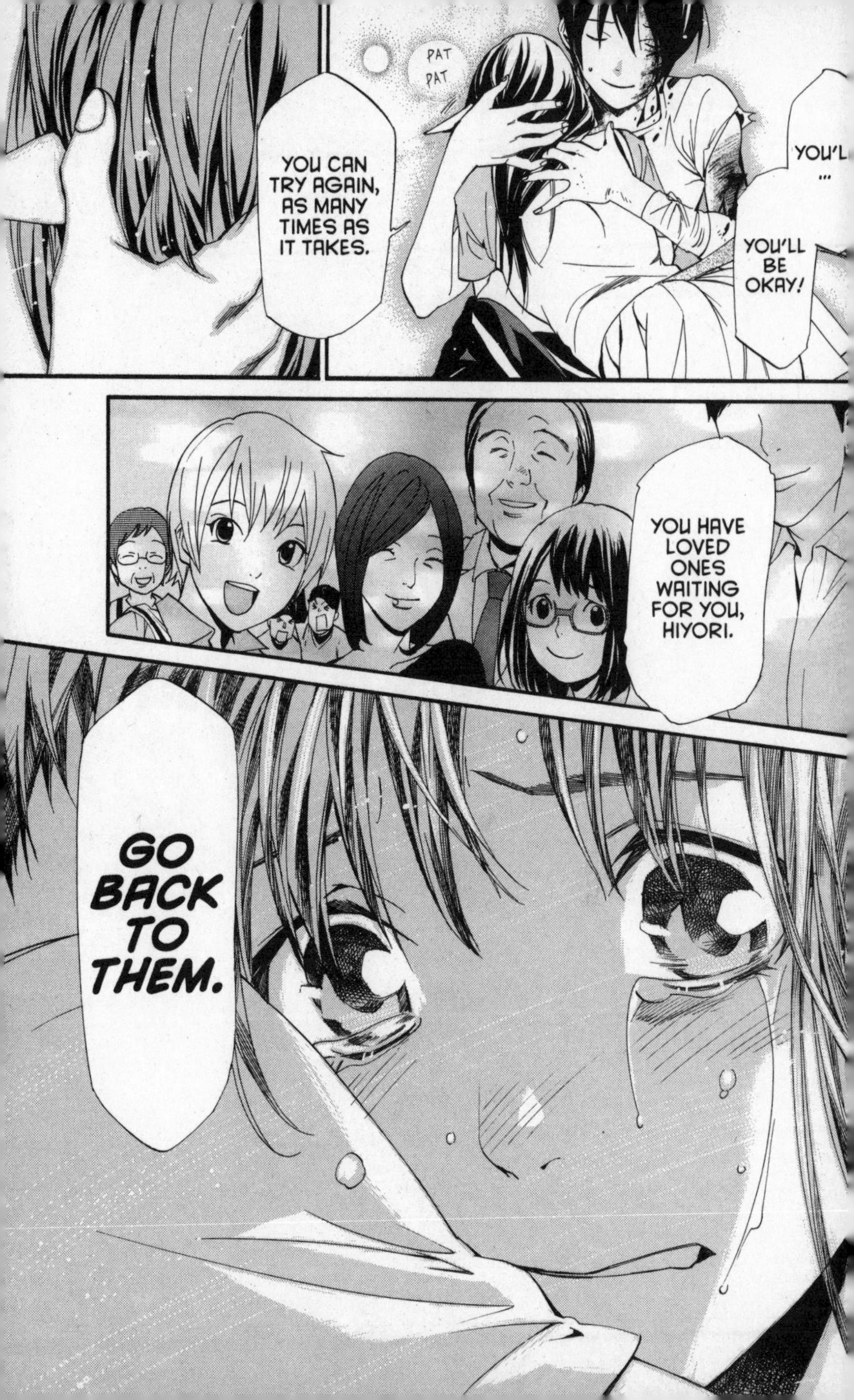
YOU'L ...
YOU'LL BE OKAY!
PAT PAT
YOU CAN TRY AGAIN, AS MANY TIMES AS IT TAKES.
YOU HAVE LOVED ONES WAITING FOR YOU, HIYORI.
GO BACK TO THEM.

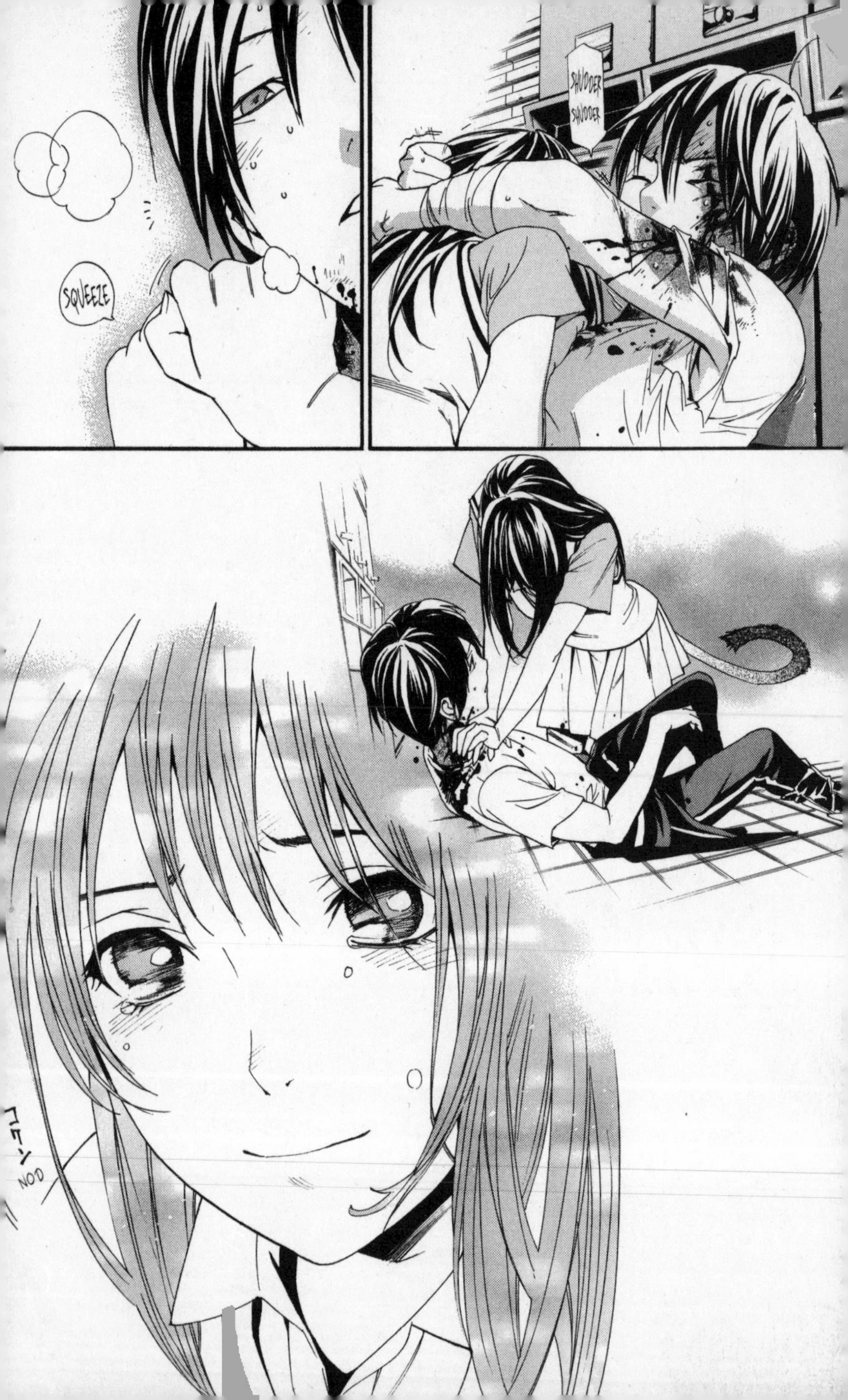
SHUDDER
SHUDDER
SQUEEZE
NOD

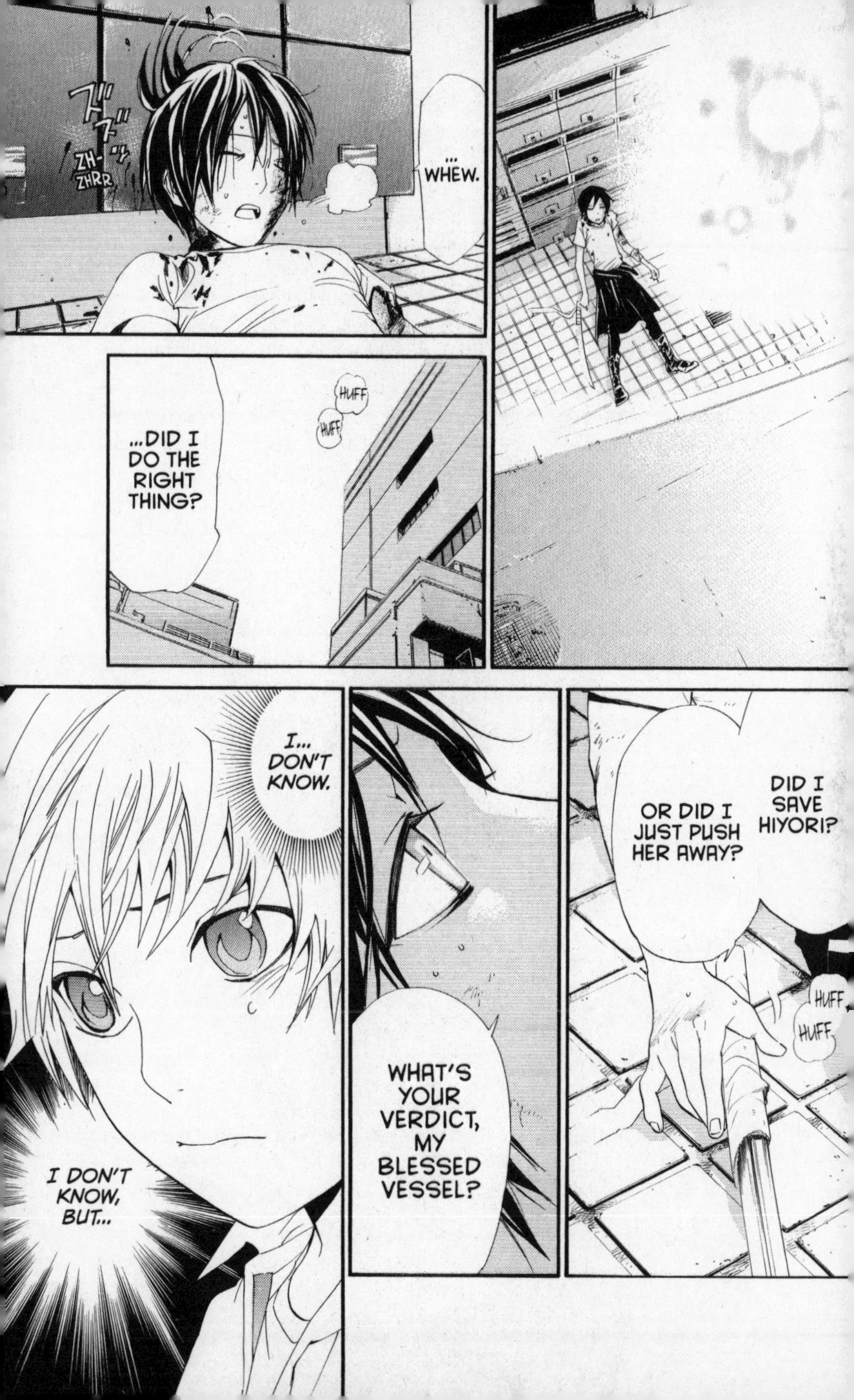

... WHEW.
ZH-ZHRR
HUFF
HUFF
...DID I DO THE RIGHT THING?
DID I SAVE HIYORI?
OR DID I JUST PUSH HER AWAY?
HUFF
HUFF
WHAT'S YOUR VERDICT, MY BLESSED VESSEL?
I... DON'T KNOW.
I DON'T KNOW, BUT...

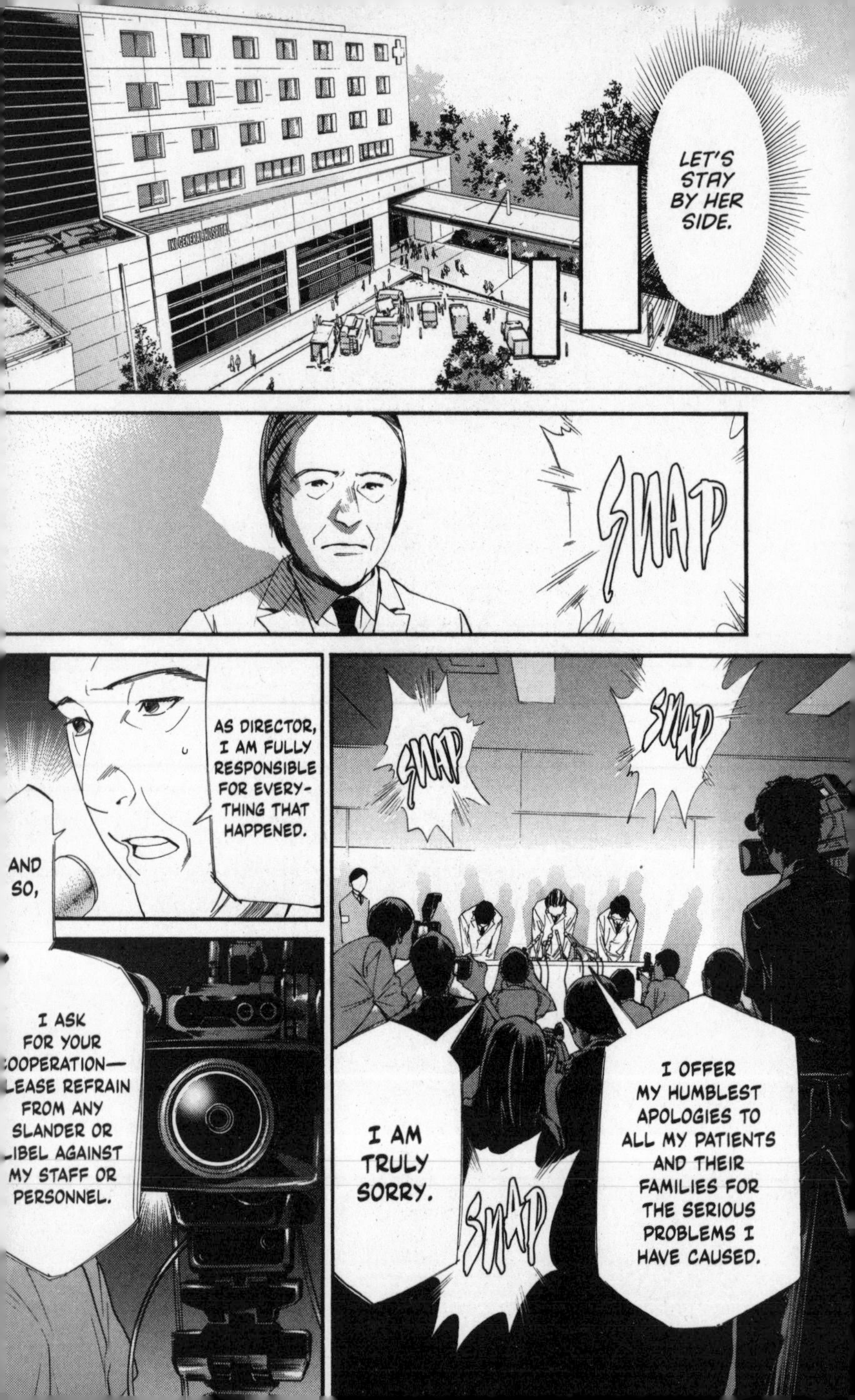
LET'S STAY BY HER SIDE.
IKU GENERAL HOSPITAL
SNAP
SNAP
SNAP
I OFFER MY HUMBLEST APOLOGIES TO ALL MY PATIENTS AND THEIR FAMILIES FOR THE SERIOUS PROBLEMS I HAVE CAUSED.
I AM TRULY SORRY.
SNAP
AS DIRECTOR, I AM FULLY RESPONSIBLE FOR EVERY-THING THAT HAPPENED.
AND SO,
I ASK FOR YOUR COOPERATION— LEASE REFRAIN FROM ANY SLANDER OR IBEL AGAINST MY STAFF OR PERSONNEL.

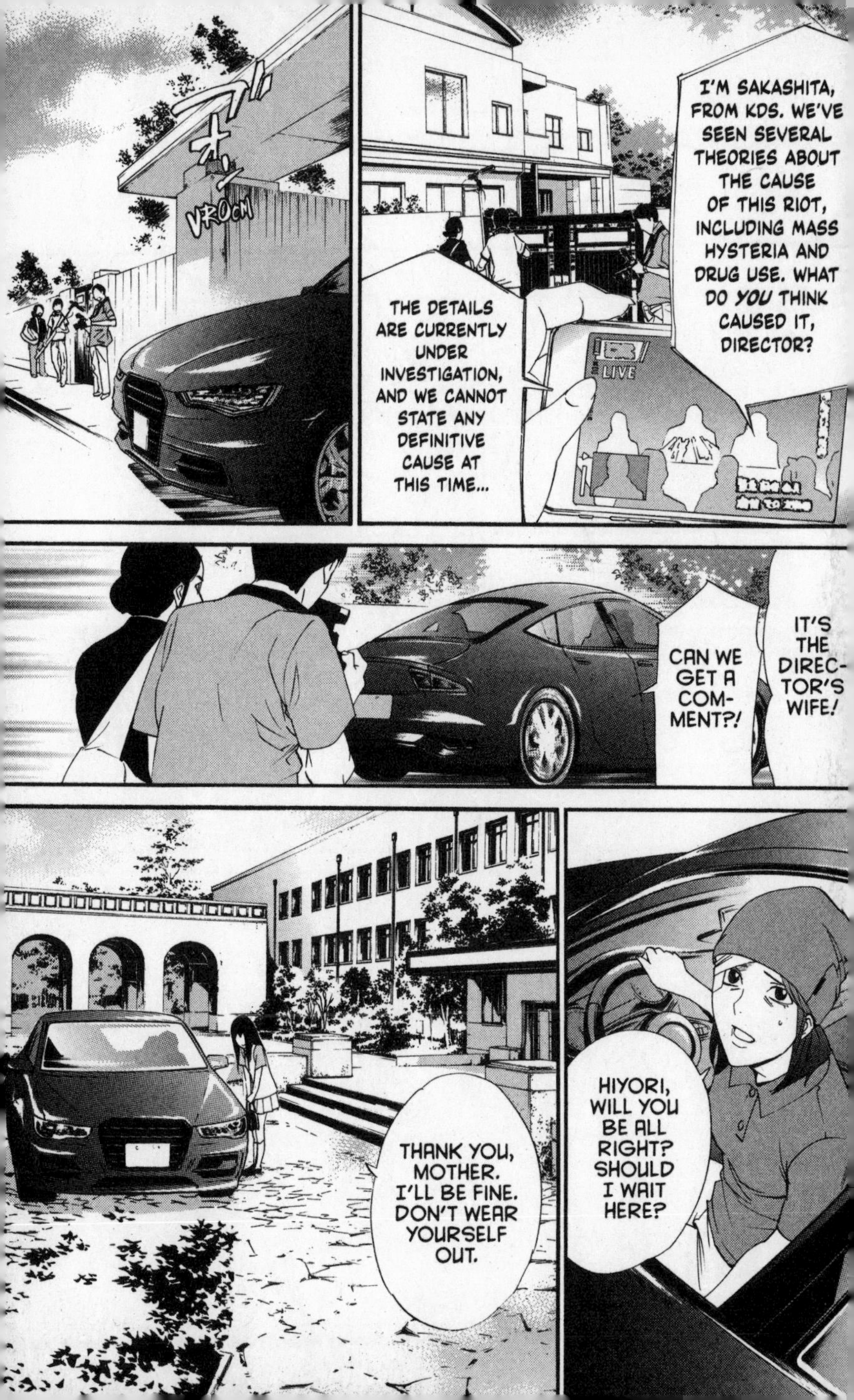
I'M SAKASHITA, FROM KDS. WE'VE SEEN SEVERAL THEORIES ABOUT THE CAUSE OF THIS RIOT, INCLUDING MASS HYSTERIA AND DRUG USE. WHAT DO *YOU* THINK CAUSED IT, DIRECTOR?
LIVE
THE DETAILS ARE CURRENTLY UNDER INVESTIGATION, AND WE CANNOT STATE ANY DEFINITIVE CAUSE AT THIS TIME...
VROOM
IT'S THE DIREC-TOR'S WIFE!
CAN WE GET A COM-MENT?!
HIYORI, WILL YOU BE ALL RIGHT? SHOULD I WAIT HERE?
THANK YOU, MOTHER. I'LL BE FINE. DON'T WEAR YOURSELF OUT.

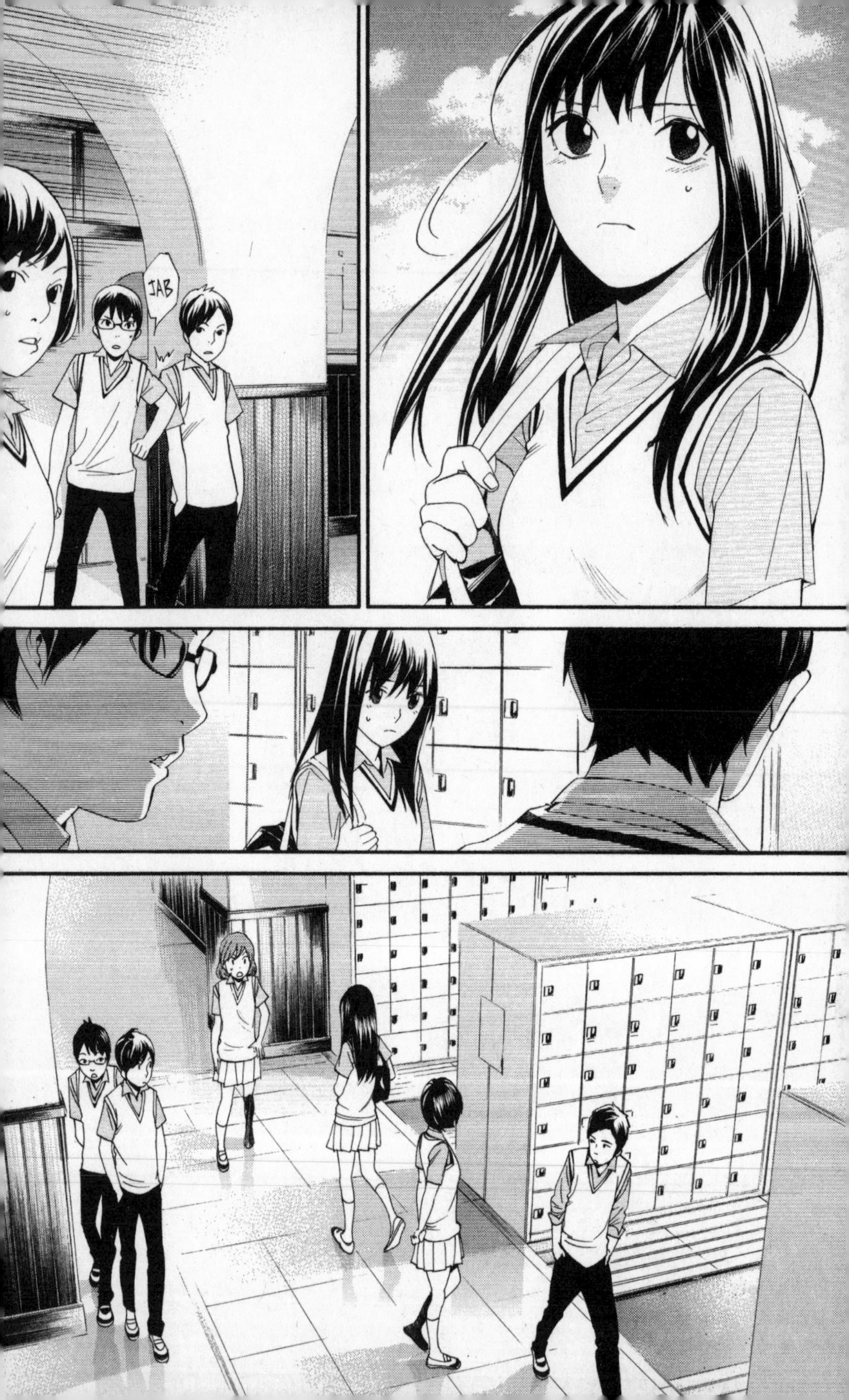
JAB

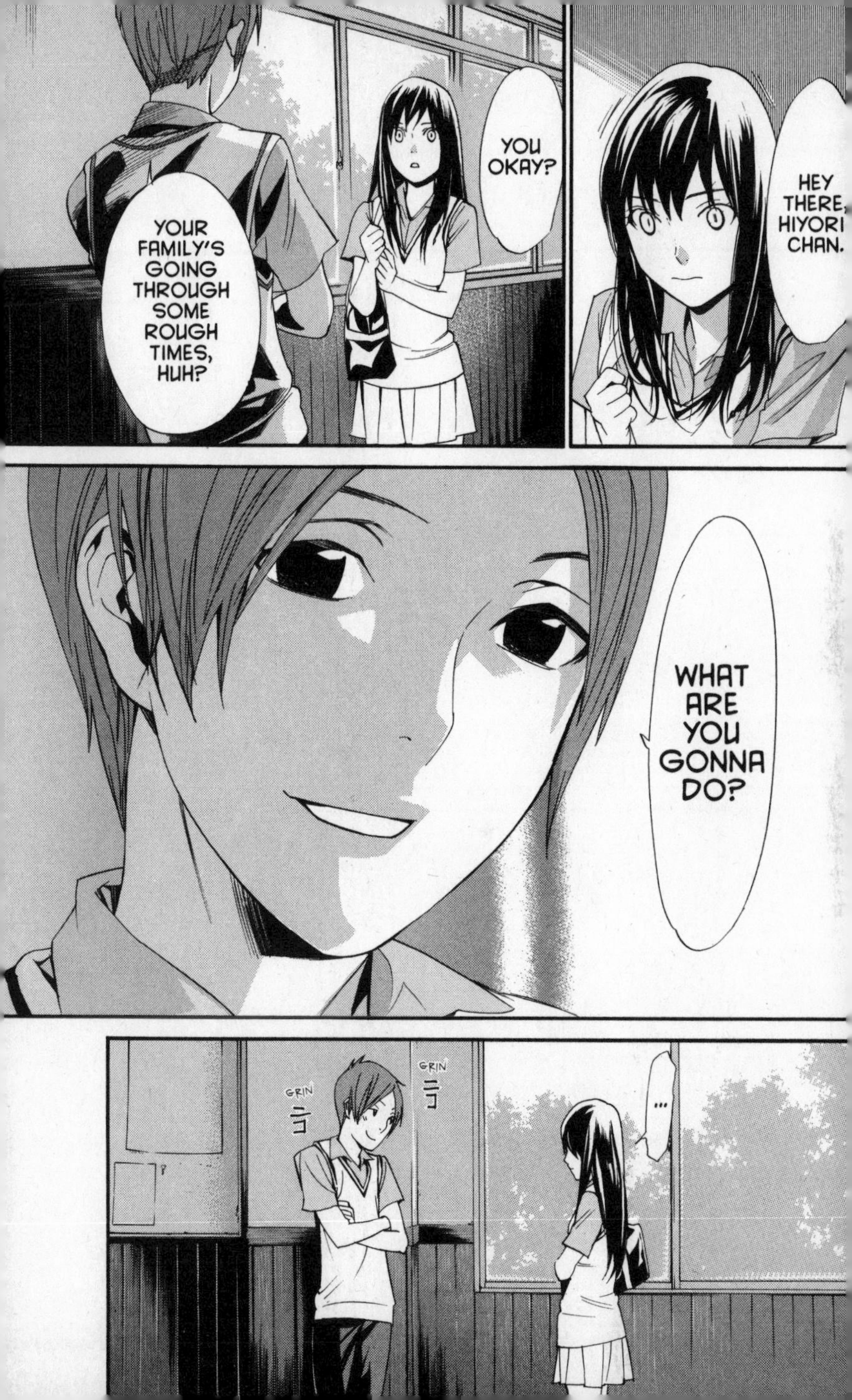
HEY THERE, HIYORI CHAN.
YOU OKAY?
YOUR FAMILY'S GOING THROUGH SOME ROUGH TIMES, HUH?
WHAT ARE YOU GONNA DO?
...
GRIN
GRIN

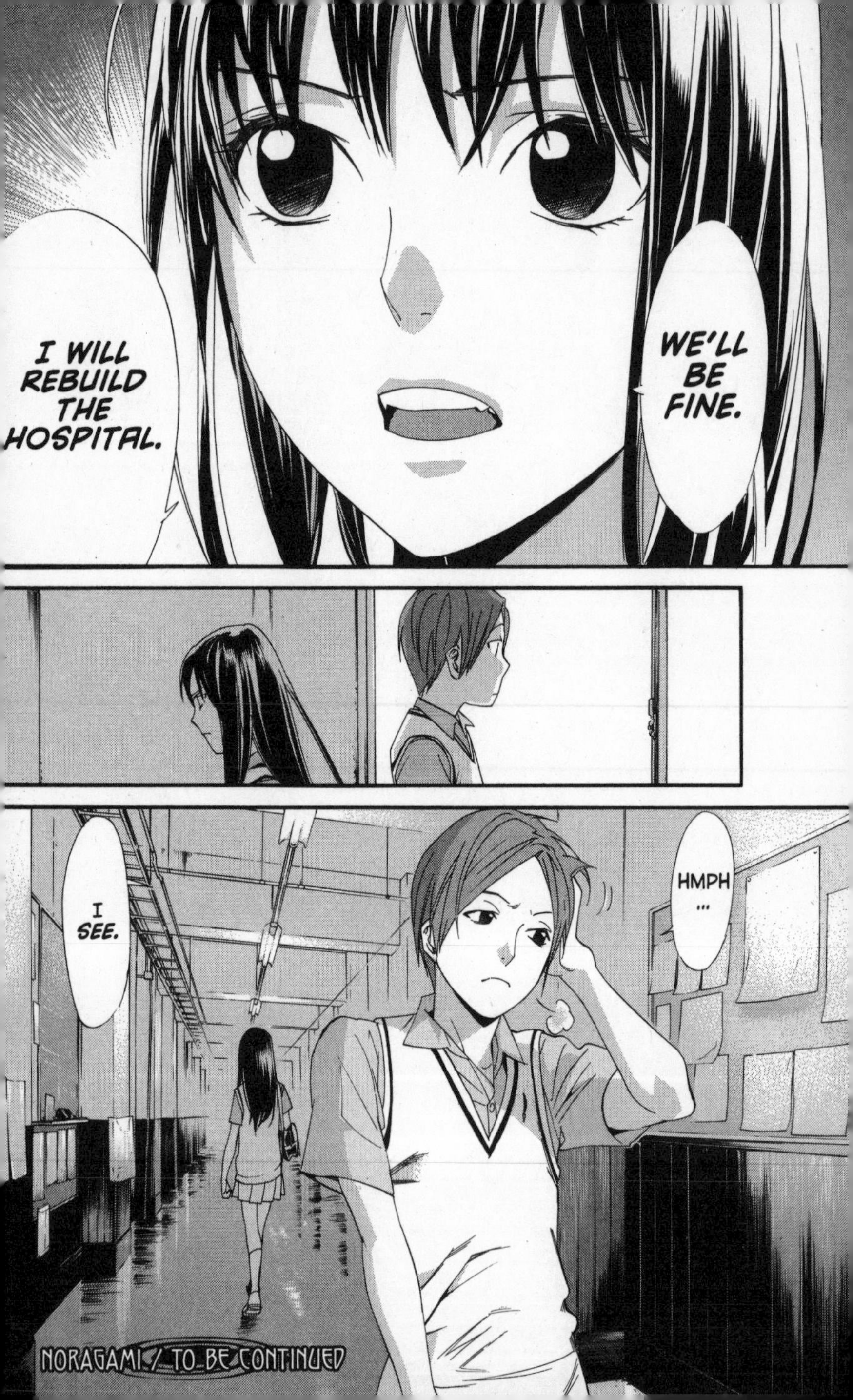
WE'LL BE FINE.
I WILL REBUILD THE HOSPITAL.
HMPH ...
I SEE.
NORAGAMI / TO BE CONTINUED

野

邑

神

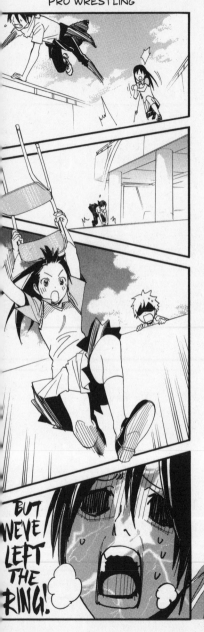

ATROCIOUS MANGA

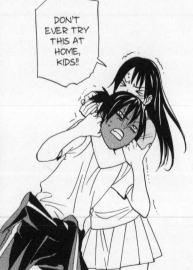

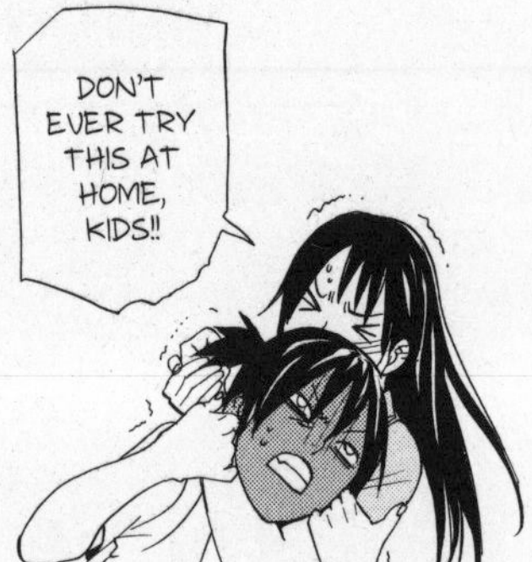
DON'T EVER TRY THIS AT HOME, KIDS!!

PRO WRESTLING

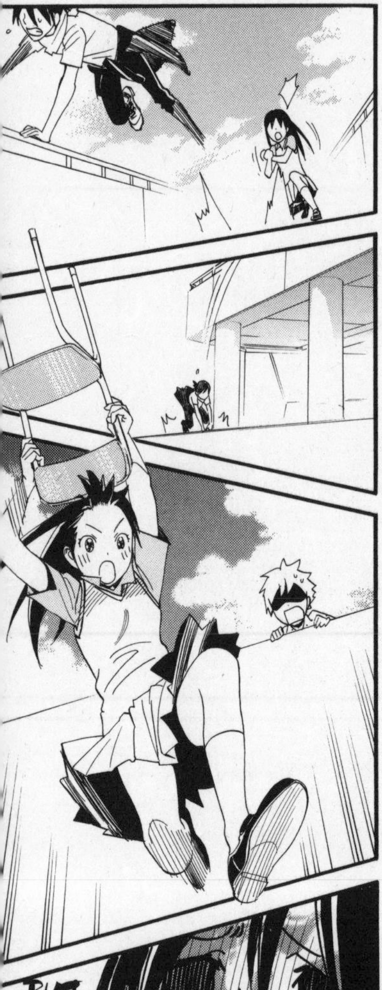
BUT WE'VE LEFT THE RING!

A OR B

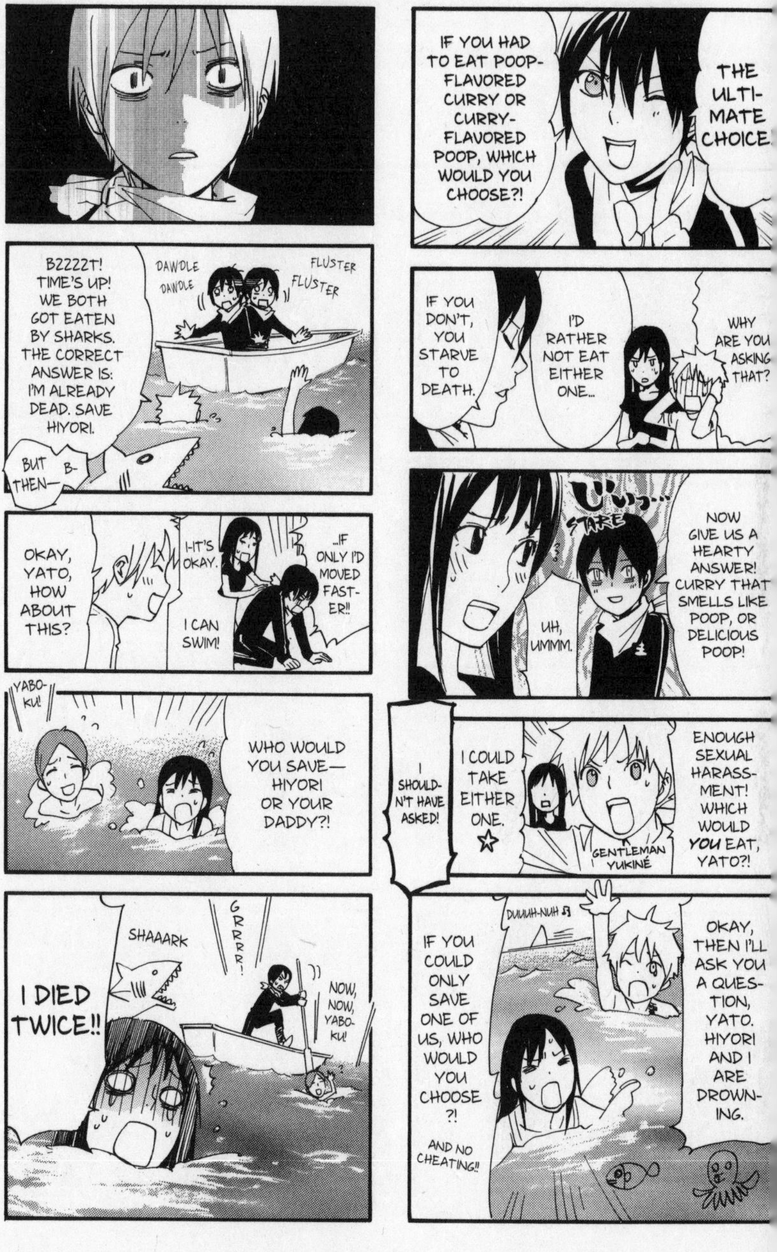
THE ULTIMATE CHOICE!
IF YOU HAD TO EAT POOP-FLAVORED CURRY OR CURRY-FLAVORED POOP, WHICH WOULD YOU CHOOSE?!
WHY ARE YOU ASKING THAT?
I'D RATHER NOT EAT EITHER ONE...
IF YOU DON'T, YOU STARVE TO DEATH.
NOW GIVE US A HEARTY ANSWER! CURRY THAT SMELLS LIKE POOP, OR DELICIOUS POOP!
STARE
UH, UMMM.
ENOUGH SEXUAL HARASSMENT! WHICH WOULD YOU EAT, YATO?!
GENTLEMAN YUKINÉ
I COULD TAKE EITHER ONE. ☆
I SHOULDN'T HAVE ASKED!
OKAY, THEN I'LL ASK YOU A QUESTION, YATO. HIYORI AND I ARE DROWNING.
DUUUH-NUH ♫
IF YOU COULD ONLY SAVE ONE OF US, WHO WOULD YOU CHOOSE?!
AND NO CHEATING!!
FLUSTER FLUSTER
DAWDLE DAWDLE
B2222T! TIME'S UP! WE BOTH GOT EATEN BY SHARKS. THE CORRECT ANSWER IS: I'M ALREADY DEAD. SAVE HIYORI.
B- BUT THEN—
...IF ONLY I'D MOVED FASTER!!
I-IT'S OKAY.
I CAN SWIM!
OKAY, YATO, HOW ABOUT THIS?
WHO WOULD YOU SAVE—HIYORI OR YOUR DADDY?!
YABOKU!
NOW, NOW, YABOKU!
GRRRR!
SHAAARK
I DIED TWICE!!

XXXX HUNTER

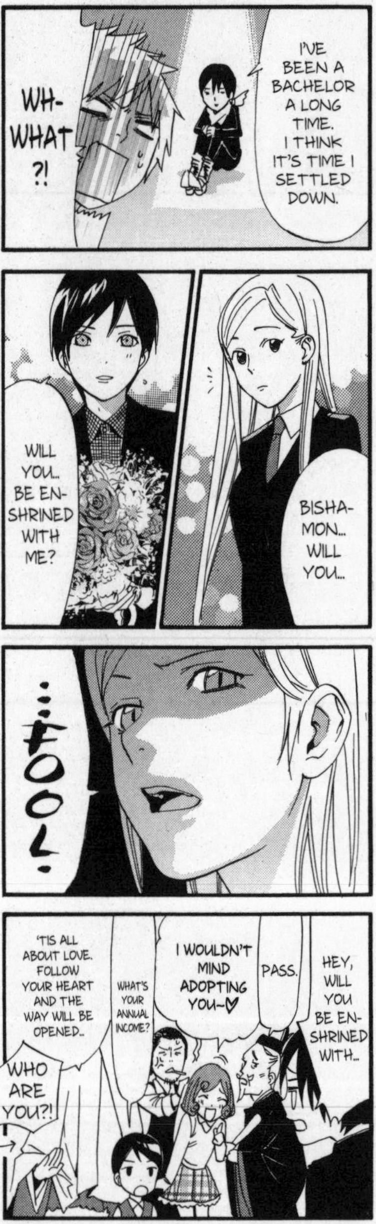
I'VE BEEN A BACHELOR A LONG TIME. I THINK IT'S TIME I SETTLED DOWN.
WH-WHAT?!
BISHA-MON... WILL YOU...
WILL YOU... BE EN-SHRINED WITH ME?
...FOOL!
HEY, WILL YOU BE EN-SHRINED WITH...
PASS.
I WOULDN'T MIND ADOPTING YOU~♥
WHAT'S YOUR ANNUAL INCOME?
'TIS ALL ABOUT LOVE. FOLLOW YOUR HEART AND THE WAY WILL BE OPENED...
WHO ARE YOU?!
TAKÉ-CHAN

HEY, PAPA

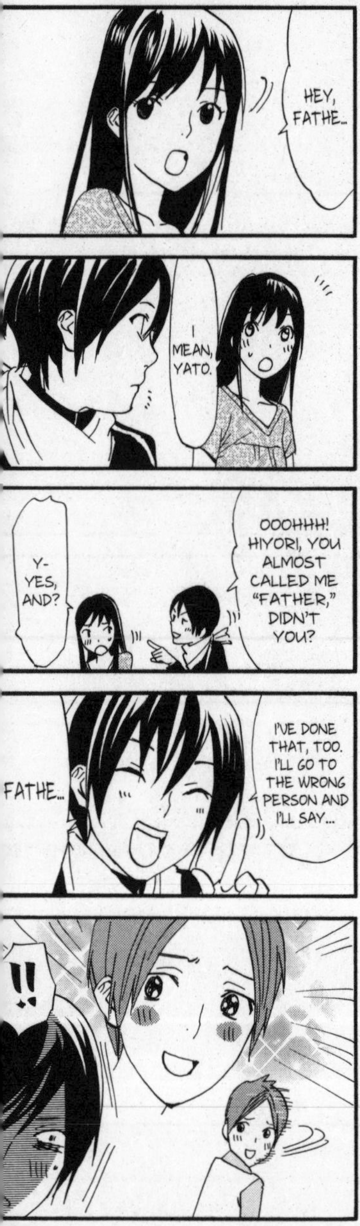
HEY, FATHE...
I MEAN, YATO.
OOOHHH! HIYORI, YOU ALMOST CALLED ME "FATHER," DIDN'T YOU?
Y-YES, AND?
I'VE DONE THAT, TOO. I'LL GO TO THE WRONG PERSON AND I'LL SAY...
FATHE...
!!

SCHOOL LOVE

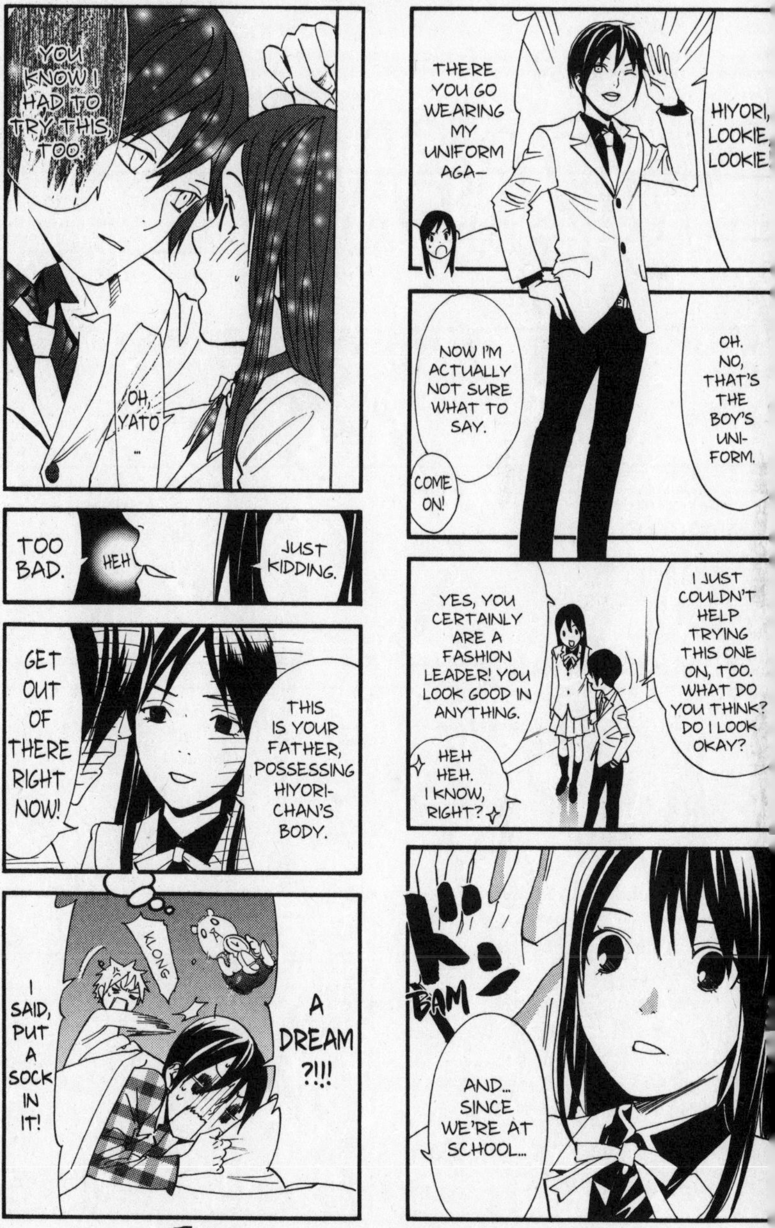
HIYORI, LOOKIE, LOOKIE.
THERE YOU GO WEARING MY UNIFORM AGA—
OH. NO, THAT'S THE BOY'S UNIFORM.
NOW I'M ACTUALLY NOT SURE WHAT TO SAY.
COME ON!
I JUST COULDN'T HELP TRYING THIS ONE ON, TOO. WHAT DO YOU THINK? DO I LOOK OKAY?
YES, YOU CERTAINLY ARE A FASHION LEADER! YOU LOOK GOOD IN ANYTHING.
HEH HEH. I KNOW, RIGHT?
BAM
AND... SINCE WE'RE AT SCHOOL...
YOU KNOW I HAD TO TRY THIS, TOO.
OH, YATO ...
JUST KIDDING.
HEH
TOO BAD.
THIS IS YOUR FATHER, POSSESSING HIYORI-CHAN'S BODY.
GET OUT OF THERE RIGHT NOW!
A DREAM ?!!!
KLONG
I SAID, PUT A SOCK IN IT!

THANK YOU TO EVERYONE WHO READ THIS FAR!

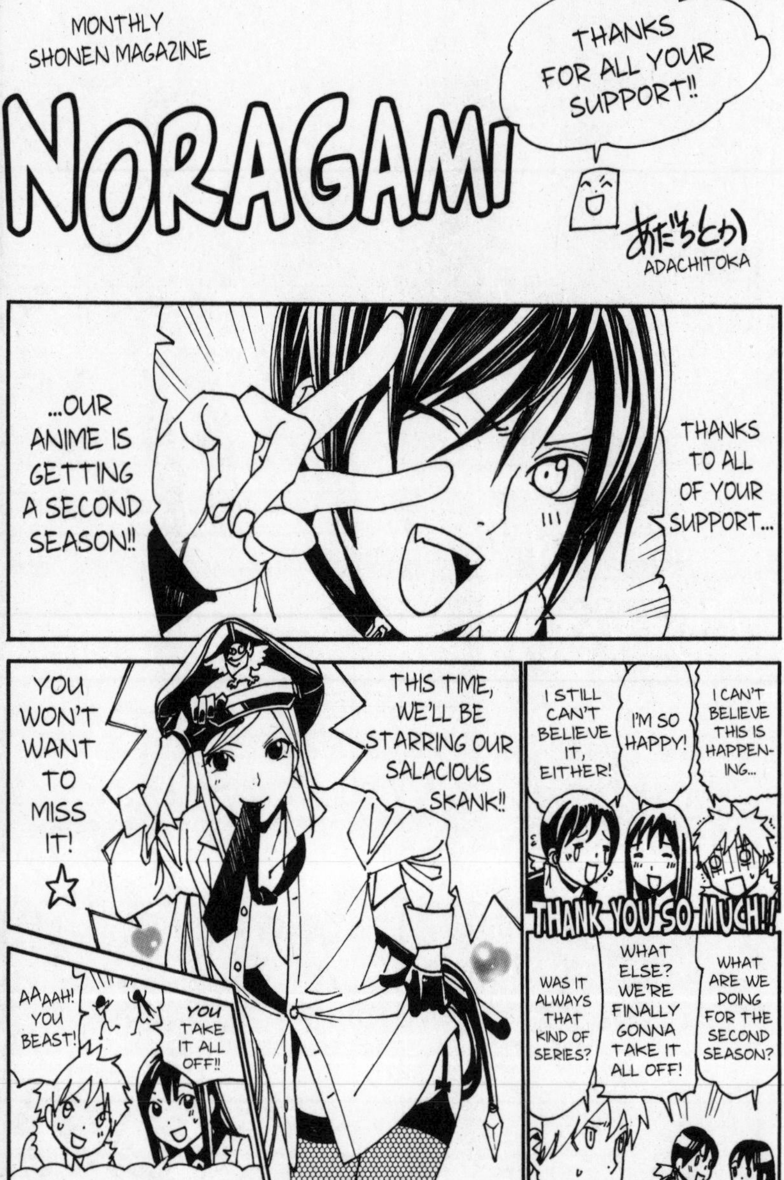
MONTHLY SHONEN MAGAZINE
NORAGAMI
THANKS FOR ALL YOUR SUPPORT!!
あだちとか
ADACHITOKA
THANKS TO ALL OF YOUR SUPPORT...
...OUR ANIME IS GETTING A SECOND SEASON!!
I CAN'T BELIEVE THIS IS HAPPEN-ING...
I'M SO HAPPY!
I STILL CAN'T BELIEVE IT, EITHER!
THANK YOU SO MUCH!!
WHAT ARE WE DOING FOR THE SECOND SEASON?
WHAT ELSE? WE'RE FINALLY GONNA TAKE IT ALL OFF!
WAS IT ALWAYS THAT KIND OF SERIES?
THIS TIME, WE'LL BE STARRING OUR SALACIOUS SKANK!!
YOU WON'T WANT TO MISS IT! ☆
YOU TAKE IT ALL OFF!!
AAAAH! YOU BEAST!
W-WE HOPE YOU ALL WATCH!!

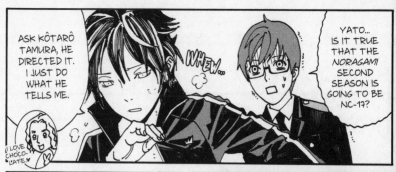

YATO... IS IT TRUE THAT THE NORAGAMI SECOND SEASON IS GOING TO BE NC-17?
WHEW...
ASK KÔTARÔ TAMURA, HE DIRECTED IT. I JUST DO WHAT HE TELLS ME.
I LOVE CHOCO-LATE.
C-COULD IT BE THE DIRECTOR PICKED UP THE WRONG BOOK AND READ TÔYA-SENSEI'S "BIOGRAPHIES OF A SKANK" FAN COMIC BY MISTAKE?!!
BIOGRA-PHIES OF A SKANK 1
TÔYA
THIS IS A DISASTER! I MUST STOP IT BEFORE IT HITS THE AIRWAVES!!!
YOU'RE TOO LATE, KAZUMA!
TUG
ANIME OUTLINE
NC-17 NORAGAMI (SEASON TWO)
BIOGRAPHIES OF A SKANK
AN UNREMARKABLE GIRL WHO SPENDS ALL HER TIME FIGHTING DREAMS OF BEING ONE OF THE LUCKY SEVEN?! HER BATTLE CRY IS 'ANYTHING TO BE MARKETABLE!' A SUCCESS STORY FILLED WITH LOVE AND BETRAYAL!
YOU'LL BE ALL THE RAGE AFTER THIS, BISHAA!
YOU'LL GET TO BE IN THE CENTER!
I WANT TO WATCH, BUT NOBODY WATCH!
YOU DO WANT TO WATCH IT.
WHA... WHAT WILL MY ROLE BE IN THIS?
THE DIRECTOR DID INDEED PICK UP THE WRONG BOOK.

※ THE NC-17 THING IS A LIE. IF YOU WANT TO KNOW HOW IT REALLY TURNED OUT, WATCH THE ANIME!

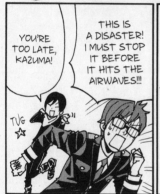

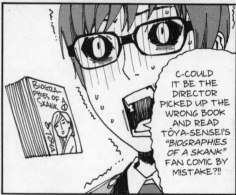

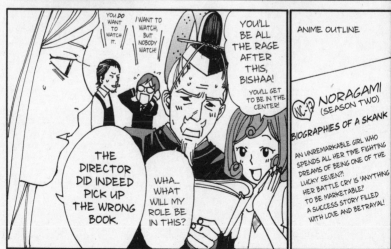

TRANSLATION NOTES

Japanese is a tricky language for most Westerners, and translation is often more art than science. For your edification and reading pleasure, here are notes on some of the places where we could have gone in a different direction in our translation of the work, or where a Japanese cultural reference is used.

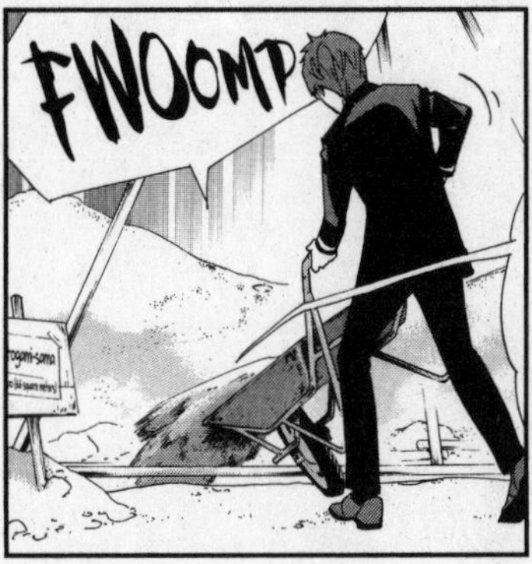
FWOOMP

Human sacrifices, page 10
The specific kind of sacrifice Yato accuses Kazuma of trying to make is called *hitobashira*, or "human pillar." The pillar in question is a live human being, who is buried near the foundation of a large construction project, such as a bridge, dam, or giant underground temple, to quell the wrath of local deities and pray for safe construction.

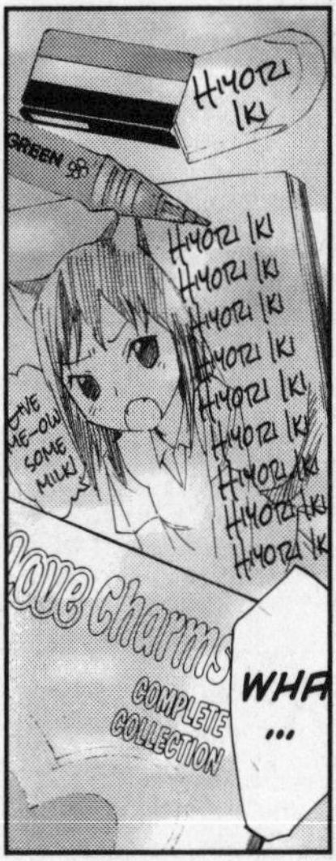
HIYORI IKI
HIYORI IKI
HIYORI IKI
HIYORI IKI
HIYORI IKI
HIYORI IKI
HIYORI IKI
HIYORI IKI
HIYORI IKI
HIYORI IKI
Love Charms
COMPLETE COLLECTION
WHA ...

Disturbing notebook, page 24
Hiyori finds this notebook to be particularly disturbing likely because the only reason she can think of for Yato to write her name so many times is that he's performing some kind of ritual that may or may not have vile consequences for her. In fact, in the Japanese, she actually called it a "curse notebook."

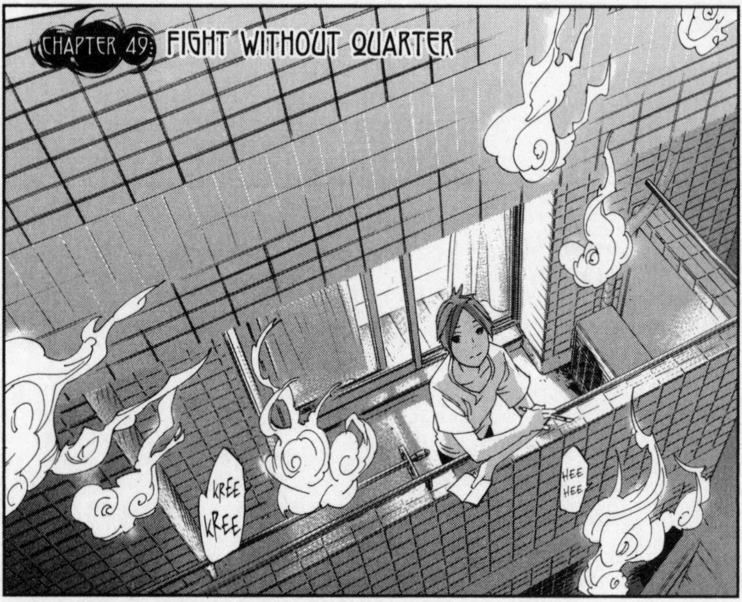
CHAPTER 49: FIGHT WITHOUT QUARTER
HEE HEE
KREE KREE

Fight Without Quarter, page 52

This phrase is translated from "*uchiteshi yamamu*," which was a slogan used in Japanese propaganda during World War II. It translates slightly more literally to "attack without stopping," but the sentiment behind it is, "We will destroy our enemy."

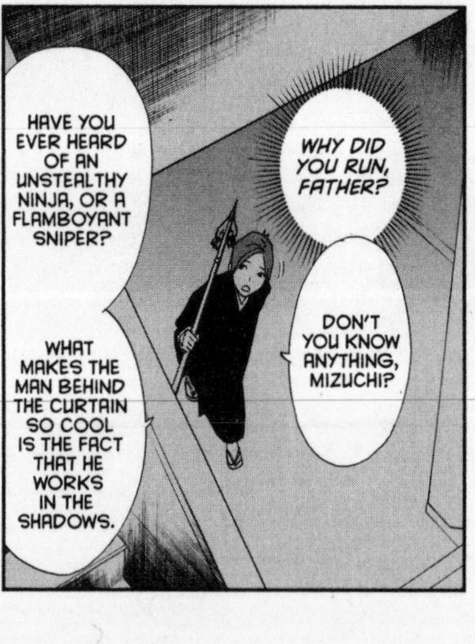
WHY DID YOU RUN, FATHER?
HAVE YOU EVER HEARD OF AN UNSTEALTHY NINJA, OR A FLAMBOYANT SNIPER?
DON'T YOU KNOW ANYTHING, MIZUCHI?
WHAT MAKES THE MAN BEHIND THE CURTAIN SO COOL IS THE FACT THAT HE WORKS IN THE SHADOWS.

Unstealthy ninjas, page 114

The translators thought it might be interesting to note that an unstealthy ninja is an oxymoron. The word *ninja* literally means "person who is stealthy."

BAM
AND... SINCE WE'RE AT SCHOOL...
YOU KNOW I HAD TO TRY THIS, TOO.
OH, YATO...

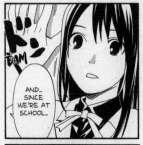

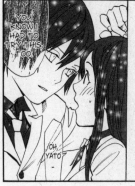

You know I had to try this, too, page 191
What Yato "had to try" is a manga and anime cliché that recently got a lot of attention on social media, known as *kabe-don*. *Kabe* means "wall," and *don* is the sound of hitting a heavy object (such as a wall), which is translated here as "bam." Often a tough guy character will bar the way in front of the object of his affection, and slam the wall as a way to get the other person's attention and look cool at the same time.

***Ningyô-yaki*, page 199**
Literally meaning "doll fry," a *ningyô-yaki* is a type of snack cake made by pouring batter into molds to make shapes. Among the most common shapes are the faces of the Seven Gods of Fortune, but they can be made to look like anything, including popular anime and manga characters. The cakes are usually filled with *azuki* red bean paste, but can also be filled with chocolate or custard. As for why the clay Lucky Seven figures would summon a dragon... well, the readers will have to refer to a different manga series, not published by Kodansha.

[illegible]

[illegible]

師

N

O

R

A

G

A

M

I

One time when I was playing at a
shrine as a kid, I found a couple
of clay figures in the bushes.
They were the size of a *ningyô-
yaki* snack cake, and they were
of Daikoku-sama and Somebody-
Else-sama from the Seven Gods of
Fortune. They were all black with
soot. I was convinced that if I
found the other five, the Dragon
would appear and grant my wish,
so I searched like crazy. Just a
memory of my eccentricity.

Adachitoka

Noragami: Stray God volume 13 is a work of fiction. Names, characters, places, and incidents are the products of the author's imagination or are used fictitiously. Any resemblance to actual events, locales, or persons, living or dead, is entirely coincidental.

A Kodansha Comics Trade Paperback Original.

Published in the United States by Kodansha Comics, an imprint of Kodansha USA Publishing, LLC, New York.

Publication rights for this English edition arranged through Kodansha Ltd., Tokyo.

First published in Japan in 2015 by Kodansha Ltd., Tokyo.

ISBN 978-1-63236-254-4

Printed in the United States of America.

www.kodanshacomics.com

9 8 7 6 5 4 3 2 1

Translation: Alethea Nibley & Athena Nibley
Lettering: Lys Blakeslee
Editing: Lauren Scanlan
Kodansha Comics Edition Cover Design: Phil Balsman